Careers
with Horses

The Comprehensive Guide to Finding Your Dream Job

By Vicki Hogue-Davies

BOWTIE
P R E S S®

Irvine, California

Karla Austin, Business Operations Manager

Ruth Strother, Editor-at-Large

Michelle Martinez, Associate Editor

Vicky Vaughn, Book Designer

Rachel Rice, Indexer

Nick Clemente, Special Consultant

Jen Dorsey, Editor

Rebekah Bryant, Editorial Assistant

Monika Stout, Production Artist

Library of Congress Cataloging-in-Publication Data

Hogue-Davies, Vicki.
  Careers with horses : the comprehensive guide to finding your dream job / by Vicki Hogue-Davies.
    p. cm.
  ISBN 1-931993-05-X (alk. paper)
  1. Horse industry—Vocational guidance. I. Title.

SF285.25.H64 2004
636.1'0023—dc22

2003028131

BowTie Press®
A Division of BowTie, Inc.
3 Burroughs
Irvine, California 92618

Printed and bound in Singapore
10 9 8 7 6 5 4 3 2

TABLE OF CONTENTS

CHAPTER 1

The Horse Industry in America

— — —

"God forbid that I should go to any heaven in which there are no horses," wrote Robert Bontine Cunninghame-Graham, Scottish horseman, writer, and adventurer, in a letter to former U.S. President Theodore Roosevelt in 1917. If the size and scope of the U.S. horse industry is any indicator, the passion for horses displayed in Cunninghame-Graham's words rings true with people today.

Though the horse industry can be difficult to quantify because of its size and diversity, separate surveys done during the last several years by three organizations show that there are almost 7 million horses in the United States. This figure includes horses used in recreation, showing, racing, breeding, farming and ranching, rodeo, polo, and police work. The American Horse Council, the trade association representing the industry nationally, put the number of horses at more than 6.9 million, following a major study released in late 1996. The National Agricultural Statistics Board, part of the United States Department of Agriculture (USDA), estimated there are approximately 5.3 million horses in the United States in its most recent survey in 1999. This figure is up 1.3 percent from the board's survey one year earlier. The American Veterinary Medical Association says in its statistical data on horse ownership from 1996, there are 4 million horses being utilized as companion animals (used noncommercially) in this country.

There are approximately 100 different horse breeds in the United States.

While the exact number of horses in the U.S. may lie somewhere between these figures—or may be even higher when taking into account potential yearly growth of the population—the industry's contribution to the U.S. economy cannot be argued. Using the 1996 American Horse Council figures, the horse industry supports more than 1.4 million full-time jobs across the country, directly produces goods and services of $25.3 billion, and has a total impact of $112.1 billion on the United States gross domestic product. These figures place the horse industry's contribution to the GDP just behind apparel and textile products manufacturing and ahead of rail transportation, motion picture services, and furniture and fixtures manufacturing.

It is no wonder that horses contribute so much, since there are approximately 100 different horse breeds in the United States. The associations dedicated to promoting and improving horse breeds in this country, such as the American Paint Horse Association, American Quarter Horse Association, and American Saddlebred Horse Association, make up an even larger number. Top horse-owning states include Texas, California, Florida, and Oklahoma. Recreational riding, showing, and racing count the largest numbers of equine and human participants (see table). Horses and the people who care for them are also involved in activities like law enforcement, working cattle, and helping the physically and developmentally disabled. Breeding, raising, and training the horses that take part in all of these activities is a cornerstone of the industry, and the businesses that supply goods and services, as well as the veterinarians, researchers, nutritionists, and other professionals engaged in improving equine health, are all major contributors.

Number of Horses and Participants by Activity

(Table courtesy of the American Horse Council)

Activity	Number of Horses	Number of Participants
Recreation	2,970,000	4,346,100
Showing	1,974,000	3,607,900
Racing	725,000	941,400
Other*	1,262,000	1,607,900
Total	6,931,000	7,062,500**

* *Includes farm and ranch work, police work, rodeo, and polo*

** *The sum of participants by activity does not equal the total number of participants because individuals may be counted in more than one activity*

The Industry's Future

While there are no overall figures available about growth of the horse industry each year, some horse organizations, such as the American Quarter Horse Association (AQHA), report continued increases in memberships and new foal registrations. (The AQHA remains the largest single breed horse organization in the world.) However, other breed organizations report that the growth of their organizations is relatively flat, which could be attributed to the state of the country's overall economy.

After several years of decline followed by marginal gains in the number of foals in recent years, Thoroughbred breeders were hit hard in 2001 and 2002 by the onset of mare reproductive loss syndrome (MRLS), which terminated hundreds of pregnancies or caused stillborn births for a significant portion of the Kentucky mare population. The overall loss was $336 million, according to a study by the University of Louisville, and the number of foals impacted in 2002 was estimated at 20 percent. Though the exact cause of MRLS is still being studied, scientists believe it is associated with horses ingesting the Eastern Tent Caterpillar. Partly in response to MRLS, the Congressional Horse Caucus was formed in 2001. The bipartisan caucus seeks to educate members of Congress and their staff about the horse industry's importance to the nation's economic, gaming, recreational, sporting, and agricultural life.

In addition to influence at the congressional level, the reach of the horse has extended to other federal areas. The U.S. Forest Service and the American Horse Council (AHC) entered into a Memorandum of Understanding in 2002, which encourages the Forest Service to identify appropriate partnership opportunities for making public lands under the agency's jurisdiction available to recreational riders and to work with AHC and its members to identify and pursue funding opportunities from nonfederal sources for trail improvements, facilities, and maintenance. In spite of increasing restrictions placed on trail use (which the memorandum seeks to help alleviate) and poor maintenance of trails, recreational riding continues to be the largest and fastest growing segment of the horse industry.

Another trend affecting the horse industry includes older citizens returning to riding. More 40- and 50-somethings, the so-called "baby boom" generation, are revisiting their childhood dreams of owning horses. Now-established

Baby boomers are flooding the recreational horse industry.

adults, overwhelmingly female, are returning to riding in large numbers. This age group is such a rapidly growing part of the horse world that some breed organizations, such as the AQHA, have added amateur competitions specifically for exhibitors in the 50-plus age range. In addition, dressage, reining, competitive endurance riding, cutting, and team penning are enjoying continued gains in popularity among all age groups. And reining debuted at the 2002 World Equestrian Games, a positive step toward making this an Olympic sport.

The horses that individuals ride are continuing to cross countries and cultures. European warmbloods, known for their pleasant dispositions, maintain their immense popularity in America for riding disciplines such as three-day eventing, dressage, and hunter/jumper events. As western riding continues to grow in popularity outside of the United States, the demand for western horses in European countries and Japan may continue to reap opportunities for trainers, breeders, riding instructors, and others familiar with the style originally developed for working purposes by the American cowboys. Additionally, Thoroughbred racing continues to grow in popularity outside the United States. Since 1999, direct exports of breeding and racing stock—from the United States to Korea—have increased five times, while exports to the United Arab Emirates tripled during the same period. Racing of Arabian horses is increasing and the high-spirited, yet gentle, horses are also making increasing inroads into the world of dressage, according to the Arabian Horse Association (AHA), even as they continue to remain a strong part of the endurance-riding world.

The way we communicate in the horse industry has also undergone significant change in the last 10 years. As use of the Internet grows throughout the world, so too is the same trend found in the horse industry. The Small Business Administration (SBA) reports that 61 percent of all small businesses among industries that use the Internet have Web sites. This statistic certainly appears to carry over to the horse industry: farms, product suppliers, breed associations, riding schools and stables, and other businesses and organizations in all areas of the industry have Web sites and more are being designed each day, allowing horse industry businesses greater exposure and creating opportunities for Web designers, programmers, and photographers specializing in horse industry ventures.

On the downside, while the rise of the Internet has made it easier for horse professionals to advertise their services, it has also been easier for less qualified people to advertise equine services. Unlike the European equine industry, the United States does not have any mandatory licensing or certification requirements for riding instructors and trainers. As is common in the horse industry, people who may not always be qualified can hang out a shingle and call themselves horse industry professionals in the area in which they practice. That said, there are currently many highly qualified instructors and trainers in this country who do not have certification. However, as the industry becomes more safety conscious, partially in response to increased litigation, and as it strives for a higher level of business professionalism, there is a growing move afoot to provide training and instruction that will enhance the quality of instruction in the industry and to have certification requirements measuring competence.

61 percent of all small businesses among industries that use the Internet have their own Web sites.

Changes related to safety are also taking place in the show ring, where all junior participants in U.S. Equestrian hunter/jumper events are now required to wear helmets certified by ASTM/SEI (American Society for Testing and Materials/Safety Equipment Institute). Concern with safety has also created several organizations whose mission is to improve safety industry wide. Three such organizations are the North American Horseman's Association, the Association for Horsemanship Safety, and the American Equine Medical Association.

Finally, as the general public becomes more comfortable with alternative therapies and holistic approaches to medicine, these nontraditional medical fields are gaining acceptance in the horse industry. Growth in the areas of equine chiropractic, massage, acupuncture, and other Eastern forms of medicine is taking place and introducing more opportunities for individuals interested in these areas. The fields of therapeutic riding and equine-assisted psychotherapy continue to expand and offer increased opportunities for riding instructors, occupational therapists, and others.

Career Opportunities

The horse industry offers a variety of career opportunities in the hands-on positions of working with horses and in areas that support the industry. Opportunities exist in such careers as breeding, showing, health and welfare, rodeo, recreation, product manufacturing, research, education, and service industries. Positions are available for people highly skilled in horsemanship, but there are also places in the industry for individuals with no direct horse experience at all.

Many people working today as trainers, riding instructors, stallion managers, farm managers, and in other high-level hands-on careers, once worked their way up the barn ladder as stable hands, wranglers, grooms, and even volunteers. These lower-level jobs, though they are characterized by long hours, hard physical work, and low pay, are often the stepping stones to lifetime careers in the industry. It is also very common in the horse industry for people with hands-on careers to work in combined positions, such as the horse trainer who also manages the barn or the riding instructor who also deals with or trains horses. Combining positions may be a requirement of the position for individuals working for someone else. For the self-employed, doing more than one job is often necessary to make ends meet.

Expect to see more growth in holistic healing and alternative equine health.

Other hands-on careers include veterinarian, where advanced education is critical; veterinary technician (assisting equine vets); farrier (caring for horses feet and legs); and massage therapist, where the ability to get along with all kinds of horses is imperative.

Outside the hands-on realm are all the other jobs that make the horse industry run. In fact, these supporting positions make up the majority of career options in the industry.

Marketing specialists promote horse businesses and products; fashion designers create clothes for equestriennes; store owners sell feed, tack, and supplies; museum curators ensure that the history of breeds or equine sports are preserved for future generations; clerical personnel help keep equine businesses humming; tack makers and leather workers produce saddles and bridles; insurance agents provide coverage for horses, horse owners, and property; and magazine editors, writers, and photographers keep horse lovers informed. Though, at first glance, working in a supporting role may not seem as attractive to the horse lover as a career that offers direct contact with horses, supporting jobs offer the chance to be involved in the industry, while in many cases, offering more regular hours and better pay and benefits.

Some horse lovers prefer the click of computer keys to the clip-clop of hooves.

Besides the distinction between hands-on jobs and supporting jobs, another useful demarcation line in the industry are those jobs designed for the self-employed as opposed to jobs done for an employer. Many positions within the horse industry require self-employment. Most farriers, some trainers and riding instructors, many veterinarians, equine accountants, bloodstock agents, photographers, writers, artists, massage therapists, braiders, equine dentists, and many more industry professionals work for themselves. Self-employment requires not only having the skills and training necessary to do the job, but also having strong business and marketing skills in order to make the business successful.

The variety of jobs in the horse industry allows for people with many different types and levels of skill and experience to find satisfying careers that will use their individual talents. As the next chapter will discuss, in order to succeed in the horse world, job seekers must assess their own interests, personalities, and inherent strengths and weaknesses before deciding upon a specific career path. Only by knowing yourself can you find a long-term career that is a good fit for you and your individual needs, personality, and skills.

CHAPTER 2

Finding Your Place

— — —

You've grown up horse crazy and know you want to spend your life working with horses. Perhaps you already have a career, but your love of horses has prompted you to seek a job in the equine industry. Before you begin contacting prospective employers, it's important to decide on the type of career you want and have a plan for achieving that goal. Many job seekers are willing to take anything they can find because they so much want to work around horses and they are afraid nothing else will come along. However, this approach is not the best road to a successful, sustainable, and profitable career. Spending time and effort now on targeting the career you want and researching the specific employers you want to work for will later pay big dividends in career satisfaction and, most likely, income.

You can begin finding your place in the horse industry by considering these questions:

- ❏ What do I expect in a horse career?
- ❏ How much experience or education am I willing to get to achieve my career objective?
- ❏ What income do I want or require?
- ❏ Where do I enter the industry to reach my goal?

What to Expect in the Industry

What you can expect in the horse industry depends very much on the type of career you choose. People who work in positions in which they have daily contact with horses obviously have different daily working lives than those who work in supporting fields without horse contact. The biggest difference, of course, is that individuals having direct contact with horses experience the joy of being around their favorite animals every day. They get to wear comfortable clothes and work outdoors—close to nature and the earth—without the confines of cubicle walls. For these advantages, they are willing to tolerate the long, irregular hours that are an accepted part of horse contact jobs, lower pay and fewer benefits, and the risk of a serious on-the-job injury that the office worker doesn't face.

If you wish to be a vital part of the equine industry, but aren't absolutely driven to see, smell, and touch horses every day, a job in a support role may offer the higher salary, better benefits, and regular hours that a hands-on job lacks. Positions in the support industry often offer a better work-life balance, which may allow you more time to spend riding trails on your own horse, perfecting flying lead changes in lessons, or taking that long-dreamed-of equestrienne vacation.

There are hundreds of jobs available in the horse industry from breeding manager to book editor.

The industry is made up of such a multitude of jobs, with different advantages and disadvantages, that there is room to accommodate the desires and skills of just about every horse lover seriously seeking a career in the industry. Just as each horse is unique, so is each person who works with a horse. People with various personalities, skills, interests, educations, and levels of horse experience—as long as they have the determination to succeed—can find a place in the horse world that is right for them. As you'll see when you read the profiles of industry professionals later in this book, many of these successful horse people were not fortunate enough to be born into the industry on farms or ranches, an upbringing that naturally fosters a horse career. Likely, many of them started out the same way as many readers of this book—with an abiding love for horses but no family connections into the industry. Through determination, creativity, and hard work, these professionals were able to turn into reality their dream of combining a love of horses with a job. If you are willing to plan your career, work hard in gaining the knowledge you need, and take the right steps toward your goals, you can have a good chance of living your dream.

Consider your personal abilities and goals before you begin a job search.

To find your place in this dynamic industry, it is important to think seriously and realistically about your own abilities, personality, and interests. Consider your experience with horses and how much time you are willing to devote to learning more about them. Consider your strengths and weaknesses. Think about the things you enjoy doing and the things you don't. Do you like working and fixing things with your hands or do you consider yourself a klutz in that area? Are you an idea person who thrives on solving problems, but you don't have the patience to implement the solutions? Are you athletic? Creative? Are you happiest working as part of a team or do you prefer working independently? Do you have trouble sitting still or do you thrive on quiet introspection?

Getting to know yourself is the first, and possibly the most important, step in identifying the career that is right for you. For example, suppose you have an assertive, extroverted personality. You know you like talking with people and your friends and family have told you that you are a good communicator. You're at your best and most alert in the morning and throughout the day, but you can't keep your eyes open past 10 P.M. You should think twice before pursuing a position as a foaling attendant or broodmare manager, where long nights of solitude are part of the job. However, you might be a good candidate for a job in sales, marketing, or public relations for an equine product manufacturer, where you'll usually work regular hours and have lots of person-to-person contact. If you have the requisite horse experience, your assertiveness and communication skills may also mesh well in a position as a riding instructor, show manager, or bloodstock agent where people skills as well as horse experience are key.

While this example is rather basic, it helps illustrate how important it is for the career seeker and the position to be a good match. It is frustrating to both employee and employer when a job and employee do not fit well, and a false start can significantly slow down or damage your progress in working toward your career goals. While this chapter only touches on the process of getting to know yourself, there are several good books on the subject that can give you in-depth insight into your own personality. One such book is, *Do What You Are*, by Paul D. Tieger and Barbara Barron-Teiger (Little Brown, 2001). The classic, *What Color is Your Parachute? A Practical Manual for Job-Hunters and Career-Changers*, by Richard Bolles (Ten Speed Press, 2003), which is updated annually, offers an education in job-hunting as well as exercises in getting to know yourself, all in one book. While neither of these books is specific to the horse industry, they provide practical advice that crosses industries and fields. Check with your local bookstore or online bookseller for these and other titles.

Ask questions of people who work in your field of interest.

After you've taken the time to examine your own personality, interests, and skills and have identified a career or careers that interest you, it is time to thoroughly research the details of those careers. While it is normal in any job to have good and bad days, the bad times will be minimized if you know what to expect going in and if the career you've chosen is a good fit for you. Here are some suggestions for starting your research.

Talk to several people who work in your field of interest, preferably not the employers, but those closer to the level in which you would enter. (Keep in mind that, at this point, you are just researching the career to see if it is a good fit for you, not seeking employment.) Let the people you speak with know you are researching the field and that you're talking with them purely for information. When making initial contact, ask for a few minutes of the person's time and explain clearly what you are doing. Have a list of questions written down. To find people in horse industry careers, contact professional associations that represent people in the field or a specific area of the industry; if you are focused on working with a specific horse breed or in a specific discipline, find the association that represents that breed or discipline. You'll find a list of addresses and Web sites for professional associations following the career descriptions; and the appendices list many breed and sport organizations. Attend horse shows, equine trade expos, rodeos, races, and other horse events to gather cards of individuals you can contact later. If time and schedules permit, ask a few targeted questions while at the event. Contact colleges for names of alumni working in the field. Talk with horse people at the barn. Let them know the career area you are interested in and see if they can suggest someone you can speak with.

Keep track of the professionals you interview. Write down their names, contact information, and details about your conversations with them. Always show your appreciation to anyone who spends her time speaking with you. If you have a formal meeting with someone, a written thank you note is the appropriate follow-up. If you speak informally to someone while hanging around the barn, be sure to show your appreciation with verbal thanks. Stay in touch with these professionals periodically. Perhaps call the veterinarian you speak to and ask a follow-up question. If you've taken someone's advice to pursue a specific kind of degree or to attend a particular clinic, drop a note to let her know. Stop and say hello to the assistant trainer at the barn where you board your horse who spent time talking with you about horse training careers. If you have always pre-sented yourself as polite and professional, most

Volunteer to learn more about possible horse careers.

people will not mind if you stay in touch; in fact, they may well be flattered by your interest in their career. If you do pursue that particular career, these same people could become networking contacts (more on network-ing in Chapter 5: Get the Job).

The horse industry thrives on the use of volunteers. Check for volunteer opportunities in your area of interest to get a first-hand feel for the job and to build up valuable experience for your resume. Spend enough time doing the job to get a real feel for the position. Volunteering is also valuable for making contacts with possible future employment opportunities. Contact placement offices at colleges, universities, and trade schools for more information.

Read, read, and read some more. Take a look at trade magazines, which are written for professionals in various fields of interest in the horse world. Also, breed and sport association magazines, consumer horse magazines, and horse books are filled with valuable information.

There are an endless number of equine Web sites on the Internet, so do a little surfing. Search your area of interest and see what you find.

Experience versus Education

Is experience more important than education in the horse industry? It depends on the job you want. For people interested in working as trainers, riding instructors, barn managers, or other highly skilled hands-on positions, the more years of experience with horses, the better. A reference from a reputable trainer, clinician, or breeder with whom you studied may be more impressive to prospective employers than a two- or four-year college degree in equine studies or equine science. However, a college degree in an equine field, along with the requisite experience, may well give you an edge over experienced candidates without college backgrounds. A degree may also be a good road into an entry-level position that allows you to prove yourself and work your way into a more responsible position. It all depends on the job itself and, to a great extent, on the employer.

Find a balance of your hands-on and mental skills.

This is the conundrum faced by job seekers looking for hands-on horse positions. Many employers welcome candidates with college degrees (though not in place of solid experience). They believe higher education makes for a more well-rounded employee with better communication, planning, and leadership skills. Other employers may be indifferent to degrees because they prefer to train their employees in their own methods or perhaps they feel that college programs neglect to teach students the practicalities of working with horses. Then, there are a few employers who may gently boot out of the barn job seekers touting their educational accomplishments. This group of employers may actually be suspicious of job seekers with college degrees, seeing them as arrogant greenhorns who rely on theory and book learning rather than on years of hands-on horse handling experience.

The bottom line in the experience versus education debate is this: If you decide to go to college and acquire an equine studies or equine science degree, be realistic in your expectations about getting a hands-on horse job. Don't expect doors to open just because of the degree; do realize that it can help you make inroads with employers if you have a degree and the requisite experience for the job, or if you are willing to take an entry-level position to prove yourself. Also, if you choose to get a degree, carefully research and evaluate the various degree programs and internship opportunities and how they will help you in relation to your long-term career goals. Be sure the program you choose offers focused training in your area of interest. If you enter college and are not quite sure exactly what career you wish to pursue, look for an equine studies program that provides a more general, overall equine education. If you are interested in a job that is very specific, such as equine massage or horseshoeing, a trade school or certificate program at a college or university may be your best bet. Perhaps you are a career changer who already has a college degree in a non-horsey field but don't have the time or interest to start over again in a four-year degree program. By taking the time to study the career you are pursuing, you can determine the best way to get educated for that job before you get started.

Another important point to think about when considering a college education is that working with horses can involve serious injury. A college education will give you something to fall back on should injury occur and you can no longer ride. Also, says Ginny Spooner, owner of J. Alden Enterprises and Huntington Beach Riding School, "If you are planning to run your own horse related business, you'll probably find that many of your clients who have the disposable income to participate in horse-related activities are well-educated themselves. Having a college education will help put you on par with them, and can allow for better communication between you."

On the other side of the fence are the careers requiring continuing education. These careers include the obvious choices requiring extensive higher education, such as equine veterinarian, accountant, and lawyer, in addition to jobs requiring specialty or trade school educations, such as veterinary technician, dental technician, or equine massage therapist. Then, there are the many other supporting jobs in the industry requiring degrees that do not necessarily have an equine focus. The public relations specialist, adver-

Many horse careers require extensive education.

tising professional, magazine editor, marketer, and architect must have at least a four-year degree to be considered for entry-level positions in these competitive fields. While an equine magazine editor would also be required to have horse experience, a degree and experience in the professional field might be more important to potential employers than a horse background. Some employers may even prefer that job candidates gain expertise in their particular field before moving to the horse industry.

Income Expectations and Requirements

The majority of people who go to work in the horse industry, especially in hands-on positions, do so because they love horses. The market is filled with individuals willing to work in entry-level positions—mucking stalls and unloading hay bales—just for the pleasure of being around horses. Add to that the number of part-timers working in the industry and salaries are further driven down. Weekly paychecks of $300 per week or lower are not uncommon for these entry-level jobs. Housing is often included, but the quality of the housing varies considerably from employer to employer. Sometimes, utilities are paid and a stall provided for your horse. Benefits like medical insurance and paid vacation, holidays, and sick leave may or may not be part of the job and benefits package.

Salaries improve in higher-level hands-on positions, but are still low when compared to similar jobs in other industries. Salaries starting at $25,000 a year or less, along with room and board, are not uncommon. Of course, there are always exceptions—such as top trainers or clinicians who earn six figure incomes each year—but these individuals are the exception and not the rule.

Support jobs in which employees feel the click of computer keys under their fingers rather than the softness of a horse's mane, generally offer higher wages with more and better benefits. Paid vacations and holidays, medical benefits, and 401K plans are common in these types of positions.

Self-employed businesspeople often spend the first couple years running in the red while they build a clientele large enough to recoup start-up costs and turn a profit. They also must pay their own medical costs and do not have paid holidays, sick days, or vacations. Bloodstock agents, tack store owners, freelance writers, farriers, some riding instructors and trainers, blanket cleaning service owners, animal communicators, and equine artists and photographers to name just a few, fall into this group.

Consider your income expectations before beginning a job search.

It is wise to know how much money you can comfortably live on before making a commitment to a career. Then, do your research to find out if you can realistically expect that income level from the career—that way, there won't be any surprises down the road. General nationwide salary information is available for many of the careers listed in this book. However, salaries can vary significantly by region and employer. For example, small mom and pop farms can't be expected to pay salaries comparable to what large-scale breeding operations may offer. To get a more detailed picture of salaries available among large and small operations in your area, review help-wanted ads online and in print publications for your region; go to the

Web site for the U.S. Bureau of Labor Statistics (www.bls.gov) for a breakdown of salaries by region; talk to placement personnel at colleges, universities, and specialty schools; or contact organizations representing the profession in which you are interested.

If you aren't sure how much money you need to live on, look at the chart below, take out a piece of paper, and write down a weekly or monthly amount for each of the areas. The numbers you write down don't have to be exact, but they should be a good general estimate. In fact, estimate slightly higher than you think you'll need to allow for possible emergencies along the way. Add up the total, and then multiply that amount by either 52 weeks or 12 months to arrive at a yearly salary. Also, don't forget to add the appropriate income tax percentage to the amount you estimate.

Plan a personal budget so you know what salary is realistic for you.

Note that this list is for personal expenses only. Chapter 6 addresses the additional expenses you may need if you're interested in starting your own business.

PERSONAL EXPENSES

- ❑ How much do I need for housing, utilities, and telephone expenses?*
- ❑ How much do I need for food and household items?
- ❑ How much do I need for transportation, including gasoline expenses and car insurance?
- ❑ How much do I need for clothing and personal grooming items?
- ❑ How much do I need for entertainment and hobbies, such as movies, books, magazines, restaurants, travel, etc.?
- ❑ How much do I need for horse expenses, including board, tack, veterinary care, food, shoeing, riding lessons, etc.?**
- ❑ How much do I need for pet care?**
- ❑ How much do I need for babysitting or schooling for children?**
- ❑ How much do I need for medical and dental benefits?*
- ❑ How much would I like to save?
- ❑ Do I have any other expenses?

* if not provided by job
** if applicable

Where to Start; How to Grow

Once you decide what you would like to do in the industry and the amount of money you can comfortably live on, where you enter the industry depends on the career you are pursuing, your education, and your level of experience.

Whatever job you are pursuing, whether it is working directly with horses or in a supporting field, it is better to target a job you have the skills for now, rather than exaggerating your skills to get a higher level position. Besides setting yourself up for failure if you can't perform the tasks of the job, plumping up your experience can be downright dangerous when a 1,000-pound animal is added to the equation. If you know in your heart that you don't yet have the necessary skills or experience to pursue that plum job as a barn manager, riding instructor, or salesperson, go for a position that is a good match for what your experience level is at the moment. Seek a job that stretches your skills and helps you to grow, but make sure it is a comfortable stretch.

Target a job you have the skills for now rather than exaggerating your skills to get a higher position.

Ask questions, observe, and learn all you can from the seasoned horse people and other professionals around you. Advancement and respect for your capabilities will come to you after you have demonstrated good performance and responsibility on the job.

Of course, to advance in a job, such opportunities must exist. This is where doing your research comes into play. Hopefully, you've chosen your opportunities carefully. Before you accept a position, make sure that the company promotes growth and advancement from within. Advancement may not seem possible if there are few positions at the top, but if the employer is reputable and the job appears to be a good place to learn and acquire experience, consider taking the job anyway. Recognize, however, that you may have to move on to move up. Some people become bitter toward their employers or so frustrated with their lack of growth in their particular situations that they leave the horse industry altogether. By going into a job with your eyes wide open, you can use that position as a stepping stone to vault you into a successful career, thus controlling your own future and avoiding job burnout.

One note on researching advancement opportunities with employers: If you are interviewing for a particular job, don't focus too much on opportunities for advancement during the job interview. The employer is looking to hire because he needs someone to address certain tasks at the moment. By learning as much as you can about the employer's operation prior to interviewing, such as size, reputation, and how long it has been in business, and by asking general questions of the employer during the interview, you can get a good idea about room for advancement.

Focus on what you can offer the company during a job interview, not what you will gain from the experience.

Also, don't automatically assume that you should take the highest-level, best-paying job you can get. It is often more beneficial to take a lower-level job with a well-respected employer than a higher-level job with a less reputable operation because there may be stronger potential for advancement and longer-term job security. Reputation is very important in the horse industry and a top employer's reputation can open doors for employees in good standing who decide to pursue jobs elsewhere.

CHAPTER 3

Horse Industry Experience

— — —

The old saying "there is no teacher like experience" can be especially true for the horse industry. When looking for a hands-on position, the job seeker can never have too much horse experience. In fact, having too little experience for the job will probably keep doors closed. The good news is that there are many ways to gain horse experience, even if you are not fortunate enough to have your own equine charge.

Start gaining experience on a local level by volunteering your time with a volunteer organization like Pony Club or 4-H. Ask around local barns to see if you can intern for a few hours each week. Consult your local college career placement office for help in finding summer stable work. Your possibilities are endless.

Internships and Other On-the-Job Training

Colleges, universities, and trade schools can often arrange internships for their current or graduating students; some college or university degree programs require students to perform an internship as a condition of graduating. Internships last for a specified period of time, for example, a summer school break, or for a set time period following graduation; they may be paid or unpaid. Speak to your college or trade school for more information on internships.

Sometimes farriers, saddle makers, leather workers, and other skilled tradespeople will agree to take on apprentices to teach them the trade in exchange for labor. Look at ads in horse publications or on the bulletin board at local tack or feed stores, ask around at the barn, or check with equine employment agencies for apprenticeship opportunities. You can also approach an expert in your field of interest and ask about the possibility of apprenticing with him.

Working students may opt to forgo college to learn on the job, providing their labor in exchange for lessons taught by an expert. While the pay may be low, room and board for students is usually provided. Typically, the professional will provide a set amount of lessons per week in exchange for help with horse care or other activities around the barn. Students with more experience may assist with training and riding instruction. It is important that both parties in these agreements clearly communicate their expectations and it is best to get such an agreement—with all the details spelled out—in writing. A written agreement allows less room for misunderstandings, which are sometimes common with working student arrangements. Also, if you pursue a working student arrangement, be sure it is with someone whose methods you respect so that you are able to follow the direction she gives you. Working student arrangements can be found through networking, advertisements in equine publications, and through equine employment agencies.

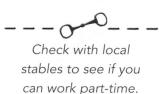

Check with local stables to see if you can work part-time.

If you would like to experience another country and culture while gaining horse industry experience, the Communicating for Agriculture Exchange Program may be for you. Since 1986, this organization has placed young men and women between the ages of 18 and 28, who have at least one year of practical experience in their chosen area, in agricultural positions in 23 countries throughout the world. The horse program includes placement in English and western disciplines, racing, veterinary, and breeding. Many jobs involve basic duties, such as mucking stalls, feeding and watering, and grooming. Participants with more advanced horse experience may find higher-level positions such as exercising, training, or instruction. Placements range from three to 12 months in length and all participants receive room and board and a monthly stipend; some may be eligible for college credit. Scholarships of $350 to $2,000 are also

Try to get an apprenticeship through a Regional Occupational Program.

available to eligible participants and may not be used for travel expenses, which are the responsibility of each participant. Contact the Communicating for Agriculture Exchange Program for application information at 112 East Lincoln Avenue, Fergus Falls, MN 56537, or visit the Web site at ca.cainc.org.

Regional Occupational Programs (ROP) are government programs that use state and federal funding to provide career guidance, training, and placement services to high school students and adults. Apprenticeships through ROP are also available. ROP programs may offer training in veterinary technology and assisting, computer programming, photography, small business management, and other areas. High school students can check with their schools' career center for more about ROP opportunities. County or state education offices and local community colleges can also provide information.

Certification Programs

Being certified or earning credentials in a field shows potential employers and clients that you are an expert in that field. Certification programs are offered for riding instructors and racehorse trainers as well as for public relations specialists and real estate agents. Earning certification may involve enrolling in a program for training and testing or simply taking a single test that measures your expertise in the field. For some fields, certification is mandatory, while it is voluntary for others. Certification programs and credentials for individual careers are included in the career listings.

Youth Organizations

Organizations targeted specifically to youth, older teens, and young adults that promote good horsemanship, citizenship, leadership, and sportsmanship skills, offer excellent opportunities for gaining horse knowledge and making contacts in the horse world. Such organizations as Pony Club, rodeo, breed and sport organizations, 4-H, and the National Future Farmers of America (FFA) fall into this category. Though having a horse or access to a horse is beneficial, it is not always required when working with such an organization. Additionally, these organizations use many volunteers. Older teens and adults may find volunteering for a youth organization to be a fun and rewarding way to gain increased leadership skills and horse industry work experience.

PONY CLUB

This international junior equestrian organization provides the opportunity to learn good horsemanship and English riding skills. Children, teens, and young adults up to 21 years of age can join. Horses and ponies

The "pony" in Pony Club refers to the age of the members, not the size of the horses.

of many different sizes and breeds are used in Pony Club activities. Although members are not required to have their own mounts, they should have access to a horse, perhaps through borrowing or leasing, to benefit fully from the organization. Pony Club members are encouraged to work their way through nine proficiency levels, each testing horsemanship and riding skills. An annual fee is required for membership and some level of parental involvement is usually expected. In addition to the volunteer efforts of parents, Pony Club utilizes other volunteers with an affinity for horses. There are more than 600 Pony Clubs in the United States and the club is represented in 30 countries. To find out more about Pony Club membership or volunteer opportunities, go to the national Pony Club Web site at www.ponyclub.org, or write to United States Pony Clubs, Inc., 4041 Iron Works Parkway, Lexington, KY 40511, for a club in your area.

RODEO ORGANIZATIONS

There are two rodeo organizations designed especially for young people through the age of 18: the National High School Rodeo Association

(NHSRA) and the National Little Britches Rodeo Association (NLBRA). The NHSRA, which has been around since the forties, was founded on two principles: to encourage youth to stay in school and to promote the highest level of conduct and sportsmanship. The goals of the organization are to stress the importance of education and to teach life skills such as leadership, responsibility, dedication, and commitment. It has an annual membership of more than 12,500 high school students from 39 states, five Canadian provinces, and Australia, and it sanctions over 1,100 rodeos each year. For more on NHSRA, visit its Web site at www.nhsra.org or write to NHSRA at 12001 Tejon Street, Ste. 128, Denver, CO 80234; (303) 452-0820.

The National Little Britches Rodeo Association, the oldest national junior rodeo association in the country, is for youth aged 8 to 18. In addition to promoting rodeo and helping members learn athletic skills in the rodeo arena, Little Britches is devoted to educating young rodeo athletes on the importance of being in top physical condition, preventative health issues, and providing a wholesome environment for western-oriented young people. Little Britches can be reached at National Little Britches Rodeo Association, 1045 W. Rio Grande, Colorado Springs, CO 80906, www.nlbra.com; (800) 763-3694.

Breed and Sport Organizations

Horse ownership is not required, though, as with Pony Club, full benefit of the organization is assured through access to a horse. Membership benefits may include participation in shows and events, opportunities to attend workshops and seminars, receipt of the organization's publication, and networking and college scholarship opportunities. Some of the breed organizations that have formal youth programs are the American Quarter Horse Association, American Morgan Horse Association, American Paint

Many breed associations and horse sport organizations offer youth programs.

Horse Association, the Appaloosa Horse Club, Belgian Draft Horse Corporation of America, and Palomino Horse Breeders of America. Check with the breed or horse sport organizations that interest you to see if they have youth programs or offer junior or discount memberships to young people.

4-H Clubs

The 4-H program, which celebrated its centennial in 2002, offers any young person through the age of 19 the chance to learn more about horses. It does not cost anything to join 4-H and many activities are available that do not require horse ownership. Programs vary from club to club and may include horse bowls that test equine knowledge, equine retreats, local 4-H horse shows, horsemanship camps, community service projects involving horses, equine arts and crafts, equine photography, writing contests and workshops, and conferences that teach equine management and leadership skills. Check with your local or regional 4-H organization for information on horse programs in your area and leadership opportunities within 4-H, or visit the National 4-H Council Web site at www.fourhcouncil.edu.

National Future Farmers of America (FFA) Organization

Students aged 12 to 21 who are enrolled in agricultural education programs are eligible for membership in FFA, whose goal is to develop leadership, career, and life skills in young people. It offers recognition and award programs and competitive team activities for students seeking careers in the horse industry. Industry partners include the American Quarter Horse Association, American Paint Horse Association, the Appaloosa Horse Club, the National Cutting Horse Association, National High School Rodeo Association, Thoroughbred Breeders Association, and racing organizations. If your high school does not have an FFA chapter, visit the National FFA Organization Web site at www.ffa.org, or write to them at P.O. Box 68960, 6060 FFA Drive, Indianapolis, IN 46268-0960. As with all the organizations in this section, FFA also appreciates the help of volunteers.

One way to add experience to your resume is through volunteering.

Volunteer Opportunities

Working in a volunteer capacity illustrates to others that you are serious about being a part of the horse world; it also allows you the opportunity to discover if a job or area of the industry is right for you. Opportunities to meet people with job leads or hiring ability are much higher if you are working among them. Demonstrating your work skills and reliability as a volunteer can impress people and open barn doors faster than if you were coming in cold. Youth, breed, and sport organizations use volunteers for assistance at shows, rodeos, races, horse fairs and expos, and other such events. Therapeutic riding programs, horse libraries and museums, trail organizations, horsemanship clinics, equine vet- erinarians, horse welfare organizations and res- cue groups, state and local horse councils, and other similar organizations also use volunteer help. The type of volunteer work available ranges from grooming horses or mucking stalls at a show barn to side walking at a therapeutic riding facility to performing administrative work for a youth group, or helping maintain riding trails for the local horse agency. To find volunteer opportunities, contact organizations listed in the appendices to this book, look at bulletin boards at tack and feed stores, read horse publications or ask around the barn.

Subscribe to association publications for your area of interest.

Informal Experience

To gain informal knowledge and experience, immerse yourself in the subject of horses. Read everything you can about them. Most importantly, read books and magazines and visit Web sites that will help you better understand the industry and the way it works. Join a horse association or local or regional horse council. Offer to help your friend with her boarded horse—clean the horse's stall or prepare the feed. Your friend will be grateful and these duties will give you a good reason to hang around the barn and talk to horse people. Visit local breeding farms, training barns, and tack and feed stores. If you are Internet-savvy, con- sider visiting horse industry Web sites.

CHAPTER 4

Your Education

— — —

This chapter discusses different continuing education options (though, in many cases, the type of education you pursue will be driven by your career choice) and it provides advice and resources on paying for your higher education. It also includes profiles of several of the equine studies and equine science programs available at colleges and universities throughout the country. (See Appendix K for an in-depth listing of colleges and universities that provide equine and agricultural degrees, accredited veterinary colleges, schools offering horse sports, and trade schools that focus on hands-on horse careers.) No matter what type or level of education you seek, remember to always present yourself professionally on applications and in person.

Trade and Specialty Schools

Trade and specialty schools provide training in specific skills or specialty areas. Schools are available for farriers, cowboys, equine dentists, insurance agents, saddle makers, massage therapists, travel agents, riding instructors, and other horse industry professionals (both in hands-on jobs and support positions). The length of coursework may range from several weeks to more than a year, depending on the level of proficiency desired in the field. These schools typically award a certificate or diploma upon completion of the program.

Trade and specialty schools provide training in specific skills or specialty areas.

Take your time and do your research when selecting a school. Ask the school if they can provide names of alumni who have agreed to speak about their experience at the school with prospective students. Ask horse people in the business if they are familiar with the school and whether it is reputable. If you find yourself unable to get information on the school's reputation, check with the Better Business Bureau in the school's area to see if complaints have been lodged. (See the figure in the section entitled "Two- and Four-Year Degree Programs" for questions to think about when considering a school. These questions can be applied to both trade schools and degree programs at colleges and universities.)

In addition to the trade and specialty schools listed in this book, check advertisements in horse publications, read the bulletin boards at the local barn or tack stores, or contact the appropriate professional associations.

Following are profiles of schools that teach dentistry, therapeutic riding instruction, equine massage, and the trade of farriery:

ACADEMY OF EQUINE DENTISTRY
P.O. Box 999
Glenns Ferry, Idaho 83623
(208) 366-2315
www.equinedentistry.com

The Academy of Equine Dentistry teaches the proper procedures of equine dentistry to prospective equine dentists, horse owners, and trainers. The academy is affiliated with World Wide Equine, Inc., a manufacturer of equine dental instruments. Students of the academy can progress through several levels of achievement leading to certification as an equine dentist. (Certification levels include Certified Equine Dentist through Certified Principal Equine Dentist.) Most courses are 50 hours long comprising five days. The number of courses and hours involved depends on the level of certification desired by the student. Written and practical examinations, letters of competence from veterinarians and Certified Equine Dentists, and proof of documented cases are some of the criteria required for certification. The cost of each five-day dental course is approximately $2,043. Students can stay in the school bunkhouse for a nightly fee of $20, or at local motels, inns, or campgrounds.

CHEFF THERAPEUTIC RIDING CENTER, INSTRUCTOR COURSE

8450 N. 43rd Street
Augusta, MI 49012
(269) 731-4471
www.cheffcenter.com

The Cheff Therapeutic Riding Center began offering instructor courses in 1971. Since that time, more than 900 students have graduated. To be accepted into the program, students must be high school graduates, at least 18 years of age, advanced riders with five years of concentrated riding experience (A and B level Pony Clubbers and graduates of approved equine studies programs are given preference), and they must have the ability to teach English riding at the intermediate level. Applicants must also show proof of CPR and first aid training. Upon arrival at the Cheff Center, students are tested for ability; failure to pass any part of the three-phase test is reason for nonacceptance into the program. The four-week-long instructor course includes two weeks of lectures on all aspects of therapeutic riding, followed by hands-on work teaching techniques. Just a sampling of the subjects includes human growth and development, disabilities, instructor responsibilities, teaching techniques, and horse selection and training. Students passing with an average between 60 and 79 percent in all subjects receive an associate instructor certificate. Instructor certificates are awarded to students who pass the course with an 80 percent in all subjects. Students passing the course with 80 percent or higher are eligible to sit for the certification exam administered by the North American Riding for the Handicapped Association (NARHA). Classes run Monday through Friday. The fee for the instructor course is $1,950, which includes a $250 registration fee, books, printed course material, and housing. Fees do not include transportation or meals.

Equissage Equine Sports Massage Therapy Certification Program

P.O. Box 447
Round Hill, VA, 20142
(800) 843-0224
www.equissage.com

Since 1991, Equissage has awarded certification to more than 4,000 equine and companion animal massage technicians around the world. Equissage's certification program consists of five days of intensive classroom study and individualized practical application. Classes are limited to 10 candidates. A background in massage therapy, though preferable, is not mandatory. The program begins with the basics of massage therapy and teaches every aspect of the discipline. The program's major emphasis is on the application of massage techniques and massage strokes, therefore students must be familiar with the basic physiology of muscles, the location of major muscles and muscle groups, and specific conditions that may affect horses when muscles are strained, tired, tense, or sore. Membership in the International Association of Equine Massage Therapists is offered to all students who complete the Equissage certification program. The cost of the program is $935 and it includes tuition, all books and materials, and a box lunch each day. Lodging and travel expenses are not included.

Pacific Coast Horseshoeing School

9625 Florin Road
Sacramento, CA 95829-1009
(916) 366-6064
www.farrierschool.com

Farrier Bob Smith established Pacific Coast Horseshoeing School in 1991 (see the profile of Bob in Chapter 9). He and forge instructor Chuck Presnall each bring over 25 years of shoeing experience to the eight-week-long farrier program. The program features three areas of study: classroom lectures and presentations, forge work, and shoeing and trimming horses. In addition to classroom discussions on such topics as anatomy, conformation, lameness, and gait faults, basic business practices for the self-employed are discussed so the students are better equipped to work in the field. School facilities include a forge and shoeing area, tool room with private lockers for each student, metal shop and classrooms. All tools and equipment are provided during the course of study. Classes are held Monday through Friday, 8 A.M. to 5 P.M.; the school is open from 7 A.M. to 9 P.M., seven days a week. Classes average 12 to 14 students each and the school holds five class sessions per year. The tuition is $4,500; an additional $50 per week fee is charged for dormitory housing. Students purchase and prepare their own meals, but the dormitory is equipped with a kitchen for meal preparation.

Two- and Four-Year Degree Programs

Community colleges and some four-year colleges and universities offer two-year Associate of Arts or Science certificates or degrees in equine studies, veterinary technology, or equine or animal science. Many of these equine degree programs are designed for students interested in specific hands-on or specialty careers, such as stable or farm management, riding instruction, training, and breeding. Two-year associate programs are also offered to those with skill in a particular field such as graphic design or computer programming who wish to join the horse industry. If you are sure of your career goal and believe you will not need to pursue further education, then a focused two-year program may be for you. If, however, you are not yet sure what you want to do or if there is a possibility you may pursue a bachelor's degree, look for an associate program with a more general curriculum and with courses that can be transferred to a four-year college or university. In either case, you should research both the career and the program, taking into consideration the areas for research discussed in the section on trade schools.

Many equine degree programs are designed for students interested in specific hands-on or specialty careers.

A four-year college degree will open more doors than an associate degree option, though it does not guarantee employment in a job working directly with horses. Four-year degrees in equine studies or science may be broad-based or concentrated in equine management, equitation instruction, equine therapy, equine research, breeding or combinations of these areas, depending upon the design of the specific program. You might consider an agricultural degree that may be combined with an equine minor. An equine degree with a business or accounting minor or even a dual major in equine studies and business may be smart choices, especially if you think you might go into business for yourself some day.

Below are some topics to consider when researching schools. You may have more questions tailored to your specific needs; don't be afraid to ask them.

- ❏ Is the program accredited and if so, by which association or organization?
- ❏ Where is the equestrian center located?
- ❏ Is the school geographically convenient or desirable?
- ❏ What type of certificate or degree does the program offer?
- ❏ How closely does the certificate or degree align with my educational goals?
- ❏ What is the length of the program?
- ❏ What is the cost of pursuing the program (including tuition, housing, horse boarding and any other fees related to the equestrian program)?
- ❏ What type of financial aid is available?
- ❏ How long has the program been in existence?
- ❏ Are there clearly stated goals for the program?
- ❏ What is the percentage of hands-on work versus theory?
- ❏ What is the balance of general education versus equine courses?
- ❏ What is the ratio of students to instructors?
- ❏ What is the education and background of the instructors?
- ❏ How current are the curriculum and teaching materials?
- ❏ What is the placement record in internship and apprenticeship opportunities?
- ❏ How successful are students in finding jobs after graduation?
- ❏ What types of positions have former students found?
- ❏ How many horses does the program have? Are students assigned their own horse or do they share one?
- ❏ Can you bring your own horse to the school?
- ❏ How much time do you actually spend working around horses?

The following is a sampling of equine studies and science programs at a variety of two- and four-year schools. The tuition figures that are given reflect the costs during the 2002-2003 school year, so check with the school for the most current tuition rates. The appendices at the back of the book offer information on additional schools that offer equine programs.

Averett University

420 W. Main St.
Danville, VA 24541
(800) 283-7388
www.averett.edu

Averett University is located in the foothills of the Blue Ridge Mountains, three miles north of the Virginia and North Carolina state lines. The school was chartered in 1859, and has offered an equestrian studies program for approximately 30 years. Students in the program learn about the care and conditioning of the horse as well as the physical conditioning of the rider; they also gain experience in riding, teaching, training, and stable management. Internships are available in various horse-related jobs, including working at farms and ranches, training, teaching, and veterinary work. Students in the equestrian program attend horse-related field trips, workshops, and clinics; they attend lectures by expert speakers; and they may take part in other horse-related activities, such as drill team. Students may bring their own horses to the school or use one of the university's 40 horses. Horse sports offered include combined training, intercollegiate dressage, and trekking. Averett's 100-acre equestrian center, located 15 minutes from the main campus, houses an indoor ring, two outdoor rings, 40 stalls, three tack rooms, pastures, cross-country trails, and more.

Degree levels offered: Associate's through master's degrees
Equine degrees offered: Bachelor of Equestrian Studies
Student population: 2,400 total; 800 traditional (full-time bachelor's students); 45 students enrolled in equestrian studies program
Number of faculty: 65 at the school; seven instructors in equestrian program
Tuition: $16,600 annually for traditional students

Black Hawk College East Campus

1501 State Hwy. 78
Kewanee, IL 61443
(309) 852-5671
www.bhc.edu

This community college in northwestern Illinois has two campuses serving several counties. For the last 29 years the Black Hawk College East Campus has offered an equine-related program designed to prepare students to enter a variety of occupations in the horse world. Credits earned at Black Hawk

College can be transferred to many four-year colleges and universities for students wishing to earn a bachelor's degree. For program activities, students may use college-owned horses or horses provided by farms in the area, or they may bring their own. Guest speakers, clinics, seminars, off-campus labs, and farm visits are also part of the equine program, and contribute to the students' overall knowledge and experience. Internships encompassing all breeds and phases of the horse industry are offered to students in the equine degree program. Horse teams at the school include a horse judging team and an intercollegiate horse show team for western riders. Horse and riding facilities include an indoor heated arena, an outdoor riding arena, 70 stalls, four tack rooms, two classrooms, and a wet lab.

Degree levels offered: Associate's degree

Equine degrees offered: Associate of Applied Science in Horse Science or Equestrian Science; certificate offered in horse science

Student population: 700 full-time students at East Campus; 70 students enrolled in the equine program

Number of faculty: 26 faculty members at the East Campus school; four instructors in the equine program with diverse experience in English and western disciplines, judging, breeding, and shoeing

Tuition: $53 per credit hour

COLORADO STATE UNIVERSITY

Department of Equine Science
105 Equine Center
Fort Collins, CO 80523
(970) 491-8373
www.colostate.edu/depts/equine

The equine science major at Colorado State University focuses on providing students with an in-depth scientific knowledge of the varied functions of the horse and how to relate those scientific principles to the growing horse industry. The degree also offers practical experience that allows students to develop proficiency in working with horses and a broad understanding of the horse industry and its relationship to the business, recreational, and production aspects of the industry. The curriculum offers a balance of mathematics, biological, chemical, and agricultural sciences, as well as social sciences and humanities. Students can choose between a concentration in industry or science, depending upon their career goals. Both the College of Agricultural Sciences and the College of Veterinary Medicine and Biomedical Science administer the equine program. In addition to its equine sciences curriculum, the school also offers a farrier program that takes at least one year to complete. CSU is on the cutting edge of research in such horse-related areas as equine reproduction, equine orthopedics, equine nutrition, and animal acupuncture. Equine internships are available with various breed organizations, shows/equine expositions, and ranches. In addition to academic studies, the school offers riding and showing through IHSA. It also has a riding instructor training program, a horse-training program, a rodeo club, a polo club, and a judging team. Horse facilities include an equestrian center two miles from the campus with two indoor arenas, one outdoor arena, a stallion lab, and veterinary care room. The school has more than 400 horses.

Degree levels offered: Certificates through post-doctoral fellowships

Equine degrees offered: Bachelor of Science in Equine Science with industry or science concentration; master's and doctoral degrees in equine nutrition, equine reproduction, equine orthopedics; farrier certificate

Student population: 24,000; 400 in the equine science program

Number of faculty: 1,520 faculty members; 12 in the equine science program

Tuition: $3,435 in-state, $12,705 nonresidents

OHIO UNIVERSITY SOUTHERN

1804 Liberty Ave.
Ironton, OH 45638
(740) 533-4551 or (800) 626-0513
www.southernohiou.edu

The Ohio University Southern campus is one of six Ohio University campuses, and the only one offering a degree in equine studies. The program incorporates a well-rounded approach to a career with horses. Students study specialized equine topics, such as equine health, equine business management and farm management, hunt seat, saddle seat, and western riding; in addition, they take courses in psychology, advertising, public relations, mathematics, English, communications, computer literacy, and more. Internships are required for the degree and can be arranged in the individual student's area of interest. Examples of internship possibilities include farm management, training, breeding management, therapeutic riding, riding instruction, veterinary assisting, and show and event management. Students majoring in equine studies may participate in team competitions in hunt seat and western riding, sanctioned by the Intercollegiate Horse Show Association. For the past three years, the Ohio University Southern Western Equestrian Team has been Reserve Champion in its region. The Ohio Horse Park, located off campus, is the home of the Ohio University Southern equine program. Its facilities include an indoor arena, a lighted outdoor arena, a dressage ring, 40-stall barn, turnout areas, and a breeding facility.

Degree levels offered: Associate's through master's degrees

Equine degrees offered: Associate of Arts in Applied Science in Equine Studies

Student population: 3,000; 62 students enrolled in the equine studies program

Number of faculty: Varies with enrollment

Tuition: $3,282 per year for Ohio residents ($1,094 per quarter) and $4,272 for nonresidents ($1,424 per quarter)

SAINT MARY-OF-THE-WOODS COLLEGE

Saint Mary-of-the-Woods, IN 47876

(812) 535-5151

www.smwc.edu

Saint Mary-of-the-Woods College is a women's college located on a 67-acre wooded campus five miles northwest of Terre Haute, Indiana. It offers several options in equine-related studies including a general equine studies major, a training and instruction major, and an equine business management major. As part of its equine studies major, students interested in therapeutic riding may obtain NARHA certification while pursuing an emphasis in therapeutic riding. Complementing classroom studies are field trips, guest speakers, clinics, horse shows, and other equine events. Internships with breeding farms, equine organizations, and businesses are available in a variety of equine areas. Opportunities to study in Ireland are also available; students enrolled in this program are hosted by the National Specialized Equestrian Training Center in Dublin, where they are placed in a work-study situation in conjunction with their particular interests in show jumping, breeding, eventing, racing, or fox hunting. The school offers competition in both English and western disciplines through the Intercollegiate Horse Show Association. Horse facilities include indoor and outdoor riding arenas, 50 stalls, laboratories, classrooms, and offices.

Degree levels offered: Associate's through master's degrees

Equine degrees offered: Associate and Bachelor of Science in Equine Studies; Bachelor of Science in Equine Business Management; Bachelor of Science in Equine Training and Instructing. Minors are offered in equine studies and equine science for pre-veterinary majors

Student population: 1,500; approximately 320 are campus-based students; almost 1,100 are students in the Women's External Degree Program; the remainder are women and men enrolled in graduate programs; 50 are enrolled in the equine studies program, including majors and minors

Tuition: $16,000 per year

TEIKYO POST UNIVERSITY

800 Country Club Road
Waterbury, CT 06723-2540
(203) 596-4631
www.teikyopost.edu

Teikyo Post University is a small private school "catering to students who put the horse first." The emphasis of the university's equine programs is on horse care, instructing, and business. Opportunities offered through the school's "Career Specialties" program include British Horse Society instructor certification in the United Kingdom, therapeutic riding instructor certification, and trigger point myotherapy certification. (Trigger point myotherapy is a treatment that relieves and controls muscular pain and dysfunction related to chronic and acute health conditions. Myotherapists use their hands, knuckles, and fingers to locate trigger points in the body, which are hypersensitive locations in the muscles that cause pain in response to stress.) Internship opportunities are available at horse publishing companies and farms in the area. Horse facilities include a nine-stall aisle leased at Rivers Edge Farm and a hunter-jumper lesson barn 13 miles from the campus. There are indoor and outdoor arenas, grass turnout paddocks, and a classroom. All riding classes and lectures, stable management classes and practicals, the instructor practicum classes, and the equestrian team practices are held at the farm. The school has nine horses for riding courses and the instructor practicum. Additionally, Teikyo Post has an IHSA team and an IHSA dressage team, an equine club, and an equine resources committee that runs seminars, lectures, and demonstrations during the school year.

Degree levels offered: Certificate through bachelor's degree

Equine degrees offered: Associate of Science; certificate or minor in equine studies; Bachelor of Science in Equine Management; a certificate in equine law is offered within the equine management degree.

Student population: 2,050 (includes day and evening students); 45 in equine studies program

Number of faculty: 31 at the school; two full-time instructors in the equine program, and six adjunct professors

Tuition: $16,950 plus student activities fee of $550 annually

VIRGINIA INTERMONT COLLEGE

1013 Moore Street
Bristol, VA 24201
(800) 451-1842
www.vic.edu

Virginia Intermont College has educated students in the equine arena since 1972. While riding is emphasized in the program, the highest value is placed on educating students to work in the horse industry. The school strives to make its equine studies program and degree valuable to both graduates and employers through a well-rounded approach that combines hands-on, real-world horse experience with a strong liberal arts core. Clinics with recognized horse industry professionals are offered, as well as seminars on topics such as liability and risk reduction, prevention and rehabilitation of equine injuries, equine career and personnel management, and American Riding Instructor certification and preparation. Internships are encouraged and a wide variety of equine professions participate, including breeding farms, camps, and riding programs. Virginia Intermont holds a U.S. Equestrian "A" rated horse show each year. Students who participate are assigned to trainers and often invited to intern or work for the trainer during the summer months or after graduation. The college has Intercollegiate Horse Show Association and Intercollegiate Dressage Association teams that have earned top honors in the school's region and zone.

Degrees offered: Associate's and bachelor's degrees

Equine degrees offered: Bachelor of Arts or Bachelor of Science in Equine Studies; Bachelor of Science in Biology with a concentration in pre-veterinary medicine; minor in equine-assisted growth and development

Student population: 900; average 130 majors and minors in equine studies

Number of faculty: 79 full-time and several part-time or adjunct faculty; six instructors in the equine program, including a licensed doctor of veterinary medicine and a PhD in equine nutrition and exercise physiology

Tuition: $18,690 per year

WILSON COLLEGE
1015 Philadelphia Ave.
Chambersburg, PA 17201
(800) 421-8402
www.wilson.edu

Wilson College, founded in 1869, offers an equine education for women interested in stable management, riding instruction, equine-facilitated therapeutics, and veterinary technology. The women's college has offered equine programs since 1983, and keeps 40 school horses as well as approximately 30 boarded student horses on its property, for use in riding lessons, labs, instruction, clinics, shows, and other activities. Horse-related facilities include 71 stalls, two indoor arenas, one outdoor arena, 20 acres of paddocks and fields, and riding trails. In addition to classroom instruction and equitation courses, field trips, guest speakers, and clinics round out the curriculum. Students also have the opportunity to participate on the intercollegiate riding team and in the eventing, dressage, drill, or western clubs. Equine internships are available and students are matched based on their interests.

Degrees offered: Bachelor of Arts and Bachelor of Science

Equine degrees offered: Bachelor of Science in Equestrian Studies with concentration in either equine management or equestrian management; Bachelor of Science in Equine Facilitated Therapeutics; Bachelor of Science in Veterinary Medical Technology

Student population: 1,000 (includes full- and part-time); 80 in equine program

Number of faculty: 35 full-time; two full-time instructors in the equine program and eight adjuncts

Tuition: $15,100 annually

Advanced Degrees

There are many professions within the greater horse industry that require advanced education. The most popular of these is equine veterinarian. The doctor of veterinary medicine (DVM) degree requires an undergraduate degree and four additional years of study at an accredited veterinary school, of which there are 28 in the United States. Other professions requiring advanced schooling of up to four years beyond an undergraduate degree include veterinary research, education, law, accounting, sports psychology, nutrition, pharmacology, chiropractic, and ethology. Many of these careers also require individuals to pass licensing or certification exams after receiving the advanced degree before they are able to work in their field.

Many careers require individuals to pass licensing or certification exams.

There are professions that do not require education beyond a four-year degree, but having a master's or doctorate degree will enable individuals to earn higher salaries and advance more quickly.

Following are a sampling of schools that offer advanced degrees in equine fields. Tuition rates are those in effect during 2003.

AUBURN UNIVERSITY
Animal & Dairy Sciences
210 Upchurch Hall
Auburn University, AL 36849-5415
www.ag.auburn.edu/dept/ads

Auburn University, a land grant university that opened its doors in 1856, is located in the hills of eastern Alabama. It is one of 28 veterinary schools in the United States. Master's and doctoral-level degrees are offered and provide advanced education and technical training in preparation for careers in public and private sectors related to animal science and technology, food science and technology, animal biotechnology, agribusiness, and university-level research and education. Areas of specialization include animal nutrition, biochemistry and molecular biology, quantitative/population genetics, and reproductive biology. Equine competition takes place via the Intercollegiate Horse Show Association, local, open, and breed shows are also offered. Horse facilities include the Horse Teaching Unit, with 50 school-owned horses, which is two miles from campus and features two lighted arenas, a reproduction lab, and a round pen.

Degree levels offered: Associate through doctorate

Equine degrees offered: Master of Science or PhD in Animal & Dairy Science with equine research; Doctor of Veterinary Medicine; Bachelor of Science; Animal Science; equine extension program

Student population: Approximately 23,000, with almost 3,000 in graduate programs

Tuition: $2,309 in-state per semester; $6,539 out-of-state per semester; Tuition and fees for the veterinary program are $9,110 for residents per academic year and $26,938 for nonresidents

SOUTHERN ILLINOIS UNIVERSITY

Department of Animal Sciences
Carbonadle, IL 62901
(618) 453-2329
www.siu.edu

Southern Illinois University in Carbondale is the second largest comprehensive university in Illinois. Founded in 1869, it maintains more than 100 academic programs that lead to associate's, bachelor's, master's, specialist's, and doctoral and professional degrees. The Department of Animal Science, Food, and Nutrition offers programs of study leading to the Master of Science degree in animal science. Programs may be designed in the areas of nutrition, reproductive physiology, biotechnology, and/or growth and development, with emphasis on horses, beef cattle, dairy cattle, or swine. Horse-related student organizations include the SIUC Equine Science Club, which sponsors events and seminars, and the SIUC riding club and equestrian team, which competes at Intercollegiate Horse Show Association events. There is also a rodeo club. Horse activities take place at the SIUC Horse Center.

Degree levels offered: Associate through doctorate and professional

Equine degrees offered: Master of Science in Animal Science with a focus in equine reproduction physiology; PhD in Physiology with equine focus; Bachelor of Science in Animal Science with equine specialization; minor in equine studies

Student population: Approximately 22,000

Tuition: $2,309 in state per semester, $6,539 out-of-state per semester. These figures do not include room and board.

UNIVERSITY OF CALIFORNIA, DAVIS

Department of Animal Science
One Shields Ave.
Davis, CA 95616-8521
(530) 752-2918
www.ucdavis.edu

University of California, Davis, is the largest of the 10 campuses of the University of California, which was chartered as a land grant college in 1868. It is second in total expenditures and third in enrollment. Master's and doctoral-level degrees specializing in equines are offered in animal science, physiology, and endocrinology. Candidates accepted into these programs are also eligible to participate in equine reproductive endocrinology research conducted by Dr. Roser, whose research focus is endocrine regulation of fertility in the mare and stallion. The school's horse facility houses approximately 30 mares and four stallions, consisting of Thoroughbred, quarter horses, Arabians and mules. The facility includes an outdoor arena, 19 outoor paddocks, a main barn with offices, stalls, breed shed, laboratory, and living quarters for two live-in students. Equine undergraduate and equine internships are also offered. The UC Davis Equestrian Center offers English and western pleasure riding and competition. The university also has a veterinary school.

Degree levels offered: Associate through doctorate

Equine degrees offered: Bachelor of Science in Animal Science with equine specialization; Master of Science in Animal Science with equine concentration; Master of science and PhD in Physiology and Endocrinology specializing in equines; Doctor of Veterinary Medicine

Student population: Enrollment at the university is approximately 29,000, with approximately 100 students in the graduate animal science program and 505 in the veterinary school

Tuition: Graduate tuition is $4,902 for in-state students per school year and $16,224 for nonresidents per year; veterinary school tuition is $11,072 for in state and $22,204 for nonresidents.

TEXAS A&M UNIVERSITY

Department of Animal Science
Kleberg Center
College Station, TX 77843-2471
(979) 845-7731
www.tamu.edu

Texas A&M University, established as part of the land grant college system, was opened in 1876, as the Agricultural and Mechanical College of Texas. Since that time, the name has changed to more accurately reflect the expanded role of the university and its tremendous growth since its inception. The initials "A" and "M" no longer represent any specific words, as the school's curriculum has grown to include agriculture and engineering, but also veterinary medicine, business, education, and many other areas. Equine-specific graduate programs at Texas A&M include studies focusing on equine nutrition and equine physiology, which may be in the areas of exercise or reproduction. The school includes an off-campus equestrian center and the Equine Pavilion, a state-of-the-art 19,000-square-foot breeding and treatment facility opened in 2002, at the College of Veterinary Medicine. Horse sports at Texas A&M include showing through the Intercollegiate Horse Show Association, polo, rodeo, and judging teams.

Degree levels offered: Bachelor's through doctorate and professional

Equine degrees offered: Bachelor of Science in Animal Science with equine science; Master of Science and doctorates in Equine Nutrition and Equine Physiology; Doctor of Veterinary Medicine

Student population: Approximately 44,000

Tuition: $46 per credit hour for residents; $282 per hour for nonresidents; veterinary school tuition and fees are $10,235 per school year for residents, $21,035 for nonresidents

College Sports Organizations

Collegiate horse sports organizations provide students the opportunity to ride and compete; horse ownership is not mandatory. If you are majoring in an equine field, however, be aware that just because a school may offer horse sports does not necessarily mean it offers equine degrees. See Appendix K for specific contact information.

INTERCOLLEGIATE HORSE SHOW ASSOCIATION

The Intercollegiate Horse Show Association promotes competition at the college level in English and western disciplines. Classes range from beginner walk-trot to advanced open equitation courses. To keep the riding field level, students are not allowed to use their own horses or tack and schooling is not permitted. Instead, riders and horses are matched through random drawings. Individual colleges host each event and provide the horses.

NATIONAL INTERCOLLEGIATE RODEO ASSOCIATION

The National Intercollegiate Rodeo Association, which is divided into 11 regions, establishes and maintains the standards for college-level rodeo. More than 135 colleges and universities have rodeo organizations on their campuses. NIRA members compete in approximately 10 rodeos a year, which offer team roping, barrel racing, breakaway roping, bull riding, and more, as they seek to make it to the College National Finals Rodeo.

UNITED STATES POLO FEDERATION

Nearly 30 colleges and universities offer polo teams for both men and women. The teams are divided into Eastern, Southeastern, Central, and Western regions, with each region holding a year-end conference tournament to decide who will go to the annual national championships. Team members ride school ponies, many of them donated to the school's polo club, and ride ponies owned by other schools when traveling to other campuses to compete.

INTERCOLLEGIATE/INTERSCHOLASTIC DRESSAGE ASSOCIATION

The mission of the Intercollegiate/Interscholastic Dressage Association is to introduce students to dressage and to nurture their continued development through competition and educational opportunities. IDA, which began in 1995 and held its first National Finals in 2002, is affiliated with the United States Dressage Federation and adheres to the rules of U.S. Equestrian. More than 20 colleges and universities, along with a handful of high schools, are currently members of IDA.

Horsemanship Clinics

Clinics offer individuals the chance to study under reputable experts and become certified trainers and clinicians in those experts' horsemanship methods. Once a person is certified, he can use the expert's name (or publicize that he was trained in that expert's methods, depending on the policy of the expert) to market himself and the business. Clinics may run for a few days or last several weeks, depending on the program.

Following are just three examples of certification programs and clinics offered by well-known horse experts. To find an expert whose methods interest you, read horse publications and books, browse the Internet, and talk to established horse people.

Natural horsemanship trainer Frank Bell offers a Partner Certification Program teaching his Seven Step Safety System (Dances With Horses, Inc., P.O. Box 819, Rexburg, ID 83440; (303) 681-3723; www.horse-whisperer.com). The length and cost of the program varies depending upon the horse experience of the student. Students attend as many three- and seven-day clinics as necessary to effectively learn and demonstrate proficiency in the method.

Centered Riding, developed by horsewoman and author Sally Swift, teaches the classic principles of riding using body awareness, centering, and imagery (Centered Riding, Inc., P.O. Box 12377, Philadelphia, PA 19119; (215) 438-1286; www.centeredriding.org). The Centered Riding Instructor's Course is open to riding instructors who are familiar with Centered Riding through attendance at a lower-level clinic or from prior work with a certified instructor. The course is seven days long.

Respected trainer John Lyons provides a certification program that teaches his conditioned response training methods (John Lyons Symposiums, Inc., 8714 County Road 300, Parachute, CO 81635; (970) 285-9797 ext. 170; www.johnlyons.com). The program, taught by his son Josh Lyons, is held in Colorado and consists of 12 weeks of study divided into three-week sessions. A limited number of people are accepted into the program and participants must bring their own horses to the sessions.

Home Study

If distance or time prohibits traveling to a school for study, home-study courses are available. Home-study courses may or may not help you get a job, but a good one can enhance your knowledge about horses or support fields, potentially making you more marketable. If you decide to go this route, choose a program by researching it thoroughly. The appendices list several schools offering equine home-study courses. Following are profiles of four schools' programs:

ASPEN EQUINE STUDIES, INC.
Equine Massage
5821 County Road 331
Silt, CO 81652
(970) 876-5839
www.equinemassageschool.com

Aspen Equine Studies offers three programs of distance study: equine massage therapy, and hydrotherapy. The equine massage program was originally designed as a classroom program and includes the study of muscles and skeletons and their actions, indications and contraindications for massage, six major strokes and occasions for each, and prevention and recognition of injury. The fee for this program is $199, plus shipping. Students completing the distance program and wishing to attend the five-day on-site massage program at Aspen Equine Studies will receive a $25 discount for the on-site program. The equine sports trainer program is offered as a natural progression for experienced massage therapists. It costs $125, plus shipping. The hydrotherapy program, targeted to professionals already working in horse rehabilitation, guides the practitioner through the proper uses of heat and ice in injury as well as the prevention and recovery of heat-related illnesses. The cost of the course is $35, plus shipping. All three programs provide a certificate upon completion.

GLOBAL EQUINE ACADEMY
P.O. Box 205
Beulah, WY 82712
(307) 283-2587
www.globalequineacademy.com

Global Equine Academy, located near the Black Hills of South Dakota and Wyoming, offers both online, on-site, and combination courses in a variety of equine subjects. Classes include equine reproduction, equine nutrition, stallion management, and equine marketing. In addition to individual classes, students can earn certificates in equine management and principles of horse training, and farrier certification. Prices vary from $375 for an eight-week-long online lecture course, to $6,975 for the certificate on principles of horse training, which includes nine lecture and four riding classes. In addition, Dickinson State University in North Dakota offers an online associate degree in agriculture sales and service, with emphasis in equine management that uses all of Global Equine Academy's online classes. Contact Global Equine Academy for more information and prices on this program.

NEW HORIZONS EQUINE EDUCATION CENTER
425 Red Mountain Road
Livermore, CO 80536-9998
(970) 484-9207
www.newhorizonsequine.com

New Horizons Equine Education Center offers distance learning for students 16 and up, from basic horsemanship through advanced principles of equine management. For example, the equine science series provides step-by-step lessons on the essentials of horse ownership, care, and management. The 10-course series explores nutrition, grooming, tack selection, health care, and other horse-related topics. Each course is divided into six lessons that include text, illustrations, and assignments. A certificate of achievement is awarded following completion of each course and a special certificate is awarded to students who satisfactorily complete the entire series. The complete series is $450 and individual series courses are $48 each with special discounts for members of the American Quarter Horse Association, the American Paint Horse Association, the Appaloosa Horse Club, and the Arabian Horse Association. New Horizons also offers special breed programs on quarter horses, paint horses, Appaloosas and Arabians. Individual courses are $48. Special interest courses in training, stable management, behavior, trailering, first aid, and other areas are available from $75 to $95. The school also offers a Young Equestrian Series for $45

PENZANCE EQUINE SOLUTIONS
200 South St.
Douglas, MA 01516
(508) 476-1317
www.kersur.net/~santa

Penzance Equine Solutions provides home-study courses on horse care and management. Courses are offered on safety horse breeds, types, and basic conformation, psychology and behavior, feed and nutrition, health care, and stable management. Students who satisfactorily complete all courses receive a certificate in Horse Care & Management; or they may take individual classes as desired. The entire certificate course is $250, plus a $35 new student enrollment fee; individual classes are $40 each. This program is recommended for older teenagers and adults. In addition to the home-study certificate and classes, Penzance Equine Solutions holds many on-site horsemanship workshops, seminars and presentations, clinics, camps, and certificate courses.

Continuing Career Options
The horse industry is always evolving. Advances in veterinary medicine, new and better horse products, and the ever-increasing use of the Internet to advertise and promote businesses are just some of the changes taking place. As a result continuing education opportunities designed to help workers stay current in the

industry and in their fields are available. Colleges and universities offer intensive short courses for equine professionals and those involved in related fields. Depending on content, these courses also may be appropriate for individuals training for careers or changing careers within the industry. Also, horse-related professional associations sponsor seminars and workshops for career professionals. To find these educational opportunities, check with a college or university in your area or contact the professional association representing your field. Following are some examples of equine short courses offered by universities. Many other schools and associations also offer short courses.

Colorado State University
Equine Sciences
Fort Collins, CO 80523-1679
(970) 491-8509 or 491-8373
www.equinescience.colostate.edu

Colorado State University's Equine Reproduction Short Courses began in 1971, with four students participating in an artificial insemination course. Today, the series has an annual attendance of more than 500. Courses are offered for veterinarians and horse owners and range from daylong classes to those that are several days long. Time in the courses is divided equally between lecture and laboratory work. Prices vary per course, ranging from $350 to more than $1,000.

Kansas State University
Department of Animals Sciences and Industry
128 Weber Hall
Manhattan, Kansas 66506
(785) 532-1240
www.oznet.ksu.edu/equine

Several times during the spring, an equine reproductive management short course is offered at Kansas State University. Some of the topics in the reproductive short course include basic mare anatomy, use of reproductive ultrasonography, artificial insemination, and equipment needs for the breeding lab. The entire course is presented in a laboratory setting using live animals. Participants have the opportunity to gain supervised hands-on experience as well as observe demonstrations. Approximately one-half of the course is devoted to hands-on learning.

The reproductive management short course is two days long and costs $250. Courses on additional topics are sometimes offered as well.

NORTH CAROLINA STATE UNIVERSITY AND THE NORTH CAROLINA HORSE COUNCIL

Extension Horse Husbandry
Box 7523, Raleigh, NC 27695-7523
(919) 515-5784
www.cals.ncsu.edu/an_sci/extension/horse/hhmain.html

North Carolina State University, with its co-sponsor, the North Carolina Horse Council, offers many short equine courses each year, including training clinics with various top trainers and a horse judging course, a new horse owner's short course, equine forage management, horse nutrition, and horse genetics. Some courses are offered every year, while others are rotated; check the Web site for current courses. Courses range from $10 to $650; most average between $50 and $75, and attendees are provided a reference manual.

UNIVERSITY OF PENNSYLVANIA

New Bolton Center School of Veterinary Medicine
Kennett Square, PA 19348
(610) 444-5800
www2.vet.upenn.edu/labs/equinebehavior

Short courses are offered at the University of Pennsylvania, targeted to veterinarians, breeding managers, and horse owners; courses include mare and stallion breeding management, stallion handling, and horse behavior. Courses range from one to two days and prices are $500 to $800, depending on the course and its length.

Financial Assistance

Many sources of financial help are available for those wishing to continue their education, no matter what level of certification or degree they seek. Scholarships, grants, loans, and work-study programs are available through horse organizations, colleges and universities, the U.S. government, and fraternal and service organizations. It takes time and research to find the best financial assistance for you and your career path.

Many scholarships and grants go unclaimed each year because students are not aware they exist or they don't know how to find them. Likewise, students are often unaware that nongovernmental organizations, such as credit unions and banks, may offer loans for continuing education. The following list of sources can help you get started as you research financial aid. These sources may provide financial aid or provide leads for finding aid. It is important to remember that many sponsoring organizations select scholarship and grant awardees based on very specific eligibility criteria, so cast your net far afield and identify several potential resources. Just a few of the eligibility requirements that may be evaluated include grade point average, involvement in equine activities, career being pursued, community involvement, financial need, and student or parent membership in the sponsoring organization. If you are interested in taking individual classes that don't necessarily lead to a degree or a short course at a university or a clinic, contact the organizations below to see if they offer financial aid options for non-degree-related activities.

Many scholarships and grants go unclaimed each year because students are not aware they exist or they don't know how to find them

COLLEGES, UNIVERSITIES, AND TRADE SCHOOLS

Ask the financial aid office at your college, university, or trade school for a list of financial assistance options. If you are planning to pursue an equine-related degree, get information from the schools you are considering about equine-specific scholarships they may offer.

STATE HORSE COUNCILS AND FARM BUREAUS

Often, individual associations offer scholarships. The Indiana Horse Council, for example, awards up to six educational grants annually of at least $500 each to residents of the state who are members or immediately related to members of the organization. For information, contact the grant coordinator at (317) 692-7115. Residents of Wisconsin who are members of the Wisconsin State Horse Council (WSHC) can apply for the WSHC Scholarship. Write to them at WSHC Scholarship, N8849 Hwy. Y, Watertown, WI 53094. The California Farm Bureau Scholarship Foundation provides approximately $75,000 in academic scholarships each year. To qualify for consideration, applicants must be residents of the state, study for a career in the agriculture industry, and attend a four-year school in California. Recipients are selected based on academic achievement, career goals, extracurricular activities, determination, and a demonstration of leadership skills. The California Farm Bureau Federation can be contacted at 2300 River Plaza Drive, Sacramento, CA 95833; (916) 561-5500; www.cfbf.com. Check with your state's horse council or farm bureau for scholarship and grant options. To find these organizations, do a web search (for example: Oklahoma Horse Council), or go to the national sites for these organizations, www.horsecouncil.org and www.fb.org.

UNITED STATES PONY CLUBS

The United States Pony Club (USPC) offers scholarships to its members through the following colleges and universities: Cazenovia College, Centenary College, Delaware Valley College, Johnson & Wales University, Lake Erie College, Midway College, Otterbein College, Salem-Teikyo University, Stephens College, University of Findlay, University of Louisville, and William Woods University. Complete details and contact information for these scholarships are available on the national Pony Club Web site at www.ponyclub.org, or write to them at United States Pony Club, 4041 Iron Works Parkway, Lexington, KY 40511. The Canadian Pony Club also offers a scholarship to members. The Todd Sandler Memorial Scholarship award consists of a two-week residential horsemanship course at the training orga-nization known as The Horse People, Inc. Contact the club at Canadian Pony Club National Office, Box 127, Baldur, Manitoba R0K 0B0 Canada; (888) 286-PONY; www.canadianponyclub.org.

FRATERNAL ORGANIZATIONS AND CORPORATIONS

Were either of your parents members of a college fraternal organization? These organizations are good sources for scholarships. Or, do either of your parents work for a large corporation that provides scholarships to children of employees? Your parent might consider contacting the employee benefits department for more information.

BREED REGISTRIES AND ASSOCIATIONS

The following registries and associations offer scholarships and grants to their members and youth members based on a variety of criteria.

- ❏ American Morgan Horse Institute awards scholarships to deserving students wishing to further their horsemanship skills in a variety of areas and riding disciplines. AMHI Scholarships, P.O. Box 837 Shelburne, VT 05482-0519; (802) 985-8477; www.morganhorse.com.

- American Paint Horse Association. During the 2003-2003 academic year, the American Paint Horse Association Youth Development Foundation awarded 35 scholarships to APHA members who are full-time students and involved in horse activities using a paint horse or who have been actively contributing to a regional club for at least one year prior to applying. American Paint Horse Association Youth Development Foundation, P.O. Box 961023, Fort Worth, TX 76161; (817) 834-2742; www.apha.com.
- American Quarter Horse Association has a large number of scholarships available to students based on a variety of criteria, including geographic location, area of study, horsemanship background, and more. American Quarter Horse Foundation, 2601 I-40 East, Amarillo, TX 79104; (806) 376-5181; www.aqha.org.
- American Saddlebred Horse Association. Scholarship recipients are chosen on the basis of academic success, financial need, involvement with American Saddlebred horses, extracurricular activities, and personal references. American Saddlebred Horse Association Foundation, 4093 Iron Works Parkway, Lexington KY 40511; (859) 259-2742; www.asha.net.
- Appaloosa Horse Club. Several scholarships for youth members and members or dependents of member studying in an equine field. Appaloosa Youth Foundation, 2720 W. Pullman Road, Moscow, ID 83843; (208) 882-5578; www.appaloosa.com.
- Arabian Horse Trust offers scholarships to high school seniors and first- and second-year college students. Recipients must demonstrate financial need and have an ongoing commitment to and interest in Arabian horses. Equine Scholarships, 12000 Zuni Street, Westminster, CO 80234; (303) 450-4710; www.arabianhorsetrust.com.
- Arabian Horse Association. The International Arabian Breeders Sweepstakes Commission (IABSC) annually awards 40 scholarships of $2,500 each to graduating high school seniors who have competed at the regional or national level on a sweepstakes-nominated horse. Scholarship recipients are selected based on merit, which includes a review of grade point average, SAT or ACT score, class rank, and extracurricular activities. Applicants must also be current members of the Arabian Horse Association at the time the scholarship application is submitted. Arabian Horse Association, 10805 E. Bethany Drive, Aurora, CO 80014-2605; (303) 696-4500; www.arabianhorses.org.

- International Buckskin Horse Association. IBHA scholarships are available to current members who have recently participated in IBHA activities. International Buckskin Horse Association, P.O. Box 268, Shelby, IN 46377; (219) 552-1013; www.ibha.net.
- Tennessee Walking Horse Breeders' and Exhibitors' Association. The TWHBEA awards eight annual $2,500 scholarships, based on academic performance and equine activities; some consideration is given to financial need. TWHBEA, P.O. Box 286, Lewisburg, TN 37091-0286; (931) 359-1574; www.twhbea.com.

SHOW AND SPORT ORGANIZATIONS

The Intercollegiate Equestrian Foundation (Hollow Rd., Box 741, Stony Brook, NY 11790; (914) 773-3788; www.ihsa.com) awards Intercollegiate Horse Show Association scholarships to IHSA members each year. The National Reining Horse Association (NRHA) provides scholarships through its sports foundation (3000 NW 10th St., Oklahoma City, OK 73107; 405-946-7400; www.nrha.com). Ask your show or sport organization if it offers scholarship or grant opportunities.

- Horseracing. The Harness Horse Youth Foundation (16575 Carey Road, Westfield, IN 46074; (317) 867, 5877; www.hhyf.org) and Harness Tracks of America, Inc. (Harness Tracks of America Scholarship Program, 4640 East Sunrise, Suite 200, Tucson, AZ 85718; (520) 529-2525; www.harnesstracks.com) offer scholarships to students pursuing careers in the horse industry, or whose parent or other relative is a racing professional. The American Quarter Horse Association awards scholarships to members involved with racing (see contact information under previous listing). The University of Arizona's Race Track Industry Program offers scholarships to its students; it also lists scholarship and financial aid information from other sources on its Web site, www.ag.arizona.edu/rtip. Additionally, the U.S. Harness Writers Association (Box 1314, Mechanicsburg, PA 17055; (717) 766-3219; www.ustrotting.com/ushwa/ushwa.htm) offers a scholarship to a college student in North America who is knowledgeable about harness racing and is interested in a career in journalism. Thoroughbred racing also offers a scholarship for an aspiring sportswriter. The Fred Russell-Grantland Rice Sportswriting Scholarship, sponsored jointly by Vanderbilt University in Nashville, Tennessee, and Thoroughbred Racing Associations of North America, Inc., provides four years of study at the university and is awarded annually to a high school senior. Contact the Coordinator of Special Scholarships, Undergraduate Admissions, Vanderbilt University, 2305 West End Ave., Nashville, TN 37203; (615) 322-2561.

❑ National FFA Organization and the National 4-H Council. Each year, the National FFA Organization awards more than $2 million in scholarships to members studying for an agricultural career (National FFA Center, P.O. Box 68960, 6060 FFA Drive, Indianapolis, IN 46268-0960; (317) 802-6060; www.ffa.org). The National 4-H Council offers grants at the local and state level for community projects but does not provide scholarships. Check with your local 4-H club for possible scholarship opportunities. National 4-H Council, 7100 Connecticut Ave., Chevy Chase, MD 20815-4999; www.fourhcouncil.edu.

❑ The American Association of Equine Practitioners Foundation. The AAEP awards scholarships to fourth-year veterinary students planning to enter an equine practice who are members of the AAEP. The AAEP Foundation also awards several youth scholarships each year to individuals from a variety of organizations, such as the National FFA Organization and the United States Pony Club. The foundation can be reached at 4075 Iron Works Pike, Lexington, KY 40511; (859) 233-0147; www.aaep.org.

RODEO ORGANIZATIONS

The National Intercollegiate Rodeo Association (2316 Eastgate North, Suite 160, Walla Walla, WA 99362; (509) 529-4402; www.collegerodeo.com/foundation.shtml), through the National Intercollegiate Rodeo Association Foundation, offers several scholarships based on a variety of criteria. The National High School Rodeo Association (12001 Tejon Street, Ste. 128, Denver, CO 80234; 303-452-0820; www.nhsra.org) offers scholarships totaling more than $133,000 each year. Scholarships are awarded to members of the organization who compete in the annual national rodeo, as well as to members based on their financial need, desire to attend college, and stated goals and objectives. Additionally, the National Little Britches Rodeo Association (1045 W. Rio Grande, Colorado Springs, CO 80906; (800) 763-3694; www.nlbra.com) also has scholarships available.

PROFESSIONAL ASSOCIATIONS

If you are entering a field that is not specific to the horse industry, such as marketing, accounting, computer programming, or law, check for scholarship information with professional associations supporting that field.

THE INTERNET

There is a wealth of scholarship information on the web. Go to your favorite search engine and type in "horse industry scholarships," "horse industry financial aid," or "horse schools scholarships" for horse-industry organizations that sponsor scholarships, grants, and loans. Or, try a free financial aid Web site, such as www.fastweb.com or www.scholarship.com. There are several such free aid information sites online. Be wary of any Internet service that charges a fee for finding or helping students apply for financial aid. While there are legitimate scholarship search services that do charge, there are many scams related to this area that operate on the Internet. Any service that charges a fee should be carefully investigated with the Better Business Bureau, your school guidance counselor, or your state attorney general's office. For more on scholarship searching and scams, go to the U.S. Department of Education's "Looking for Student Aid" Web site at www.ed.gov/prog_info/SFA/LSA.

LOCAL RESOURCES

Community, civic, and religious organizations can be excellent sources of information about private scholarships, as can banks and credit unions. Nongovernmental loans for students may be offered through these institutions. Finally, check reference sections of public and school libraries that maintain financial aid information.

GOVERNMENT LOANS

The U.S. Department of Education is the largest single provider of student financial aid in the country. Approximately 70 percent of the student aid awarded every year comes from the Department's programs. In 2000-2001, government assistance—in the form of loans, grants, and work-study programs—amounted to $61 billion. Loans must be repaid with interest, and grants are not repaid. Work-study programs provide jobs to help students pay for their education. The U.S. Department of Education publishes an informative online student handbook about its financial aid program; called

The Student Guide, Financial Aid from the U.S. Department of Education. It provides details on assistance available, eligibility requirements, repayment options, and how to apply. You will find the guide at the following web address: www.ed.gov/prog_info/SFA/StudentGuide. Note that not all schools accept all forms of federal financial aid. Check with your school's financial aid administrator to find out what it accepts.

Following is an overview of the loans and grants available:

- ❑ Federal Perkins Loans. These loans borrowed from and repaid to schools offer a low interest rate to undergraduate and graduate students. The loan is made with government funds, with a share contributed by the school. Depending on the level of financial need and other factors, undergraduate students can borrow up to $4,000 for each year of study, with a maximum of $20,000 borrowed as an undergraduate. Students engaged in graduate or professional study can borrow up to $6,000 per year, with a maximum of $40,000, which includes money borrowed as an undergraduate.

- ❑ Stafford Loans. There are two types of Stafford Loans available—direct loans from the federal government and Federal Family Education Loans (FFEL) from private lenders. Usually, schools participate in one Stafford loan program or the other. Eligibility requirements and loan limits are the same for both programs, with loan repayment options and administration of the loans being the major differences. Both subsidized and unsubsidized loans are available (subsidized loans are based on financial need while unsubsidized loans are not). Loan amounts vary according to school year and other factors.

- ❑ PLUS Loans. These are awarded to parents of students rather than to the students themselves. Like Stafford loans, they are available as direct loans or as FFELs. Parents must undergo a credit check and students must meet federal student aid eligibility requirements. The yearly limit on a PLUS Loan is equal to the cost of attendance minus any other forms of financial aid. By law, the interest rate on these loans will never exceed 9 percent.

- ❑ Federal Pell Grants. Pell Grants are awarded to undergraduate students based on financial need. School costs, full- or part-time attendance, and length of attendance are taken into account when considering the amount of the grant. Eligible students may receive one Pell Grant in a year, with maximum amounts available dependent on program funding.

(The maximum grant for the 2002-2003 award year was $4,000.) The U. S. Department of Education guarantees enough money to participating schools to pay the Pell Grants of all eligible students. Unlike loans, Federal Pell Grants do not have to be repaid.

❏ Federal Supplemental Educational Opportunity Grants (FSEOG). FSEOGs are for undergraduate students with exceptional financial need. Students are awarded these grants based on the availability of funds at their particular school, with no guarantee that every eligible student will be able to receive a grant. Students can receive grants from $100 to $4,000, depending on need and funding levels.

❏ Federal Work-Study. The Federal Work-Study Program provides jobs for undergraduate and graduate students who demonstrate financial need. Students in on-campus jobs usually work for their schools, and may or may not work in jobs related to their majors. Students in off-campus jobs typically work for nonprofit organizations or public agencies. However, some schools also have work-study agreements with private, for-profit employers. Total amounts awarded through this program depend on financial need, funding levels, and when the application is made. Students are usually paid hourly, though some graduate students in higher-level work-study jobs may be salaried. Wages are equal to or greater than the federal minimum wage.

CHAPTER 5

Get the Job

— — —

You've done the necessary homework on the area of the horse industry in which you would like to work. You also know what career path you're interested in following. You've decided on the type of schooling or training that you'll need to reach your goal. Now, how do you find job opportunities and what tools do you need to get an interview and the job?

When in doubt, remember that personal relationships are vital. Make contacts at your local stables and with equine professionals for future leads. Don't hesitate to use your school's resources like career placement offices. Remember to keep building bridges with each new contact.

Finding Job Leads

There are many different ways to find job leads, some better than others. Networking with people in your chosen field, according to the U.S. Department of Labor, is the best way to find employment. You can use cold calls and mailings, equine industry employment agencies, listings through professional associations or alumni groups, college job fairs, equine expos, and help wanted ads to assist in the job search. Having a multi-faceted approach that leans heavily on the more proactive job search methods, such as networking, will help you get employed.

Networking

Ideally, your job search should begin once you've decided on a career and even before you've finished acquiring whatever combination of education and experience you will need to pursue that career. This is where networking proves its importance. If you followed the advice in Chapter 2, and stayed in touch with the professionals you met and spoke to while researching potential careers, one of your first steps in your job search will be to let these people know that you are now actively seeking employment. Pull out that list of networking contacts and get in touch! Try to speak in person, if possible, with most of your contacts, either on the telephone or face-to-face. Ask if they can provide any information or advice—or potential leads—for your job search. Know what you want to say before you make contact, but try to keep your call short so you don't use too much of the person's time. It's helpful to have a short "sales pitch" written out that tells your contacts about the type of position you're seeking and offers highlights of your education and experience. You might want to practice on a friend or family member first, to make sure your delivery is fluid and conversational. For people you don't know well or are uncomfortable approaching in person, write a letter reminding them how they know you and include your resume.

Try to speak in person, if possible, with most of your contacts, either on the telephone or face-to-face.

When contacting your networking list:

❑ Remind the person who you are and where you met.

❑ Indicate that you have just graduated college, completed training as a working student, etc., and are now seeking a job.

❑ Be specific about what type of job you are seeking.

- Offer brief details about the highlights of your education or experience. For example, "I just graduated with a bachelor's degree in equine science from XYZ University. The focus of my studies was on reproduction and I spent summer internships at the Great Horses breeding farm working for breeding manager Jane Jones." Then, give a concise description of your duties, such as, "I was responsible for helping with care of 20 broodmares, foal sitting, and assisting with artificial insemination."
- Ask if she might know someone who is looking for an employee with your skills and experience.
- Thank her sincerely, whether or not the conversation is helpful.
- Ask politely if she will contact you if she hears of something for which you might be a good fit.

If a networking contact is also a potential employer, don't ask about possible employment opportunities with the company or barn; if there is an opening and she is interested in you, she will mention it when you let her know of your availability. If you ask them directly for employment, and for some reason she does not think you are a good fit for the operation, you will have put her on the spot, potentially making for an awkward situation. If you have maintained polite, professional contact with the people on your networking list, they will probably be more than happy to give you advice or keep an eye out for an appropriate position. Remember to ask everyone you speak with for names of other possible contacts you might approach. Also, if you are in school, let professors and other students

Remember to ask everyone you speak with for names of other possible contacts you might approach.

know what type of employment you're seeking. Let your horsey friends know that you are interested in a particular job within the industry. The more people you tell, the better chance you'll find someone who knows someone who's hiring.

Always remember to thank anyone who helps you and remember that networking works both ways, so be willing to help others in the future, if they should request it.

COLLEGE PLACEMENT OFFICES, CAREER FAIRS AND ALUMNI ASSOCIATIONS

School placement offices provide counseling on conducting job searches, honing interview skills, and preparing a resume. They maintain job listings and may be able to help you find a position. Visit your school placement office for more information. Colleges also hold career fairs usually encompassing a variety of industries and fields at which employers set up booths to meet with prospective employees. Check with your school about career fairs in your area. If you are a career changer who is also a college graduate, contact the alumni association of your alma mater and inquire about possible career services and job listings.

EQUINE EMPLOYMENT SPECIALISTS

Agencies are available to help job seekers find employment in the horse industry; they also can provide valuable advice on pursuing horse industry careers. Here is information on four such agencies:

- ❑ Equimax; www.equimax.com or call (800) 759-9494. Equimax maintains a list of horse industry jobs that is updated daily, as well as a list of job candidates that is provided to employers. The charge to job seekers is $45 to $70, depending on the level of service requested. It also provides valuable job search information on its Web site and through its compact disc, *The Career Game*. The CD is provided free to those who sign up for the service, or it can be purchased separately for $9.95.

- ❑ Equistaff; www.equistaff.com. This online job service is paid for by employers and is free to job seekers. After registering, applicants can search jobs and add their resumes to the system to get their pertinent information and qualifications listed for possible employers. The site also contains tips on writing cover letters and other aspects of job hunting.

- ❑ Professional Equine Employment; www.equinepros.com or call (800) 733-6008. Following a detailed application process, Professional Equine Employment places job seekers in positions throughout the horse industry. The only charge to applicants is a $40 nonrefundable processing fee ($75 charge to nonresidents of the U.S.).

- ❑ The White Horse Agency; www.equusuk.co.uk; Tel: 07967 388597. The White Horse Agency is based in the United Kingdom, but offers placements throughout the world. The site is updated weekly with new job listings.

PROFESSIONAL ASSOCIATIONS

Professional associations provide job leads to members either through postings on their Web sites or through printed listings. (For example, the American Veterinary Medical Association lists jobs for veterinary personnel on its site.) While associations representing professions directly related to the horse industry may be good sources of jobs for the industry, they may be a long shot to find a public relations job in the horse industry through an association representing public relations professionals, or a marketing job in the industry from an association representing marketing professionals as these organizations represent professionals in all industries with the horse world playing just a small part. However, if you are trying to build experience in your field prior to entering the horse industry, then professional associations for your field are good places to look for employment.

COLD CALLS AND MAILINGS

Do research on the industry employers you would like to work for and then contact them directly, either by phoning or sending a letter and resume. Do this even if they have no advertised openings. If you get someone on the telephone, briefly go through your sales pitch, letting him or her know how you would benefit his or her operation. If they are not interested, thank them politely and ask them if they know of anyone else you might contact. If they don't have any openings now but may in the future, find out if they'll grant you an interview anyway. The employers are more likely to keep you in mind if they've had personal contact with you and you've made a good impression. When approaching potential employers through the mail, send a professional looking, well-written resume accompanied by a personal cover letter. Do not use e-mail to approach employers unless you've first found out through your research that the employer accepts resumes this way. If you're unsure about an employer's policy, err on the side of caution: send your resume the old-fashioned way, or call to find out the preferred method of submitting your resume. If an employer does accept resumes via e-mail, a cover letter is still required and it should not be any less formal than one you would send through the regular mail. However, don't worry about trying to scan your signature for electronic cover letters—it's okay to send them without. Also, keep in mind that if you are transmitting a resume via e-mail, use standard fonts, as some fonts may not be available to the person reading the file and they might convert to code instead.

When approaching potential employers through the mail, send a professional looking, well-written resume accompanied by a personal cover letter.

Classified Advertisements

Horse industry print publications as well as the multitude of horse-related Web sites carry classified advertisements from businesses and these should not be overlooked in a job search, especially if they are found at the local or regional level or if they represent a specific area of the industry. When looking on the web for employment, try searching with words or phrases such as "equine employment," "jobs with horses," or any combination of "jobs" or "employment" and "horses" or "equines." However, keep in mind that depending on publication schedules, ads may be out of date by the time you submit your resume. The same is true of Web sites, depending on how often the site is maintained. Also, in a tight job market, employers who run advertisements may literally receive hundreds of resumes, so the importance of a targeted, professional resume cannot be overemphasized.

Preparing your Resume

Who is the intended audience for your resume? How do you create a resume that will impress employers? Take some time to consider your audience and map out the content, format, and style of your resume before you send it to prospective employers.

Resume Target Audience

Most prospective employers will require a resume to get an overall view of your education and experience and to determine if you have the qualifications for their open position. If you've never met the employer before, she will almost certainly want to see a resume; if you know the employer through your networking channels, she will still most likely want to see a resume to get an idea of your specific skill set. If the employer hasn't asked for one by the time of the formal interview, bring a few copies to your meeting. Doing so will give the employer something to refer to and to develop questions from and it will demonstrate that you are thinking ahead in a professional manner. Bring at least three copies in case the employer asks for more.

Composing Your Resume

To write your resume, sit down and list everything about your background and experience that could possibly be applicable to the job you want. Don't limit yourself to paid work experience and education. Instead, think of all the ways in your daily life you have gained experience and demonstrated your abilities. Did you demonstrate teaching and leadership skills by instructing a class or by tutoring? Did you demonstrate your public speaking ability through the starring role in the high school or college play? Did you lead your team to victory as the captain of the local soccer team? While you will not list everything you have ever done on your resume, after you make your list, you'll select the accomplishments that best demonstrate your background and abilities for a particular job. You can create more than one list of experiences based on the types of jobs you are pursuing and interchange them to target your resume to a particular employer.

Add to your list any continuing education, including college, trade school, clinics, etc., and the degrees or certificates you have received. If you were on the dean's list in college, graduated with honors, or won any awards, be sure to include that information. Also, write down extracurricular activities—such as participation on the debating team or working as editor of the school newspaper—that will help demonstrate communication, leadership, or other skills.

Include any jobs you've held, whether during the summer or part-time, as an intern, student or apprentice; or even if they were in a different industry or field. Include any community service or volunteer work that you may have performed. Note the skills you used at these jobs and your most important accomplishments. Also include any performance-based honors or awards employers may have given you.

List everything about your background and experience that could possibly be applicable to the job you want.

Add 4-H or Pony Club memberships, riding lessons, experience caring for your own horse, collegiate equestrian experience, and any other experience that illustrates your background with horses. Include any professional associations or breed or horse sport organizations that you are a member of and note any offices you might have held.

Now that you've developed your list, read through it and consider how the skills and experience you have acquired can be applied to the job you want. Don't try to use everything on the list; just include those things that will make you an attractive candidate for the job. Don't just list your achievements; also explain what you did and how your skills contributed to the success of the organization. You may need to vary your resume, depending on the position for which you are applying, especially when various combinations of jobs are involved.

If you have a lot of overall horse experience and are applying for a position as a breeding manager, rather than focusing on riding skills or ability, emphasize your education and any experience with mares or foals or with stable management. Also, think about the skills you have that are not directly related to horse experience, but can help you in the job. For example, management and organizational skills can help you keep breeding records on the mares and foals.

If you are pursuing a position teaching hunt seat to beginners, emphasize your riding ability and experience in that discipline. Include ribbons you've won, any riding background in other styles or disciplines, and any teaching experience you may have, even if your teaching or tutoring experience is not in riding. Emphasize the ways you've used your communication skills in previous jobs or in college.

If you're applying for a job as a stable manager that also includes riding instruction, you'll want to include experience and applicable skills for both of these areas. If stable management is 80 percent of the job and riding instruction is only 20 percent, then emphasize your qualities for the stable manager position first, followed by your qualifications for teaching.

Avoid cluttering your resume with irrelevant information. For example, the picture you took of your horse that won first place in a photography contest is worth mentioning if you are seeking a job as a photographer or with a publisher of equine magazines. However, it won't help you get a job as a nutritionist for a feed company or exercise rider at the track.

Think about the skills you have that are not directly related to horse experience, but can help you in the job.

If you are a career changer, you have other important considerations to keep in mind, such as how much of your prior experience applies to the horse industry career you are seeking. For example, if you have worked 15 years as an administrative assistant for a toy company and are now seeking an entry-level job as a groom or stable hand, many of the details of your previous experience will not need to appear on your resume. An owner of a breeding barn or riding school will probably not care about the travel arrangements you made for the boss of your toy company or how fast you can type. He might, however, be interested in the organizational and communication skills you demonstrated in your previous career, as well as any office management experience you may have, because these skills can also be utilized at the barn. Someone who is highly organized is likely to keep the tack room in good shape and ensure that supplies do not run out. A person with strong communication skills probably won't forget to notify the barn manager if a horse becomes lame or ill, and will probably work well with others, including clients. If the employer is forward thinking, he will also realize that an applicant who has managed an office may be able to transfer those leadership and coordination skills to a stable management position, after she has acquired the necessary horsemanship experience.

If you are completely changing careers, highlight relevant experience up front and leave the rest of the details out.

The point to remember is this: if you are completely changing careers, highlight relevant experience up front and leave the rest of the details out.

For someone changing industries, but who is planning to work in the same field, such as moving from a marketing position in the auto industry to a marketing position in the horse industry, previous work experience is directly relevant to the new job, so it should be detailed on the resume. For example, if you received a merit award for helping to implement a marketing plan that resulted in increased sales of luxury cars to a specific demographic group, then highlight that in your resume. This will help demonstrate your expertise in the field of marketing, and this expertise can be carried over to the marketing of horse products.

Structure

Whether you first highlight your education or your experience depends upon the type of job you are pursuing, how much education you have, and whether you are changing careers. Generally, whatever is most likely to catch the eye of prospective employers should appear first. People applying for hands-on horse positions should usually list their horse experience before their education. If you are pursuing a job in a supporting industry that requires a degree, such as journalism or accounting, and have little experience in the field, list your education first. Career changers should emphasize experience first if they are changing industries but not fields. However, if they're starting over completely in a new field and new industry, they might wish to show their education or training in the new field first, along with any skills demonstrated in a previous career that could be applied to the new job, rather than listing previous experience that is unrelated to the new career. In other words, you should highlight your strengths.

The next thing to decide is whether your resume will be a reverse chronological one or a functional one. A reverse chronological resume lists all your work experience, starting with your most recent employer and works backward from there. A functional resume lists your skills and experience by type, and then briefly lists places and length of employment. The reverse chronological resume is most often used by people with much applicable and recent work experience, whereas the functional resume may be more appropriate for students with little paid work experience or for employees who have moved from job to job or who are changing both industries and fields. The Monster.com Career Center Web site suggests not using a functional resume except in "emergency" situations, i.e. where you have little work history or have changed jobs excessively (some managers are bothered when they cannot see a career progression. Basic examples of the three types of resumes are given on pages 82 and 83.

People applying for hands-on horse positions should usually list their horse experience before their education.

When using a chronological resume, if you have had success in a particular job that closely demonstrates experience for the job you are pursuing, list that job first, whether or not it is your most recent job. It is more important to present your most applicable experience first, than to stay with a particular structure that will not showcase your appropriate skills.

Length

One page is usually sufficient for a resume, especially for people starting out in the working world. Employers who are wading through piles of resumes to find suitable candidates will appreciate someone who gives them a concise, to-the-point read. Even career changers with longer work histories may need only one page to adequately convey their experience if they include experience relevant only to the new position. To stay current with both your experience and the relevant technology you may have used in your past jobs, focus on the last 10 to 15 years of your work history. If you have relevant experience prior to that time frame, list it. If you're an experienced employee, it is more important to have a resume that adequately reflects your experience and accomplishments than to force yourself to pare it down to one page. In only rare instances should a resume be longer than two pages.

Design Dos and Don'ts

When preparing your resume, keep it simple and easy to read. Use common fonts, such as Times New Roman or Helvetica, and set the default font size at 11 or 12 points. Use a 14- or 16-point font for your name and contact information, which should be centered at the top of the page. Set margins to 1 inch all around. Don't mix several fonts or be tempted to add color, graphics, or other strong design elements. Bold headings or headings slightly larger than the body text are common and acceptable. Use bullets when listing your experience or skills. Print resumes on high-quality white or off white resume paper.

General Dos and Don'ts

Do keep sentences short and to the point. Do include a summary of qualifications that emphasizes the skills that are directly related to the position you are seeking. Do have someone else review your resume for flow, logic, typos, and other errors. If necessary, hire a professional resume writer to help you with your resume. The relatively low cost (approximately $50 to $150) is well worth the payoff for those who are not confident in their own resume-writing abilities.

If necessary, hire a professional resume writer to help you with your resume.

Don't include personal information such as hobbies, marital status or birth date, unless they relate directly to the job. Don't use personal pronouns. Do not include a statement saying, "References Available Upon Request." This phrase is now considered passe, according to the Monster.com Career Center Web site and other resume-writing experts; employers know that references will be provided if requested.

Cover letters

All resumes should be mailed with a cover letter. This introduces your resume and is the first thing employers read when they open your envelope; so making a strong impression through a well-written letter is essential.

Include the position you are applying for (include a reference code if requested) and how you learned about the job. If someone is referring you, be sure to mention that person's name; this may help put your material on the top of the stack.

Tailor the cover letter to the job being advertised and emphasize the accomplishments that qualify you for the job, without rehashing your resume. You may wish to lead in with a broad statement of your overall credentials, followed by a bulleted list of strengths or list of projects in which you demonstrated your experience and qualifications.

Mention why you are interested in the job and how you will be of benefit to the employer. Say something about the employer that will show that you have familiarity with their operation. For example, "While studying for my equine science degree, I researched many Thoroughbred breeding farms throughout Kentucky and was impressed with the quality of your operation." Then give some specific details that you learned about the operation that honestly impressed you. It is important to have really done your homework here and not to make flattering statements that you cannot back up.

Close your cover letter with an active statement that requests an interview.

Close with an active statement that requests an interview and gives a general time frame on your availability or mentions you will follow up with a telephone call to answer further questions. End by thanking the reader for her time and consideration. Don't forget to sign the letter, unless it is being sent via e-mail, in which case, no signature is required. Check spelling, grammar, and punctuation after completing the letter so that you make a positive and professional first impression.

If you are sending your resume cold, meaning you are not responding to an advertisement or have a referral, and if you are not sure that the business even has an opening, then your cover letter should be slightly different from that mentioned above. Prior to sending your materials, do a little homework about the operation so that you can write clearly about how your skills will benefit the company. Check to see if the company, organization, or farm has a Web site that may provide an overview. Also, find the name of the person who would most likely be doing the hiring. Address the cover letter to that person. Do not send out cover letters and resumes addressed, "To Whom It May Concern" or "Dear Sir or Madam." This lack of attention to detail shows the recipient that you can't be bothered to do the work it takes to find his name. Open your letter by introducing yourself and mentioning specifically what type of job you are seeking; then lead into your qualifications for the job.

Other Job-Hunting Materials

A well-written resume and cover letter are not the only materials you'll need as you look for a job. Here are a few more items that may be important.

BUSINESS CARDS

Have a set of simple business cards made up that give your name, address, telephone number, and e-mail address. You can go to the local print shop and have a large quantity made, or make your own cards and print them off your computer with special business card paper available at the local office products store. Carry your cards with you at all times—you never know when you'll meet someone who can help you in your job search—and hand them out liberally. Let everyone you give a card to know what type of position you're seeking. Also, include your business card when mailing your resume to prospective employers.

REFERENCES AND REFERENCE LETTERS

Prepare a list of former employers, professors, and any other professional contacts willing to attest to your experience in a particular area and to your character and ability as an employee. Have the reference list ready to provide upon request. At some point, when job candidates are serious enough to interview, they will be asked for references. Be sure your references agree to speak on your behalf before you add them to your list. The list of references should give each person's name, title, and contact information; and it should briefly describe your relationship with that person. (For example: Sam Smith is the owner of the Flying Z Dude Ranch. I worked two summers for him as a trail guide.)

When you go on interviews, bring along copies of reference letters to give to the interviewer.

Letters of reference are valuable to have as well. Ask three or four of your best references to write a letter on your behalf. When you go on interviews, bring along copies of these reference letters to give to the interviewer (more on this in "The Job Interview" section below).

Work Samples

Certain types of jobs require samples of your work. This is true for graphic designers, writers, editors, architects, and others. The career breakdowns in Part II will tell you, by career, whether samples or a portfolio are required. If you have a professional-looking Web site that contains work samples, you may wish to direct the employer to your site. However, ask whether she would prefer to view your samples in print or online.

The Job Interview

You've followed up on job leads, have all your printed materials prepared, and are looking forward to your first interview. To make a good impression, be a few minutes early, dress neatly and appropriately for the job; wear a suit to interviews for office positions, even if the company has a casual dress code. (It is much better to be overdressed than to arrive for an interview underdressed.) However, the one exception is a barn job: don't show up at the barn in a business suit! Instead, wear clean, casual clothes to the barn. If you will be riding during the interview, wear clean riding clothes and polished boots. Bring a folder to leave with the employer that includes a clean copy of your resume, a business card, letters of recommendation and samples of your work (if appropriate).

Work on your body language during interview practice sessions. Sit up straight, but don't be stiff.

Prior to the interview, consider the questions an interviewer may ask. Plan how you will respond to the questions and the examples you will use to highlight your experience. If you are especially nervous about the interview, spend time rehearsing for it. Have a friend or parent ask questions that you think the interviewer might ask, and practice answering them. Work on your body language during these practice sessions. Sit up straight, but don't be stiff. You want to appear relaxed during the interview even if you are not (and most people are not). You can also practice answering questions to a tape recorder to get a feel for how you sound. This will help you to eliminate the "ums," "uhs," and "uh-huhs" from your vocabulary and it will let you know if you are coming across strong and confident or nervous and meek.

Let the employer set the pace for the interview, then follow her lead. Be interested and alert, look the interviewer in the eye, and answer questions in a clear, lively voice. Employment specialists say that most employers form a lasting impression of job candidates in the first few minutes of an interview, so be sure to get off to a strong start with the first question you are asked. If it is an open-ended question, such as, "What can you tell me about yourself?" come back with a clearly thought out answer that highlights how your experience and strengths will benefit the employer and that provides specific examples showcasing your knowledge and experience. Don't respond to this critical first question by giving a rote description that sounds like it came right out of your resume.

At some point during the interview, you will be asked if you have any questions. Be sure to have several questions prepared, or you will come across as disinterested or unprepared. Don't ask questions about salary and benefits, as you want the focus to be more on how you can benefit the company or operation, rather than what the company or operation can do for you. Some questions to ask (if provided they have not already been answered in the interview) might include: What is the employee culture like? What is a typical day like? What skills and qualities are most important in an employee? What projects are coming up in the next few months? Why is the job available? What is the next step? When will you select someone? When the interview is over, shake hands with the employer and reiterate your interest in the position. If she doesn't tell you when she expects to make a decision, be sure to ask, so that you will know when to follow up.

Immediately following the interview, send a thank-you note. The note can be in the form of a typed business letter or it can be handwritten on an attractive note card. Wait a few days beyond the date the employer said she would make a decision, and then follow up with a telephone call. If you don't get the job, thank the employer for considering you and let her know that you would appreciate being kept in mind should other opportunities arise in the future. Even if you are disappointed about the outcome, be gracious and polite. The horse industry is large, but it is not so large that you can afford to burn bridges, especially if you are seeking employment in a particular industry segment.

Wait a few days beyond the date the employer said she would make a decision, and then follow up with a telephone call.

For more information on beginning a job search, preparing a resume, writing cover letters, or interviewing, visit the public library. There are many books that go into great depth on these topics. Or, go to a job search Web site such as www.monster.com. While these books and Web sites will not be specific to the horse industry, they provide in-depth general information that can help you in your horse industry job search.

Figure 2: Sample Cover Letter—With Job Opening

Mandy Brown
1212 Jones Drive, Anytown, Kentucky 12345
(213) 123-4567, mbrown@website.com

May 30, 2004

Ms. Kathleen Smith
Breeding Manager, Heavenly Horses Farms
2222 Kentucky Rd., Bluegrass, Kentucky 23456

Dear Ms. Smith,

I recently learned from Jack Jones, owner of Great Horses Farms in Ohio, that you are looking for an assistant broodmare manager.

This June, I will graduate from college with a Bachelor of Science degree in Equine Science from XYZ University, with a concentration in the area of reproduction and breeding. During school, I worked at the university teaching facility and performed internships at Great Horses Farms, working with the breeding manager. My responsibilities included helping with general care of 20 broodmares, assisting with both artificial insemination and live cover breeding, and foal sitting.

Additionally, I have cared for my own horse since I was 10 years old, participated in Pony Club, and was a member of 4-H, focusing on leadership as well as equine activities. The enclosed resume details my experience and background.

I have researched several Thoroughbred farms during my job search and am most impressed with the quality of your operation and your strong standard of broodmare care. I believe that with my targeted experience in the area of breeding, as well as my broad knowledge of horses, I would be an asset to your farm and someone who would continue to uphold Heavenly Horses Farms' high standards.

Thank you for your time in considering my qualifications. I will call you next week to further discuss my qualifications for the position.

Sincerely,

Mandy Brown

Figure 3: Sample Cover Letter— "Cold"

Mandy Brown
1212 Jones Drive, Anytown, Kentucky 12345
(213) 123-4567, mbrown@Web site.com

May 30, 2004

Kathleen Smith
Breeding Manager, Heavenly Horses Farms
2222 Kentucky Rd., Bluegrass, Kentucky 23456

Dear Ms. Smith,

I am contacting you because I am seeking employment at a Thoroughbred breeding farm as an assistant breeding or broodmare manager. After researching several Kentucky Thoroughbred farms for my job search, I am most impressed with the quality of your operation and your strong standard of broodmare care.

This June I will graduate from college with a bachelor's degree in equine science from XYZ University concentrated in the area of reproduction and breeding. During school I gained experience at the university teaching facility as well as performing internships at Great Horses Farms, which is located in Ohio. My responsibilities included the following:
* helping with general care of 20 broodmares
* assisting with artificial insemination and natural breeding
* foal sitting.

Additionally, I have cared for my own horse since I was 10 years old, participated in Pony Club, and was a member of 4-H, focusing on leadership as well as equine activities. The enclosed resume details my experience and background. I have also enclosed a letter of recommendation from Ms. Spring, the breeding manager at Great Horses Farms.

I believe that with my targeted experience in the area of breeding as well as my broad knowledge of horses, I would be an asset to your farm and someone who would continue to uphold the high standards of Heavenly Horses Farms.

Thank you for your time in considering my qualifications. I will call you next week to discuss possible employment opportunities.

Sincerely,

Mandy Brown

Figure 4: Chronological Resume

Name
Street Address
City, State, Zip
Telephone Number
Cell Phone w/Voicemail
E-mail Address

Objective
If you include an objective statement, be specific about the type of job you are seeking. For example: *Seeking position as hunter-jumper trainer at medium-to-large training barn.* Do not include a statement about general goals.

Summary of Qualifications
Include three or four qualifications that directly highlight your skills for the position you are seeking.
- Assistant trainer of hunter-jumpers at (add name of well-known training barn).
- Trainer of own horse who has won at junior levels.
- Other supporting statement

Work Experience
2000-2003 Job Title, Operation Name, Address
    Duties of the job; start all sentences with an active verb
1997-2000 Job Title, Operation Name, Address
    Duties of the job; start all sentences with an active verb
1995-1997 Job Title, Operation Name, Address
    Duties of the job; start all sentences with an active verb

Other Horse Experience
- Use bullets to add interest.
- List any horse skills and experience not discussed elsewhere.
- Include volunteer work and clubs, such as 4-H and Pony Club.

Education
Degree Achieved, School Name, City and State, Year Graduated
Degree Achieved, School Name, City and State, Year Graduated

Figure 5: Functional Resume

Name
Street Address
City, State, Zip
Telephone Number
Cell Phone w/Voicemail
E-mail Address

Objective
Seeking position as hunter-jumper trainer at medium-to-large training barn.

Summary of Qualifications
Include three or four that directly highlight your skills for the position you are seeking.
- Assistant trainer of hunter-jumpers at (add name of well known training barn)
- Trainer of own horse who has won at junior levels
- Other supporting statement

Experience

Training: List all experience starting with active verb; Use bullets if desired

Riding: List all experience starting with active verb; Use bullets if desired

Horse Care: List all experience starting with active verb; Use bullets if desired

Stable Management: List all experience starting with active verb; Use bullets if desired

Employers
2000-2003 Job Title, Operation Name, Address
1997-2000 Job Title, Operation Name, Address
1995-1997 Job Title, Operation Name, Address

Education
Degree Achieved, School Name, City and State, Year Graduated
Degree Achieved, School Name, City and State, Year Graduated

CHAPTER 6

Starting a Business

— — —

The horse industry is filled with people who are their own bosses. Equine artists, bloodstock agents, breeders, veterinarians, massage therapists, farriers, writers, and those involved in other occupations either choose to work for themselves because of their own desire for independence, or they work in a job that typically dictates self-employment. Most people who start a horse business do so because they have a passion for the animal or they have grown up around horses and horses are what they know best. Being successful at running a business, however, takes much more than knowing and loving horses. A solid business plan and solid business management skills are critical. According to the U.S. Small Business Administration (SBA), the number one reason businesses fail is because of poor planning and management. To be a success in your horse business, you must first be a good businessperson.

Get Educated

Before starting a business, get some basic business skills under your belt. While in college, minor in business or, if you're in a degree or certificate program, take business courses such as finance, accounting, and marketing. Doing so will help you, whether you start your own business immediately after graduating or take a few years to get some solid work experience under your belt. You can also take business classes at the local community college or adult school or go to the Web site for the SBA (www.sba.gov) to see what courses they offer. The SBA is a gold mine of information for people wishing to go into business for themselves and it can be a valuable resource as you plan and start your own enterprise. Read books, business magazines, and online articles on business methods and how to plan and get started. Surf the Internet for sites that address small business concerns. It is also wise to talk to an equine business consultant for the ins and outs of successfully starting and running a horse business. If you don't know any equine business consultants, ask around at the barn and tack store or read horse publications to locate one.

Following are a few books that specifically address the topic of horse businesses:

- ❏ *Complete Guide for Horse Business Success*, by Janet E. English, C.P.A. (Equine Research, 1995)
- ❏ *Growing Your Horse Business*, by Lisa Derby Oden (Blue Ribbon Consulting, 2000)
- ❏ *The Horse Equestrian Business*, by Julie Brega (J.A. Allen & Co Ltd., 1999)
- ❏ *Running A Stable As a Business*, by Janet W. McDonald (J.A. Allen & Co Ltd., 1995)
- ❏ *Starting & Running Your Own Horse Business*, by Mary Ashby McDonald (Storey Communications Inc., 1997)

Legal Structure of Business

An important decision to make about your business is its legal structure, which is determined by a variety of factors, including the type and size of the business, whether it is a one-person operation or has employees, its legal restrictions, and potential tax advantages and disadvantages. Talk to your

CPA or a small business attorney; she will offer advice on the best structure for your business based on the individual factors relating to it. There are three basic types of business structures.

A sole proprietorship is a business owned by one person. It is the simplest and least costly way of getting started. All profits go to the owner and are claimed on the individual's tax return. The downside is that all risk goes to the owner as well. If you should be sued and lose the judgment, both your personal possessions and your business assets can be taken.

A partnership is a business owned by two or more people. The profits as well as the risks are shared between the owners. Like the sole proprietorship, profits are claimed on the owners' tax returns. While a general partnership can be formed simply through an oral agreement between the parties, it is smart to have a partnership agreement drawn up legally by an attorney to avoid potential conflicts. The agreement should stipulate such details as: type of business, length of the partnership, how much was invested by each partner, how profit and loss will be divided, what each partner will be paid, and what will happen should a partner die or become incapacitated.

Legal structure is determined by a variety of factors, including the type and size of the business, whether it is a one-person operation or has employees, its legal restrictions, and potential tax advantages and disadvantages.

The corporation is the most complex business structure to set up, because there are more regulations and higher taxes involved. The advantage to a corporation is that, as a separate legal entity, the business is taxed separately and can be sued in its own name, meaning that your personal assets are not vulnerable. Liability is generally limited to stock ownership, except in cases of fraud. If you own a small business, talk to your CPA about the possibility of setting it up as an "S" corporation. With this arrangement, you will pay taxes at the lower rate of a sole proprietorship or partnership, but you will have the liability protection that comes from being incorporated.

Other Legal and Insurance Considerations

In addition to structuring your business for tax purposes, there are other legal matters to consider. For example, what are the zoning or licensing laws in your area? If you are planning to keep horses as part of your business, find out about which local ordinances or environmental or health laws apply. Also, if you will be operating a hack stable or riding school, have an equine attorney prepare a liability release for riders to sign. A signed release is absolutely critical for protecting your business should a rider be injured and bring a lawsuit against you. In addition, get advice and help from this attorney about any other contracts you may need. The following books cover the topic of horses and law, and were written by equine attorney Julie Fershtman: *Equine Law & Horse Sense* and *MORE Equine Law & Horse Sense* (Horses & the Law Publishing; 1996 & 2000).

Insurance for horses includes major medical coverage, mortality insurance, and loss-of-use insurance (which will help pay the bill when a horse becomes ill or injured).

Horse business owners must also consider the type of insurance needed for horses, facilities, riders, and employees. Insurance for horses includes major medical coverage, mortality insurance, and loss-of-use insurance (which will help pay the bill when a horse becomes ill or injured). If you cannot afford to replace a horse in case of death, you might consider mortality insurance. Coverage can be limited and expensive, so find out first what causes of death are included in the coverage. Loss-of-use insurance covers horses that are injured and can no longer perform in a specific area. Also, consider whether having any insurance at all makes sense. (If your business has several horses, the cost of insurance premiums for all of them may be more than the price of replacing one or two horses). Talk to an equine insurance agent to find out what the policies cover and what restrictions apply; this will help determine if insuring your horses is a good investment. To find insurance agents who specialize in horses, talk to other horse owners in your area, look in classified listings in horse publications, or do a Web search under "equine insurance" or "horse insurance." Also, see the profile of Jorene Mize, equine insurance broker, in Chapter 15.

Property and liability insurance are critical. Property insurance protects your business facilities and supplies against fire, theft, and other losses. Liability insurance protects horse businesses in case of rider injury. Although it is required in some states, you should consider purchasing it even if it is not mandatory. Some horse organizations may offer group policies, so check with equine organizations in your state. If your business will have employees, you might consider providing health insurance. This will not only benefit your employees, but may benefit you through increased employee retention and fewer sick days.

Developing a Business Plan

The key to starting a successful business is in the planning. Preparing a business plan forces aspiring business owners to carefully think through every element of the business, from where it will be located to how it will be financed to what customers will be charged. At a minimum, writing the plan is valuable to help identify weaknesses, document goals and objectives, and help measure your progress toward achieving your goals. At its best, the plan will be the document you continue to consult when managing the growth of your business. Also, be aware that if you apply for money to invest in equipment or facilities for your business, a business plan will be an important part of your loan package. In addition, the Internal Revenue Service will want to see your business plan should you or your business be audited. New partners who are brought into the business should be shown the plan so they can understand the operation's goals, objectives, financial structure, and other important details.

A business plan will be an important part of your loan package if you apply for money to invest in equipment or facilities for your business.

The following paragraphs will help you address many aspects of your business before you begin writing your plan. How simple or complicated a plan is usually will correlate with the simplicity or complexity of the business itself. Freelance writers working out of their homes who have minimal start-up costs and no employees should not need a long complicated plan. On the other hand, someone starting a mid-size riding school, who is planning to hire stable hands, grooms, and riding instructors, and purchase a string of horses, will have a longer, more in-depth plan. If you need help with your business plan, talk to a CPA specializing in horse-related businesses or to an equine business consultant. For an in-depth tutorial on developing a business plan that you can tailor to meet your horse industry needs, visit www.sba.gov.

Elements of a Business Plan

Figure 6: Table courtesy of the U.S. Small Business Administration

1. Cover sheet
2. Statement of Purpose
3. Table of Contents
4. The Business
   A. Description of Business
   B. Marketing
   C. Competition
   D. Operating Procedures
   E. Personnel
   F. Business Insurance
   G. Financial Data

II. Financial Data
   A. Loan Applications
   B. Capital Equipment and Supply List
   C. Balance Sheet
   D. Breakeven Analysis
   E. Pro-forma Income Projections (Profit & Loss Statements)
      Three-year Summary
      Detail by month, first year
      Detail by quarters, second and third years
      Assumptions upon which projections are based
   F. Pro-forma cash flow
      Follow guidelines for letter E

III. Supporting Documents
   A. Tax returns of principals (for last three years)
   B. Personal financial statement
   C. Franchise contract and all supporting documents provided by the
      franchisor in the case of a franchised business
   D. Copy of proposed lease or purchase agreement for building space
   E. Copy of licenses and other legal documents
   F. Copy of resumes of all principals

BUSINESS DESCRIPTION

Think about what product or service your business will provide and what market needs it fills. Consider the area of the country you are in and whether there is room for a business like yours. For example, if you are planning on working as a veterinarian or farrier in a specific division of the industry, is there a demand in your region or is the market tapped out? Depending on the type of business you're planning, especially if it is a supplier of goods or services to horse owners, you might leave surveys at tack stores, feed stores, riding, and training schools describing your product or service and asking whether it is something horse people would use or buy. What are the opportunities for growth in your area? Consider whether you will work out of your house or if you need to buy or lease space elsewhere. You will also need a name for your business. If you use a fictitious name, you may be required to register that name in your county.

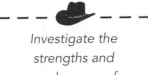

Investigate the strengths and weaknesses of your competition.

COMPETITION

Who is your competition and how do your products or services differ from what the competition offers? What are the strengths and weaknesses of your competitors? How does the competition advertise and market their businesses? Study your competition to answer these questions. It's helpful to keep a file on each of your major competitors, including notes about their businesses, promotional materials, and pricing information. Keep track of what your competitors are doing, when they are having promotional events, how they are advertising, and when they are having sales or specials.

MARKETING

Long before you hang that "open for business" sign on the door, have your customer base identified and make sure you have a plan for attracting and keeping them. Who are your customers? How will the business attract and keep customers? How will the business be marketed and advertised? What image will the business project and how will that image be built? How will you price your services or products to remain competitive yet stay profitable? Consider the bottom line of what you need to earn to live comfortably, then do your homework to find out what your customer base can afford, what your competitors are charging and how high the demand is for your product or service. Think about how and where you will advertise your services.

Prepare mailing lists of potential customers and a list of horse events and other places where the customers you want to attract can be found. Volunteer with youth organizations or breed and sport associations as a way to find customers while demonstrating your commitment to the industry.

Prepare mailing lists of potential customers and a list of horse events and other places where the customers you want to attract can be found.

Establish a brand identity for your business from day one by incorporating a common look into all of your marketing materials. Consider having a logo created that is unique to your business and that customers will come to instantly recognize as yours. Incorporate your logo or look into your business cards, stationery, Web site, brochures, flyers, newsletters, promotional giveaways (such as refrigerator magnets and memo pads), and any other collateral marketing materials.

Advertise your business in the telephone book, local newspapers, regional or national horse publications, and on local radio and television programs. Sponsor an event, such as an art contest for amateur equine artists; or, organize a seminar on horse care. Be creative as you think of ways to get out and reach potential customers.

OPERATIONS

What days and hours will you work? Depending on the business, this may be driven by your customer base. If you own a braiding service, your hours will be dictated by the need to have horses ready to show in the morning, which means you may be up working most of the night. Consider how the business will run day-to-day and how many employees it will require. Will you actively manage the business every day or will you hire management help? What benefits will be offered to employees? How will records be kept and inventory tracked?

FINANCES

Consider the one-time expenditures you will have to get your business started. Do you have the money on hand or will you need to finance these purchases? In addition to money for capital expenditures, you should have enough money saved to cover your operating expenses, salary, and personnel costs (if you have employees) for one year. Prepare a budget that projects your income and costs over the next one to three years. Personnel costs will include not only salaries but also any benefits that you offer. In addition, consider the type of accounting system you will use to keep the books balanced.

CHAPTER 7

Breeding Careers

— — —

This chapter highlights typical careers exclusive to the world of horse breeding. These hands-on positions require a high level of skill and extensive experience with horses. There are many other occupations at horse breeding farms that support breeding operations, but they are not listed here because they are not exclusive to the breeding industry. Such careers include farrier, groom, stable hand, trainer, and farm office worker. See the other chapters or consult the index for more positions that support breeding.

To find positions in horse breeding look for internships through your college or university career office, contact breeding farms, get in touch with equine employment services, and network at horse events. Keep in mind that a career in breeding requires skill, dedication, and the ability to work long and unusual hours. The rewards are many, though, when you help bring new life into the barn.

Artificial Insemination Technician/ Breeding Technician

ABOUT THE JOB

Artificial insemination technicians and breeding technicians work on breeding farms or for breeding research organizations and assist veterinarians with impregnating mares artificially. Technicians also help breeding managers collect semen from stallions, handle and ship semen, and perform other duties. They must be knowledgeable about breeding equipment and equine anatomy, and have good record-keeping skills to keep track of the mares that have been bred and the specimens used in the impregnation process.

EDUCATION AND TRAINING

A two- or four-year degree from an accredited veterinary technician program with a focus on large animal breeding and artificial insemination is required. Most states also require certification or licensing. (See Chapter 9 for more on the veterinary technician profession.)

SALARY

A recent survey by the North American Veterinary Technician Association (NAVTA) shows the average salary for veterinary technicians in equine practice is $20,057.

RESOURCES

North American Veterinary Technician Association
P.O. Box 224
Battle Ground, IN 47920
www.navta.net

Breeder/Breeding Farm Owner

ABOUT THE JOB

Breeding enterprises range from single stallion or mare operations to full-scale equine reproduction farms. Some people breed as a hobby, part time, or in conjunction with another type of horse business. However, others work at breeding full time and hire employees to assist with breeding operations. Horse breeding involves a significant investment in money and time and those interested should pursue the career only after careful thought and planning. The breeding business is not for amateurs—those considering the profession must have strong horse knowledge and handling skills. In addition, they must be able to assess the quality of breeding stock; be knowledgeable about breeding practices; and have sales, marketing, and business management skills. The hours are long and the payoff is not guaranteed.

Many people who successfully enter this field have years of experience in other hands-on horse careers. They may be trainers, judges, equine veterinarians, or longtime horse owners. Others target breeding as their career choice from the start and learn the ropes through apprenticeships in breeding operations or via entry-level positions.

EDUCATION AND TRAINING
A degree in equine reproduction or equine science as well as in-depth business training is helpful.

SALARY
The median annual salary for animal breeders is $22,650.

RESOURCES
Check out breed associations and publications pertaining to the horse breed you wish to work with as well as general horse magazines and books. Recommended books on horse breeding are:
- ❏ *Modern Horse Breeding: A Guide for Owners* by Susan McBane (The Lyons Press, 2001)
- ❏ *Storey's Guide to Raising Horses: Breeding/Care/Facilities* by Heather Smith Thomas (Storey Books, 2000)

Breeding Manager/Broodmare Manager/ Stallion Manager

ABOUT THE JOB
Breeding managers oversee horse breeding as well as the care of stallions and mares. Farms may have separate broodmare and stallion managers or an overall breeding manager, depending on the size of the operation. On very small farms, the farm manager may fill the roll of breeding manager. Breeding managers are responsible for the overall health and welfare of the horses, and their

duties may include collecting and shipping semen, artificially inseminating mares, and performing lab work. Breeding and foaling seasons are the busiest times of year for breeding managers; they are often on call and must work around-the-clock. Some breeding managers live at the facility where they work, with room and board part of their overall benefits.

People wanting to be breeding managers must have strong horse knowledge and handling skills. They must have experience with live coverage, or natural, breeding as well as with artificial means of breeding; strong record-keeping skills; and knowledge of equine genealogy and blood-typing. They also must be attentive to the special health needs of mares in foal and have foal-handling skills. In addition, they should have good people skills, enabling them to work effectively with clients seeking breeding and stud services.

EDUCATION AND TRAINING
Increasingly responsible positions at a farm or on-the-job training as an apprentice make for a strong background in breeding management. A master's degree in equine reproduction or equine science is also a good way to get a foot in the door.

SALARY LEVELS
Average salaries for experienced breed managers are in the range of $25,000 to $35,000, with housing often included.

RESOURCES
If you graduated from an equine program, contact your college or university job placement office as well as equine employment agencies such as Equistaff (www.equistaff.com) and Equimax (www.equimax.com). Also, review help wanted advertisements in print and online horse publications and directories.

Career Spotlight

DOUG GERARD, BREEDING MANAGER

Doug Gerard is breeding manager for the Cedar Ridge Stallion Station, a division of Casey Hinton Quarter Horses, Inc., in Whitesboro, Texas. This 80-acre ranch focuses on breeding, training, and showing reining and working cow horses in competition. Doug grew up on a ranch in South Dakota and has been involved with horses his entire life. Because of his strong horsemanship background, pursuing a career with horses was a natural progression for him rather than a conscious decision. Before coming to Cedar Ridge, he worked as a quarter horse trainer and breed manager for a small farm in Wisconsin. When not working, he and his quarter horse mare, Ritzy Rhinestone, participate in team rop-

ing on the ranch. Doug has a degree in agricultural business; he also has taken short noncredit courses on breeding.

Q. What does your job as a breeding manager involve?

A. Day-to-day, I oversee health care for the broodmare band, which is the main focus of my job. We may have 120 mares with babies during breeding season. I coordinate the breeding collection of studs. We do all artificial breeding, as there is not as much risk of injury as with live coverage breeding.

Q. What did you do prior to your current career?

A. I trained and rode horses. I knew I wasn't going to set the world on fire as a trainer, so I focused on breeding instead.

Q. How many hours a week do you usually work?

A. I am on call all the time. My hours worked per week average anywhere from 70 to 90. Seventy hours is pretty common.

Q. What do you enjoy most about your work?

A. I enjoy doing a good job. Having people tell me I'm doing a good job is a plus. I like the challenge and the people I work with. I enjoy getting a tough mare bred.

Q. What do you like least about your work?

A. It's hard working with people who don't understand breeding, but they try to breed horses anyway. Some people don't understand the dedication it takes. You have to be there when you need to be there. Some people don't want to take the time or do the things they need to in order to do breeding right.

Q. What is your most memorable moment as a horseman?

A. There are many: getting an embryo out of a mare we've been working on for a year and a half, the first time I collected from a futurity champion. The horses are a great blessing, as are the people trusting their mares and stallions to us. I watched a woman who was picking her mares up from us; she was crying as we loaded them. She said to me, "I've never had my mares look so well when I came to pick them up." Those are the types of moments that are memorable.

Q. What is the most rewarding part of your job?

A. Knowing I've done a good job and am successful at what I'm doing is rewarding. Also, trying to get a mare in foal as soon as possible and knowing when I go in at night that I've done what needed to be done that day.

Q. What is the most challenging part of your job?

A. Getting up every morning at 4:30 A.M. and being in good humor is a challenge. I get to look at some beautiful mornings; I just don't get to linger over them.

Q. What do you think is the biggest achievement of your career?

A. Being right here working with the people, and the caliber of horses we work on.

Q. What advice would you give to someone interested in a career in horse breeding?

A. I'd say don't do it if you don't like to put in long hours. If you want a 9 to 5 job, don't do it. The rewards are great, though—like taking great horses and breeding them and maybe producing the next champion. Even though the horses don't stay here long, we keep track of what they do. Another reward is getting to enjoy both horses and people.

Q. What education and experience do you recommend for someone interested in breeding?

A. A lot of people out there who know more about the technical side of breeding have a college degree in the field, so I recommend going to college. Also, if you can get a job during breeding season on a farm, you'll learn as much there as anywhere.

Q. What personality traits should a person have who is considering this field?

A. You need to be a hard worker, and also a little laid-back. You need to be able to roll with the flow because nothing works out the way you plan.

Q. Is there anything else you'd like to say about your career in the horse industry?

A. This job is as rewarding as anything I've ever done. If you like horses and people, you would enjoy breeding. You get to talk to people all over the country, from someone in New Jersey in the morning to Maryland in the afternoon. If you love horses, what better job can you do?

Equine Theriogenologist

About the Job

A theriogenologist is a board-certified veterinarian who specializes in the field of reproduction. Theriogenology is the study of the physiology and pathology of male and female reproductive systems, and the clinical practice of veterinary obstetrics, gynecology, and semenology. An equine theriogenologist is someone who specializes in horses. Equine theriogenologists work in private practice and for breeding farms; colleges and universities and corporations also employ them. (For information on related careers, see the entry for reproductive physiology specialist in Chapter 17.)

Anyone interested in the career of equine theriogenology must have a strong educational background and be comfortable with hands-on equine health tasks like birthing, semen harvesting, and surgery.

Education and Training

A Doctor of Veterinary Medicine with specialized training and American Veterinary Medical Association (AVMA) board certification in theriogenology is required.

Salary

According to AVMA statistics for 2001, the mean annual salary for equine veterinarians in private practice was $108,405; the salary for veterinarians employed by colleges and universities was $83,059.

Resources

American College of Theriogenologists
P.O. Box 3065
Montgomery, AL 36109
www.theriogenology.org

Society for Theriogenology
P.O. Box 3007
Montgomery, AL 36109
www.therio.org

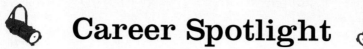 # Career Spotlight

DALE PACCAMONTI, DVM, MS, DIP ACT
EQUINE THERIOGENOLOGIST

Dr. Dale Paccamonti is an equine theriogenologist in the School of Veterinary Medicine at Louisiana State University. He has worked in the field for 18 years and at the university for 15 years. His interest in theriogenology was sparked during his years as an undergraduate, when he worked as an artificial insemination technician with dairy cows, and at veterinary school at Michigan State University, where he took courses in reproductive physiology. After receiving his DVM, Dr. Paccamonti spent four years in a mixed practice on the East Coast and did considerable work with dairy cattle. He decided to further his education to specialize in theriogenology and was accepted into a residency program at the University of Florida, where he worked with a group of theriogenologists. Although he worked with various animals, he found the equine work most interesting. This interest led to his position at Louisiana State University after he received his board certification.

Q. What is your job?

A. I teach veterinary students the specialty of reproduction, do research in various aspects of reproduction, and work as a clinician in the hospital. Duties in the hospital include evaluating fertility and treating infertility in mares and stallions, breeding mares through natural coverage and artificial insemination, performing embryo transfers, handling obstetrical problems, assisting mares with problems during pregnancy, freezing semen, and diagnosing pregnancies.

Q. How does this career differ from that of a reproductive physiology specialist?

A. A reproductive physiologist has an advanced degree in reproductive physiology but is not trained to diagnose and treat disease, nor is he legally permitted to do so. A veterinarian specializing in reproduction or theriogenology is trained to diagnose and treat various diseases and ailments.

Q. What is your typical workday like?

A. I arrive at the office at 7:30 A.M. After checking and answering e-mail for a half hour, I begin seeing patients with the students, working through cases in the hospital and those presented during the day. I answer numerous phone calls with questions about reproduction in all species, but most questions are about horses; the second most common questions are about dogs. On some days, I go on field calls to horse farms for breeding work. I generally finish with cases about 5:30 P.M., and then return to the office to return phone calls and answer e-mail that I wasn't able to get to during the day. I also squeeze research projects in among all that.

Q. What do you enjoy most about your work?

A. I enjoy the successes—the infertile mare we get pregnant, the healthy foal we deliver after a difficult pregnancy.

Q. What do you like least about your work?

A. I don't like the failures—the infertile mare we can't get in foal, the foal that dies because of problems during pregnancy.

Q. What other horse industry experience do you have?

A. I worked on an Arabian farm during high school, where I fed, cleaned stalls, and helped with breeding.

Q. What is the most rewarding part of your job?

A. Getting a problem mare pregnant, delivering a healthy foal, teaching motivated students, and the intellectual stimulation of research.

Q. What is the most challenging part of your job?

A. Trying to solve infertility, especially when the cause is not known.

Q. If you could do it over, is there anything you would have done differently to reach your career goal?

A. I would have obtained a PhD, which provides a different perspective on research and gives you the training to get started initially; it also helps to obtain funding for research endeavors.

Q. What advice would you give to someone interested in the field?

A. Try to get as much experience as possible. Work at a breeding farm to get horse experience; ride with a vet. The more you know what it's all about and what the possibilities are, the better you will be able to make a good career choice.

Q. What education and/or experience do you recommend for someone interested in working in equine reproduction?

A. One should get a doctor of veterinary medicine degree and licensing; board certification in theriogenology is important for some positions. I would recommend a PhD for academic positions.

Farm Manager

ABOUT THE JOB
Farm managers run the day-to-day operations of breeding farms. They ensure the horses are cared for, manage personnel, and oversee everything from fence mending and barn painting to repair of farm equipment. The hours are long and irregular, especially during breeding and foaling seasons, when farm managers are on call and sometimes work around-the-clock. The majority of the farm manager's time is spent outdoors or in a barn, though time may be spent in the office fielding phone calls from clients inquiring about breeding services. On smaller farms, farm managers may also act as breeding managers and oversee all stallion and broodmare care. Farm managers live on-site with room and board, which is often part of their overall compensation.

In addition to having horse skills and knowing the characteristics of the horse breeds they work with, farm managers must be good record keepers and understand pasture and schedule management.

EDUCATION AND TRAINING
On-the-job training in the form of an apprenticeship or working as a stable helper is excellent education. A bachelor's or master's degree in equine science or equine reproduction is important; business classes are also helpful.

SALARY
The median annual salary is $27,084.

RESOURCES
Check equine employment agencies and advertisements on the Internet and in regional and national horse publications and directories.

Foaling Attendant

ABOUT THE JOB
Foaling attendants could be described as the midwives of the breeding world. They watch pregnant mares for signs of labor, and they often stay up with the mares at night—when the horses most often give birth—to help the animals through the birthing process. Foaling attendants are trained to

recognize the signs of labor and impending birth, check that the foal is in the correct position, and recognize any problems that may require a call to the veterinarian. Attendants spend time grooming and petting the mares prior to labor so that the horses will come to trust them, as mares are extremely protective of their foals. Depending on the size of the breeding operation, foaling attendants may keep an eye on a large number of mares at any one time. Some foaling attendants work for several smaller farms and may travel from barn to barn in the same night to check on mares due to foal. Following births, foaling attendants observe the mares and foals to make sure that the foals stand when they should and nurse correctly.

Sometimes foaling attendants take on night watch duties, administer medications, clean breeding equipment, and perform other duties. Being patient, enjoying solitude, having stamina, and being a "night person" benefits those interested in working as foaling attendants.

In addition to professional foaling attendants who train specifically for this career, a foaling attendant job can be a viable entry-level position for the person interested in working her way up into a position as a breeding or farm manager. Sometimes breeding farms will hire students or interns to work as foaling attendants under the close supervision of breeding managers.

EDUCATION AND TRAINING
Training in equine studies or equine science and an apprenticeship with an experienced foaling attendant or breeding operation are recommended.

SALARY
Most foaling attendants earn minimum wage and more with experience.

RESOURCES
Check equine employment agencies as well as help wanted advertisements in print and online horse publications.

Career Spotlight

THERESA JONES, FOALING ATTENDANT

Theresa Jones has worked as a professional foaling attendant for 16 years. Before becoming involved in the breeding world, she trained and showed horses. But once exposed to her first delivery, she knew she had to get involved in the foaling process. After working in the field, Theresa wanted to learn more so she got a job working with a veterinarian specializing in equine reproduction, where she worked full time for seven years. Since that time, she has written a book on foaling *The Complete Foaling Manual* (Equine Research, Inc., 1996) and also offers an Internet advice column on the topic. Both the book and column are designed to help horse owners throughout the world with their mares and foals.

Q. What does your job involve?

A. My job involves monitoring mares and determining when they are close to foaling, being with them and assisting during delivery if necessary, and providing postpartum care for the mare and her new foal. I also provide care for sick or weak newborns or mares with problems in the postpartum period.

Q. How did you get your first job in breeding?

A. After I saw a mare foal for the first time and decided that I wanted to learn more, getting a job was easy because not many people want to stay up with mares all night, every night. My first job was on a large Thoroughbred breeding farm.

Q. What was a typical workday like when you worked at foaling full-time?

A. My typical day was spent going on farm calls with the veterinarian all day. He provided overall equine care but specialized in reproduction. When the farm calls were done, I would then go to the farms where I was responsible for foaling mares. Sometimes I had mares at only one farm, but frequently I needed to check mares at three or four farms. There were times when I spent all night traveling between farms and checking on mares, because each farm had at least one mare that looked close to foaling.

Q. How many hours a day do you typically work?

A. When I worked for the veterinarian full time in addition to foaling mares, I basically worked around-the-clock from January through June. I would work with the veterinarian during the day and then watch mares at night. On a lucky day, I could go home for a couple of hours to shower and change clothes. Even when I could take a few hours off, which was usually on a Sunday, I was on call for the mares I was responsible for foaling, or I'd go on emergency calls with the veterinarian.

Q. What do you enjoy most about your work?

A. I enjoy working with the mares and foals. The mares are usually incredibly brave and dignified, and the foals are just too much fun!

Q. What do you like least about your work?

A. Never getting enough sleep.

Q. What is your educational background?

A. I finished one year of college and had two years of nursing school.

Q. What is your most memorable moment as a horsewoman?

A. There have been many memorable moments with mares and foals. Probably the most memorable was successfully delivering a foal who presented with his head down between his front legs. Every time I would reposition his head, he would move it right back down between his legs. It was a difficult delivery but finally accomplished, and the foal was fine. That foal went on to win approximately $200,000 as a racehorse.

Q. What is the most rewarding part of your job?

A. Nursing a sick or weak foal back to health.

Q. What is the most challenging part of your job?

A. Successfully completing a difficult delivery.

Q. What advice would you give to someone interested in a career as a professional foaling attendant?

A. Anyone who wants to work as a foaling attendant should be prepared for long, boring hours with bursts of excitement, panic, sadness, and extreme joy.

Q. What education and experience do you recommend for someone interested in working in this field?

A. Overall experience with horses and knowing horses are extremely important for a foaling attendant. Any medical background is also very helpful.

CHAPTER 8

Communications and Creative Careers

— — —

This chapter introduces professions that keep horse lovers and the horse industry informed; it also showcases careers in which creativity is a key component. Because many of these positions require the ability to convey messages about the horse world, the positions in this chapter typically require strong communication and writing skills. While most of these jobs do not involve direct horse contact, they may require horse knowledge and experience. Equine product manufacturers, magazine and book publishers, breed and sport associations, training barns and breeding farms, and other horse industry operations are all potential employers for those seeking to enter communications or creative fields. Successful freelancers in these positions will have business and marketing skills in addition to professional expertise in the field.

Advertising Specialist/Manager

About the job

An advertising specialist/manager plans and oversees advertising campaigns for associations, retailers, manufacturers, event operators, and others. She typically works for an agency, but may be employed on staff at a larger association or horse-related business. While some advertising agencies specialize in the horse industry, few, if any, support the horse world exclusively. If you are considering a career path in advertising, be prepared to work with clients in other industries as well. Many advertising agencies are full-service organizations, meaning that in addition to offering advertising, they also handle marketing and public relations.

Advertising professionals recommend that people wanting to break into the field focus on the advertising field first and the specific industry second. Gaining experience through an internship or entry-level position with a top advertising agency will make it easier for you to target specific agencies specializing in the equine industry or other horse-related businesses or associations. Extensive horse experience is not required, but having a general knowledge of the horse world will help you understand your client's needs.

Education and training

This job requires a four-year degree in advertising, marketing, mass communications, or public relations. Internships within the field are highly recommended. Some top agencies offer in-house training programs for advertising personnel.

Salary

The median yearly salary for an advertising and promotions manager is $55,940.

Resources

American Advertising Federation
1101 Vermont Ave, NW, Suite 500
Washington DC 20005-6306

American Association of Advertising Agencies
405 Lexington Ave., 18th Floor
New York, NY 10174
www.aaaa.org

Career Spotlight

HOLLY DAVIS PARKER, ADVERTISING AGENCY PRESIDENT

Holly Davis Parker is president of the Idea Flight advertising agency, which specializes in the horse and aviation industries. Idea Flight's horse-related clients include producers of packaged goods, such as grooming and nutritional products, and considered-purchase products—more expensive items like barns, trailers, and fencing. Hers is a full-service agency, offering advertising, marketing, and public relations to its clients. Holly has worked in the advertising field for 15 years. Prior to starting her own agency, she worked as a copywriter.

Holly, who owns two horses, has ridden since she was a child. She has competed in both western and English disciplines and currently focuses on dressage and eventing. Her horses include Waypoint Charlie (named for a navigation term), a 10-year-old Thoroughbred gelding, now retired; and McLendon, a 15-year-old, 17.3-hand Clydesdale/Thoroughbred cross. Her love for her equine charges is evident in the way she describes the horses' unique personalities. "Waypoint Charlie is, as my husband David says, 'a lap horse.' He'd love to come in, hang out on the couch and watch the game on television. McLendon is reserved and rather proper, kind of like a butler, but he's slowly loosening up."

Q. What does your job involve?

A. I started out as an advertising copywriter, one-half of the creative side of the advertising business. Now that I head an agency, I'm more of a generalist. I still do some of the creative work, but I am also heavily involved in strategic planning for current clients, supervision, administration, and new business growth.

Q. What is your typical workday like?

A. I'm happy to say that there is no typical workday, which keeps things interesting. I work about 60 hours a week. I travel on average 18 times a year to see distant clients and attend trade shows, including consumer events such as Equine Affaire, and competitions such as Quarter Horse Congress and the Rolex Kentucky Three-Day Event. When I'm in the office, my time is split among coming up with creative concepts and writing, strategic planning, agency management, account supervision, and getting new business. Agency life brings with it a pretty big ebb and flow. For example, most of our full-service clients wish to have calendar-year marketing plans. So every fall gets pretty crunched with planning, doing creative work, selling, and then implementing those plans for the following year. But then we shut down for two weeks over the holidays to take a breather. Somehow, I still manage to ride regularly enough to compete lightly.

Q. What do you like most about your job? What do you like least about your job?

A. I love creating a great campaign that works better for the client than anything they've ever done before. That's the big passion and payoff for me. What I like least is doing our own agency's marketing. I have no problem tooting my clients' horns, telling the world how wonderful their products are, but ironically, I get bashful about doing it for our firm. I have to force myself to do it. If I had my druthers, all our business would come by referral.

Q. What is the most rewarding part of being an advertising/marketing communications professional?

A. Creating a zinger—one of those dead-on messages that's both intelligent and visceral that grabs the target by the heart and won't let go.

Q. What is the most challenging part of your career?

A. It's always a challenge justifying the critical role of creativity in a successful marketing campaign to people who don't believe in it.

Q. What is the biggest achievement of your career?

A. Personally, it has been starting an agency with zero clients and zero funding, and growing it into a real business with real employees and accounts that my mother recognizes! For clients—the achievements that really count—it's honestly hard to pick just one. We've been fortunate to make a huge, positive difference in the businesses of a number of clients, and that's the big job-satisfaction payoff for all of us here.

Q. What is the biggest obstacle in your career?

A. I guess the biggest obstacle was actually learning the craft in the first place. The creative sequence in the College of Communication at the University of Texas at Austin where I attended school is extremely difficult and competitive, and surviving that was no picnic. If you think about it, we teach children to draw within the lines, grass is always green, and elephants are always gray. This does not foster creative thinking! So I struggled for a while to connect with the right side of my brain. Sure, I'd always done well in writing in school, but coming up with breakthrough concepts that grab someone's attention in under three seconds and then persuades them to buy is hard!

Q. If you could do it over, is there anything you would have done differently to reach your career goal?

A. I would have colored outside the lines and made my elephants pink.

Q. Do you feel it is necessary to have direct horse experience to go into equine advertising?

A. No, you don't have to have direct horse experience, but it helps. First and foremost, you have to know the job you're doing, whether it be creative, public relations, or whatever. And it's best to get strong experience outside the industry, because: (a) it will give you hugely valuable experience that you'll need; and (b) it gives you a broader range of experience, often with larger companies, which will help your resume tremendously.

Q. How will having direct horse experience benefit people going into the equine advertising field?

A. My best analogy is this: A group of people at an agency is put in charge of selling toothpaste for a client. It's an easy bet that every one of them has used toothpaste regularly over the last few decades, and thus has a personal connection with the target market for toothpaste. Now let's take that same talented group of people, and give them horse clippers to sell. If they do their job correctly, they'll delve into why those clippers are superior, and will do their best to convey it memorably to the target audience. However, if just one member of that team is a horse person, the job becomes a thousand times easier—and more cost-effective—for the client. Taking that one step further, I think copywriters, specifically, really need to know horses, because the horse industry has a language all its own. If you know horses, really know horses, you can add all those little touches that say, on behalf of your client, to the target market: I AM YOU. The more the audience identifies with the advertiser, the more likely they are to buy. People buy from people they like, and often the only chance a company has to be a likable "person" is through advertising. So, an agency that employs a talented team that includes horse people can offer clients both better cost and a stronger creative approach.

Aside from creative, the other area where it really helps is in public relations. Can you imagine calling on editors (who surely know horses) and talking about a new product, service, or development on behalf of your client and not knowing about horses?

Q. Do you ever have direct contact with horses as part of your job?

A. While I certainly don't have the contact that a veterinarian, riding instructor, or farm manager has, I do have some contact. I get to attend a lot of great equine events as part of my business. I market our agency to the horse industry by way of my competition horses and I test products on my horses—either testing new products a client is coming out with, or giving our team hands-on experience with a new client's products.

Q. What kind of education and experience do you recommend for someone going into advertising?

A. At the level our agency operates, I expect a four-year degree from either a major university or a well-regarded smaller college in advertising, marketing, mass communications, or journalism (for public relations positions). That's sufficient for entry-level. For higher-level positions, I strongly prefer to hire people with agency experience, but I'll consider crossovers from the client side or, rarely, the publication side. If they are to work on an equine account, I strongly prefer that they ride as a hobby. Clients looking for marketing managers are going to want a four-year degree plus experience either on the client or agency side, and horses as a hobby will usually be a plus, but not a necessity. High-end consultants and talented freelancers will have similar education and experience, but there are also a plethora of horse-loving freelancers making a reasonable living cranking out inexpensive client-directed ads, catalogs, and other material. For that, you just need to know how to use graphics programs on the computer.

Q. What strengths or skills do you believe a person should have who is considering this field?

A. There is a place for nearly every type of personality and skill set in advertising, marketing, and public relations. For example, within a traditional ad agency, you have account planning (good for those who can see the big picture and plan moves ahead of time), account service (where excellent customer service skills play the biggest role), creative (good for artists and writers and other creative types), media planning (good for organized people who aren't afraid of basic math), market research (those interested in science and psychology), public relations (good for journalism majors with excellent people skills) and event planning (at its most basic, someone who likes to throw a good party and doesn't mind chasing down every last detail to make it perfect).

Q. What do you think is the future job outlook for your field within the horse industry?

A. Advertising, marketing, and public relations will be around as long as we have some form of free market economy. Rather than the specialty becoming obsolete, you need to guard against your mind aging along with your body. To a large extent, it's a young person's profession, but as long as you keep thinking young and have a passion for the business, your decades of experience will be highly valued. Regarding the horse industry specifically, there aren't many clients who have both the vision and the market potential to allow you to create marketing for them, so it will always be somewhat limited at the top of the game, from the agency/firm side of things. However, if you work directly for the client as a marketing manager, you will always have options.

The pay above any entry-level position is sufficient to afford at least a modest horse habit. Job security on the agency side is rather poor—jobs come and go with the agency's client roster—but generally speaking, there are plenty of jobs to go around for reasonably talented individuals when the economy is good. With good performance, job security is higher on the client side, but you only get to work on one set of products for one company. It's enjoyable from the agency side because the view is always changing as we focus on projects for a variety of clients.

Q. What advice would you give to people who want to work in this field solely within the horse industry?

A. First and foremost, if you want to be good at your job, get experience in the field outside the horse industry. Land an internship or entry-level position at the best firm you can, and work your tail off. Advertising, marketing, and public relations are all exceptionally rewarding, challenging, and flat-out fun fields to be in, but they all require a few years of paying dues. So take the modest salary, work hard, and learn as much as you can about all the facets of the business. Three to five years seems like a long time, but it will pass in a flash, and by then, if you've been working hard and are in the right place, you should be seeing some payoff both personally and financially.

Q. What advice would you give to someone interested in starting her own business within this field?

A. If you really want to run your own firm someday, put in a few more years working your way up the ladder to get more senior experience, and then get ready to make the leap. At that point, you'll have one of two choices: you can operate as a consultant or freelancer, working for both agencies/public relations firms and clients, or you can take the harder route and build your own agency or firm, hiring employees and so forth. Either way, to operate in the horse industry, you'll need to make contacts by attending shows and talking to horse people.

Q. Is there anything else you would like to say about your career?

A. My father said something very wise to me that applies here. He has always loved his job (flying), but became surrounded by a whole lot of cranky retired people when we moved to Florida in the late 1970s. It took him a little while, but he finally figured out what the problem was: they hated their jobs for some 30-plus years, and by the time they made it to retirement, they were permanently angry. His advice was to find a job you love most days, because it's far more fulfilling to spend your life doing something you love than having double the pay at a job you hate. So if you love horses to the ends of the earth, you can find a way to make a living around them—sometimes even a decent living.

Announcer

ABOUT THE JOB

Announcers work at horse shows, rodeos, races, and other horse events by keeping live audiences and television and radio listeners informed. Announcers at shows and rodeos are self-employed and paid per event. They may travel frequently, work irregular hours and many weekends, and must market themselves constantly in this competitive field to maintain steady work. Racing announcers are employed by individual racetracks and are required to hold special licensing. Many announcers were once participants themselves and have in-depth knowledge of horses and the sport or discipline they cover.

Horse expertise is essential for announcers, as are strong speaking and communication skills. Announcers must be very comfortable in front of an audience; in some situations, such as the rodeo, being a bit of an entertainer is important, too. In addition, they must know how to operate technical equipment, either their own or the equipment of the venue at which they are working.

Announcers are generally scheduled far ahead of the event, so begin looking for work at least one year in advance of the show or rodeo season. Contact sport, breed, and rodeo organizations for information on upcoming events. Race callers should contact individual racetracks for information on hiring. (Racetracks are listed in Appendix G.)

EDUCATION AND TRAINING

A four-year degree in communications or attendance at a broadcasting school is helpful.

SALARY

The median annual salary for announcers is $20,270.

RESOURCES

International Professional
Rodeo Association
P.O. Box 83377
Oklahoma City, OK 73148
www.iprarodeo.com

Career Spotlight

CREED ROBERTS, RODEO ANNOUNCER

Creed Roberts has worked as a rodeo announcer for four years. He has also announced at horse shows and bull riding events. In addition to announcing, his rodeo background includes competing in bareback riding during college and raising rodeo-bred cattle with his partner in South Texas. This Texas-born cowboy hasn't yet turned rodeo announcing into a full-time career, opting to work at the family business during the week, but he dedicates much of his time to the sport of rodeo. Creed has two horses that help him with penning cattle: Dunny, a 19-year-old quarter horse, and Kalala, a 24-year-old quarter horse. Creed is a member of the Professional Rodeo Cowboys Association, the United Professional Rodeo Association, and the Rodeo Stock Registry of North America.

Q. What made you decide to go into announcing?

A. I wanted to educate the crowd in all the aspects of rodeo. I found that a lot of our spectators still did not understand the rules, the techniques, or the lifestyle of rodeo cowboys.

Q. How did you get your first job in rodeo?

A. After I graduated from college, I visited my hometown rodeo. They have a 10-week summer series. All of the rodeo committee members were dear friends of mine. I asked them if I could announce a few rodeos for them next year. As the year got closer, they called me up and I announced all summer long. I rented the sound equipment and netted $25 per rodeo. I eventually was able to afford my own sound equipment. These friends are the ones who definitely got me going.

Q. What did you do prior to your current career?

A. I was going to college and riding bareback horses. I worked for the

Forage Heifer Development Center while I was attending Stephen F. Austin State University in Nacogdoches, Texas.

Q. What is a typical workweek like?

A. I work all week in our family business. We sell PVC pipe and fittings to the plumbing and utility wholesale industry, and I cover all of our accounts in Central and South Texas. On Friday afternoons, I head out to the rodeos. Most of my rodeos are in Texas and Louisiana. I always show up about five hours before the start of the rodeo, which gives me plenty of time to set up the sound system, get my microphone check out of the way, and adjust to any problems if any arise. I then get with the committee chairperson and go through the whole rodeo with him to ensure that we are on the same page. Then, it is off to find the funnyman [rodeo clown] and run through his act and his jokes to make sure we sound sharp and funny. I then visit with the stock contractor about what animals are in the performance and who his bullfighters, pickup men, and judges are. Finally, I sit down with the secretary and find out about our contestants and the order of events.

Q. How many hours/days per week do you typically work?

A. I sleep about five hours per day, so you can do the math! Between announcing rodeos, taking care of my rodeo cattle, the family business, and my family, there is always plenty of work to be done.

Q. What do you enjoy most about your work?

A. I enjoy the kids. Rodeo is such a kid-friendly sport. I love to watch the kids smiling. If they are not having fun, then we, as contract personnel, are not doing our jobs.

Q. What do you like least about your work?

A. I don't like being away from my family. It is tough to bring them with me to every rodeo. So I am away from them quite a bit.

Q. What is your educational background?

A. I have a bachelor's degree in animal science, I'm trained as an artificial insemination technician, and I attended the Rodeo Academy.

Q. What is your overall background with horses?

A. We own a couple of horses because we work around cattle all the time. The horses make our job a lot easier on penning the cattle. I have grown up around horses all my life. I have a dun horse that I am really fond of. He always does what I ask of him and he never complains. My kids are itching to get into horse events, so I'm sure we will be adding to the pony herd.

Q. What is your most memorable moment in rodeo?

A. Being able to work with the National Professional Bull Riders in Victoria, Texas was great. They are the top bull riding organization in Texas. That event was extra special because my dad was able to run my sound for the two-day event. It was a joy to have him work for me for a change. We truly had a great time.

Q. What is the most challenging part of your job?

A. Making sure that all the personnel are on the same page. It takes all areas of rodeo to have a successful performance. So, that means the producer, the committee, the stock contractor, the clown, and the announcer must know what is going on and when. Not easy to do.

Q. What is the biggest achievement of your career?

A. I haven't hit my big achievement yet, but I'm on course. The high point right now is being involved with Bob Tallman and his crew with Buckers, Inc. and the Rodeo Stock Registry of North America.

Q. What is the most challenging obstacle in your career?

A. It's been hard juggling work, cattle, rodeos, and family. My days are only so long, and I try to fit 35 hours into a 24-hour day. Time is, for sure, my obstacle.

Q. What advice would you give to someone interested in rodeo and announcing?

A. You have to be dedicated and you must love the sport of rodeo. Read the publications about rodeo and rodeo-related topics. Talk to as many contestants as you can to find out who they are and where they come from. (This will help you fill dead air while you are on the microphone.) Learn about rodeo. You will find out how much you don't know about rodeo when you announce your first show. You have got to be the encyclopedia of rodeo.

Q. What education and/or experience do you recommend?

A. Go to an announcing workshop. International Professional Rodeo Association announcer Sam Howry puts one on twice a year called Rodeo Academy. It teaches all the aspects of becoming a successful rodeo announcer. Also, take classes in communication. Learn to have confidence when speaking in front of large groups. You also want to learn how to speak more clearly and how to protect your voice. Another way to get experience is to jump in feet first. Announce as many rodeos as you can. Start with high school and junior rodeos, which are more relaxed and a great training ground for becoming a professional announcer. Also learn about music, which has become one of the most important parts of professional rodeo. Get a sound system that is clear and simple to operate.

Q. What personality traits should someone have who is considering this field?

A. You should be outgoing, so you can relate to the audience. You must learn patience, because you work with many people and it is easy to blow your cool. Stay calm. Have a positive attitude. Your attitude can be heard through the speakers, so make it a positive one. Look good. Act and dress the part. Be accountable. Be on time all the time, because being late will cost you the job next year.

Q. If you could do it over, is there anything you would have done differently to reach your career goal?

A. I would have asked for help. I have a lot of people around me who would have helped me out; I just never asked for it. I have learned that people in this industry are eager to help. Next time, I will utilize them.

Q. What else would you like to say about your career?

A. I have been truly blessed to have a career in rodeo and to have a family that loves me and supports me. Rodeo is one of the select fields that groups family, fun, and hard work under one title. I am grateful for that. Rodeo is finally getting the credit it deserves. We are on national television on a regular basis and are portrayed in arenas across the globe. We are dipping into the spectator world and plucking out a whole new group of audiences. The coverage of rodeo is becoming more accurate, which helps our sport. Thanks to people who write about rodeo—in books like this one—it will help bring out an understanding of rodeo and other topics related to the cowboy way of life.

Art Director/Graphic Designer

ABOUT THE JOB

Art directors and graphic designers develop visual images for magazines, advertising campaigns, and other printed and online material. They use various software packages to design magazines, brochures, newsletters, advertisements, and more. Art directors may often supervise graphic designers, who assist with design and layout. They work with editors, writers, and project managers from the beginning of a project to its publication. Since art directors and designers help select photographs for magazines, advertising, and marketing pieces, a discerning eye for quality photos is important. By studying the layout of horse magazines and advertising pieces, you'll learn what appeals to horse enthusiasts.

Many people in this field work as freelancers on a contract basis for magazines, associations, and businesses. In fact, according to the U.S. Bureau of Labor Statistics, 60 percent of graphic designers (across all industries) are self-employed. A strong portfolio and good marketing and networking skills are necessary for freelance success.

Individuals with these jobs must be computer savvy and must stay current with graphic design software. Horse knowledge is not required, but it is helpful when selecting photos and creating designs that will appeal to a horse-loving audience. Should you choose to freelance, you will be responsible for budgeting both your time and money. Attention to detail, strong organization, and basic accounting skills are necessary.

EDUCATION AND TRAINING

A two- or four-year degree in graphic arts or graphic design, a four-year degree in communications with strong graphic arts experience, or training at a specialized art school is necessary.

SALARY

The American Institute of Graphic Arts/Aquent Salary Survey 2002 reports a median annual salary of $60,000 for art directors, $40,000 for graphic designers (mid-level), and $53,000 for freelance graphic designers.

RESOURCES

American Horse Publications

Internship and Student Mentoring Programs
49 Spinnaker Circle
South Daytona, FL 32119
www.americanhorsepubs.org

American Institute of Graphic Arts
164 Fifth Avenue
New York, NY 10010
www.aiga.org

Artist

ABOUT THE JOB

Equine artists create original artwork using a variety of techniques. They work in watercolor, oil, pencil, bronze, silver, clay, and other substances. Some specialize in a specific breed or area, such as Thoroughbred or rodeo, while others take a more generalist approach.

Artists may sell prints or sculptures to the horse-loving public, illustrate for magazines and books, accept portrait commissions from horse owners, design jewelry; or produce greeting cards, T-shirts, coffee mugs or other items featuring their illustrations. Most artists are self-employed and work either full- or part-time at their talent. The amount of money they make is determined by the amount of time they put into creating and marketing their work.

Successful equine artists recommend developing a unique approach to your art that makes it different from what is already out there. Imagination, determination, and marketing ability are all essential. While it isn't necessary to be an expert rider, a strong appreciation for the beauty of the horse and knowledge of equine anatomy and conformation are critical to success.

EDUCATION AND TRAINING

A two- or four-year degree or higher in graphic arts, fine arts, commercial arts, or training at a specialized art school is helpful, though some successful artists are self-taught or have studied with a mentor. Business classes or a minor in business are also helpful for self-employed artists.

SALARY

The median annual salary for fine artists is $32,870.

RESOURCES

The American Academy of Equine Art
c/o Kentucky Horse Park
4089 Iron Works Parkway
Lexington, KY 40511
www.aaea.net

American Horse Publications
Internship and Student Mentoring Programs
49 Spinnaker Circle
South Daytona, FL 32119
www.americanhorsepubs.org

Artist's and Graphic Designer's Market
F&W Publications
1507 Dana Ave.
Cincinnati, OH 45207

Career Spotlight

SHERRIE ENGLER, EQUINE ARTIST

Sherrie Engler credits her start as an equine artist to her first ride atop her grandfather's horse when she was a toddler. She has been drawing horses and dreaming about them ever since. Now, through her artwork that Sherrie sells through her business, Headed West, she shares her love of horses with others who also appreciate the beauty and spirit of this animal. She began working full-time as an equine artist in the late nineties and has sold more than 3,000 prints during that time. Sherrie is currently horseless, but enjoys visiting the horses owned by her friends next door whenever she feels the need to "love on" a horse. She grew up riding her grandfather's Missouri Fox Trotter and later owned a quarter horse that she showed in western pleasure classes and, mostly, enjoyed taking out on the trail.

Q. What media do you work in and what type of art do you create?

A. I paint with pencils, which give an illustration effect to my work and provide vivid color. I'm able to do greater detail with them. I also illustrated two equine books, which launched my work as being collectible. My first book, *Photos & Drawings for Equine Conformation & Anatomy*, has over 200 illustrations of my artwork. Many artists and college students use this book to study the way muscles and bone structure create the overall look of the horse.

I very rarely take commissions, since most new work I create becomes a part of the five collections of prints I sell. I create whatever comes out of my head—quarter horses, racing, horses with children as well. My most popular collection is "Heartstrings." It features the tender moments that most horse owners can appreciate.

Q. How difficult is it to work full-time as an equine artist?

A. Many equine artists find it hard to make a living being only an artist. They work full-time at something else and do this part-time or have spouses who make a full-time living. However, it is possible if you know how to market yourself or are willing to learn. For example, you can market yourself by putting work out where a lot of people will see it—listing things on e-Bay or marketing for the holiday season. Diversify. Treat art as a business. Take advantage of all your marketing opportunities. Look slick and professional when packaging your product and in your Web design and catalogs. Brand your business with your color scheme, name, and logo. If you want to make a living as an artist, you must either become a businessperson or hire someone to promote your work.

Q. What is your educational background?

A. I have a graphic design degree with a minor in equine science.

Q. What is your typical workweek like?

A. I work easily 40 hours a week. Each day I check my e-mail and Web site for orders; the rest of the day involves shipping, paperwork, and replying to my customers. I usually spend about five hours a week actually creating new art.

Q. How does having direct horse experience benefit people who want to become artists?

A. You need horse experience, and I think most equine artists have one-on-one experience with horses. The part of you that loves horses shows through in your artwork. There are many good technical artists who create equine art, but I think their art is missing the heart of the horse. Art can take a brief moment that a horse lover experienced and bring it to life on paper forever. That's what sets your work apart from other artists. So many of my customers say, "Your work put on paper what my heart has known through my horse."

Q. What strengths or skills should a person have who is interested in this field?

A. You need determination and marketing skills, and you must have a different approach from everyone else. For example, my approach is to use pencils instead of paint. Making your own style of art is the most important thing you can do for yourself. Your art should look like yours, not another artist's.

Q. What do you think the job outlook is for equine artists?

A. There is a lot of interest out there in showing and owning horses. Potential markets for artists include people who own horses; the quarter horse and paint horse industries, which are expanding; horseracing is a whole other market—people want to buy prints of racehorses on the track. Prints are more affordable now and technology is having a huge effect on the market. Being able to produce your own prints is the key to being a successful equine artist now, but it is also important that you set a high standard in reproducing your work.

Q. What education and/or experience do you recommend for someone going into the field?

A. Get a graphic arts degree as well as marketing and technical computer skills. My graphic design degree has been the most beneficial to me; I don't have to ask someone if what I'm doing will be appealing to the public. Also, four years of college will help you do everything in the most professional way possible.

Q. What is the most rewarding part of being an equine artist?

A. Sharing my love of horses with other horse lovers.

Q. What is the most challenging part of being an equine artist?

A. Finding time to draw everything I want to draw.

Q. What is the biggest achievement of your career?

A. My first book is my biggest achievement. It took more than a year to illustrate over 200 drawings for that book. I also learned more about how a horse is put together through the process, and that has served me well in my artwork since.

Q. What is the most challenging obstacle in your career?

A. Learning how to manage my time. I'm not always able to draw when I want to, so I have had to learn that I have to manage my time and still be able to find the time to draw.

Q. How has your family assisted you in your career?

A. My daughter Chelsey is one of my inspirations. She was quite the dress-up queen as a little girl, and quite a bit of my "Heartstrings" collection is based on her. What's not to love about a little girl dressed up with a pretty horse?

My husband, Eric, has been very supportive and together we both learned to write HTML code so I could design and develop my own Web site to sell my work. In the beginning, it took both of us to run the site. I don't think I ever could have learned so much without his help. My mom has also been a big influence in my life. She never tired of looking at my art or hanging it on the walls when I was growing up. She made special arrangements for art classes when I was growing up, and, as a single parent, she fostered my love of art in such a way as to make it a part of who I am today.

Q. Is there anything else you would like to say about your career?

A. Affordability is key especially in the beginning. As you become more popular and collectible, prices can go up; but if somebody wants to put your art on his wall, it should be affordable. I think a lot of artists assume only rich people buy art. I have learned that is very far from the truth. If you make your work affordable, you will sell to all horse lovers.

Editor: Books

ABOUT THE JOB

There are several different types of editors. Book editors work with writers on books that are in publication. The acquisitions editor is responsible for acquiring new titles for the publishing company. The managing editor generally oversees the entire book development process, from working with the writer during the writing phase to production and publication. Copyeditors carefully read manuscripts for accuracy in spelling, grammar, punctuation, style, and coherence. Production editors prepare manuscripts for the various phases of the production process. There are a few book publishers that specialize in equine topics, with all or the majority of the books they publish dedicated to equines.

Publishing houses may use freelance editors for overflow work. Writers themselves sometimes hire freelance book editors directly as they try to get their manuscripts in top shape before being seen by agents or publishers. Freelance editors must use their networking and marketing skills to get work, either marketing themselves to publishing houses or promoting themselves to writers through advertisements in writers' magazines and other means.

Book editors should have excellent communication and grammar skills and be detail-oriented. Depending on the publisher, horse expertise may or may not be required.

EDUCATION AND TRAINING

Four-year degree in journalism or English.

SALARY

The median annual salary is $37,550.

RESOURCES

Writer's Market
Writer's Digest Books
1507 Dana Ave.
Cincinnati, OH 45207
www.writersmarket.com

Editor: Magazines, Newspapers, Newsletters, and Journals

ABOUT THE JOB

Editors have overall responsibility for the direction and production of their publications. They set editorial policy and style, create story calendars, assign stories to writers, edit stories, write columns and features, choose photographs and artwork, and work with the art director to determine the look of the publications. Editors work with advertising staff to make sure the publication is attractive to both advertisers and readers; she also interacts with other departments, including production and circulation. Top editors on a publication are responsible for managing staff, handling budgets, preparing business plans, and tackling other administrative duties. They stay up-to-date on the latest industry developments by attending industry events and conferences.

In addition to editing and writing skills, successful publication editors have excellent communication, organizational, and people skills. Readers of horse publications are passionate about their favorite topic and many are experienced horse people. In order to understand, enlighten, educate, and entertain this knowledgeable audience, it is essential that publication editors have a strong horse background. Editorial jobs can be found with horse associations or with local, regional, national, and international publications.

EDUCATION AND TRAINING

A four-year degree in journalism, English, or communications is essential.

SALARY

The median annual salary for magazine and periodical editors is $42,560; the median for newspaper editors is $37,560.

RESOURCES

American Horse Publications
Student Internship and Mentoring Programs
49 Spinnaker Circle
South Daytona, FL 32119
www.americanhorsepubs.org

Career Spotlight

MOIRA C. HARRIS, MAGAZINE EDITOR

Moira C. Harris is editor of *Horse Illustrated* magazine and group editor for BowTie, Inc. equine division. She has been the editor of *Horse Illustrated* since 1996 and started with the magazine in 1993 as an associate editor, working her way up from there. As group editor of some of the company's other equine magazines, she oversees *Horses USA, Quarter Horses USA, Young Rider*, and *Hobby Farms*. Prior to joining BowTie,

Inc., Moira edited college textbooks, freelanced as a rock music reporter, and worked as an account assistant for an advertising agency. Moira, who grew up in Southern California, has ridden since she was a child, starting out in western and soon switching to hunt seat. She currently competes in the jumper division with her Irish Thoroughbred, Ballymena. In addition to her magazine work, Moira has written several books, including *Dressage By The Letter: A Guide For The Novice*, originally published by Howell/Macmillan; *Mastering the Art of Horsemanship: John Lyons's Spiritual Journey* (Bowtie Press, 2003); *Keep It Simple Series Guide to Caring For Horses* (Dorling Kindersley, 2003); and *Born In The USA: A Celebration of America's Horses* (Globe Pequot, 2003).

Q. What does your job as a magazine editor involve?

A. Well, editing, obviously. But "editing" is different for every magazine. Sometimes we get manuscripts in and they're pretty much ready to go. Others need significant reorganization and even rewrites. I usually am pretty moderate, unless the article is weak, and then I'm brutal about making it better, gutting the piece and building it back up. I coach my freelance writers and photographers. I select every photo that goes in the magazine, and I do a little bit of writing. I manage my staff, and do all those administrative duties (budgets, business plans, employee reviews, meetings). I also work in tandem with our advertising staff to make sure that we are providing a product that the readers enjoy, and the advertisers want to participate in. I interface with all the other departments, such as production, design, circulation, and human resources. I also travel to trade shows and horse expos. The buck stops here, basically, no matter what the situation.

Q. What is your typical workday like?

A. There's a lot of phone and e-mail communication. There are loads of meetings. I typically get on the computer and see what arrived overnight. I check my schedule and see where we are in the process, what deadline we are up against. I will undoubtedly attend at least one meeting a day. I field questions from the staff and talk to the group publisher. Sometimes I just have my lunch at my desk while I copyedit. I will sift through about 7,000 slides a month looking for appropriate photos for the issue. I work with the art director to develop the look of that month's issue. I brainstorm with my managing editor, who is a great second lieutenant.

Q. How many hours/days per week do you typically work?

A. I work a regular day basically. I know some editors stay longer. My horsey life continues outside the office, so I need to stay on schedule for that!

Q. What do you enjoy most about your work?

A. The fact that I have my passion—horses—married to my vocation. I've been involved with horses on and off since I was 9 years old, but I've learned so much more by being in the business. I love the fact that I am educating and entertaining my readers. It's fulfilling.

Q. What do you like least about your work?

A. The regular "administrative" work that virtually everyone has to go through at their jobs. I wish I didn't have to attend meetings or do the "paperwork" end of things. I'm a creative person, and that goes against my grain!

Q. What is your educational background?

A. I have a bachelor's degree in communication arts, with emphasis in newspapers, ironically. I wasn't really interested in magazines in school. I wanted to be a reporter. My school had an equine science program, so I took those classes as elective courses. I also have an art background, and attended classes at the Art Center/College of Design. This really helps with understanding page layout and graphics, as well as photo composition. Who would have thought that would come in handy? You just never know!

Q. When did you know you wanted to go into publishing?

A. Since I was in 4th grade. I always knew I wanted to write. I wrote a book when I was 10 about my friend's horse, Rare Girl. I also illustrated it. I have no idea whatever became of it.

Q. What sparked your interest in horses?

A. When I was really little, we used to go to Fresno, to visit my grandmother and grandfather. They had a vineyard that was right across the street from a quarter horse farm. I would immediately run through the rows of vines to get to the horses, and would spend all day feeding and petting those that would venture close enough to the fence. I was hooked right then.

Q. Where do you train?

A. I train with Pacific Coast Jumpers, and my trainers are Joe and Katie

Lifto. What I like about working with them as my trainers is that they go for the whole "sports psychology" aspect of riding. They want us to be mentally ready and they are so great at getting us to focus and have fun, too.

Q. What is Ballymena like?

A. Ballymena, or Missy, is a workaholic. She's nearly 17-hands tall, a bright bay, gorgeous girl that just makes my heart skip a beat. She LOVES to jump. She is also incredibly sweet natured, and totally level-headed for such a hot tamale. That's her Irish side. She can occasionally be bossy, but overall is a perfect match for me. Trainer Joe calls her my Cinderella horse.

Q. What is your most memorable moment as a horsewoman?

A. I can't really pinpoint one. I might have to say meeting Charlie, my first horse, for the first time. My riding instructor found him for me, and we drove the 100 miles to Vista, California, to check him out. I remember seeing him, when he was 11 years old, standing in the crossties all beautiful, in his prime, and just saying, "I can teach you so much." And he did. I also remember my first horse show when I was 10, how proud my dad was. He braided my hair in two pigtails and I got to ride my favorite school horse, this ancient rangy Thoroughbred named High Fleet. I came home with ribbons and a little trophy. It was such a great memory.

Q. Why is having horse experience necessary to be successful in your field?

A. It is necessary because while you can learn some on-the-job, the industry has a distinct lingo, a way of operating. It's a sport, it's a lifestyle, and it's animal health and welfare. You can be a great editor, understand grammar and style, proofreading, sentence structure, page layout, publishing . . . but if you don't have the equine knowledge, it's nearly impossible to be a "voice of authority" for the nation.

Q. Do you have direct contact with horses as part of your job?

A. We sneak off to horse shows about every month. I meet some of the top riders, trainers, and professionals at shows. Otherwise, we don't physically have contact with horses as part of the job.

Q. What is the most rewarding part of being a magazine editor?

A. It is having someone approach me and say they've had something good happen as a result of reading the magazine. That and having someone say they read my column every month. It makes me feel like I make a difference.

Q. What is the most challenging part of being a magazine editor?

A. It is challenging always keeping it fresh, keeping the topics that run from year to year exciting.

Q. What is the biggest achievement of your career?

A. The biggest achievement for me is that under my leadership, *Horse Illustrated* has become the nation's—make that the world's—largest horse publication.

Q. What is the most challenging obstacle in your career?

A. The challenge is producing a magazine with tighter time restraints, while still trying to maintain the quality.

Q. What has driven you to excel in your career?

A. I want to be the best that I can. My parents always told me I was born to put words to paper. I can't think of doing anything else.

Q. What education and/or experience do you advise for someone interested in a magazine career?

A. Stay away from English or creative writing, unless you want to be a freelance writer or book author. You really need the hands-on courses such as editing, reporting, mass communication history, law, and interpersonal communication—the things that a mass communications degree provides. That doesn't mean stay away from writing, because you'll need clips to show potential employers. I'd also suggest taking any horse-related courses you can find in your area. Some stables offer them, even.

Q. What personal strengths or skills should a person have who is considering this field?

A. A person should be organized, first and foremost. They should be attentive to detail and have creativity and a sense of humor. An editor should look outside the industry to bring in fresh ideas, too.

Q. What advice would you give to someone who wants to become a writer or magazine editor within the horse industry?

A. If you just want to write, you don't necessarily need a degree. You can just have natural talent and horse knowledge. However, if you want to be an editor, get a degree in communications, with emphasis in publications. Be prepared to start at the bottom, and maybe supplement your entry-level salary with a second job. Contact the magazines closest to your area: most magazines are not going to look at an unsolicited resume from across the country for a junior editor's position. Learn a computer page layout program, such as Quark XPress.

Q. If you could do it over, is there anything you would have done differently to reach your career goal?

A. I can't think of anything, really. I feel quite lucky to have everything fall into place.

Q. What do you think the job outlook is for editors of equine magazines?

A. There's definitely a finite universe out there for print editors, but the Internet will probably open up a host of new opportunities that weren't there before.

Q. To what professional or horse-related associations or organizations do you belong?

A. I belong to U.S. Equestrian, the nation's sporting organization, and American Horse Publications.

Q. What other career-related experience do you have?

A. I've been a publications judge for the Western Association of Magazines; I've been a guest speaker on the topic of getting started in magazine publishing at various horse expos, too.

Q. Is there anything else you would like to say about your career or your life with horses?

A. Horses keep me cash poor, but I wouldn't have it any other way!

Photographer

ABOUT THE JOB

Photographers spend the majority of their time working outdoors, capturing special moments at races, shows, rodeos, and events. They create portraits for horse owners and sell their work to magazine and book publishers, product companies, and others. The majority of photographers are in business for themselves, rather than as full-time staff members at a magazine or business. Earnings for photographers are directly affected not only by the quality of their work, but also by their marketing ability.

Artistic ability and technical ability, good eyesight, and patience are key in this field. Depending on the type of work you choose to do, travel may be frequent or infrequent. Many event publications are now going online, with results posted soon after a race or competition is over. This requires photographers to deliver digital shots almost immediately, which means they might spend all day shooting an event, then rush to the computers to download photos and send them off to editors.

Equine photographers should understand horse behavior and movement as well as the sports they are shooting. Being able to set up shots that show the horses and riders at their best, while not interfering with their performance, is critical. Photographers who can supply well-written copy or captions with their photos may find themselves gaining additional work since many editors like to see complete packages.

EDUCATION AND TRAINING

A two- or four-year degree in fine arts, trade school technical training, or on-the-job training is essential. Classes on equine anatomy are helpful, as are business classes.

SALARY

The median average salary for staff photographers is $23,040.

A poll by the Equine Photographers' Network, an organization of freelance equine photographers, shows that the majority of respondents work part-time as equine photographers, or full-time as general photographers, not exclusive to the horse industry. Only 19.51 percent of respondents work full-time as equine photographers. Of respondents, 67.44 percent said their earnings in 2001, from equine photography were under $10,000; 16.28

percent earned between $10,000 and $20,000; 6.98 percent earned between $20,000 and $30,000; and 4.65 percent earned between $30,000 and $40,000. From there, the earnings jumped up to between $70,000 and $80,000 for 2.33 percent of respondents and another 2.33 percent reported earning more than $90,000.

RESOURCES
Equine Photographers' Network
www.equinephotographers.net

Professional Photographers of America
229 Peachtree St., NE, Suite 2200
Atlanta, GA 30303
www.ppa.com

Photographer's Market
F&W Publications
1507 Dana Ave.
Cincinnati, OH 45207

American Horse Publications
Internship and Student Mentoring Programs
49 Spinnaker Circle
South Daytona, FL 32119
www.americanhorsepubs.org

Career Spotlight

DANA GOOKIN-OWENS, PHOTOGRAPHER AND WEB DESIGNER

Dana Gookin-Owens works full-time as a freelance photographer and Web designer in northern California. She grew up on a cattle ranch and started riding horses before she could walk. Along the way, Dana also developed an interest in photography and decided to combine her two passions into a career. She started her photography business twelve years ago, Dana Gookin Photography, shooting horse shows to build her reputation. Her business grew from there. In addition to horse photography, she also shoots family and high school senior portraits and the occasional wedding. Three years ago, Dana also began designing Web sites for farms and other horse businesses as well as non-horse-related companies. In addition, she designs advertising layouts and flyers.

Dana has two horses, Maximum Attraction (or Cruiser) a seven-year-old quarter horse gelding, and Marauders Showdown (or Calvin) a seven-year-old paint. She competes in western pleasure, showmanship, horsemanship, and hunter under saddle. About her horses she says, "Calvin is into everything, turns on faucets, lets himself and everyone else out of their stalls. Cruiser is very quiet, but loves to be loved on."

Q. What does your job as an equine photographer involve?

A. I travel to ranches and farms, working with the owners to get the best possible background and the results they are looking for. I also develop and print photos and do image manipulation of photos, including backgrounds, removing halters, people, and more.

Q. What does your job as a Web site designer involve?

A. I try to work closely with clients to achieve the image they are trying to portray. Work includes gathering information, designing, scanning photos, uploading to the site, and submitting to search engines.

Q. What experience and education do you have that prepared you to be successful as a photographer and Web designer?

A. I worked at a newspaper. I was assigned to photograph the sports events, which included rodeos, horse shows, and gymkhanas. I am mostly self-taught in horse photography. For Web design, I took several classes, including HTML and Adobe Photoshop. I also went to junior college and have attended lots of seminars.

Q. What is your typical workday like?

A. Hectic, very hectic!

Q. How many hours/days per week do you typically work?

A. I typically work 8 to 12 hours a day, between the computer and photo sessions. I usually work 5 to 6 days a week

Q. Do you feel it is necessary to have direct horse experience to break in as an equine photographer or an equine Web designer?

A. Yes, having horse experience will help you understand what the client is trying to achieve with photos and Web sites. Knowledge of the breed and discipline that you're photographing will help you get the perfect shot that the horse show competitor will buy.

Q. What steps should someone who is trying to become established as a freelance photographer and/or Web designer take to make it happen?

A. Work with experienced horse photographers and have knowledge of horses and the discipline you are planning to shoot. Web design would require knowledge of the Internet and the software programs you plan to use. Have lots of patience and don't give up.

Q. What type of education and experience do you recommend to someone going into photography or Web design?

A. For photography, one needs knowledge of basic photography and cameras, as well as horse experience. For Web design, I would recommend a more formal education in graphic design, such as through a college or trade school.

Q. What personality traits should a person have who is considering these fields?

A. Lots of patience.

Q. What do you think the job outlook is for these fields within the horse industry?

A. That is hard to say. Hopefully, more stallion owners, trainers, and others with horse businesses will see the importance of advertising on the Internet.

Q. What do you like most about your job? What do you like least about your job?

A. I like to be creative. I like working with horses and people. Least has to be the paperwork.

Q. How much travel is required of someone in your profession?

A. That would be a personal preference.

Q. What is your most memorable moment as a horsewoman?

A. Placing fifth in horsemanship at the World Championship Paint Horse Show.

Q. What is the most rewarding part of your career?

A. When a client is in tears of joy over the photos I've taken or Web site I've designed.

Q. What is the most challenging facet of your career?

A. The hours that are involved.

Q. What has driven you to excel in your career?

A. The love of horses and happy clients.

Q. If you could do it over, is there anything you would have done differently to reach your career goal?

A. I would have had a formal education in graphic design.

Public Relations Specialist

ABOUT THE JOB

Public relations specialists work for show and sport organizations, breed associations, and horse businesses either directly, through public relations firms, or as self-employed consultants. The field of public relations includes media relations, marketing communications, community relations, investor relations, publicity, and employee communications. Public relations practitioners seek to create good will for their organizations through use of media, special events, publications, and marketing collateral material. People in this field act as spokespeople in the media for the organizations they support. Publicists promote a specific event or individual. Senior public relations professionals serve as advisors to top management on how best to promote the organization, its messages, and its goals.

Good judgment, an outgoing personality, strong writing talent, and excellent communications skills are necessary to work in this field. While horse experience is not necessary, it is helpful for understanding an equine organization's goals and audience. As in any industry, "speaking the same language" as your client or audience makes the job easier.

EDUCATION AND TRAINING

A bachelor's degree in communications, public relations, advertising, journalism, or English is essential. In addition to a degree, an internship working in public relations is strongly recommended. Certifications for public relations professionals are offered by two organizations: The Public Relations Society of America and The International Association of Business Communicators (see Resources). While certification is not required, it will make you more marketable in this competitive field.

SALARY

The median annual salary for public relations specialists is $41,010.

RESOURCES

Public Relations Society of America
33 Irving Place
New York, NY 10003-2376
www.prsa.org

International Association of Business Communicators
One Hallidie Plaza, Suite 600
San Francisco, CA 94102
www.iabc.com

Publisher: Books

ABOUT THE JOB
Equine book publishers produce books about various horse-related topics. To be successful, they must carefully assess their target market to be sure there is a need for the types of books they wish to publish. Solid planning, business management, and financial skills are also required. Some book publishers are one-person operations, but larger publishers may employ editors, designers, marketing and sales professionals and others to help run their businesses. As a result, strong people management skills are important. Book publishers also need to be good communicators to deal effectively with printers, bookbinders, distributors, and equine booksellers.

For publishers who also write their own books, strong horse knowledge and experience, or excellent research skills, are essential. Even publishers who employ others to do the writing must have horse industry knowledge to determine the size, scope, and interests of their potential audience.

EDUCATION AND TRAINING
A degree in journalism, English, equine studies (or other area of equine expertise), business or marketing, or other field significant to the horse industry is essential. Prior experience as a book industry intern or working for a book publisher is a requisite.

SALARY
Depending on the size of the publishing company, salaries can range from $50,000 up to $500,000.

RESOURCES
Publishers Marketing Association
627 Aviation Way
Manhattan Beach, CA 90266
www.pma-online.org

Publisher's Weekly
360 Park Ave. South
New York, NY 10010
www.publishersweekly.com

Publisher: Magazines, Newspapers, Newsletters

ABOUT THE JOB

Like equine book publishers, magazine publishers must assess their market to find out how large the demand is for the type of magazine they wish to publish. Many small and regional equine magazines start up every year, but they often fail because the publishers have not done their homework. Rising paper and postage prices as well as increasing printing costs also may affect the success of new magazines and other periodicals.

Successful publishers must have strong planning and business management skills, editorial know-how, and sales and marketing ability to attract advertisers and subscribers. At large magazine operations, the owner and publisher are often two separate people. At small magazines, the publisher is usually the owner and may also be the editor. Strong horse experience is essential for publishers who also act as editors. Even publishers who hire editors with horse experience should be familiar enough with the audience to effectively set the strategic direction for their publication.

EDUCATION AND TRAINING

A degree in journalism, equine studies (or other area of equine expertise), business, or other field significant to the horse industry is essential. Prior experience as an intern or working for a magazine or other periodical is a requisite.

SALARY

Depending on the size of the publishing company, salaries can range from $50,000 up to $500,000.

RESOURCES

American Horse Publications
49 Spinnaker Circle
South Daytona, FL 32119
www.americanhorsepubs.org

Magazine Publishers of America
919 Third Ave.
New York, NY 10022
www.magazine.org

Video/Film Editor

ABOUT THE JOB

Video and film editors use their editing expertise to help in the production of equine videos, shows featuring horse sporting events, and films. Sometimes, the same person may act as the camera operator and the editor. (This is especially true for the self-employed.) Large operations may have separate camera operators and editors. Sometimes, the footage must be edited quickly if it is to be broadcasted immediately, so it's important the technical expertise is mastered. While horse experience is not required, an understanding of equine behavior and movement will be beneficial to the final product.

Editors must know how to operate technical equipment. In addition, they must be able to turn raw footage into flowing, coherent productions complete with audio, graphics, and text, so a creative and artistic eye is critical.

EDUCATION AND TRAINING

Attendance at a vocational or photography school, two- or four-year college or university degree, or on-the-job training is important.

SALARY

The median annual salary for video/film editors is $36,910.

RESOURCES

Media Communications Association International
401 N. Michigan Ave.
Chicago, IL 60611
www.itva.org

Videographer/Camera Operator

ABOUT THE JOB

Videographers create product videos for manufacturers, record horse performances at events, make educational and other films, produce sales videos for breeding farms, tape student riding lessons, and more. Camera operators work at sporting events and other venues by capturing images on film, or they film scenes for television and movies. One-quarter of the people in these fields are freelancers, according to the U.S. Bureau of Labor Statistics. Salaried camera operators are typically employed in the television and film industries and belong to the appropriate unions.

Many freelance videographers are also horse photographers, or they may do video work outside the equine industry to keep business up. Marketing, networking, and business skills are necessary to succeed as a self-employed businessperson. Artistic ability, good eyesight, strong hand-eye coordination, and an understanding of camera equipment are required of all successful videographers and camera operators. While detailed horse knowledge is not necessary, a basic understanding of equine behavior, conformation, and movement is very helpful.

EDUCATION AND TRAINING
On-the-job training, attendance at vocational or photography school, or a two- or four-year college or university degree is important.

SALARY
The median annual salary for videographers and camera operators is $28,980.

RESOURCES
Media Communications Association International
401 N. Michigan Ave.
Chicago, IL 60611
www.itva.org

Web Designer and Web Site Manager

ABOUT THE JOB
Web designers create Web pages for associations, farms, and businesses. Using specialized Web design software, they work with their clients or employers to determine the look and feel of a site. Many freelance Web designers and full-time designers working for small businesses or associations act as Web site managers, which means they are responsible for regular maintenance and updates to the sites. As a result, they must understand Web programming languages, the technical workings of the Internet, and how Web sites are hosted. At larger companies, these two functions may be split into two positions.

This field is growing as more horse businesses go online. People entering the field must be computer savvy and stay current in the constantly changing world of software and computers. Aspiring freelancers should have marketing and business skills as well as the money to invest in computer equipment and software, which can involve considerable costs. Horse experience is not required. However, as with many jobs in this chapter, horse experience will help you better understand the desires of your horse industry employer or clients.

EDUCATION AND TRAINING

Two- or four-year degree in graphic arts or graphic design, with classes focusing on the Internet; or training at a specialized art school.

SALARY

The American Institute of Graphic Arts/Aquent Salary Survey 2002 reports a median salary of $50,000 for Web designers.

RESOURCES

American Institute of Graphic Arts
164 Fifth Avenue
New York, NY 10010
www.aiga.org

Writer: Advertising and Marketing Copy

ABOUT THE JOB

Copywriters develop written pieces for advertising, marketing, and public relations campaigns. Items they produce include brochures, direct mailers, newsletters, print ads, videos, and sales scripts. Copywriters may work directly for equine businesses or organizations or for the advertising, marketing, or public relations agencies that support them. Many copywriters gain experience working for someone else and then turn to freelancing, selling their talents to businesses, associations, and agencies. It is unlikely, though, that you will find enough freelance copywriting work in the horse industry to support yourself full-time. Writing copy for other industries and diversifying into other areas, such as writing articles for equine magazines, are ways you can maintain work full-time as a freelancer.

Aspiring copywriters must have a portfolio of their work to show prospective employers or clients. If you do not have a portfolio of school-work or work produced as an intern or part-timer, you can acquire samples by volunteering your writing services to a nonprofit organization or doing pro bono work for a small business. Copywriters should have enough horse knowledge to convincingly speak the language of their audience.

EDUCATION AND TRAINING

A bachelor's degree in advertising, communications, public relations, English, or journalism is required. Internships are recommended. Some larger advertising agencies have training programs for copywriters.

SALARY

The American Institute of Graphic Arts/Aquent Salary Survey 2002 reports a median annual salary of $50,000.

RESOURCES

American Association of Advertising Agencies
405 Lexington Ave., 18th Floor
New York, NY 10174
www.aaaa.org

American Marketing Association
311 S. Wacker Drive, Suite #5800
Chicago, IL 60606
www.marketingpower.com

Writer: Horse Magazines and Books

ABOUT THE JOB

Many horse industry writers are freelancers who place their stories in local, regional, national, and association publications; they also write horse books. While large magazines and some horse associations may keep writers on staff, many publications rely on freelancers who have strong knowledge of horses. Writers query publications and book publishers with ideas on the latest in horsemanship, training, medicine, or other topics of interest. Those writers who prove themselves to magazine editors may find themselves receiving regular assignments.

Working as a freelance magazine or book writer is not an easy way to make a living. Many writers do it on a part-time basis or diversify into other writing arenas, such as public relations, advertising, and marketing. Writers with photographic talent may be at an advantage because they can present magazines with complete packages that include both story and photos.

Most magazines want to see published clips of a writer's work when considering story ideas. Book publishers considering a proposal will want to see a list of writing credits. Writing for the school newspaper or magazine, or contributing articles to your local newspaper are good ways to obtain publishing credits. Strong interviewing and research skills, adherence to deadlines, and marketing and communication skills are important for freelance writers.

EDUCATION AND TRAINING

Bachelor's degree in journalism or English for staff writers is typically required. Though a degree is not required for freelance writers if they have good writing skills and equine knowledge, it is always helpful.

SALARY

The median annual salary is $42,450.

RESOURCES

Writer's Market
Writer's Digest Books
1507 Dana Ave.
Cincinnati, OH 45207
www.writersmarket.com

American Horse Publications
49 Spinnaker Circle
South Daytona, FL 32119
www.americanhorsepubs.org

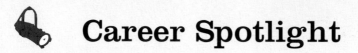

Career Spotlight

PATTI SCHOFLER, FREELANCE WRITER

Patti Schofler has worked as a freelance writer for more than 15 years. A sampling of some of the equine magazines she has contributed to include *Chronicle of the Horse*, *International Arabian Horse*, *Practical Horseman*, *Dressage Today*, *Arabian Horse World*, and *Western Horseman*. In addition, she writes in areas outside the horse world to supplement her magazine income. Patti is a graduate of the United States Dressage Federation's "L" (Learner Judge) Judges Program. She manages dressage shows and judges schooling shows in addition to writing. She earned a bachelor's degree in history with minors in political science and English; she also holds a paralegal certificate.

Patti lives with her husband, who is "non-horsey but perfectly supportive," on a 15-acre ranch in California. Her horses include Star, a 22-year-old Arabian gelding (Patti bought him as a yearling and, together they earned a United States Dressage Federation bronze medal) Fanny, a 12-year-old Arabian/Oldenburg mare that Patti bred; and Novio, an 8-year-old Dutch Warmblood that acquired on a trip to the Netherlands. Other ranch inhabitants include two miniature donkeys and three cats.

Q. What does your job as a freelance writer involve?

A. I write in as many capacities as I can. I write for horse magazines. I write as a freelance publicist. I recently have taken on a nonprofit human services agency as a client, for whom I do public relations and fund-raising. I have also worked as a paralegal, which of course entails considerable writing.

Q. What did you do prior to your current career?

A. I have always written in one way or another. I was a reporter for the *Chicago Tribune*, a publicist for United Airlines, and a family law paralegal.

Q. What is your typical workday like?

A. Fortunately, there are not many typical days. I may work on one project one day, or a half day, and then switch to another. Although I might wear the hat of a show manager one day and the hat of a magazine writer the next, I'm usually writing. The hours vary according to how much work I have.

Q. What do you enjoy most about your work?

A. I love interviewing and researching.

Q. What do you like least about your work?

A. Finding work.

Q. How necessary is it to have horse experience to write about horses?

A. I think it is absolutely necessary, if only to get good story ideas. Riding and writing are continual learning experiences, and if you're not around horses, you don't have the perspective to ask the right questions and put the answers in the proper context.

Q. What sparked your interest in horses?

A. It seems like it's something that has just always been there, and I have no idea where it came from because I didn't grow up around them. I grew up in Chicago.

Q. What is your most memorable moment as a horsewoman?

A. When Star was 15, we tried a competitive trail ride and he camped for the first time. He has a lot of trail experience for a dressage horse, but didn't have special conditioning for this ride. We rode through a wildness area, past feral horses, through creeks. He just did it all, and had perfect vet checks. We were eliminated because we came in too early. He was such fun.

Q. Do you have contact with horses as part of your work?

A. No. I've found that most of my stories are done from phone interviews. However, story ideas come from contact with horses.

Q. What is most rewarding about your work?

A. Doing a good interview that I know will make a great story.

Q. What is most challenging?

A. Getting work and making the story worthy of the interview.

Q. What is your biggest achievement as a writer?

A. I've had some interviews that I consider my greatest achievements. Also, winning the Chronicle of the Horse Best Feature of the Year award in 1999.

Q. What personal strengths or skills should an aspiring writer have?

A. A good ear to hear what people are saying and a good eye to recognize a story.

Q. What advice would you give to aspiring writers?

A. Find a few areas in the horse world that interest you and focus on those. I don't think you can write successfully about every aspect of the horse world.

Career Spotlight

ANGELIA ALMOS, BOOK AUTHOR

Angelia Almos is the author of *Horse Schools: The International Guide to Universities, Colleges, Secondary Schools and Specialty Equine Programs* (1st Books, 2002). She has pursued freelance writing seriously as a full-time career for the past four years. In addition to her book, Angelia writes arti-

cles on the subject of horse schools and exercises her more creative side by writing short and long fiction on horses and non-horsey topics like science fiction. She began riding at the age of five, had her first horse at 10, and has competed in gymkhana and jumping. Angelia taught riding at a summer camp and currently coaches young riders in jumping at the barn where she rides. Her horses include Southern Belle, a 13-year-old Anglo-Arab/ Hanoverian that Angelia show jumps; Lady Kristy, a 16-year-old Anglo-Arab diagnosed with navicular disease and retired to her parents' New Mexico ranch; and Ginger, a 17-year-old Shetland Pony that Angelia bought for her daughter. Angelia and her family live in northern California.

Q. What made you decide to become a writer?

A. I turned to writing after deciding not to pursue a hands-on horse career. I wanted to find something that I enjoyed and could primarily do from home. I knew that, besides working with horses, I most enjoyed creating stories and writing. I love to combine my two main passions of horses and writing as often as I can.

Q. What motivated you to write *Horse Schools*?

A. I was motivated by my own experience in looking for a horse school and realizing how badly a guide like this was needed. I made the decision to write *Horse Schools* after starting an e-mail networking list for people looking for horse schools. After answering the same questions over and over again, I decided that *Horse Schools* needed to be written. When I originally undertook the task of writing it, I didn't realize how large a job it was going to be. It turned out to be about three times larger than I had originally thought.

Q. What does your job involve?

A. My job involves hours of writing and rewriting. I have two computers; one is in my office and the other is an old laptop. I prefer to write on my laptop as I can move it where I need to be in the house, and this allows me more time to write. I do most of my rewriting on paper, as it's easier to catch the grammar, spelling, and punctuation mistakes on hard paper. If I'm doing major restructuring I'll do it on the computer so I can cut and paste. Lots of research is involved because whether I'm working on fiction or nonfiction, I like to make sure I have some idea of what I'm writing about. When writing about horses, it's fairly easy as I either know the answers or know where I can go to find the answers. My job also involves lots of promotion and marketing. If your book is published, either traditionally or as a self-publishing venture, you have to be willing to promote it.

Q. What is your typical workday like?

A. I don't actually have a typical workday, but I usually get up early and check my e-mail. I respond to anything that is urgent and file away other e-mails to be answered later. If I worked late writing, I will look over what I wrote, edit, and change a few things. After taking my daughter to school, I'll head to the stable, where I school Belle in the arena, or I'll take her on a long trail ride. In the early afternoon, along with collecting my daughter from school and caring for her, I may work on marketing and promoting the book. By 3 P.M., I'm usually on my laptop and in-between house chores, I'll write and edit. About 6 P.M., I stop for the night, unless I'm on a roll, then I'll write through the evening, until about 10 P.M. when I make myself go to bed.

Q. How many hours/days per week do you usually work?

A. It depends on the project. At the height of gathering data and writing for *Horse Schools*, I easily worked 10 hours a day, seven days a week. When I'm working, I tend to focus all of my energy on that project and I can't do anything else as long as I'm awake. When I don't have looming or huge projects like *Horse Schools*, I work five days a week and average about five hours a day with writing and editing. However, getting story ideas and doing all the plotting in my head, as all writers experience, goes on 24/7.

Q. What do you enjoy most about your work?

A. I enjoy creating characters and watching their stories unfold. Nothing gives me more satisfaction than turning out a line of dialogue or writing a description that gives my stomach little butterflies when I reread it.

Q. What do you like least about your work?

A. Having a scene in my head, trying to get it onto paper, and not being able to write it as I see it. Or writing myself into a corner.

Q. What is the most rewarding part of writing on horse topics?

A. For nonfiction, it's knowing that I'm helping kids pursue their passion or when someone learns something from my writing. It's rewarding when people look through my book and find schools that are perfect for them that they wouldn't have found otherwise or that would have taken them a lot of research to find on their own. For fiction, it's when someone gets totally involved in the story and can't wait to find out what happens next; or when a reader can relate her own experiences with the main character's experience.

Q. What is the biggest achievement of your career?

A. The biggest achievement would be seeing *Horse Schools* written, following through and publishing it on my own, and getting it out and recommended by the horse industry magazines.

Q. What is the most challenging obstacle in your career?

A. Time. I have a daughter, a husband, and many other interests. When you work for yourself, and have no one but yourself to answer to, it can be difficult to make the time that is required to get the work done. The other obstacle is getting a publisher to believe in your work as much as you do. On the creative side, the biggest obstacle is that little monster inside you telling you that what you just wrote is no good, you're a horrible writer, no one will ever want to read this so you should give it up and get a real job.

Q. What education and experience do you recommend for someone interested in becoming a writer in the horse industry?

A. Read a lot. The number one thing that any writer needs to do is read more than they write. Taking college classes and joining writers groups can also help any writer develop and improve her writing skills. Most colleges offer English or journalism degrees. You can also specialize and get a writing degree in creative writing, fiction writing, creative nonfiction writing, professional writing, and more. The majority of jobs for an employer in the writing industry do require that the applicant have at the minimum, a bachelor's degree.

Freelance writers don't have to have a degree. However, to write in the horse industry, they need to practice their horse skills often. The more hands-on activities they do, the more fodder for their writing. If they have a love for horses, it will show up in their writing. Writers need to be able to research, especially if they write horse fiction books for adults or teens. Nothing bugs a horse person more than picking up a book with a horse on the cover, getting into the story, and then finding a glaring horse error. If someone chooses to write about horses, he should make sure he has a passing knowledge of horses and the field he chooses to place his book in.

Q. What personality traits should a person have who is considering this field?

A. A writer should have a lot of self-discipline, as you will, for the most part, be working on your own without a boss looming over your shoulder. You are your own boss. It's way too easy to get tired of a project and put it on the back burner, especially if it's something you haven't sold beforehand and there isn't anyone waiting for you to finish it. The only way to get published is to write—and write a lot.

You need to be able to budget your time and work with your personality. Some writers do better working slowly and steadily, while others prefer waiting until the last minute and then punching it out quickly. Each method will work as long as you meet your deadlines. The difference between focusing on books rather than articles is that the time allowed to write a book is much longer, so you need to set your own mini deadlines or you might find yourself coming up on the deadline with only half the book finished.

Q. Is there anything else you would like to say about your career in the horse industry?

A. I love what I do! Anyone interested in pursuing a writing career, whether fiction or nonfiction, needs to have a lot of perseverance. It can be easy to give up after receiving the 100th rejection letter. I've always felt that writing is similar to acting in the number of auditions and rejections that it takes and the tough shell you have to develop so you don't take the rejections personally. If you keep writing, and keep working on improving your own writing craft, you will be published eventually, whether you're picked up by a traditional publisher or you believe in your project enough to self-publish it.

CHAPTER 9

Equine Health and Welfare Careers

— — —

Most careers listed in this chapter involve daily contact with horses and require strong hands-on horse experience and often a master's or doctoral degree. People in these careers focus on the overall physical and mental health of horses, and do a large portion of their work on-site at barns and stables. The hours can be long and demanding. Though veterinarian is perhaps the most well known career concerned with equine health and welfare, many other jobs also concern themselves with equine well being. As you can see, there are several opportunities in the health and welfare field including chiropractor, animal welfare worker, and animal communicator. Other positions involved with equine health and welfare, but which are more focused on research or education, are highlighted in Chapter 17.

Acupuncturist

ABOUT THE JOB

Equine acupuncturists are licensed veterinarians who have undergone additional training in acupuncture. Most veterinary acupuncturists who treat horses use acupuncture in conjunction with traditional veterinary medicine. Some equine veterinary acupuncturists practice acupuncture exclusively or they may combine it with other Eastern healing approaches. In addition to the equine medical training required, a strong understanding of horse behavior and an ability to handle all kinds of horses are important.

Acupuncturists insert small needles under the skin to stimulate specific points on the body, causing physiological changes and helping the body heal itself. Acupuncture is used to relieve arthritis pain, improve balance, treat gastrointestinal disorders, correct leaning, help with reproductive problems, treat chronic lameness, and more. In severe cases, electro-acupuncture may be used. This procedure stimulates points by running electrical currents through the needles, stimulating the body's own pain-relieving substances.

Veterinary acupuncture schools report that the field is growing: they are seeing an increase in students over the past several years. This may be due to acupuncture's increased acceptance among horse owners, as the public in general grows more comfortable with holistic approaches to medicine.

Acupressure, which stimulates points without needles, may be practiced by those with specialized acupressure training who are not veterinarians.

EDUCATION AND TRAINING

A state-licensed DVM with additional training in veterinary acupuncture is required. Competition to get into veterinary school is intense, as there are only 27 accredited colleges of veterinary medicine in the United States (see Appendix K). High school science coursework, an internship, or part-time job working with horses and strong grades in college pre-veterinary studies will increase your chances of being accepted to a veterinary school.

Training programs for licensed veterinarians in equine acupuncture are offered by Colorado State University School of Veterinary Medicine, the International Veterinary Acupuncture Society, and the Chi Institute in Florida. There is no certifying body for veterinary acupuncture at this time and the AVMA does not formally recognize any certification from any program. However, if you receive a certificate of completion from a veterinary acupuncture program, the AVMA will consider you "certified" from that particular program.

SALARY

According to American Veterinary Medical Association statistics for 2001, the mean annual salary for equine veterinarians in private practice is $108,405.

RESOURCES

International Veterinary Acupuncture Society
P.O. Box 271395
Ft. Collins, CO 80527-1395
www.ivas.org

The American Academy of Veterinary Acupuncture
66 Morris Avenue, Suite 2A
Springfield, NJ 07081
www.aava.org

American Academy of Veterinary Medical Acupuncture
Colorado State University Veterinary Teaching Hospital
300 West Drake Rd.
Fort Collins, CO 80523
www.aavma.org

American Association of Equine Practitioners
4075 Iron Works Pkwy.
Lexington, KY 40511-8434
www.aaep.org

Animal Communicator

ABOUT THE JOB

Animal communicators seek to improve the lives of animals through better human/animal understanding. Some specialize in a particular species of animal, such as the horse. They use telepathic means to try and discover what horses think, feel, and want; their goals are to improve behavioral issues and to discover if the animal is in pain (though they do not seek to be an alternative to proper veterinary care), among other goals. Horse owners often call upon communicators when more traditional methods of problem correction have failed; sometimes, veterinarians refer them. Communicators may work with the horse in person or do consultations from a distance once they have received basic facts about the horse, such as name, age, location, etc.

Many communicators say they have been communicating with animals since they were children, while others became interested in animal communication later in life, usually after experiencing a personally difficult time or episode of spiritual discovery. Experienced communicators believe that everyone is born with the ability to communicate with animals, but they must first learn to trust their own intuition. What is key is to be able to put aside preconceived notions about animals and to have an open mind about alternative ways of thinking and healing.

EDUCATION AND TRAINING

Animal communicators come from a variety of educational backgrounds. Some have backgrounds in psychology, others are ministers or spiritual healers, and some breed or train horses.

SALARY

Communicators charge per session, with sessions ranging from a quarter of an hour to an hour or more. Charges range from $25 to $100 and up per session.

RESOURCES

An Internet search or trip to the local bookstore will uncover several books on the subject. One by Penelope Smith, who helped found the animal communication field in the early 1970s is entitled *Animal Talk: Interspecies Telepathic Communication* (Beyond Words Publishing, Inc., 1999). Lydia Hiby, (see Career Spotlight) has published two books on animal communication.

Career Spotlight

LYDIA HIBY, ANIMAL COMMUNICATOR

For 20 years, Lydia Hiby has talked to animals and given their messages to owners. Though she communicated with animals as a child, she had a healthy degree of skepticism about people who were in business as animal communicators. That changed, however, when Lydia, who was educated as an animal health technician and worked as a show groom at a large hunter/jumper barn in New York where she was born and raised, met an animal communicator who came to talk to the horses.

After Lydia observed Beatrice Lydecker, the renowned communicator, work with the horses and discussed her dog with her, Lydia's skepticism about animal communication vanished. She moved to California, worked at a veterinary clinic during the week and accompanied Lydecker to ranch calls on weekends. It took Lydia more than three years before she was comfortable working as an animal communicator full-time. Today, she has an international reputation in the field. She does phone and live consultations with animals and animal owners, gives seminars and lectures, and is the author of two books: *Conversations with Animals*, co-written with Bonnie Weintraub (New Sage Press, 1998), and *More Conversations with Animals* (NewSage Press, 2003). Lydia has been featured in the *Wall Street Journal*, *Los Angeles Times*, *Washington Post* and has appeared on *Late Night with David Letterman*, *The Tonight Show with Jay Leno*, and *48 Hours* among other shows. She spends her spare time riding the trail on Winter Chocolate, a Trakehner-Thoroughbred cross, and caring for several other animal companions, including two llamas, a goat, and a collie.

Q. How does animal communication work?

A. Much of my work comes from veterinarians, who send their clients to me. People come to me because they want to know what their animals need, from the minds of the animals themselves. If I am doing a phone consultation, I ask for the name, age, color, breed, and location of the animal. Then, I look at a map or other image of the animal's location and quietly call the animal by name in my mind. The animal's name is like her own personal radio frequency that I dial into. Every animal has her own frequency. Once I've dialed the animal in, I ask her what she wants to tell me. Then I open the conversation up to the owner, and ask what he wants to know. Sometimes animals have a message they want to give. They talk to me through pictures, emotions, physical sensations, and symbols and I turn it into words that the owner can understand. There are some animals that are "old souls" and I can actually hear them talking in my head. For example, my goat is an old soul. Once, when I was in the barn with her, she kept saying, "snake." When I looked, I found a snake in with the llamas.

People call me a "medical intuitive." I am educated as an animal technician and my original direction was to be a veterinarian. I give animal owners information they can take back to their veterinarian, farrier, or trainer. I also consult on when it is time to put an animal to sleep.

Q. How do you handle the skepticism you encounter?

A. I don't do anything differently. I just try to tell people as judiciously as I can that their animal is trying to tell them something and I try to get a lot of detail. I have a policy that, if someone is unhappy with the results of a consultation, I will give them their money back. Recently, a woman was skeptical about the consultation with her animal companion and I sent her check back to her. She later called and wanted to return the check to me because she had come to believe in what I had said. I didn't want the money back, however. My satisfaction was in knowing that she had opened up to having a deeper relationship with her animal companion.

Q. What do you charge for a consultation?

A. I charge $30 for a 15-minute consultation per animal. I try to keep prices low. If an animal needs veterinary care or some other method of care, I would prefer people spend their money on that.

Q. What is a typical week like?

A. Much of my work is with show horses, show dogs, and show cats. Two-thirds of it is with horses. When I do live consultations, I might do several horses at the same barn or I might go to a dog club that is sponsoring me. A couple days a week, I have open phone hours from 10 A.M. to 10 P.M. with clients who have prepaid my fee. Once a month, I teach a one-day class to train people how to better communicate with their animals.

Q. What is your overall background with horses?

A. I've ridden since I was 10. I belonged to the Pony Club and later taught Pony Club classes. I was mostly involved with hunter/jumpers on the East Coast. I did show jumping and A-circuit shows and also worked as a show groom.

Q. What do you enjoy most about your work?

A. Hearing from people that I've helped them with their animals. Knowing the animals I've consulted with are better; working with pet owners who are open to the possibility that there is something deeper in their pets.

Q. What do you like least about your work?

A. Having to discuss putting animals down with the owners. Sometimes, the veterinarian and others will tell the person that there is no quality of life, yet the owner isn't sure what to do, so she'll consult me. The animal might tell me that he is not ready to go yet and I have to relay this to the owner. It is very difficult.

Q. What is your most memorable moment?

A. There was an iguana in California who was getting sick and no one could discover why. I don't feel as comfortable working with exotics; but this owner called me for a consultation and I had no idea we were talking about an iguana. I had an image of licking the floor. Then the owner told me that her iguana liked to lick the floor, which is when I discovered we were talking about an iguana! It turned out the owner used a toxic cleaner on the floor. During my consultation, the iguana kept saying "sweet potatoes." It turned out that sweet potatoes heal the liver and the iguana was "telling" me what he needed. I have learned that animals will let you know what they instinctually need. This iguana was such an amazing spirit. We took this nine-foot long exotic animal to a pet fair once and people passing by would immediately start feeling his personality. He was an old spirit and a real lesson to me.

Q. What is the most rewarding part of being a communicator?

A. All of it is great—including being part of the process. I'm just honored to be the messenger. It keeps getting more interesting; it keeps getting deeper and the insight comes through better. The animals are more tuned in.

Q. What personality traits should someone have who is considering animal communication?

A. They should be very empathic, able to put themselves in the animal owner's place or the animal's place. When someone comes to me, he is laying himself open for whatever comes out of my mouth, so I must relay the message to the owner with grace and humility.

Q. What advice would you give to someone interested in this area?

A. Have a mentor; team up with an established communicator. Ride along with your mentor and compare notes. Remember that you have to deal with people as well as animals, so be sure that you have that skill.

Pick an aspect and make it your own in an area you know about. Don't try to work with too many species or in too many areas. Now, I work mostly in areas that I know, such as, medical difficulties, with dogs, cats and horses. For example, I don't work with lost pets anymore or with animals that have passed over. These are not my areas and I can't get enough details on them to be comfortable.

Q. What else would you like to say about your work?

A. Horses are not misunderstood, but they can be better understood. If many people who own horses, and other animals, would get to know their animals on a deeper level, they could learn so much more. Horses have learned to deal with humans and they give us so much. When people are open to the possibility that animals are much deeper than most people believe, this knowledge can establish a very powerful connection between human and animal, which will greatly broaden our respect of and love for our animal companions.

Chiropractor

About the job

Equine chiropractors manipulate their patients' spinal columns to correct misalignment, which relieves pain and allows better performance. Like veterinarians, farriers, and other equine health professionals, they usually travel to where their patients are located. Animal chiropractors are either veterinarians who have taken specialized chiropractic training, or they are human chiropractors with training in animal chiropractic. Some veterinary chiropractors practice both traditional equine medicine and chiropractic, while others strictly work as chiropractors. Those who are educated as doctors of chiropractic (rather than as veterinarians) may work with both humans and animals or may work exclusively with animals depending on their preference. Many chiropractors may include into their practices other forms of non-traditional medicine, such as acupuncture.

Chiropractors must know how to behave around horses and have a strong understanding of equine anatomy. Like other self-employed professionals, they should have strong marketing and business skills to ensure their practices thrive.

Education and training

A DVM with training in chiropractic, or Doctor of Chiropractic with training in animal chiropractic is required, as is state licensing in the respective field and certification through the American Veterinary Chiropractic Association

Salary

Salary is dependent upon location and whether the chiropractor also works on human clients.

Resources

American Veterinary Chiropractic Association
442154 E. 140 Rd.
Bluejacket, OK 74333
www.animalchiropractic.org

Career Spotlight

CHERYL RICKETTS-MULVEY, DOCTOR OF CHIROPRACTIC

Cheryl Ricketts-Mulvey has helped people and animals feel better through chiropractic for more than seven years. She began by treating people, but because of her love for horses and repeated requests by horse-owning patients to treat their animals, she decided to gain additional training in animal chiropractic. After attending the Options for Animals chiropractic school in Illinois, Cheryl received certification to practice animal chiropractic. Now, the majority of her practice consists of horses and dogs. She also treats cats, goats,

pigs, cows, mules, some exotic animals such as llamas and emus, and even the occasional chicken. Every week, Cheryl sees from 75 to 100 horses, 50 dogs, and 30 people.

Cheryl and her husband, Finbarr Mulvey, own Olde Mission Chiropractic, in San Marcos, California. Finbarr treats only people, including rodeo cowboys on the Professional Rodeo Cowboy's Association circuit. Cheryl's human patients include many riders and she often treats riders and their horses together by bringing portable chiropractic equipment to the barns housing her equine patients. Cheryl owns five horses that she keeps at her home.

Q. How did you get into the chiropractic field?

A. While I was a medical student, majoring in biomedical sciences, I was in a bad car accident. I got horrible migraine headaches and had severe neck pain requiring pain injections in my neck, which didn't even help. I turned to a chiropractor as a last resort when nothing else worked to treat my pain. I had always been skeptical of chiropractors; in fact, I called them "quacko-practors." After my treatment, I felt so much better that I switched to studying chiropractic. I now, of course, swear by chiropractors.

Q. What is your typical workday/workweek like?

A. I'm up at 6 A.M. to feed and clean my horses and get my young daughter, Ireland, ready. I see 25 to 30 horses in a workday and am at the first client's barn early. I travel three days a week to outlying and coastal areas and try to see as many horses as I can on these days. Because I work for myself, I can work as many hours as I want, or as few.

Q. What does a treatment regimen for a horse involve?

A. With most horses, I do the exam and first visit adjustment and then a follow-up in four to six weeks. For horses at higher competitive levels, such as Grand Prix or Olympic horses, I might do the follow-up in two weeks, when I feel I have to be really aggressive. If a horse is doing really well, I'll do a three-month follow-up. After that, I recommend a minimum one-year maintenance adjustment. When riders have their horses adjusted, they also become trained to know when the horse doesn't feel quite right. When they feel the difference, they'll call me for another adjustment. Prevention is so important.

Q. What do you enjoy most about your work?

A. Treating horses is my favorite part of the job. Horses are my comfort zones. I have a strong respect for them even if a horse is lunging, kicking, bucking, or biting. I'm comfortable and carry on calmly. I get to be outside 10-15 hours a day with horses and still I'm not tired. If I had to do the same number of hours indoors with people, I would be exhausted. I also enjoy treating riders and working with the horse and rider to help balance them as a team. They come to me because they have a passion for riding.

Q. What do you like least about your work?

A. Trying to juggle my schedule and keep everyone happy. I can only do so much in a day, but I hate to say no when someone has a horse with a problem. Some people want to add a horse during my visit, but I can't do it because my schedule is so tight and I have to see the next client's horse. People's animals are like their kids, and I hate saying no.

Q. What is the most rewarding part of being a chiropractor?

A. Doing a good job and seeing the animals get better. The second time I come, after I've helped an animal the first time, he remembers and will run right up. Animals are more than eager for you on the second visit. And they are very honest about their pain—if an animal limps it is because she is hurting.

Q. What is the most memorable moment in your career?

A. This question is hard to answer because every day, something amazing seems to happen. Seeing a horse I treated win a Grand Prix is memorable. One of the first horses I ever adjusted had terrible behavioral and physical problems. They had to shoot darts into his stall just to sedate him. He was really mean and aggressive. The owners said that if I couldn't help him they were going to put him down. I saw the horse four times. That horse is pulling carts now, showing, and doing parades. All of his nastiness went away.

Q. What is the biggest achievement of your career?

A. The success I've had. I never thought I would be as busy as I am or have so many people hear about me. Some people drive from as far away as Arizona and Nevada to let me see their horses. That always amazes me. People tell me after I've treated their animal that "now I have my horse back," or "I have my dog back." I always wonder what I did. In my mind, all I did was adjust them. Also, the response from veterinarians is wonderful. I get many referrals from veterinarians. Also, the achievement is in the people. I will see the animals of established clients in the middle of the night if necessary. I always remember that they are the people who supported me when I first started in this business.

Q. How long have you ridden and in what disciplines do you ride?

A. I've ridden since I was four, when I got my first pony. Growing up, I rode with my grandfather and competed on the "A" circuit. I've done a little bit of everything: hunters, jumpers, eventing and western pleasure, reining, and more. Currently, I'm focusing on more formal dressage. I have five horses: a Thoroughbred hunter/jumper, and pleasure horse; an off-the-track Thoroughbred who is becoming a jumper; an Oldenburg for more formal dressage; an Appaloosa reining horse; and a pony for my daughter. I've broken and started horses myself, though not as much anymore. I've found that if you do the proper groundwork with horses, nothing bad ever happens once you get on.

Q. Why is having horse experience necessary to be successful?

A. You can't be successful working on horses without horse experience. I do this because I love horses. My motivation is not to make money, but rather because I love animals. Because of my love for horses, people have said I have a very calming presence around horses. I'm not nervous, so I relax them. Also, most clients only want horse people around their horses. Clients have interviewed me on my horse background before letting me treat their horses. Having horse experience will help provide you with the instinct to know how to read the horse and how to be safe. If you don't know horses and you want to do this for the money, you will not be successful. You have to love what you do and love horses, or why are you doing it?

Q. What advice would you give to people who want to become equine chiropractors?

A. Spend a lot of time with horses. Volunteer at a stable or a veterinarian's office. Travel with a chiropractor, if possible. Love what you do; it has to become part of your life.

Q. Is physical strength necessary?

A. You don't need strength to be an equine chiropractor. (I am small at 5' 1".) It is all about speed and using your body properly. You have to be fast. The less mass you have, the more speed you must have.

Q. What personality traits should a person have who is entering this field?

A. They should be outgoing and caring, have a strong personality but a gentle hand. You also have to be flexible when working with animals who can be unpredictable at times. Animals can sense weakness, so people need to be strong, but not overbearing. They should be sensitive and willing to cry with clients who are upset. You have to know how to deal with people whose animals are in the last stage of their lives. Also, you need strength of personality to deal with some horse owners. You are at risk of being injured when working with horses, so you have to discipline the horse without offending the owner.

Q. Is there anything else you would like to say about your career or your life with horses?

A. I'm still waiting for the best to come and I'm looking forward to showing horses again.

Equine Dentist

About the job

Equine dentists perform preventive maintenance and correct problems with the teeth that can cause pain and affect performance. This profession continues to evolve as more people recognize the importance of a healthy mouth to overall equine health. In the not-so-distant past, dentistry consisted of filing the sharp points on the horse's teeth and not much more. As technology and standards in the field improved, so has the demand for well-trained dental practitioners.

There are currently two career paths to practicing equine dentistry: 1) education and licensing as a veterinarian with further studies and/or certification in equine dentistry; or 2) training and certification through an equine dental school. Do your homework before committing to a particular career path. For example, it is illegal in many states for non-veterinarians to practice dentistry, so check your state's regulations. In states where non-veterinarians are able to practice dentistry, technically, they are required to work with a veterinarian, most notably when invasive procedures or sedation are involved. The general position of the equine veterinary community is that equine dentistry should be performed only by licensed veterinarians or by certified veterinary technicians, and under the supervision or employ of veterinarians. (In reality, there is a higher demand for equine dentists than there are veterinary dentists to fill it, so qualified people trained in dentistry who are not veterinarians often have no trouble finding work.)

All equine dental practitioners should have experience working with a wide variety of horses and strong horse-handling skills. They should also be familiar with equine anatomy. Professionals in the field recommend that anyone interested in this career observe a properly trained equine dentist at work before making a commitment. This will help you decide if the field is right for you.

Education and training

DVM degree and licensing, with advanced training or certification in equine dentistry is required. Another choice is attendance and certification through an equine dental school (see Appendix K or check with the American Association of Equine Practitioners for American Veterinary Medical Association-approved technical schools that may offer training).

Apprenticeship with a practicing equine dentist, for both veterinary and non-veterinary practitioners is essential.

Salary

Equine veterinarians earn an average of $108,405 per year, according to a 2002 survey by the American Veterinary Medical Association.

Resources

American Association of Equine Practitioners
4075 Iron Works Parkway
Lexington, KY 40511
www.aaep.org

International Directory of Equine Dentistry
P.O. Box 1040
Glenns Ferry, ID 83623
www.equinedentistry.com

International Association of Equine Dentistry
www.iaeqd.org

Career Spotlight

RICHARD O. MILLER, EQUINE DENTIST

Richard O. Miller, DVM, has dedicated his professional life to veterinary medicine, eventually specializing in equine dentistry. Born and raised in Southern California, Dr. Miller attended college at Washington State University, where he also completed veterinary school. Throughout his career, he saw a great need for equine dentistry and eventually became a rare veterinary specialist in the field. Still living in Southern California, Dr. Miller now practices only equine dentistry and is passionate about promoting the importance of thorough dental care for the well-being of horses. Although he has no horse of his own at this time, he has 50 years of experience in most horse-related disciplines, and is most comfortable with hunter/jumpers and racehorses.

Q. What made you decide to go into the field of equine dentistry?

A. There was no one else doing it well on the whole planet, other than a handful of technicians, and the need was so great.

Q. How did you get your first job in this profession?

A. With difficulty! Veterinarians were afraid to use my services and trainers were afraid to use me because they felt that veterinarians were totally untrained—which was the case.

Q. What did you do prior to your current career?

A. I practiced equine veterinary medicine for 15 years in pediatric/reproduction in Lexington, Kentucky, and for 11 years on the racetracks of Southern California.

Q. What does your job involve?

A. Ninety-five percent is equilibration and edontoplasty with emphasis on longevity, comfort and performance. Equilibration means placing everything on the same plane and edontoplasty is the forming and shaping of teeth. We also do exodontics [tooth extraction], periodontal procedures, and composite fillings.

Q. How many hours/days per week do you typically work?

A. We typically work 5 days a week when at our home base in Orange County, California, but when one is on the road and expenses are considerable, we work 10 to 20 days consecutively without a break. Typically, work days are 10 to 12 hours, not including travel time.

Q. What do you enjoy most about your work?

A. We are actually improving the well-being of our patients and the results are often immediate.

Q. What do you like least about your work?

A. The financial return is less than half of general practice incomes and sometimes clients can't appreciate your contribution unless they are present at the time of the dental intervention.

Q. How did you become trained in equine dentistry?

A. None of this training was available in vet schools and, even now, only four schools offer any training. My experience came through contacts with the 10 to 12 technicians on the planet who had carried the information through the last hundred years (the "dark ages").

Q. Do you have any other horse industry experience?

A. I was owner/manager of Summerhill Farm in Lexington, Kentucky, from 1963 to 1976. Emphasis in the spring was on boarding and breeding thoroughbred broodmares. Summer to winter, we emphasized our hunter/jumper competitions and Pony Club. Several years of polo and fox-hunting were included in there someplace.

Q. What is your overall background with horses?

A. Over 50 years with some experience in most disciplines, but I'm most comfortable with hunter/jumper and racetrack.

Q. What is your most memorable moment in the horse industry?

A. Delivering a Northern Dancer foal following a difficult dystocia [slow to progress labor].

Q. What is the most rewarding part of your job?

A. That I can make profound changes in the lives of my patients almost immediately.

Q. What is the most challenging part of your job?

A. Educating clients about the need for proper and complete dentistry.

Q. What is the most challenging obstacle in your career?

A. Other veterinarians who think that our work is useless, scientifically unproven, excessive, and invasive—not much different from the human scene 150 years ago.

Q. What education and/or experience do you recommend for someone interested in working in equine dentistry?

A. There are two very good private schools available to veterinarians and technicians but most people still learn by the tried-and-true method dating from the Middle Ages—the guild system, where an apprentice learns from a master and then becomes a journeyman.

Q. What personal strengths or skills do you believe a person should have who is considering this field?

A. Strength can be important, but 100-pound females compete favorably with 220-pound males in the same manner that they do in most equestrian disciplines—with finesse. In any case, a good horsemanship background is advantageous.

Q. What is the biggest achievement of your career?

A. Educating people about the need for dental procedures.

Q. If you could do it over, is there anything you would have done differently to reach your career goal?

A. Yes! I would have been born 40 years later! The world was not ready to receive the message about equine dentistry since the profession had literally died after the cavalry quit and the tractor replaced the horse on the farm.

Farrier

ABOUT THE JOB

Farriers play an integral role in the well being of horses. By shoeing and shaping the feet of horses, they can correct problems involving gait, stance, and lameness. Farriers are usually self-employed, with shops set up in their own vehicles. The hours are long and the work is physical. Also, farriers sometimes have to cover a large amount of territory to reach their customers. Some farriers specialize in specific horse breeds or in certain areas, such as with racehorses or hunter/jumpers. Farriers in the racing profession must be licensed through the home state's horseracing licensing body.

Prospective farriers should be familiar with horse anatomy—in particular the hoof, foot, and leg—and be willing to work in conjunction with veterinarians to identify and treat problems. They should also have a strong working knowledge of horses and have the skills to handle a variety of equine (and human) personalities.

EDUCATION AND TRAINING

Beginners in the field often work as apprentices for experienced farriers and learn the trade strictly through these apprenticeships or by observing experienced farriers. The majority, though, attend a specialized farrier school, followed by an apprenticeship. The length of time spent in a farrier school varies, depending on the level of education and certification desired. (See Appendix K for a list of farrier schools.) Both the American Farrier's Association and the Brotherhood of Working Farriers Association offer professional certification to farriers.

SALARY

In their November 2000 edition, the *American Farrier's Journal* reported a national average salary (before expenses) of $58,536

RESOURCES

American Farrier's Association
4059 Iron Works Pike
Lexington, KY 40511
www.americanfarriers.org

Brotherhood of Working Farriers Association
14013 East Hwy 136
LaFayette, GA 30728
www.bwfa.net

Career Spotlight

JERRY BAKER, FARRIER

Jerry Baker has cared for the feet and legs of horses for 35 years. Born in Montana, where he grew up on a grain and cattle ranch, Jerry has been around horses since the day he was born, though he didn't start to fully understand equines until many years later. Although Jerry spent four years in college majoring in agricultural business, he is self-taught as a farrier. Prior to his work as a farrier, he held a variety of jobs: bartender, dishwasher, and farm laborer; he also worked on an oil pipeline and spent a couple of years in the military. It was during his two-year stint in the U.S. Army that Jerry, stationed in Kansas in 1965, met a farrier who introduced him to the trade. More than three  decades later, Jerry still enjoys the work and his life with horses. In addition to shoeing horses, Jerry raises Thoroughbreds and quarter horses. He currently lives in Louisiana.

Q. What does your job involve?

A. Horsemanship. It is the most important aspect of being a farrier, followed by people skills and business skills, such as scheduling and accounting. If you really want to be on the top of your game—the kind of farrier people seek out—you must constantly read, study, observe, and associate with other farriers.

Q. What is your typical workday like?

A. My typical workday has changed drastically from when I started out 35 years ago, working on rodeo and pleasure horses. Today, I work with world-class jumpers and racehorses, but I still do some "backyard" shoeing. There is a wide variety of possibilities in shoeing that can range from draft horses, to Arabian show horses, to staying with the typical trail ride horse; it just depends on your niche.

On a typical day, I get up early, around 5:30 A.M. or 6 A.M., for quiet time and at least 30 minutes of reading. I play out my day in my mind, because I work on the same horses all the time. I think about what it will be like, even though I know each horse personally and how to interact with each one. It may sound funny, but I know my horses so well that I can tell what kind of day it will be the minute I walk in the barn. I try to get to the first horse by 8 A.M. and work until lunch. When I'm shoeing horses, I may do runners in the morning and jumpers in the afternoon; maybe I'll do a corrective job. It's important to study horse pathology, physiology, and conformation (how the horse is built) so I can enhance his movement, support, and function to the top of his game. In the late afternoon, I load my truck with the used supplies of the day and go back to my blacksmith shop, where I make anything I'll need for the days ahead.

It's important to learn the skills of blacksmithing so that you can make any shoe necessary that will help a horse in his way of going (performing). I also work on my skills for a couple hours and take time to think about how to do my job with more efficiency. Then it's wind-down time. I go home, eat supper, do the billing, and rest.

Q. To what professional organizations do you belong?

A. Louisiana Metalsmiths Association, past president; American Farrier's Association; Southern Farrier's Association; Gulf Coast Blacksmith Association.

Q. How many hours/days per week do you typically work?

A. Eight to 12 hours a day, five or six days a week. It just depends on which week it is.

Q. What do you enjoy most about your work?

A. I love what I do because of the horses and the people who own them. Most have been with me for a long time.

Q. What do you like least about your work?

A. I don't enjoy those hard days in deep mud and heavy rain.

Q. What made you decide to go into this field?

A. Just meeting the right person at the right time. I went into the U.S. Army in 1965, and was stationed at Ft. Riley, Kansas, where I met Dan Adcock, a cook and horseshoer from Oklahoma. We did rodeo together two years later and became friends. With his encouragement, I began studying to be a farrier. I had no training, no knowledge, no nothing, but the guts to try, and the people he worked for gave me a chance to work on their horses. Upon returning to Montana, I shoed our own rodeo horses and soon the jackrabbit telegraph let others know and the phone began to ring. This included roping, race, barrel, and pleasure horses. In the late '60s, there were no inside barns so it was a short season, April through September. I kept trying it there for a while and then moved to Colorado, and took a job riding pastures, roping, and doctoring sick calves. Then, I moved to Minnesota, where I did a lot of show horses, and finally to Louisiana, where I could work year-round.

Q. What is your overall background with horses?

A. Growing up on a ranch, my experience with horses started pretty young, but I was over 35 before I began to understand how a horse thinks, why he behaves the way he does, what he feels, what he likes and doesn't like. I worked with horses on the ranch, starting with young horses (and some that weren't so young). I did amateur rodeo and was high school state and district champion in 1965, and in college, was team captain and president of the rodeo club.

Q. Do you have any of your own horses?

A. I am currently raising Thoroughbreds for racing and quarter horses for the joy. I love running the nursery and watching the young ones progress.

Q. What is your most memorable moment as a horseman?

A. That's easy—the day I met Burney Chapman of Lubbock, Texas. [Burney Chapman was a world-renowned farrier, perhaps best known for reintroducing the heart-bar shoe for therapeutic use on foundered or laminitic horses.] He came to work on a horse in my area and I picked him up at the airport and had the pleasure of getting every question answered that I'd had for 20 years. He was such a great man to patiently listen and answer, when he surely did not have to. He also encouraged me to continue my education, and that changed my life forever. It's like Burney said, "knowledge is like a pile of horse manure. If you just leave it piled up, it'll kill the grass. But if you spread it around it will do some good." The late Burney Chapman influenced many farriers and I was lucky enough to be one of them.

Q. What is the most rewarding part of being a farrier?

A. This answer is also easy. The best part of my job is making a horse comfortable so he can perform his job with efficiency. A comfortably footed horse is a happy horse; when that horse is happy, I'm happy. It is a real reward.

Q. What is the most challenging part of being a farrier?

A. The discipline. You have to study people, horses, and life. You must honor your work, be on time, and be pleasant when everything around you isn't.

Q. What is the biggest achievement of your career?

A. The word "horseman" can now go on my tombstone without reservation.

Q. What is the most challenging obstacle of your career?

A. Burnout. Most people don't make this career last 35 years.

Q. What education and/or experience do you recommend for someone interested in becoming a farrier?

A. For the basics, go to a school and study under an instructor with integrity. Then, apprentice with a top-notch farrier for a minimum of two years to learn the practical application of the knowledge you acquire from your own studies. You will have to learn on your own a great deal about pathology, physiology, and conformation. Go to all the clinics you can, especially the American Farrier's Association's national convention.

Q. What personal strengths or skills should a person have who is considering this field?

A. If you are a good horseman going in and you observe the Golden Rule, you can excel.

Q. If you could do it over, is there anything you would have done differently to reach your career goal?

A. I didn't have a lot of options growing up, but I learned the meaning of "cowboy up." Life led me in this path, and I've learned from my experiences, but I don't look back. Yesterday is yesterday. It's history.

Q. What do you think the overall job outlook is for farriers?

A. Excellent. You can shoot the moon. People with horses will always need someone with the skills and horsemanship to care for them, and people will hire the best they can afford.

Humane Investigator

About the job

Humane investigators work for governmental agencies or nonprofit organizations and look into cases of alleged animal abuse. They also seek to educate the public about the humane treatment of animals and attempt to correct abusive situations by educating abusers before arresting them. Animal control officers working for government agencies may be trained law enforcement professionals who can legally remove abused horses and make arrests. Full-time investigator positions are available with larger humane organizations and governmental animal control agencies; part-timers and volunteers also hold many investigative roles.

Humane organizations sometimes receive complaints of abuse from well-intentioned individuals that turn out to be false—a horse may be unusually thin because of illness and is actually under a veterinarian's care, or horses are out to pasture and are dirty or muddy but within the range of reasonable caretaking—so investigators must have horse experience to recognize if abuse is indeed occurring. If they are working for an organization that does not deal exclusively with horses, they should also have experience with other animals.

People wishing to get into this field must have strong empathy for horses and other animals, be dedicated to reducing animal suffering, and be able to work in tough and emotionally distressing situations. They should also have good communication skills to deal with horse owners, and strong organizational and written skills to keep records and prepare reports that may be used as legal evidence.

Education and training

A two- or four-year degree in animal science, equine studies, or justice administration is necessary. State certification is required for governmental animal control employees. Certification may require passing a physical abilities test, medical exam, and background investigation. Also, specialized training in recognizing animal abuse, which is available through The Humane Society of the United States and the American Society for the Protection of Cruelty to Animals, is helpful. A national cruelty-training academy focusing exclusively on horses is offered by Code 3 Associates.

SALARY

The National Animal Control Association's 2000 salary survey of animal control officers reported a starting yearly salary ranging from $13,236 to $44,149.

RESOURCES

The Humane Society of the United States
2100 L St. NW
Washington D.C., 20037-1598
www.hsus.org

American Society for the Prevention of Cruelty to Animals
424 E. 92nd St.
New York, NY 10128
www.aspca.org

Code 3 Associates
Equine Investigations Academy
P.O. Box 1128
Erie, Colorado 80516
www.code3associates.com

National Animal Control Association
P.O. Box 480851
Kansas City, MO 64148
www.nacanet.org

Equine Humane Rescue Organization Founder/Owner

ABOUT THE JOB

Owners of equine humane and rescue organizations are dedicated to reducing the suffering of horses, both domestic and wild. Owning an organization is hard, emotionally draining work, with little financial incentive. The rewards come from knowing that you are helping to end abuse and suffering toward horses. Humane organization owners manage investigations, rehabilitation, adoptions, animal care, fund-raising, employees and volunteers, public relations, and other business aspects. In small organizations, the owner may be the only full-time employee, relying on volunteers and part-timers to help with day-to-day operations and investigations. Large humane organizations may have employee managers, investigators, animal care workers, and others to assist, leaving the owner to be concerned with the higher-level aspects of running the organization like fundraising, public relations, and overall management.

The owner of a humane or rescue group needs good communication skills to recruit volunteers and work with animal control officers, state agencies, and horse owners. Public relations and fund-raising skills are necessary because nonprofit organizations rely on donations of money, food, land, services, and equipment to continue operating. People interested in starting an equine rescue organization should have strong experience with horses and should first volunteer or take a position with an existing organization to gain experience.

EDUCATION AND TRAINING
A degree in equine studies or science is helpful, as is training in recognizing horse abuse and handling abused animals.

SALARY
Salary is dependent upon the size of the organization.

RESOURCES
Search for humane and rescue organizations on the Internet under "hoofed animal humane organizations" or "horse rescue organizations," or other combinations involving "horse" and "humane," "welfare," or "rescue." You can also read equine publications or purchase a copy of the Horse Industry Directory from the American Horse Council, which includes a list of equine welfare groups.

Career Spotlight

HELEN MEREDITH, FOUNDER OF UNITED PEGASUS FOUNDATION

As the founder of the United Pegasus Foundation, Helen Meredith devotes herself to rescuing and caring for retired racehorses. To her, horses are beautiful creatures and this enchantment led her to pursue a professional lifetime with them. Before devoting herself to rescuing racehorses from the horse slaughter industry, Helen had an impressive career in horseracing. Living in England in a family of four children, she recalls petting the gypsy horses in the fields nearby. Since she was 15 years old, she has worked with Thoroughbred racehorses, serving apprenticeships with Sir Mark Prescott in England and John Cunnington in France and working with Northern Taste and Contessa de Loir. For two years, she worked with the great

Thoroughbred breeder Marcel Boussac. She has trained many winning Thoroughbreds and was the assistant trainer to trainer Jonathan Pease. Helen rode in approximately 100 amateur races in France and became one of the leading amateur riders. In 1989, she came to the United States and met and married another Thoroughbred trainer, Derek Meredith, who stills trains racehorses at Santa Anita Racetrack in California. Together, they trained the 1993 Breeders' Cup Sprint Winner, Cardmania. In 1994, Helen founded the United Pegasus Foundation to care for, rehabilitate, and adopt out retired racehorses.

Q. What made you start the United Pegasus Foundation?

A. In 1991, I saw a newscast about the horse slaughter industry and I was shocked when I learned how many Thoroughbred racehorses were being dumped when they could not race anymore because of injury, or because they were too old or too slow. Even the broodmares and stallions were being dumped because they were no longer producing championship horses. Every year, thousands were sent to slaughter. I have worked with Thoroughbred racehorses since I was 15 years old, and they have filled my life with many pleasures. I never dreamed they would end up at a slaughter plant. So in 1991, I decided I would try to make a difference by helping these horses that had nowhere to go and to educate the public about the horse slaughter industry.

Q. What does your job involve?

A. When I first started, I did everything, including looking after the horses, bookkeeping, creating newsletters, and raising money. Now, even though I have more help, I still seem to be doing everything.

Q. What is your typical day like?

A. Unfortunately, I do not live on any of our farms, because my husband still trains racehorses, so we live near Santa Anita Racetrack for his convenience. My day starts with either an hour drive to our Hemet farm or a two-hour drive to our Tehachapi farm. I usually get up about 5:30 A.M. and hit the road. Once at the farm, I help feed the horses and make sure they are all okay. I still help clean the stalls and paddocks, medicate the horses if needed, and work with certain horses. I also answer the telephone and show people around who come to visit or who are looking to adopt a horse. Of course, my mind is always working, thinking of how we are going to raise enough money to keep United Pegasus going. This is the hardest job of all.

Q. How many hours/days per week do you typically work?

A. I work seven days a week, six days at the farms and one day at home to catch up on paperwork, phone calls, etc. I work between 12 to 14 hours a day and longer if necessary.

Q. What is the most rewarding part of your work?

A. The most rewarding part of my job is watching some of the Thoroughbreds that I rescued. They might have had severe leg injuries and would not have had a chance if we had not taken them in. When I see them out in their paddocks running, jumping around, and playing with their buddies, it gives me the warm feeling that all my hard work was worthwhile.

Q. What do you like least about your work?

A. When I have to make the decision to euthanize a horse, especially if that horse has been with us for many years, it is often heartbreaking.

Q. What is the most challenging part of your work?

A. I often wonder where the next dime is coming from to cover all the bills. Our overhead is tremendous and people think the racetrack industry and the owners largely support us. Even though we do receive some funds from these sources, it is not nearly enough to make a dent in our overall expenses. These racehorses are their owners' responsibility from the day they are born.

Q. What is the biggest achievement of your career?

A. I think my biggest achievement was to reach every goal I had in life. I wanted to work with racehorses and learn everything about them. I learned how to groom and ride them on the training grounds in the mornings. I then went on to riding them in amateur races in France and won quite a few races. One race I rode in featured the best lady riders against the best jockeys. I finished third in this race and was presented with a beautiful bouquet of flowers by Princess Anne and had my photo taken with her. My father was there that day and he was very proud of me.

I have worked with some of the best Thoroughbreds in the world and was lucky to travel to many countries with them while they were racing. I also trained four horses in France, on which I won 12 races on the flat and over the jumps.

Q. What has been the most challenging obstacle you've faced working in horse rescue?

A. Fund-raising has always been the biggest challenge. It is very difficult to convince many of these owners to support their racehorses after their racing careers have come to an end. Sometimes, this means a lifetime commitment of support; however, if we can retrain these horses for a second career, their owners' support would only be needed for a short period of time, depending on the horse's state when we receive him. The other challenging thing about horse rescue is learning how to say no. We cannot accept every horse out there, especially when we receive a dozen calls on some days from owners who want to donate their horses. In most cases they are looking to dump their horses so that they can free up their barns for younger horses.

Q. What education and/or experience do you recommend for someone interested in working in equine rescue?

A. I always advise people who want to start an equine rescue organization to research money sources first. Horses are always around, the money is not. Finding your own property is critical in starting your rescue group, as it is your foundation and headquarters for rehabilitating and placing horses. Start small because it is better to save five horses and care for them properly than to save 50 horses and not be able to feed them.

Q. Is there anything else you would like to say about your career in the horse industry?

A. For me, horses are the most beautiful creatures in the world and when I see them perform with stamina and elegance, it often brings a tear to my eye.

Equine Humane/Rescue Organization Worker

ABOUT THE JOB

Like owners of humane organizations, people who work for humane and rescue groups do it to help end animal suffering, not to get rich. In addition to humane investigations, which is discussed separately in this book, workers for humane and rescue groups work under veterinary guidance to rehabilitate horses; handle daily care, feed and groom; perform basic training so they can place horses in loving homes; handle adoptions; and perform office work and facility maintenance.

Humane/rescue organization workers may have a variety of skills and levels of horse experience depending upon their duties. Many humane and rescue workers are part-timers or volunteers.

EDUCATION AND TRAINING

A degree in equine studies or science is helpful, as is training in recognizing horse abuse and handling abused animals.

SALARY

Volunteer or minimum wage and above depending on experience and size of the organization.

RESOURCES

Humane and rescue organizations working with horses can be found by searching the Internet under "hooved animal humane organizations," "horse rescue organizations," or by using other combinations involving "horse" and "humane," "welfare" or "rescue;" reading equine publications; or purchasing a copy of the *Horse Industry Directory* from the American Horse Council, which includes a section on equine welfare groups.

Identification Technician

ABOUT THE JOB

Identification technicians aid in the battle against horse theft by freeze marking, tattooing, or implanting microchips in horses. Technicians may be self-employed or work for companies specializing in horse identification. They travel to the barns and farms where client horses are located, check horse records to confirm ownership, fill out paperwork about the horses and horse owners, and apply the applicable identification methods to the horse so they can send records to the appropriate state agencies and breed registries.

Licensing and certification requirements vary by state, so check with your state veterinary office or association. In some states, the implanting of microchips is considered an invasive procedure and may only be performed by a veterinarian or the horse owner.

EDUCATION AND TRAINING
Training by a veterinarian or a degree as a veterinary technician in addition to the appropriate licensing or certification is required.

SALARY
Veterinary technicians in this industry earn an average of $35,833 per year according to the North American Veterinary Technician Association.

RESOURCES
AVID Inc. Equine Division
3179 Hamner Ave.
Norco, CA 91760
www.avidid.com

Kryo Kinetics Associates, Inc.
P.O. Box 12490
Tucson, AZ 85732-2490
www.horseweb.com/kka

Massage Therapist

ABOUT THE JOB
Professional equine massage therapists work on horses for the same reason massage is used on humans—to increase comfort and relieve pain. Equine massage helps keep horses sound and performing at their best. It also may be used to reduce soft tissue injuries, reduce stiffness and increase flexibility, enhance muscle tone and range of motion, shorten post-event recovery time, invoke relaxation in stressed horses, and improve behavioral problems brought on by discomfort or pain. Veterinarians may refer horse owners to

massage therapists and, conversely, massage therapists alert veterinarians if a problem goes beyond their realm. Massage therapists are self-employed businesspeople who pick up much of their work through networking at horse events, barns, racetracks, and by word of mouth. Massage sessions normally last for approximately one hour and therapists may see as many as seven or eight horses in a day.

Being comfortable around horses is key in this career. People with solid, hands-on knowledge of horses and anatomy, as well as human massage therapists who are also horse people are good candidates for this profession.

EDUCATION AND TRAINING
Training through an equine massage school (see Appendix K), or a state-certified program in human massage with additional training in equine anatomy is essential. No licensing is required at this time.

SALARY
A recent survey by the Equissage school of animal massage reported that the average rate for an equine massage session is $57.50. Sessions generally last approximately an hour. This rate may vary widely depending on the area of the country. Another factor in pricing services is whether the track or barn you are calling on is familiar with equine massage and its benefits. Those familiar with this service may easily pay $75.00 or more per session, according to Equissage.

RESOURCES
International Association of Equine Sports Massage Therapists
P.O. Box 447
Round Hill, VA 22141
www.iaesmt.com

International Equine Trigger Point Myotherapist Association
249 Mountain Rd.
Granby, CT 06035

TT.E.A.M. Training International
P.O. Box 3793
Santa Fe, NM 87501-0793

Veterinarian

ABOUT THE JOB

According to American Veterinary Medical Association statistics, there are more than 60,000 veterinarians in the United States. Of these, the majority—more than 45,000—are in private practice. This ratio holds true for equine veterinarians as well, with the majority of them in private practice, traveling to perform exams, give inoculations, diagnose and treat ill or injured horses, perform reproductive procedures such as artificial insemination and embryo transplants, birth foals, and perform surgeries. Private practice veterinarians are usually on call; if there are several in the same practice, that duty is divided up. Though the work is physically demanding, the hours are long and can include weekends and nights. However, the rewards of the work outweigh the downsides, say many veterinarians. Veterinarians working in racing require special licensing through the racing board or commission for the state.

Though being a private practice veterinarian is what many people probably imagine when they consider working in this field, equine veterinarians are also employed in the government sector, and at universities and corporations. For example, a veterinarian employed by the federal or state government may work to eradicate the spread of infectious disease or enforce animal protection laws; corporate veterinarians develop new products, including food and pharmaceuticals; veterinary schools employ equine veterinarians to perform research or to teach. While many of these positions have less hands-on horse contact, the upside is that they also provide shorter and more predictable working hours.

A good understanding of horse behavior and how to handle horses is essential to being an equine veterinarian.

EDUCATION AND TRAINING

Four years of pre-veterinary study, plus four years of veterinary school to achieve a DVM (or VMD) degree, followed by passing a state licensing exam is required. Competition to get into veterinary school is intense, as there are only 28 accredited colleges of veterinary medicine in the United States. High school science coursework, an internship or part-time job working with horses, and strong grades in college pre-veterinary studies will increase your chances of being accepted to a school. Veterinarians who plan to teach or do research may also earn a PhD. Corporate veterinarians may need additional training in their area of specialty and government practitioners are required to pass the civil service exam.

SALARY

According to American Veterinary Medical Association statistics for 2001, the mean annual salary for equine veterinarians in private practice is $108,405; the mean first-year salary for veterinary college graduates in equine private practice was $28,526.

RESOURCES

American Association of Equine Practitioners
4075 Iron Works Pkwy.
Lexington, KY 40511-8434
www.aaep.org

American Veterinary Medical Association
1931 N. Meacham Rd. #100
Schaumburg, IL 60173-4360
www.avma.org

Career Spotlight

Josh Hill, Doctor of Veterinary Medicine

Josh Hill, DVM, is an equine veterinarian who has been in practice for three years. He works with six other vets at Barrone Veterinary Clinic in Sunset, Louisiana, which offers full-service equine treatment and surgery. Born and raised in Iowa, Josh was first exposed to horses through his mother, who rode hunters and jumpers. Along with his brother and sister, he began to ride at age six, and by eight, he was actively showing in American Quarter Horse Association English and western events. When Josh was 15, he knew he wanted to become an equine vet, having had many favorable experiences in his interactions with the vets caring for his horses. At 19, he began training horses and, in college, he showed in reining. He earned a bachelor's degree in animal science and his DVM from

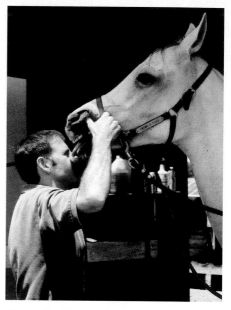

Iowa State University. Josh continued the family tradition by marrying a horsewoman, deSaix Tankersley Hill, a riding instructor and barn manager he met while making a horse call. Together, they live in Louisiana, and are both very active in the equestrian world. (See profile of deSaix Tankersley Hill in Chapter 18.)

Q. Do you work in a particular area of the industry?

A. I work in surgery and the treatment of high performance horses—racehorses, hunters, jumpers, etc. I multi-task in all areas of veterinary medicine, including preventive care and emergency treatment, lameness issues, pre-purchase exams, reproduction, anesthesiology, and surgery.

Q. What other horse industry experience do you have?

A. I was an assistant trainer for an AQHA judge for three years in high school. I worked at Iowa State University's horse barn for five years doing reproductive work. I've worked at various boarding stables—showing and training my horses and judging open shows and Intercollegiate Horse Show Association shows.

Q. What does your job involve?

A. Pre- and post-race treatment of racehorses, surgery, barn calls, reproductive work, preventive care, treatment, and surgery.

Q. What is a typical workday like?

A. The day begins with morning rounds at the racetracks from 7:00 A.M. to 10:00 A.M. From 10:00 A.M. to noon, I make road calls. In the afternoons, there are more road calls, sick horses, and emergency care. If it is a race day we have pre- and post-race care. The day typically ends at 6:00 P.M. to 7:30 P.M., barring emergencies.

Q. How many hours per week do you typically work?

A. 65 to 70 hours per week.

Q. What do you enjoy most about your work?

A. I most enjoy being able to bring a horse back from the brink by fixing his problems and restoring him to health.

Q. What do you like least about your work?

A. The long hours.

Q. What is your most memorable moment as a horseman?

A. Getting into vet school and getting my DVM.

Q. What is the most rewarding part of your career?

A. The satisfaction I get from helping people and their horses with their problems.

Q. What is the most challenging obstacle in your career?

A. The practice location being so far from my home state has been difficult. Also, it's been hard being in an area where very few people know me or of my accomplishments in the horse industry.

Q. In addition to education, what type of experience do you recommend for someone interested in being an equine vet?

A. Get your hands dirty and start at the bottom—cleaning stalls, grooming, caring for horses—and ride around with a practicing vet before you enroll in vet school. The more you hang out around horses and equine vets, the more information you will gather that will prove invaluable in not only getting into vet school, but succeeding in getting your DVM.

Q. What advice would you give to someone considering a career in this field?

A. Make sure it is what you really want to do and that you are willing to invest the time.

Veterinary Assistant

ABOUT THE JOB

Veterinary assistants help veterinarians with a variety of duties. They schedule appointments, accompany veterinarians on rounds at barns and farms, clean and set up instruments, and assist with physical exams. They may perform many of the same duties in private veterinary practice as veterinary technicians, except for those duties that do not require professional licensing as a technician. Many times the two titles are used interchangeably, which is technically incorrect (see following listing). In larger practices that have both veterinary technicians and veterinary assistants on staff, the technician may supervise the assistant. Because veterinary assistants often learn their skills through on-the-job training, their level of expertise is determined by the needs of the veterinarians who train them.

The work the assistant is expected to perform will determine the amount of horse experience needed. Assistants performing many of the same duties as veterinary technicians will be expected to have higher levels of horse knowledge.

EDUCATION AND TRAINING

On-the-job training and/or completion of a certificate program is necessary. There are certificate programs in veterinary assisting and a few of the schools that offer accreditation to veterinary technicians offer an assistant program as well; essentially, this is an abbreviated version of the programs offered to technicians. The American Veterinary Medical Association does not accredit programs for veterinary assisting.

SALARY

The median salary for veterinary assistants is $23,070.

RESOURCES

American Veterinary Assistants' Association
1709 Blue Rock Street
Cincinnati, OH 45223
www.avaa.bigstep.com

Veterinary Technician/Technologist

About the job

Veterinary technicians/technologists assist veterinarians in a professional capacity. They execute laboratory tests, accompany veterinarians on rounds to barns and farms, act as surgical nurses, educate clients, give anesthesia, set up instruments, perform physical exams, and manage the veterinary office. They may also work for breeding operations assisting with horse health care and reproduction.

Strong horse handling skills and a good understanding of equine behavior are important in this position, as well as strong communication skills for working with equine veterinarians and horse owners.

Education and training

A two- or four-year degree in an accredited veterinary technician/technologist program is required. (Though the term "veterinary technician" is commonly used for all individuals accredited in this field, the American Veterinary Medical Association and the North American Veterinary Technician Association define "veterinary technician" as someone receiving a two-year AVMA-accredited degree in a veterinary technician or technology program and a "veterinary technologist" as someone who graduates with a bachelor's degree in an AVMA-accredited veterinary technician or technology program.) There are currently 80 programs in the United States accredited by the American Veterinary Medical Association.

Salary

The most recent survey of its members from the North American Veterinary Technician Association, gives these average salaries for veterinary technicians/technologists in the following areas: private equine practice, $26,250; industry/sales, $35,833; vet tech education, $33,254; university/college, $30,512; diagnostic/research, $37,410.

Resources

North American Veterinary Technician Association
P.O. Box 224
Battle Ground, IN 47920
www.navta.net

Career Spotlight

MINDY FOWLER, VETERINARY TECHNICIAN

Mindy Fowler is a certified veterinary technician and has been working for Anoka Equine Veterinary Services in Elk River, Minnesota since 2002. The practice consists of eight veterinarians and several veterinary technicians and other staff members who provide both field and hospital care to hundreds of equines each week, from miniatures to draft horses to donkeys and mules. There is even an occasional llama in the mix.

Mindy attended the University of Minnesota at Crookston, where she earned her bachelor's degree in two majors, equine science and animal industry management. While at the university, she showed in western pleasure through the Intercollegiate Horse Show Association. She still rides western today and also "dabbles in hunt-seat." Mindy received her veterinary technician degree from the Medical Institute of Minnesota and has her CVT certification in the state of Minnesota and Oklahoma. Anoka Equine is her first job working for a large animal practice.

Q. What does your job involve?

A. I primarily work in the lab as a technician. I check for new blood work coming in, run tests for Coggins, study CBC's to check white blood cell platelets (this shows if a horse is dehydrated or has an infection), look at blood chemistry, and set up for surgery. Some of the other veterinary technicians in the office go along on field calls to help with testing or handling unruly horses.

Q. How many hours a day do you work?

A. I am scheduled for eight, but usually work 10.

Q. What do you enjoy most about your work?

A. Seeing the horses go home feeling better than when they came in. Seeing a happy horse.

Q. What do you like least about your work?

A. Having to euthanize a horse. The worst part is when a doctor says there is nothing more he can do for a horse after spending months trying to save him and it's better to let him go. That is the hardest part.

Q. What made you decide to become an equine veterinary technician?

A. All my life I wanted to be a veterinarian. I realized that here at Anoka Equine, I can do much of the veterinary work without being married to my job. I also didn't want the responsibility of the veterinarian, who has to make that final call and say there is nothing more he can do. As far as being an equine vet tech, I've always loved horses and ridden pretty much my whole life, so I wanted to work in an equine practice.

Q. What sparked your interest in horses?

A. As a child, I got into a car accident with my grandmother. Shortly afterward, I saw a young girl riding a paint and I found it very comforting. I always wanted to be a part of it.

Q. What is your most memorable moment with horses and in your career?

A. Winning the regional competition in college for the Intercollegiate Horse Show Association show team. As far as my work last summer, we had a two-month premature foal named Micro here. The foal required 24-hour care for three months, but he grew up to be a happy horse.

Q. Why is having hands-on horse experience necessary to be successful as an equine vet tech?

A. The actual lab work and technician training are the same whether you are working with large animals or small. But, to work with horses, you must know how to handle them for safety's sake.

Q. What is the most challenging part of being a veterinary technician?

A. The biggest challenge for any technician is knowing what the doctor wants before he or she wants it. You have to be a mind reader to keep up with them. That is the goal of the technician.

Q. What advice would you give to someone who wants to become an equine veterinary technician?

A. Spend all the time you have outside of school riding with a veterinarian and/or working at a barn learning to restrain the horses.

Q. What personality traits should prospective equine veterinary technicians have?

A. Be fun-loving, have a positive attitude, be easy to work with—at large animal hospitals you must work as a team—enjoy being challenged and motivated, and always be willing to learn something new.

Q. Is there anything else you would like to say about your career?

A. It's the best decision I ever made. It's important in life to have a job you love. I love getting up every morning and coming in to work.

CHAPTER 10

Events, Judging, and Training Careers

— — —

Wherever you find horses, you'll find people wishing to test their riding and athletic skills along with the prowess of their horses, as well as people supporting these athletic competitions. Showing is the second largest area of the horse industry in terms of number of competitors, while rodeo has a strong following of its own. The main sanctioning body for equestrian competitions in this country is U.S. Equestrian, formerly U.S.A. Equestrian. The international sanctioning body is Federation Equestre Internationale, which establishes rules and regulations for the conduct of international equestrian events in jumping, dressage, eventing, driving, vaulting, and endurance riding. The largest rodeo organization is the Professional Rodeo Cowboys

Association (PRCA). The Professional Rodeo Cowboys Association sanctions nearly 700 rodeos. These rodeos, as well as many of the hundreds of rodeos that are sanctioned or not sanctioned by smaller rodeo organizations, follow the rulebook of the PRCA.

Key to most of the following careers is an in-depth knowledge of the sport and its rules, as well as excellent horsemanship and riding skills. To get that knowledge, immerse yourself in the sport by reading all you can about it, visiting shows and rodeos, volunteering, talking to people in the sport, and getting involved in its youth organizations. High schools, colleges, and youth groups (such as 4-H) hold horse show competitions and rodeos. See the appendices for contact information on high school and collegiate organizations that promote horse showing and rodeo.

Association Directors

ABOUT THE JOB

Directors of horse breed and sport associations run the day-to-day operations of their organizations. There are over 100 different breed and sport organizations in the country, some of which are small (consisting mostly of volunteers) and some which are larger (with paid staff members). Association directors plan and manage horse shows and other similar events. Staff members may also register horses, lobby, do promotional work, educate horse owners, and produce publications and literature. One person may wear several hats in performing the various duties or many staff members divide the duties, depending on the size of the organization.

Most of the work is performed in an office and there is little horse contact. General office and computer skills are necessary. Depending on the position, horse experience may or may not be required. Even if it isn't a requisite, it is still a good idea when applying to a breed or sport organization to have basic knowledge about the breed or sport, to show that you have done your homework.

EDUCATION AND TRAINING

Education varies from a high school diploma to an advanced college degree, depending on the position.

SALARY

Salaries vary by position; some association directors and staff are strictly voluntary.

Career Spotlight

BETH BEUKEMA, PRESIDENT, INTERSCHOLASTIC DRESSAGE ASSOCIATION

Beth Beukema has served as the president of the Interscholastic Dressage Association since the organization became an official national association in 2001. She has also been the department chair of Equine Studies at Johnson and Wales University in Providence, Rhode Island, for over 20 years. Her lifelong love of horses led her to acquire a master's degree in equine exercise physiology. Beth has over 30 years of experience in dressage and combined training as a competitor, a judge, and a professional educator. Growing up mostly in Cambridge, Massachusetts, Beth has always been involved with horses. Currently, she owns three Dutch warmbloods imported from the Netherlands. Their ages range from three to 23 and they are trained from second level through FEI.

Q. What is the role of the Interscholastic Dressage Association in the horse world?

A. The association sets standards and framework for dressage competition for both college teams and individuals that lead to regional and national awards.

Q. What does your job involve?

A. I organize the all-volunteer, nonprofit educational sport association, by interacting with fellow board members, regional representatives, coaches, and students.

Q. What is your typical workday like?

A. There is no such thing as a typical workday.

Q. How many hours/days per week do you typically work?

A. This varies tremendously, depending on the time of year.

Q. What do you enjoy most about your work?

A. The people.

Q. What do you like least about your work?

A. Typing.

Q. What made you decide to go into this field?

A. My love of horses and I enjoy working with people.

Q. What other horse industry experience do you have?

A. Over 30 years experience in dressage and combined training as a judge and competitor. I also am a professional educator in the equine industry.

Q. What is your background with horses?

A. I have worked in various aspects of the industry, including breeding, training, teaching, judging, competing, and riding.

Q. What is your most memorable moment as a horsewoman?

A. I've had too many wonderful moments to name a single standout.

Q. What is the most rewarding part of leading the Interscholastic Dressage Association?

A. Seeing the growth and interest from a handful of teams in an informal organization to a well-functioning national organization with teams throughout the country.

Q. What is the most challenging part of your job?

A. Finding the time to get it all done.

Q. What is the biggest achievement of your career?

A. Directing the Johnson and Wales University Equine program for 20 years.

Q. What is the most challenging obstacle in your career?

A. Time.

Q. What has driven you to excel in your career?

A. My Type-A personality.

Q. What education and/or experience do you recommend for someone interested in working for a horse-related association?

A. Minimum of a bachelor's degree in equine studies or animal science and business courses.

Q. What personal strengths or skills should a person have who is considering association work?

A. Organizational and people skills and the ability to multi-task.

Q. If you could do it over, is there anything you would have done differently to reach your career goal?

A. Not a thing.

Q. In very general terms, what income do you believe someone working for an association can expect?

A. In volunteer organizations, nothing. In organizations with paid directorships, from $24,000 a year and up, depending on the size of the organization.

Q. Is there anything else you would like to say about your career or your life with horses?

A. It's extremely rewarding when your advocation is also your vocation. You need to love what you do to succeed in it.

Braider

ABOUT THE JOB

On show day, a skillfully braided mane not only enhances the appearance of the horse, but it also demonstrates to judges that the rider is serious about her sport. Professional braiders are experts in braiding the perfect manes (and tails) in a variety of styles, the most well known being the hunter-style "knotted" braid. Braiders sell their services at horse shows and spend nighttime and early morning hours braiding prior to shows. They braid yarn, or sometimes heavy thread, into the mane to hold the braid in place. Some of the other tools and equipment braiders use are step stools, pulling combs, braid pull-throughs, gel or water, clips or clothespins, rubber bands, and aprons or belts for holding braiding equipment. Braiders also provide mane and tail pulling services and may offer clipping and other grooming services as well. Pulling is sometimes done at the same time as braiding, if needed, or prior to show day.

People interested in working as professional braiders must have nimble fingers and be comfortable working with a variety of horse personalities. Networking and marketing skills are necessary to find business, especially when just starting out. It is a good idea to have photographs available of horses you have worked with that demonstrate your expertise. Most braiders combine braiding with other jobs in the horse industry; others braid part-time.

EDUCATION AND TRAINING

On-the-job training or experience braiding your own horse's mane or the manes of your friends' horses. Professional braiders sometimes give clinics at horse expos and other horse events or hold private clinics.

SALARY

Professional braiders and show grooms charge an average of $20 to $40 per mane and slightly less for tails. Most pros say they can braid a mane in 30 to 45 minutes; less time is required for tails, as only part of the horses' tails are braided.

RESOURCES

To polish your braiding skills or to learn how to braid, Lucky Braids offers a video, (*Better Braiding*) as well as clinics. You can visit the Lucky Braids Web site at www.luckybraids.com.

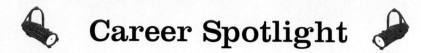

Career Spotlight

RUTHANN SMITH, PROFESSIONAL SHOW BRAIDER AND PRODUCT MANUFACTURER

Ruthann Smith, owner of Lucky Braids, braids the manes and tails of today's best show horses. Counted among her clients are Olympic and World Champion show jumping riders Peter Wylde, Michael Matz, Katie Monahan-Prudent, and George Morris; Olympic dressage bronze medalist Dottie Morkis, and World Pairs Driving Champion Jimmy Fairclough. Through her company, which was officially founded in 1999, Ruthann sells her own line of grooming products and offers a video and two-day clinics on braiding and grooming. She writes on the topic of top turnout. Plans are also in the works for a grooming and braiding school where students can hone their skills alongside top professionals. Ruthann has worked as a professional braider since 1977, when she was only 11 years old. She has taught clinics since 1993.

Q. What does your job involve?

A. My job is multifold. I braid, teach clinics, write, speak at trade shows, and develop and market products for healthy turnout.

Q. What is a typical day like?

A. When braiding, I am usually on the ladder 10 P.M. to noon, working very fast. Of course, I need to be relaxed to quiet the horse and achieve my rhythm. My braiding order is a careful balance. If a horse is silly, I might need to do him while the barn is quiet even if the horse shows late. There is lots of traveling and it is not so unusual for me to only get three hours of sleep. It is rare to be able to sleep well when I've got a full schedule of braiding horses.

Q. What is your horse industry background?

A. When I was nine, I took care of Monoco, who was first in the country and fifth in the world in dressage. When I moved to hunters and jumpers, I took care of Peter Wylde's first Grand Prix horses while he trained with George Morris. Once I started braiding full-time, I circulated in top barns, working atop the ladder, watching all the best grooms get their horses in top shape. Once I started teaching clinics, I realized how rare it is that horses are well cared for, so I started campaigning at trade shows, sharing the best methods, and getting people excited to take good care of their horses.

I made my video and entered the product manufacturing and marketing end of the industry. I then realized that most manufacturers don't know horses and make products that are really unhealthy for them. So, I continue to develop specialized and healthy alternatives.

Q. What is the biggest achievement of your career?

A. The biggest achievement of my career was braiding Dutch. I had heard about his mean aggression—it was legendary—and you couldn't get into his stall. The first time I tried to braid him, he threw me into the wall several times as I was just getting him on the cross-ties. I had to let go of my fear to figure it out, but I realized he was also afraid. So I rubbed his eye to calm him and got some knots in his neck. I had the rider to hold him and soothe his mind by rubbing his eye! We'd quiet him, I'd braid, and then he'd start to inflate. I'd stop and she would rub his eye again, softening him. We kept cycling this way. Once, at the New England Equitation Championships, where there is a small, scary and slippery ring, there was a scheduling glitch. We had two braiders on his mane, one on his tail, someone tacking him up, and another person holding him. He went into the ring and nailed it! I was not happy about the scheduling problem, but the fact that he left that hurried grooming situation in a relaxed and focused state was a real measure of how much confidence he had gained. He proved that cupping the eye with the palm of your hand and rubbing can turn the most fearfully aggressive horse into a buttercup.

Completing the *Better Braiding* video was a big achievement for my teaching skills. That video was not only an instructional feat, but technically, it was difficult. For example, if the horse shifted his weight, he was out of frame.

Developing a product for solving tail rubbing was also monumental. Everyone knows a horse that rubs. Every solution to date may take away the itch, but it dries the skin, ultimately feeding the cycle. My product takes away the irritant and inflammation, and then it nourishes the skin of horses that rub themselves raw.

Q. What is the most challenging obstacle in your career?

A. The most challenging obstacle in braiding has been taking care of my body. I've had lots of injuries and sometimes they happen without time to heal. But I learned to stretch, stand square (it is so tempting to twist your back as you move down the crest), and I even found a chiropractor who is a whiz with wrists. (If you look to a chiropractor be sure that he has special sports medicine training. There's not a lot of training with appendages in school—wrist accuracy requires post-grad sports medicine study.)

The most challenging obstacle in teaching was learning how to effectively communicate the fine motor skill. It took me a long time to learn how to speak to people's inclinations. My video breaks the whole process into graduated steps, while showing each part three times, building, and reviewing. Anyone can learn this.

Everything about manufacturing has been difficult. You can't imagine how many problems arise and how long things can take to get done. It's one issue after another—and that is the norm. To go into manufacturing, you have to have a strong stomach, incredible fortitude, and patience.

Q. What advice would you give to someone interested in braiding?

A. You can make the most beautiful braids, but that does not qualify you to be alone in the barn at night. Safe and quiet handling skills are paramount.

Make it your business to learn from the very best professionals and stay aware of everything around you. Keep learning. And always be humble to the fact that the craziest accident can happen at any time. Also, don't go pro until you are a great braider. Your reputation begins when you start. Be sure to have enough miles on the ladder that you can do a beautiful job consistently before you take money. Then, come out of the gate and charge the going rate—it is much easier than raising your prices later.

If you are interested in manufacturing horse products, know that it will consume your life. Branding, packaging, advertising, public relations, marketing, bookkeeping, riding the cash flow—it can take everything you have.

Q. What personal strengths or traits are valuable?

A. To be a braider, you must be hardy and have unrelenting discipline. Stamina and 400 percent reliability are essential. Whatever happens, the horses need to be braided on time and without getting them plugged. As a manufacturer, you must have great organizational and multi-tasking skills. The product has to be high quality, distinctive, and effectively branded.

Q. What is the job market like for braiders?

A. Good braiders are always in demand because so few people take the time to do it well. The thing is, though, you have to practice a lot. It takes time to get good.

Q. What rate can braiders expect to charge?

A. First, don't go pro until you are proficient. The going rate is $40 per mane and $30 per tail. How much money you'll make is relative to what you can do and how carefully you schedule yourself. Most barns have a few braiding jobs during the week, but lots on the weekend. Don't get in over your head. Think ahead. Be organized. As far as manufacturing products, plan on slaving and spending more money than you can imagine!

Q. What professional associations do you belong to?

A. I belong to no associations. I am in the thick of it all. However, growing up, I was a 4-H'er and highly recommend it as well as Pony Club. If a group promotes sound horsemanship, try to learn everything you can.

Q. If you could do it over again, what would you do differently?

A. I would have learned to save my body sooner. Keeping fit and keeping the body in line are so important. Manufacturing is tough, but I love that I am able to help the horses be more comfortable in their skins. Every setback has had a reason in the big scheme of things. As far as teaching, I love what I've put together on that front; it works really well.

Q. Is there anything else you would like to say?

A. Remember that proper turnout is a measure of respect for horses. Be sure to always take good care. The horses should come first. They try so hard to take care of us.

Horse Show Course Designer

ABOUT THE JOB

Horse show course designers design and build the courses for competitive horse events. Because building a course is a carefully planned and executed process requiring a high degree of expertise in the particular horse discipline, course designers are often competitive riders in the sport or trainers, judges, show managers, or other participants of high standing in their area. Typically, they design courses in addition to working in other areas of the showing world. Course designers must be present as officials at shows for which they have designed courses. U.S. Equestrian provides licensing for course designers who have demonstrated the knowledge and experience necessary to build suitable courses.

To become qualified as a course designer, become an expert in your discipline and its rules and regulations. Start out by talking to local stables and finding out about small schooling shows in the area and who designs the courses. Network with stable owners and show managers and let them know of your expertise in your discipline and of your interest in course design.

EDUCATION AND TRAINING

A high school diploma and college degree in an equine field are helpful, though not required. Expertise in your discipline and licensing through U.S. Equestrian for rated shows.

SALARY

No information available.

RESOURCES

U.S. Equestrian
4047 Iron Works Parkway
Lexington, KY 40511
www.usef.org

Horse Show Judge

ABOUT THE JOB

Horse show judges evaluate the talents of horses and riders in thousands of shows held throughout the country every year. They are experts in the disciplines and divisions they judge, which include hunter and jumper, western horsemanship, harness, equitation, saddle seat, breed divisions, and trail classes. Becoming a licensed judge is a long and involved process; it takes a great deal of equine expertise and dedication as well as a willingness to spend a lot of time on the road traveling to various shows.

To become qualified as a horse show judge, educate yourself in the discipline you wish to judge and learn the rules of judging. Read books and other publications, study the U.S. Equestrian rulebook, and attend judging clinics and classes. U.S. Equestrian holds national clinics each year on judging. The United States Dressage Federation offers an educational program for aspiring judges in that sport. Some breed organizations require specialized training for those interested in judging breed competitions, so check with the breed organization for their requirements. Look into judging schooling shows (preferably outside your area so you are not judging your former competition) where you can gain valuable experience. To be considered as a schooling show judge, you will need to provide detailed background of your riding, training, and showing experience, as well as strong references.

EDUCATION AND TRAINING

A high school diploma and college degree in an equine field are helpful, though not required. Classes in judging, expertise in your discipline, and licensing through U.S. Equestrian are necessary.

SALARY

Judges are paid a flat fee per show (often around $300), as well as travel and other expenses.

RESOURCES

U.S. Equestrian
4047 Iron Works Parkway
Lexington, KY 40511
www.usef.org

United States Dressage Federation
220 Lexington Green Circle, Suite 510
Lexington, KY 40503
www.usdf.org

Career Spotlight

ELIZABETH A. VARS, HORSE SHOW JUDGE

Elizabeth A. Vars performs as a judge of hunters and hunter seat equitation, holding cards with the New England Horsemen's Association and U.S. Equestrian. Growing up on a small farm in tiny Ashaway, Rhode Island with her mother, horse trainer Beverly Gifford Vars, Elizabeth spent her life around horses. She began riding when she was only three years old. As a child, she had fun galloping around the countryside, and fox hunting with the Tomaquog Valley Hunt Club. She also competed in hunter and equitation divisions in shows in nearby Connecticut, New York, and Massachusetts. Elizabeth attended a small college preparatory school, The Williams School in New London, Connecticut, before graduating cum laude with a Bachelor of Arts in English from Randolph-Macon in Ashland, Virginia. In addition to judging horse shows, Elizabeth also

has a demanding real estate career specializing in equestrian property, and she continues to compete on her own show hunter, an off-the-track Thoroughbred named Brown Wrapper.

Q. What other horse industry experience do you have?

A. I have been a freelance writer for the *Horsemen's Yankee Pedlar* and *The Chronicle of the Horse* (I won one of their yearly journalistic awards for an article I submitted about professional braiders). I have braided horses professionally. I opened my own traveling consignment shop when I was 18. I also worked for S&S Saddlery (now known as The Country Saddler) in New Jersey, and on the road. I managed the photographer's booth for both James Leslie Parker and Cathrin Cammett, and traveled up and down the East Coast and to California with them.

Q. How did you become involved in judging?

A. It was a natural extension of having been in the horse world since the age of three. My mother, Beverly Gifford Vars, is a trainer, and I don't think I have her patience to teach. Judging better fits my personality. I enjoy watching competitions and I feel that, as a judge, I am giving back something to the sport at the same time.

Q. What is a typical day like when judging a show?

A. Long. Typically, I will get to the show 15 to 30 minutes prior to the start, only to be told that the warm-ups aren't finished, so it'll be another 15 minutes until the start of the show. Then, depending upon what ring I am given to judge, I will get my cards in order. For example, if I am in a "big eq" ring, I'll look at the course and start creating different tests so that when I'm asked for one later in the day, it is readily available. That way, I will not hold up the show in any way with judge's block.

Q. How many hours/days per week do you work?

A. Everyone who knows me will say too many! I really couldn't put a number to the hours I work, but I can tell you that I haven't gone on a proper holiday in over three years. I am also a realtor specializing in equestrian properties in North Kingstown. Like the horse world, real estate is a very demanding career. Between my involvement in my real estate business, riding my show hunter, judging, and enjoying a few hobbies, I don't have time left for much sleep!

Q. What do you enjoy most about judging horse shows?

A. Spending the day with horses, even if I am not competing.

Q. What do you like least about judging?

A. Waiting. A horse show is just that—a show. It's not a practice or a dress rehearsal, but it's an actual event. I, as a rider, do not allow a judge to wait for me. I usually am the person to volunteer riding the course first in my division, if for no other reason than to get the class started. In the past, shows had a posted order that everyone adhered to, barring the occasional trainer/multiple ride conflict. Now, riders wait for their entourages before looking at a course diagram. It's outrageous!

Q. What is your most memorable moment in the horse industry?

A. Watching my sister, Hillary, compete at Madison Square Garden and celebrating afterwards at the party at Tavern on the Green. It was a family affair. Our father had purchased the horse, Nicholas, as an investment. Our mother was our trainer and took my sister everywhere to get qualified and promote her as a junior rider. I'm Hillary's biggest cheerleader and it was such a great moment for her! A close second was riding in the A/O division at the Washington International Horse Show on that same horse my sister rode at the Garden. Nicholas wasn't a hunter, but we got qualified and had a blast.

Q. What is the most rewarding part of judging?

A. Watching a really great ride by either a professional or an amateur. Or better yet, watching a kid who has had a really lousy horse show (falling off or riding a bad pony) who just keeps with it and finally nails the last class. I love kids like that because they are usually the ones who love every aspect of having a horse or pony. They like mucking out the stalls and helping out and they are bound and determined to get it right. Those kids are rare nowadays.

Q. What is the most challenging part of judging?

A. Having a class that is so awful that you have to choose the best of the worst. Mason Phelps once told me that judges never learn how to pick fourth through sixth and I think that is very true.

Q. What is the biggest achievement of your career?

A. Being regarded as an honest and fair judge.

Q. What is the most challenging obstacle in your career?

A. Time. Or, I should say, lack thereof.

Q. What advice would you give to someone interested in judging?

A. I mainly stress the importance of doing the student judging—lots of it, more than you think you need! Just because you think you have been in the business a while and can tell the good from the bad and that judging is easy, it is different when you're sitting in a chair doing it. Your cards need to be organized and contain enough information so if a rider or trainer or parent wants to discuss a round, you can look at the card and give an answer, whether they agree with it or not. Great trainers/riders do not necessarily make great judges.

Q. What experience/education do you recommend for someone interested in working as a show judge?

A. Have a mentor and be a sponge to all the knowledge around you.

Q. What personality traits should a person have who is considering this field?

A. I think that an individual should be highly organized, efficient, energetic, interested, proactive, and motivated.

Horse Show and Rodeo Manager

ABOUT THE JOB

Managers of horse shows and rodeos direct the overall planning and implementing of these events. They may be employees of horse associations or organizations or they may be freelancers experienced in event management as well as the particular sport. Horse show and rodeo managers are responsible for hiring personnel, finding event sponsors, directing workers, and taking care of all the details that make an event successful, from assigning stalls to bringing in vendors. The show or rodeo manager is the point-of-contact who handles all problems as well as resolves any disputes that may arise. Like others working in official and managerial positions in the showing and rodeo worlds, show and rodeo managers are people who have been involved in the sport for a long time, often as competitors, administrators, or both.

Excellent leadership and people skills, assertiveness, and organizational capability are required to manage a horse show or rodeo.

EDUCATION AND TRAINING

A high school diploma and college degree in an equine field are helpful, though not required. Management classes are also helpful. Expertise in your discipline and certification through U.S. Equestrian for shows or PRCA for rodeo are important.

SALARY

No information available.

RESOURCES

Breed, sport, rodeo, and show associations. See appendices for listings.

Horse Show and Rodeo Secretary

ABOUT THE JOB

Secretaries for horse shows and rodeos are official personnel who handle many of the administrative and clerical duties involved in staging such an event. A secretary is a key component in the event's success, because he or she handles most of the paperwork surrounding shows and rodeos and accepts and organizes entries. Secretaries prepare program and prize lists, record contestant times and information, and coordinate and correspond with show and rodeo officials. Show secretaries are responsible for ribbons and trophies while rodeo secretaries calculate payoffs and pay the cowboys when they are finished riding.

Many show secretaries have been competitors themselves or have been otherwise closely involved in showing or rodeo and have worked their way up to the secretarial position. Excellent organizational and communication skills are necessary for show and rodeo secretaries.

EDUCATION AND TRAINING
A high school diploma and college degree in an equine field are helpful, though not required. Classes in judging are important. Expertise in showing or rodeo and certification through U.S. Equestrian or PRCA are also critical.

SALARY
No information available.

RESOURCES
U.S. Equestrian
4047 Iron Works Parkway
Lexington, KY 40511
www.usef.org

Professional Rodeo Cowboys Association
101 Pro Rodeo Drive
Colorado Springs, CO 80919
www.prorodeo.com

Horse Show Steward or Technical Delegate

ABOUT THE JOB
Horse show stewards have oversight while on show grounds to ensure that the rules of showing are enforced; they report to the appropriate officials any violations that might invalidate a class. They also investigate suspected rule violations, ensure events are run as required, oversee drug testing, and measure animals required to be measured. The stewards also must report back on the competitions, in writing, to U.S. Equestrian, including any offenses

or rule violations committed by competitors or exhibitors. In addition to these duties, technical delegates inspect the courses and arenas to ensure that all technical details satisfy regulations and may instruct the show organizers to make adjustments to the course if necessary.

Like judges, show stewards and technical delegates must have strong experience in the horse and horse show world and an in-depth familiarity with the rules of showing to become licensed. Strong references are required for the licensing application process.

EDUCATION AND TRAINING

A high school diploma and college degree in an equine field are helpful, though not required. Expertise in your discipline and licensing through U.S. Equestrian are required.

SALARY

No information available.

RESOURCES

U.S. Equestrian
4047 Iron Works Parkway
Lexington, KY 40511
www.equestrian.org

Career Spotlight

KAREN GOLDING, STEWARD, SHOW JUMPING TEAM MANAGER

Karen Golding's experience working in the horse industry spans more than three decades. As a show steward, she ensures that show rules are enforced. She holds U.S. Equestrian and Federation Equestre Internationale stewards licenses. As a team manager for the U.S. Equestrian team, she oversees the care of the team's jumpers at international competitions. She worked for Michael Matz, a three-time Olympian in show jumping, (including a silver medal at the 1996 Atlanta Olympic Games) for many of her years in the sport. For Matz, she managed the barn and groomed horses. She worked at such competitions as the Olympics, Pan Am Games and FEI World Cup Final. This all-around horsewoman is also skilled in acupressure and ultrasound therapy. Like so many accomplished horse people, Karen has been around horses since she was a child, when she got her first pony.

Q. How did you get your first job?

A. I met Bernie Traurig in England, and he asked me to groom for him for six months. That was 33 years ago.

Q. What is your typical workday like?

A. If I am stewarding, I get to the show grounds early. I work 10 hours a day. When I'm traveling with the team working a show, it's easy to have 18-hour days. I'm checking the horses, watching the riders, generally overseeing, answering questions, looking at the prize list, etc.

Q. Do you enjoy the travel involved in the showing world?

A. The circuit goes from January through November and I'm pretty much on the road all the time. I enjoy the travel. The people I work with and see are like an extended family. Whether I'm stewarding or managing the team, I'm traveling. For example, in 1993, I ended up being chief steward at the World Cup in Las Vegas. If I hadn't done that, I would have gone as team manager. Either way, I will be there.

Q. What is the most rewarding part of your work?

A. Seeing a horse turned out well. A lot of it is a case of self-gratification; just being part of it all is gratifying. The riders may get the glory, but I am behind the scenes helping to make it happen.

Q. What is the most challenging?

A. The horses are the simple part. It's the people with attitudes who are challenging.

Q. What is the biggest achievement in your career?

A. The respect I have from the worldwide horse community. I know so many international personalities. We can talk about show jumping and have rapport. There is a lot of self-gratification in that.

Q. Is there anything you would have done differently?

A. I don't think so. I was very fortunate with the people I work for.

Q. What advice would you give someone who wants to work in showing in the horse industry?

A. Be the best you can be. I started off being a groom. I wanted to be the best groom and I wanted things to be perfect. At first, I blamed Michael Matz, my employer, for being nitpicky. Now, I'm the same with people who work for me. Take pride in what you do. Be a sponge and soak everything up so that you learn.

Q. What education do you recommend?

A. Get as much experience as you can. I think college equine programs are good things. But you can't graduate thinking you know it all. Have an open mind and common sense.

Q. What personal strengths or skills should someone interested in show team management have?

A. Have people skills. You are the buffer between owners and riders, trainers and grooms. Be a therapist.

Q. Is there anything else you would like to say?

A. I feel I am very lucky. I've been involved with some incredible horses and incredible people. I've been to five Olympic Games and 17 World Cups as team manager.

Professional Rider

ABOUT THE JOB

Professional riders are hired by horse owners to show horses in athletic competitions. They may be hired to ride, to ride and train, or to ride, train, manage the barn, and handle other duties. Professional riders need a specific level of showing and riding expertise depending on the wishes of the horse owner. However, some horse owners may be willing to work with a talented amateur who has never competed as a professional rider, while others may require only professional riders qualified to ride through the Grand Prix level. U.S. Equestrian defines a professional rider as someone who "accepts remuneration for riding, driving, showing in hand/in halter, training, schooling, conducting clinics or seminars, instructs in equitation or horse training. An amateur does not receive any remuneration for the services mentioned."

If you are interested in becoming a professional, it is important to establish yourself first as a talented amateur with an impressive resume; this will make it easier to market your services as a professional.

EDUCATION AND TRAINING

A high school diploma is minimum. A college degree in equine studies or other equine area is helpful, though not required.

SALARY

According to a 2003 survey performed by the Equistaff horse industry employment service, riders reported making $19,705 annually. Fourteen percent received housing benefits, 29 percent received medical and dental benefits, and 14 percent received additional nontraditional benefits.

RESOURCES

For more on the difference between amateur and professional status, contact:
U.S. Equestrian
4047 Iron Works Parkway
Lexington, KY 40511
www.usef.org

Rodeo Clown/Bullfighter/Barrelman

About the job

Rodeo clowns and bullfighters keep competitors safe by distracting bulls. They also entertain the crowd by engaging in freestyle "fighting" with bulls. Barrelmen also distract bulls by jumping into their barrels when a bull gets too close and sometimes acting as a line of defense between the bull and clown, as they are batted around in their barrels. Clowns also entertain and amuse the crowd by performing tricks and stunts. Rodeo clowns, bullfighters, and barrelmen must be in top physical condition. Large rodeos may hire separate professionals, while small rodeos may have just one person who can do it all.

People interested in working at rodeos as cowboy protectors and entertainers must be in top physical condition; they also must be agile, able to think on their feet, and make quick decisions under extreme pressure.

Education and training

Those interested should attend a rodeo, bullfighting, or clown school (there are several in the United States). Check on the Internet under "rodeo schools," "rodeo bullfighting schools," or "rodeo clown schools," or contact the American Professional Rodeo Clown and Bullfighters Association. Certification is also offered through PRCA.

Salary

Clowns and other rodeo entertainers are paid per performance or rodeo. PRCA clowns can earn into the hundreds of dollars per rodeo with some commanding as much as $750. Some may also be paid for their mileage and receive endorsements and sponsorships. Bullfighters generally receive $35 to $100 per rodeo event or more.

Resources

Professional Rodeo Cowboys Association
101 Pro Rodeo Drive
Colorado Springs, CO 80919
www.prorodeo.com

Career Spotlight

F.J. "SCOOTER" CULBERTSON, PROFESSIONAL RODEO CLOWN/
BULLFIGHTER; RODEO JUDGE FOR THE PROFESSIONAL RODEO
COWBOYS ASSOCIATION

Scooter Culbertson has pursued his passion of working in rodeo for over 30
years, between police work and working in the oil fields of his home state of

Texas. Born and raised outside of
Corpus Christi, Scooter spent his
boyhood around horses and cattle
on farms and ranches. When he discovered he could make money riding and fighting bulls, he got
involved in the rodeo and never
wanted to leave. In 2002, Scooter
was voted by peers and audiences as
the Risky Business Bullfighters
Association Barrelman of the Year. Unfortunately, the physical toll of bullfighting has taken Scooter out of the arena as a bullfighter, but he continues
to enjoy entertaining the crowd as a barrelman. He also judges rodeos
whenever he can and owns a dance hall in Bandera, Texas.

Q. What do you currently do?

A. I'm co-owner of the second oldest dance hall/cabaret in Texas.
Although I'm retired from cowboy protection, I still do barrelman work and
judging for rodeos. I also advise up-and-coming bullfighters.

Q. How long have you done rodeo work?

A. I've got over 20 years of experience, on and off, over the course of 30
years. After 24 different broken bones, five concussions, a dislocated jaw—
twice, internal injuries, and a torn-off right ear, I'm retired from bullfighting. I never want to stop being in the arena though, so I still am a barrelman
and do judging, too.

Q. What did you do in rodeo?

A. I was a rodeo clown and bullfighter. My primary job was to provide cowboy protection by placing myself in between cowboys and bulls and diverting the bulls' attention. As a barrelman, my job is to keep the crowd amused with jokes, funny antics, and comedy skits involving explosions, fireworks, and clown cars.

Q. What does working as a rodeo clown/bullfighter involve?

A. Distracting the bull so the fallen cowboy can get to safety. A rodeo clown needs to pay close attention to the bull and the action in the arena. He must react correctly and without hesitation. In addition to cowboy protection, the clown is there to entertain the crowd with style and humor.

Q. What does working as a rodeo judge involve?

A. Being knowledgeable about all the rodeo sports. Although there are rodeo judging schools and seminars, a lot of judges have been raised on working ranches and around rodeos, so they've already learned all the rules.

Q. What is a typical workday like?

A. When I am a rodeo clown/bullfighter/barrelman, I start out by loading up all my supplies and traveling to the rodeo. Once there, I unload and check in with the contractor. It's then important to relax and focus on my game plan. I also have to put my face on and stretch to get physically ready. At times, bullfighters are asked to help behind the shoots with various tasks, such as untying calves.

As a judge, I have to arrive at the arena early to do a lot of prep work before the event begins. I select the drawing of bulls and riders. I measure roping pins, ropes, and barrel distances for racing. I place the steers' names into the hat and let the riders pick the "luck of the draw" to determine which steers they will ride and when. Once the events begin, I am in the judges' stand in the middle of the arena, and then I judge.

Q. When you worked in rodeo, what were your typical hours and work-days per week?

A. Typically, rodeos take place over the weekend. The short ones are usually Friday and Saturday; the longer ones may last from Thursday through Sunday. My role in the arena usually lasts a couple of hours per rodeo day.

Q. What do you enjoy most about the work?

A. It's a great feeling when I hear the audience applaud in apprecia-tion of my efforts. But the greatest feeling is when the cowboys express how much they appreciate my work. It's subtle—maybe a nod or wink or a high-five—but it means a lot. I also enjoy the kids who come up to me for photos and autographs. It's wonderful to have made a difference in their day.

Q. What do you like least about the work?

A. The pay. You have to do this work for the love of it. There are not too many who can make a lot of money doing it.

Q. What is your educational background?

A. I graduated from Del Mar College in police science and became a police officer. I also went to rodeo judging school.

Q. Where were you born? Where did you grow up?

A. I was born and raised in Texas, a little north of Corpus Christi.

Q. When did you know you wanted to work in rodeo?

A. Since childhood. I always worked on farms, rounding up cattle, picking cotton, and harvesting grain. By the time I was 16, my friends and I would jump on the backs of the bulls in the squeeze shoots. Older guys would come back from the rodeo telling us about how they were getting paid for riding the bulls, so we decided to join them.

Q. Do you ride horses, and, if so, how long have you ridden?

A. I did a lot of riding while doing ranch work as a kid and young man. I was never good with roping, though. I'd like to get into riding again now. I used to have two quarter horses for working, but my favorite horse was an Appaloosa named Speckle because he was the most spirited.

Q. Do you have direct contact with horses as part of your job?

A. Not as a clown, but I do judge bareback, saddleback, and roping events.

Q. What is the most challenging part of working as a rodeo clown/bullfighter?

A. The physical aspect of it all. It's hard to maintain your body over a period of time. Trying to compete with the new, younger guys is also a challenge.

Q. What is the biggest achievement of your career?

A. Winning the Risky Business Bullfighters Association's 2002 Barrelman of the Year award, which is voted on by both the crowds and my peers.

Q. What is the most challenging obstacle in your career?

A. The injuries. Although I've fought bulls with broken ribs, my injuries usually require recuperation time. My worst incident put me out for nine months—I suffered a severe concussion that led to some memory loss.

Q. What has driven you to excel in your career?

A. I don't like failure. My ultimate goal always was to be recognized in whatever I chose to do.

Q. What education and/or experience do you recommend for someone interested in being a rodeo clown/bullfighter or judge?

A. Learn the trade by going to a bullfighting/rodeo school, or have a couple fighters help you learn. Check with the rodeo crowd in your area to find a nearby school. Then, do an internship at a practice pen in your area. Get permission from the stock contractor and the fighters to join them and have them watch over you. Then, move on to the arenas.

Q. What personal strengths or skills should a person have who is considering working in rodeo?

A. You must be in top physical condition due to the danger and activities involved in rodeo. Mentally, you must be sharp and able to make snap decisions under pressure. You must accept the dangers and stress!

Q. What advice would you give to someone who wants to become a rodeo clown, bullfighter, or judge?

A. Whatever you choose to do in life, you have to have these three things: mind, heart, and ability. Without them, you won't have success or enjoyment.

Q. If you could do it over, is there anything you would have done differently?

A. Yes. Although rodeo work was my passion, people convinced me to pursue other career and personal options throughout my life, so my rodeo work was scattered over the years. If I did it again, I would not have quit doing the rodeos. I think I could have gone farther if I didn't have all those interruptions.

Q. What do you think the job outlook is for rodeo?

A. It's good, but remember, a bullfighter's years are limited. It takes eight to 10 years to reach the top level, and then only eight to 10 years after that before you get too physically beat up and have to retire to being a judge or barrelman. The market is flooded with fighters and clowns, so it is competitive. Younger guys are always coming along.

Q. How are rodeo clowns, bullfighters, and judges paid?

A. You make a bid on each performance. The rates are flexible, depending on the size of the show. Some guys can make a full-time living with nationwide sponsorships, but these are rare. Most bullfighters need another source of income.

Q. Is there anything else you would like to say about your life in rodeo?

A. If you love it, do it. Get the rush; make people laugh. If I could do it full-time, I would.

Rodeo Cowboy

About the job
Rodeo cowboys compete in bull riding, bareback bronco riding, saddle bronco riding, calf roping, and wrestling. Women also compete in these sports through the Professional Women's Rodeo Association (see appendices for contact information) and in barrel racing at most rodeos. Some cowboys make their living in the rodeo arena while others compete only on weekends and hold jobs as trainers, ranchers, or other related professions. Full-time rodeo cowboys live a transient life, with a majority of their time and energy spent traveling from one rodeo to another, often driving through the night, and pulling the horse trailer to make the next competition. Rodeo cowboys often form "buddy systems"—they'll travel to rodeos with other competitors, share expenses and take turns behind the wheel. The buddy system can foster lifelong friendships and helps make the rodeo community a tightly knit one. While rodeo cowboys pursue the lifestyle for a variety of reasons, including the excitement and the camaraderie, another lure is the potentially high compensation: earnings for top cowboys can run into the hundreds of thousands of dollars per year. After the travel and injuries have taken their toll, many rodeo cowboys retire as competitors but stay involved in the sport as judges, stock contractors, or instructors to other potential competitors.

If you haven't grown up around rodeo, as many contestants have, you can get started by first learning all you can about the sport. Visit rodeo Web sites and read books and other publications. Attend rodeos and observe or, better yet, act as a volunteer and get to know people on the rodeo circuit. If possible, find a mentor. Also, get involved in youth, high school, and collegiate rodeo organizations.

Education and training
While a college education is not required to compete in rodeo, rodeo organizations such as PRCA strongly encourage higher education.

Salary
Top PRCA cowboys earn from the high tens to hundreds of thousands of dollars per year, though the average cowboy earns far less than that.

RESOURCES
Professional Rodeo Cowboys Association
101 Pro Rodeo Drive
Colorado Springs, CO 80919
www.prorodeo.com

Professional Bull Riders, Inc.
6 South Tejon Street, Suite 700
Colorado Springs, CO 80903
www.pbrnow.com

American Junior Rodeo Association
4501 Armstrong St.
San Angelo, Texas 76903
www.home.gte.net/ajra/

Rodeo Judge

ABOUT THE JOB

Judges in rodeo usually come up through the ranks of professional rodeo cowboys. Rodeo judges score competitions, ensure the rules are followed, and are responsible for insuring the humane treatment of the animals used in competition. Rodeo judges must know the PRCA rulebook, which is strictly adhered to, and also attend the Wrangler Pro Officials Program. According to PRCA, the program was "designed to ensure fair and equal treatment of all contestants."

Judges may be PRCA employees who spend much of their time traveling to rodeos from coast-to-coast and everywhere in-between, or they may be "reserve" judges who generally work within their own areas of the country.

EDUCATION AND TRAINING

A high school diploma and college degree in an equine field are helpful, though not required. Experience in rodeo and training through the Wrangler Pro Officials Program and other rodeo judging seminars is necessary, as is licensing through PRCA.

SALARY

No information available.

Professional Rodeo Cowboys Association
101 Pro Rodeo Drive
Colorado Springs, CO 80919
www.prorodeo.com

Trainer and Clinician

ABOUT THE JOB

Trainers (and assistant trainers) perform everything from basic starting under saddle to advanced training and finishing of horses, depending on their knowledge and level of experience. Trainers may prepare horses for athletic competition or train the horses to be safe and reliable mounts for their owners. They often have strong backgrounds as competitive riders and sometimes combine competition with their training. Trainers work long hours, often seven days a week, during competition seasons. They may train horses at their clients' barns or farms, or work out of a training barn where clients' horses are boarded and clients come to them. Some trainers live on-site and room and board is part of their overall compensation package. Trainers often augment their incomes by working in other complementary areas of the horse world: as professional riders, riding instructors, horse agents, judging, appraising, consulting, and managing barns. Some top trainers are also clinicians who teach their training methods at equine expos, shows, and at other horse events.

Strong riding, horse handling skills, and knowledge of equine behavior are necessary for this position. Marketing and business skills are also important for trainers, as they are often self-employed. Other helpful personal attributes include having good people skills for working with clients and getting out in front of a group (for clinicians) and having a great amount of patience. (See entry for racehorse trainers in Horseracing section.)

EDUCATION AND TRAINING

On-the-job training as an apprentice to an established trainer, participation in clinics, trade school attendance, or college degree in equine studies or science, with classes in training methods are helpful. Certification from a reputable trainer or clinician is helpful in attracting clients, however, no licensing or certification is required for trainers, except for those working in the horseracing industry (see Chapter 11 for more on racehorse Trainers). Business and marketing classes are also helpful for people aspiring to work as trainers, because many trainers are self-employed.

SALARY

Trainers average $25,828 per year, according to a 2003 survey by Equistaff, an online job horse industry job placement agency. Twenty-three percent of trainers receive housing; 15 percent said that they received benefits such as medical and dental insurance; 38 percent received extra benefits such as riding, boarding, breeding rights, and use of a vehicle. Clinicians charge fees per clinic and may also charge for travel, lodging, food, and other expenses.

RESOURCES

Breed and sport organizations for the breed or sport you wish to work with, horse publications, and directories.

Career Spotlight

ANDREA MONTGOMERY, RIDER AND TRAINER

Andrea Montgomery trains dressage horses and works with horse owners wishing to learn the art of dressage. She and her husband, Tom, also own the Imperial Knights Production Company, a jousting group that performs more than 75 shows a year at Renaissance fairs, corporate events, and high schools. Tom trains the knights and works with the jousting horses. Andrea and Tom have three horses: a 12-year-old Thoroughbred named Hobie, an eight-year-old quarter horse named Leo (used for jousting in tournaments), and a seven-year-old Friesian named Othello (used in shows as a trick horse and to demonstrate dressage movements). They live in Norco, California.

Q. How long have you worked with horses?

A. I've always worked with horses. I've been riding for 30 years. My first job was as an instructor and it evolved from there. I had my own lesson barn on Maui, where I grew up, until I got tired of that because it is kind of limited there. It is an island, after all. I wanted to ride horses and travel, so I hooked up with the Lippizaner stallion show through a classified advertisement. They hired me over the phone. I worked with them for six years, riding in the show and training horses, which is where I met my husband. When we left, we started the Imperial Knights; I've also been training horses and working as a riding instructor. In 2003, though, we did go on a three-month tour with the Lippizaner show again, to England, Scotland, and Northern Ireland.

Q. How did you first get involved with horses?

A. I started riding when I was about eight years old. My family bought this big ranch and then decided we needed horses. The first horse we bought was a palomino quarter horse. I did 4-H and showed. At 13, I got my very own horse that was all mine, a Thoroughbred. We were living on Maui then and I used to ride with the clinicians at the Maui Horse Center, which is where I learned dressage.

Q. What is your typical week like?

A. During a typical week, I go to clients' farms and work their horses. I usually ride several horses a day and then work our horses; I do office work for the company, arrange events and clinics. I do dressage clinics where I give six to 10 lessons a day.

I also work the Imperial Knights' events. We do about 75 shows or more a year at renaissance fairs and corporate events. We do a drug free educational program at schools. Prior to the jousting tournament, we play games of skill and I do a demonstration with my Friesian "war horse." We do tricks and demonstrate moves that horses used while in battle with knights. That's how dressage moves were developed, as battle maneuvers. It turned into an art form from there, when knights realized these highly trained horses were too valuable to take into battle. I am also the "master of horses" at the shows and generally supervise everything, as well as catching the horses when the jousting knights fall off (all part of the show, of course!).

Q. What do you enjoy most about your work?

A. I most enjoy the day-to-day work with the horses. They are so glad to see you. I love riding and the horses. I am pretty grateful that I can make my living with horses. I like just hanging out with them. Sometimes, I think I should have been a professional show groom because I just want to touch the horses and be around them all the time.

Q. What do you like least?

A. People who do unsafe or unhealthy things with their horses. Unfortunately, the horse world has its share of unscrupulous people. I think that's why we have our own barn, so we can do our own thing. I'm all about the benefit of the animal and it's frustrating to see people who don't care for their horses. I've seen people at stables who come to see their horse every two weeks, ride him into the ground, put him away wet, and leave him standing in the stall for the next couple of weeks until they decide to show up again.

Q. What is your most memorable moment as a horsewoman?

A. There have been so many! I've had a few really great moments working with students and seeing a light bulb go off when they get something. I get chills seeing that. I've been working with a student who is going to the World Equestrian Games in endurance in the fall. I've been working with her for four years. It is awesome that she has gone so far.

There was a recent performance on my horse that was very memorable. I performed at a show called Dressage in the Wine Country in Santa Rosa, California, in 2003. I had trained the horse myself from the beginning and we did dressage moves and tricks. Five thousand people were on their feet screaming and clapping following the performance. On the last tour with the Lippizaners, we performed in front of Princess Anne in Scotland. I'll never forget that.

Q. What is the biggest achievement of your career?

A. Having our own business. Not only is it successful, but also we're able to make a living at it. I love being able to do what I love to do

Q. What is most rewarding about your work?

A. I like best working with both horse and rider and getting the rider to ride her horse better. I prefer working with both, rather than just going out and riding someone's horse.

Q. What is the most challenging obstacle in your career?

A. Being true to myself and not getting caught up in the politics.

Q. What advice would you give to someone interested in working with horses as a rider, trainer, or instructor?

A. Start learning immediately. It takes years to learn and is a lifelong commitment. Be committed to horses. Be prepared to work hard. Try and get a working student position. There are some great working student opportunities; you can learn a lot. Work hard and "shovel a lot of poop." Don't take on a career with horses lightly—horses are forever. I've been riding all my life and the horses still teach me something every day. Learn as much as you can, read, use all the information out there.

Q. What personality traits should someone have who is considering these fields?

A. Patience. I'm very patient with both people and horses. I see a lot of people who lose their temper with their horses when it is not the horses' fault that something has gone wrong, but theirs. Be levelheaded and find your way through the maelstrom. Stay on your path; focus on what you want to do with your horses and not what everyone else is talking about. Have your own mind.

Q. If you could do it over, is there anything you would have done differently to reach your career goal?

A. I had wanted at one time to be an English teacher. I had a full scholarship to go to college, but I didn't go because I was working with horses. The college education would have been something to fall back on should I have needed it. So, if I could do it over, I would have finished my education. I do regret that a little.

Career Spotlight

SHERI M. KUSABA, ASSISTANT TRAINER

Sheri M. Kusaba is an assistant trainer for J. Alden Enterprises in Huntington Beach, California. Like many people working in hands-on horse jobs, Sheri doesn't work exclusively as a horse trainer. She also instructs students at Huntington Beach Riding School, part of J. Alden Enterprises, and engages in horse sales. She has worked in her current position for six years.

Q. How did you get into horse training?

A. As a child, I always liked horses. I rode, took lessons. When trainer Scott McFall asked me to ride different horses for him, I was glad to. Then he moved to J. Alden and I was hired as well, and here I am now.

Q. What does your job involve?

A. It is a combination of training and riding instruction. I also take care of the horses with feeding and medication. I deal in horse sales for additional income.

Q. What is your typical workday like?

A. Everyday is different. There is a pattern to each day but they are all different, not monotonous. With horses, because they are animals, things happen that are not expected and this changes what I do within that day. I like that in my job. I don't like routine.

Q. How many hours/days per week do you typically work?

A. I am scheduled for 40 hours and five days a week. Some days are shorter than eight hours and some are longer. The hours vary depending on horse shows and if there are any horse problems.

Q. What do you enjoy most about your work?

A. Riding and training and being around the kids. Also, being in the fresh air and sun, rather than a cramped office with air-conditioning.

Q. What do you like least about your work?

A. The money. Also, it isn't a dependable kind of job, so you have to work with what you've got, including the sometimes long hours.

Q. What is your educational background?

A. I have a high school diploma and a few college classes.

Q. When did you know you wanted to work with horses?

A. As a child I wanted to be a jockey, but then as I got older, I just knew I wanted to be around horses all the time.

Q. In what disciplines do you ride?

A. Only English, but I would like to try western.

Q. What are the names and ages of your horse(s)?

A. I have one horse at the moment. His name is Ricky and he is six years old.

Q. What is your most memorable moment as a horsewoman?

A. Watching the children grow up and win in the show ring. There is one girl I have been teaching for as long as I have been here. She won an equitation jumping class; in this class, the judge rates the rider's posture. For her to win that class made me feel like I accomplished my job.

Q. What is the most rewarding part of your work?

A. Being outside and around horses all day.

Q. What is the most challenging part of your work?

A. The time that goes by so fast and the physical strain the work takes on your body.

Q. What is the biggest achievement of your career so far?

A. Having the parents of my students respect my opinion and knowledge.

Q. What is the most challenging obstacle in your career?

A. To learn more.

Q. What advice would you give to someone who wants to become a riding instructor and/or trainer within the horse industry?

A. Stick with it. Learn as much as you can about horses. Go wherever you can and watch others; take what you can get. You will probably start at the bottom, so do a good job and help others and they will help you. Keep riding.

Q. What education and/or experience do you recommend for someone interested in a career as an instructor or trainer?

A. In addition to horse experience, a degree in business helps for becoming organized, especially if you work for yourself. You should be able to talk to people, as you have to be able to communicate with people to network and to buy and sell horses.

Q. What personal strengths or skills should a person have who is considering this field?

A. People skills and teaching skills.

Q. What are your career goals for the future?

A. To do more riding and maybe open my own business.

Q. What did you do prior to your current job?

A. I did odd jobs, working for my parents and friends. I worked for the Knott's Berry Farm amusement park. None of those jobs lasted.

Q. If you could do it over, is there anything you would have done differently to reach your career goal?

A. No. In looking back at the jobs I have had, I can see they made me a better person for my job now.

Other Horse Show and Rodeo Personnel

ABOUT THE JOB

In addition to the horse show and rodeo positions discussed in detail above, there are many other people who work in the two areas. Some of them are paid employees and some are volunteers, often depending upon the size, scope, and level of the show or rodeo. Large shows and rodeos may have personnel filling all of these positions while smaller shows and rodeos combine positions where one person is doing several jobs.

Additional personnel working horse shows include other officials such as a president or executive director, a treasurer who oversees all financial matters, arena crew to set up and tear down the jumps and courses, workers to set up booths and stalls; plus announcer, organist, photographer, publicist, security personnel, stall manager, ringmaster, paddock master, emergency personnel, veterinarian, and farrier. Concessionaires provide food and drinks and vendors sell their products.

A highly important person in the rodeo world is the stock contractor, who supplies the horses, Brahma bulls, cattle, and calves for rodeo events. Rodeos often use the services of local stock contractors because they're familiar with them and the animals do not have to be shipped for long distances. Other rodeo personnel include pickup men, photographers, maintenance and ground staff, security personnel, concessionaires, timers, chute personnel, and emergency medical personnel, vendors, performers including trick riders and ropers, and other entertainers. Positions at rodeos may be voluntary or paid, depending on the size and scope of the rodeo and level of competition.

Visit horse shows or rodeos and talk to people in different jobs or volunteer at a local show or rodeo to get an idea of the employment available.

EDUCATION AND TRAINING

Education and experience will depend upon the particular job, and it can vary from high school to advanced degrees, plus various licensing or certification.

SALARY

Salary varies depending upon the position.

RESOURCES

Horse shows or rodeos, breed and sport organizations, horse publications.

CHAPTER 11

Horseracing Careers

— — —

Horseracing in the United States is a multibillion-dollar industry that employs more than 472,000 people throughout the country. Flat track racing, followed by harness racing, are the most popular forms of the sport. While Thoroughbreds are the most popular breed of horse for flat track racing, quarter horses, Arabians, Paints, Appaloosas, standardbreds, and even mules also have strong followings. Standardbred trotters and pacers are used in harness racing. A handful of tracks on the East Coast of the United States also feature steeplechase racing, in which jockeys lead their horses in jumps over fences and other obstacles.

There are several career opportunities in racing besides the obvious career of jockey. Help prepare the horses for a day of racing as an exercise rider. Combine a love of horses and music as a bugler. Exercise your business skills in racing administration. There is truly something for everyone in racing.

The types of jobs the racing industry generates are as varied as the skills, experience, and personalities needed to fill them. In addition to the hands-on jobs that probably come to the minds of most horse lovers, such as trainer, jockey, groom, and exercise rider, the industry generates thousands of positions in public relations, marketing, sales, accounting, information systems, and human resources. Pari-mutuel workers who manage and take bets, as well as simulcasting personnel who ensure the widest possible audience for races, are critical to the industry. Concessionaires, ushers, groundskeepers, security guards and others all contribute to the day-to-day operations of tracks.

Racing officials, who are present at every race, are responsible for ensuring that races are run fairly and safely for the betting public. Following is a general list of racing officials required to oversee races. Additional officials (see list below) may also be present at race meets at the discretion of the racing commission. Titles and positions vary slightly for harness racing:

- steward (three at each meet)
- racing secretary
- horsemen's bookkeeper
- judge, including paddock judge and patrol and placing judge
- horse identifier
- clerk-of-scales
- outrider
- starter
- timer/clocker
- official veterinarian
- racing veterinarian

This chapter focuses on the official/managerial positions, the hands-on horse careers and pari-mutuel jobs. Because every track, state racing commission, and trainer does things a little differently, actual positions and responsibilities of these positions will vary. Generally, large tracks and racing barns will offer more specialized positions while smaller tracks and barns may combine positions. If you are interested in working in racing as an accountant, sales person, photographer or other professional field that is found throughout the horse industry, read this chapter to get a general understanding of the racing world and then see the chapters that discuss those specific fields in detail. People interested in employment in concessions, ushering, grounds keeping, and security should contact individual racetracks in their area for more information on hiring. Some tracks hire people as young as 16 for concession and ushering positions. Most of these jobs are seasonal or part-time, but they can provide valuable racetrack experience and a foot in the door.

Be aware that racing is a world in itself and can be difficult for an outsider to break into. Having contacts or growing up in racing is a big advantage. According to racing professionals, the best way to break in if you don't have contacts is to network, network, and network. Hang around the track and get to know people. Stop by in the morning during exercise hours and ask questions (without getting in the way, of course). Find out who the players are in your area and in the industry. Read industry publications such as *Thoroughbred Times*, *The Blood Horse Source*, and *Hoofbeats* for contact information and potential job openings. Schools with racing programs often offer placement assistance to their students in managerial or other official racing positions. Three schools with programs that educate students for careers in racing include the University of Arizona's Race Track Industry Program, the University of Louisville's Equine Industry Program, and the Agricultural Technical Institute at Ohio State University at Wooster. Young people ages eight to 16 who are interested in racing can join Kids to the Cup (120 So. First Ave., Arcadia, CA 91006; www.kttc.org). This nonprofit organization seeks to educate young racing fans and future industry employees. The Harness Horse Youth Foundation (16575 Carey Rd., Westfield, IN 46074; www.hhyf.org) is a nonprofit educational organization for young people interested in harness racing. Also, contact equine employment agencies for possible opportunities in racing (see Chapter 5 for agencies) and the personnel offices of area racetracks or your state's racing commission for more information on hiring practices. All racetrack personnel are required to be licensed through their states; licensing requirements vary from state-to-state.

Bloodstock Agent

ABOUT THE JOB

Bloodstock agents advise clients in and negotiate prices and sales agreements for the purchase or sale of Thoroughbred horses. They are self-employed and rely on their knowledge of horses, the racing industry, and bloodstock markets to help racehorse owners and potential owners make the wisest decisions. Agents also arrange for trailering of horses, insurance, veterinary checks, and transferring of ownership paperwork. Successful agents have a strong knowledge of horse conformation, pedigree and value, as well as an understanding of the basics of breeding, training, and overall equine health. Many agents provide additional services, such as stallion advertising and promotions, breeding services, arranging partnerships and syndicates, pedigree research and analysis, and international sales and shipping. Other agents may specialize in one of these particular areas.

In addition to being knowledgeable about horses and the racing industry, excellent people and business skills and expertise in networking and marketing are important.

EDUCATION AND TRAINING
A four-year degree in equine studies, with additional business classes, or a degree in business or marketing is required.

SALARY
Commission on sales and purchase transactions (usually 5 percent) and/or retainers for ongoing consulting services.

RESOURCES
Publications such as *Thoroughbred Times*. Also, state and local Thoroughbred owners and breeders associations.

Bugler

ABOUT THE JOB
If you are a musician who loves horses and doesn't mind being in front of a crowd, a job as a racetrack bugler might be for you. The bugler plays "The Call to the Post" (also known as "Boot and Saddles" for its historic use alerting cavalry troops to saddle and bridle their horses) prior to each race. Buglers may play at several racetracks and fairs and hold other employment as well, or they may be hired by a single racetrack to play the bugle and also perform other tasks. Some buglers use trumpets or other horns rather than bugles. Knowledge of racing may or may not be required, depending on the track.

EDUCATION AND TRAINING
High school diploma, or more, and training as a musician.

SALARY

No information available.

RESOURCES

Racetracks and other equestrian events.

Charter

ABOUT THE JOB

This individual is a harness racing official who charts each race. This official prepares charts that show the names of the horses and drivers, date and place of the race, track size, track condition, track temperature, type of race (trot or pace), order of finish, and individual time of each horse.

EDUCATION AND TRAINING

A four-year equine degree with a racing, administrative, or managerial focus, and an internship in horse racing or extensive experience in horse racing.

SALARY

No information available.

RESOURCES

Universities with racing programs, racing publications, area racetracks, and state racing commissions.

Clerk-of-Scales

ABOUT THE JOB

These important racing officials are responsible for overseeing jockeys, jockeys' attendants, and the jockey room. The clerks-of-scales weigh jockeys and equipment before and after races to verify their weight. They also verify that jockeys have current licenses issued by the racing commission. They report to racing stewards if jockeys arrive late or do not present themselves to be weighed in; when jockeys are under-or overweight; or if a jockey dismounts before reaching the scales. The clerks-of-scales also oversee the security, regulation, and conduct of jockeys and their attendants in the jockey room and supervise the jockeys' valets and the issuing of equipment to each jockey. The clerks-of-scales assume the duties of the jockey room custodian in the absence of that employee. Following the day's racing, the clerks-of-scales report on the weights carried in each race.

In addition to racing knowledge, it's important to have managerial, communication, and organizational skills.

EDUCATION AND TRAINING
A four-year equine degree with a racing, administrative or managerial focus, as well as an internship in horse racing, or extensive experience in horse racing.

SALARY
Salary is dependent upon the region of the country and track.

RESOURCES
Universities with racing programs, racing publications, area racetracks, and state racing commissions.

Clerk-of-the-Course (Harness Racing)

ABOUT THE JOB
Clerks-of-the-course verify and maintain the registration and eligibility records of all horses. They also view races and maintain records of race results for each racing day. Clerks-of-the-course record details of all races, including horses entered, positions of horses at the finish, names of scratched or ruled-out horses, recorded times, and any penalties, protests, or appeals.

EDUCATION AND TRAINING
A four-year equine degree with a racing, administrative, or managerial focus and an internship in racing, or experience in racing.

SALARY
Salary is dependent upon the part of the country and track for which you work.

RESOURCES
Universities with racing programs, racing publications, area racetracks, and state racing commissions.

Clocker

ABOUT THE JOB

Clockers are racetrack officials who time racehorses during training workouts. They record the distance and time of each workout and prepare a list of the workouts for the steward and the racing secretary following the conclusion of training hours. They also post workout times for the public and provide the information to the news media. This position requires excellent organizational and record-keeping skills.

EDUCATION AND TRAINING

Extensive experience in racing, or a four-year equine degree with a racing, administrative, or managerial focus and an internship in racing.

SALARY

Salary is dependent upon the region of the country and track for which you work.

RESOURCES

Universities with racing programs, racing publications, area racetracks, and state racing commissions.

Exercise Rider

ABOUT THE JOB

Exercise riders exercise and condition horses for racing. They work under the supervision of racehorse trainers and sometimes use this position to gain experience toward becoming jockeys. Riders must have excellent riding skills and the ability to break from the gate and gallop racehorses around the track while properly pacing them. The weight limit for exercise riders may vary, depending upon the trainer. However, exercise riders do not have the strict weight restrictions imposed on them that jockeys do and their weights can be quite high in comparison to that of jockeys. Some riders are former jockeys who can no longer live with the constant demand of keeping their weight down, so they either returned to exercise riding or chose exercise riding over racing. Riders may exercise as many as 10 horses during morning exercise hours.

In addition to working for racing stables, exercise riders also work at breeding farms helping to train and develop young horses for racing. Riders working at farms may be expected to help out with many other duties in addition to riding, such as caring for horses and stable management tasks. Some exercise riders may work at the track as well as at the farm.

EDUCATION AND TRAINING
A high school diploma and extensive experience with horses are necessary.

SALARY
Median salary is up to $20,000 per year, with housing sometimes included. Exercise riders may receive a small percentage of purses or bonuses tied to their horses' success.

RESOURCES
Check out *Thoroughbred Times* and other racing publications for industry contacts. Local racetracks may be able to provide publications listing the names and pertinent information on the trainers, owners, and jockeys on their racing circuit.

Career Spotlight

MIMI DAVIS, EXERCISE RIDER

Mimi Davis has exercised racehorses for 22 years. She works at Keeneland and Ellis racetracks in Kentucky, as well as at Payson Park in Florida. While she has worked at many tracks up and down the East Coast, Mimi likes the Kentucky-Florida route she presently works. She has ridden horses since her grandmother introduced them to her at age four. In addition to Thoroughbreds, Mimi has also worked with quarter horses and saddle horses. Mimi was born and raised in Kentucky, was a member of the Keeneland Pony Club, and attended the University of Kentucky. She has no horses of her own at this time.

Q. What does your job involve?

A. At my present job, I ride seven days a week on the horses my boss selects. I also help keep things going along in the shed. We all pitch in. I might set tack or other equipment, walk horses, graze horses, ship horses, put on bandages, hold for the blacksmith, vet, or chiropractor and help to direct them if there is something wrong with a horse or something needs to be addressed. When necessary, I also ship out of town with our horses if they need to stay a few days. There, I will groom, ride, walk, vet, and saddle the horse for the race. Basically, I am a traveling assistant. I also drive the truck and trailer. I have my own old trailer and truck, and Alison, my boss, also has one.

Q. For whom do you exercise horses?

A. I am fortunate enough to work for Alison Register, a friend and terrific horsewoman. Alison owns Macoma Farm. I am technically paid by Alex G. Campbell, Jr. and by Alison. Alison is one of the good people today who gives her employees respect and trust. We have the best crew in the country working in our barn.

Q. What is a typical day like?

A. Typically, I am in the barn at Keeneland by 5 A.M. and finished by 10 A.M. I leave early at times to go to Macoma Farm to bring horses in and feed. Next, on to Timbertown Farm to ride a few we have in lay up [resting or being rehabilitated from an injury] for Mr. Campbell or Layton Register. At Keeneland, I do anything necessary to keep things running along. I ride, do laundry, walk horses, move the magnetic blanket to horses needing it, set up tack and other equipment, and pony horses to the track with or without riders. When necessary, we all clean the stalls, get the pony ready or just about anything else, even finding loose dogs, to get things done before the track closes. I ride five to 10 horses in a morning.

Q. How did you get started as an exercise rider?

A. I worked for a man I had known all my life. I began breaking yearlings for Johnny Ward working at Domino Stud in the afternoons until he decided I could work mornings, also. I was fortunate in that I knew how to sit on a horse pretty well before starting out exercising. That meant I would not fall off so easily. Lucky me.

Q. What other racing or horse industry work have you done?

A. I have worked in several other positions throughout the 22 years I've been galloping horses. Along with exercising, I worked as an assistant trainer to several very good trainers. I have held my own trainer's license and raced one horse I purchased as a yearling and later sold. I have worked the sales at Keeneland on and off since I was in college. I worked as an outrider for about three years. I loved that job and owning my own horses, but the pay was minimal, and most tracks don't offer benefits. I learned a lot when I was outriding, and I also learned that I was a decent horsewoman myself. I worked in the racing office at one point and I also proofread catalogue pages for the sales staff. I've broken yearlings many times on various farms. I take pride in any work I do, and, in particular, my work with horses.

Q. How many hours per week do you work?

A. I only work around 40 hours a week—sometimes more when I have shipped with a horse. It's not like the days as an assistant, putting in 80 hours and more a week.

Q. What is your overall background with horses?

A. My grandmother came to our house when I was only four years old and asked if my brother Kent and I would like to ride horses. We said "yes" and that was that. I went to the barn seven days a week from then on, although we did ride less during winter. My grandmother was a horse-woman. Her mother was a horsewoman. She expected me to learn how to do everything. And I did. Any good horse person will tell you that you will never know everything and that you'll learn every day when dealing with horses. This is true. You stop being good when you stop learning.

Q. What do you enjoy most about your work?

A. I love to ride horses. In particular, it gives me great pleasure to see a horse improve under me. Whether he is a young horse who is learning or an old horse trying to get past a problem. I just love to see them happy and going in the right direction.

Q. What do you like least?

A. What I like least is the fact that the Thoroughbred business is just that—a business now. The real horsemen cannot survive unless they go P.R. The horses are suffering; there are fewer truly good horsemen and it trickles down the barn from riders to grooms to hot walkers. It is too in-depth to go into here, but suffice it to say that I wish it were a sport again.

Q. What have been your most memorable moments as a horsewoman?

A. Working as an outrider at the fairs in Massachusetts. I never missed a loose horse. I caught a loose horse during a race as the horse was heading into the horses that were running. The loose horse was running the wrong way and probably would have collided with one or more of the other horses. I saw a problem in the race before it happened, backtracked, and managed to catch the horse from behind, an almost impossible task. I would not normally chase a loose horse from behind. I realized the danger of the situation and thought I could keep him away from the other horses if I could get close. Fortunately, I had the best ponies, and very fast ones. I caught the horse on the offside and ran him past the field. And, it was memorable that day, when the jockeys' wives thanked me for saving their husbands. I choked up and tried not to cry, I was so touched and proud of my horse. It was very exciting and very gratifying to know the people I worked with appreciated what had just occurred. The gate crew even gave me a pat on the back. Everyone on the backside knows everyone else. At the fairs you work closely, so injury to anyone was personal. Being responsible for keeping people safe is really awesome when you perform well.

Q. What is the most rewarding part of your career?

A. I truly enjoy riding, just sitting on a horse. I love it when the horse pricks her ears, squeals, and enjoys the work she does. It is great. Adding to that is if the horse wants to be a racehorse and can run. You really feel great!!

Q. What is the most challenging part of your career?

A. Dealing with people. That is true in any career, I am sure. I am a people person, but the animals are the easy part.

Q. What is the biggest achievement of your career?

A. I'm not sure I have reached my greatest achievement. I am proud of the work I do every day and hope I know when it is time to stop. Riding is extremely physical as well as mentally taxing. When it is time to quit, it is time to quit. At this point, I would have to say that watching a horse excel while you are working with him and participating in his training is an achievement in itself.

Q. What is the most challenging obstacle in your career?

A. The biggest obstacle for me has been myself, realizing that I am good at what I do and going ahead and doing it. I have a college degree I never used. This is my gift.

Q. What advice would you give someone interested in being an exercise rider?

A. I suppose the one piece of advice I would give to anyone, whether she has ridden a horse before or not, would be to work with yearlings and break young horses before going to the racetrack. If you don't mind grooming on the track or hot walking first, you'll see what a horse will have to face later in life.

Q. What type of experience should the person get?

A. Any type of work or sport around a horse gives you something to learn. No matter the breed or business, you can learn something that will help you down the line.

Q. What personality traits should a person have who is considering this field?

A. I don't believe there is one particular type of personality that excels in exercise riding. Each person will be good at something different that will suit the different types of horses. The horses have personalities themselves.

Q. Is there anything else you would like to say about your career?

A. I am proud to be a "racetracker." We are hardworking, industrious vagabonds who appreciate and love horses.

Handicapper

ABOUT THE JOB

Handicappers decide the odds on horses for each race. They are employed by racetracks and sometimes are hired seasonally; or they may work as freelancers and provide handicaping information to newspapers and racing publications. Successful handicappers have a thorough knowledge of racehorses, including their training, pedigree, temperament, and past performances. They also know the records and weights of jockeys or drivers and racing conditions, which enables them to analyze the data and estimate the probable finishing order for each horse in a race. For maiden races, handicappers use breeding and qualifying time data to set odds.

EDUCATION AND TRAINING

Extensive knowledge of horseracing.

SALARY

Full-time handicappers start between $25,000 to $30,000 per year.

RESOURCES

Daily Racing Form
100 Broadway 7th Floor
New York, NY 10005-1902
www.drf.com

The Jockey Club Information Systems
821 Corporate Drive
Lexington, KY 40503
www.tjcis.com

Harness Driver

ABOUT THE JOB

Harness drivers sit in sulkies, the small carts pulled by standardbred pacers or trotters.

Standardbred racing is contested in two gaits—the pace and the trot, with the majority of them contested at the pace. Pacers move the legs on one side of their body in unison: left front and rear, and right front and rear. Trotters move with a diagonal gait; the left front and right rear legs move in unison, as do the right front and left rear. The best drivers can drive in both pacing and trotting races. Drivers in harness racing do not have height or weight restrictions, though the average weight is between 150 to 165 pounds. Some drivers are trainers and/or owners of the horses they drive, while others are catch drivers (similar to jockeys who drive for different trainers and owners and do not train their own horses). Agents are not found in harness racing as they are in Thoroughbred racing because catch drivers negotiate their own terms with trainers and owners. The best drivers may be named to drive multiple horses in the same race; from there, they negotiate the best terms with owners and trainers.

The most successful harness drivers are experienced trainers. The best way for aspiring drivers to gain experience is to work with a successful trainer. Also, the United States Trotting Association offers a school for people interested in amateur racing.

EDUCATION AND TRAINING

A high school diploma and working student arrangement with a trainer are essential. All drivers are licensed through the United States Trotting Association and there are different levels of licensing, depending on the age and experience of the driver.

SALARY

The standard driving fee is 5 percent of the purse, though drivers may negotiate other arrangements.

RESOURCES

United States Trotting Association
750 Michigan Ave.
Columbus, OH 43215
www.ustrotting.com

Horse Identifier

ABOUT THE JOB

Horse identifiers are racing officials who are responsible for ensuring that the correct horses are racing. They check tattoo numbers under the animals' top lips, as well as sex, color, and markings, and compare those against registration, eligibility, or breeding documents, as necessary. Identifiers report any discrepancies to racing stewards or paddock judges. They also supervise the tattooing, branding, or other identification method approved by the breed registry and the racing commission for horses located on racetrack grounds.

Horse identifiers are very knowledgeable about the characteristics of the breed of horse they identify, including colors, markings, and other features such as cowlicks and whorls. When not actually in the paddock looking at horses, identifiers spend much of their time in the office doing paperwork.

EDUCATION AND TRAINING
Extensive experience in racing, or a four-year equine degree with a racing, administrative, or managerial focus and an internship in racing are important.

SALARY
Salary is dependent upon the part of the country and track for which you work.

RESOURCES
Investigate universities with racing programs, racing publications, area racetracks; see state racing commissions for information on hiring practices.

Career Spotlight

BARBARA BORDEN, HORSE IDENTIFIER

Barbara Borden works as a horse identifier at several Kentucky racetracks: Ellis Park, Keeneland, Churchill Downs, and Turfway Park. She has worked in the field since 1988, starting out as an assistant identifier before rising to become the top horse identifier approximately 11 years ago. Her job at these four major tracks keeps her busy year-round. Although the horse identifier position was originally a state job working for the Kentucky racing commission, Barbara is now employed at the racetrack. Barbara hasn't had a horse of her own for years, but she loves the many horses she sees each week in the paddock prior to the races.

Q. What do you do in your job?

A. Horse identifiers do just what the name implies—identify each horse that runs in each race. I've got a program that lists horse tattoos, horse markings, and other identifiers. Prior to each race, in the paddock, I examine tattoo numbers on the horses' upper lip, markings, and cowlicks to make sure the horses that I have listed are the horses in the paddock getting ready to race. I look at an average of 100 horses a day. I come in around 8 A.M. and, when not at the paddock, I spend most of my time in the office, doing paperwork and checking registration certificates. Registration certificates are likened to a birth certificate for people (with the horse's registration number could be compared to the person's social security number). The horse carries this number with him all his life. The registration certificate includes birthdate, the sire and dam of the horse, as well as markings, cowlicks, or swirls in the horse's coat. For horses without white marks, cowlicks are used for identification. Every horse has at least one cowlick on his head and one on either side of his neck. The registration number begins with the last two digits of the year the horse was born. That two-digit number becomes part of the lip tattoo. Racehorses cannot be tattooed prior to age two, but they are tattooed before making their first start.

Q. What happens if you suspect the wrong horse is in the paddock?

A. When a foal is registered initially, between six and nine months of age, photos are sent to The Jockey Club. When it's time for the tattoo technician to tattoo the horse, we take additional photos and send those to The Jockey Club. If it isn't an obviously different horse, I contact The Jockey Club. They would describe what they see in the photos and I compare their description to what I'm seeing. If I believe it is the wrong horse, I recommend a scratch to the steward. When wrong horses are sent to the paddock, the trainers are fined. Most of the time they are honest mistakes, and it is very hard to pin switches down to absolute cheating, because it's hard to prove. We all want to keep it honest and aboveboard.

Q. How did you get involved in racing?

A. I grew up in Cleveland, gravitated to the racetrack there, as did my siblings (my brother is a jockey and my sister a trainer). I went to the track one summer to walk hots and decided not to continue my studies in music. I worked as a groom, galloped horses, worked for the Daily Racing Form, and then when a job in the horse identifier's office opened up, I took it. A lot of identifiers at tracks get thrown into the job or the new guy gets shuffled into it because it entails a lot of paperwork and responsibility, so many people don't want it. I was lucky enough to have a mentor, the person who had previously worked in the job. People don't always realize that identifying is not all black and white. You have to take the paperwork and the horse and try to put them together. Sometimes it can be a judgment call in the paddock area because you have to interpret the descriptions. It came in handy that I was trained and worked with someone who was good at it.

Q. What do you enjoy most about your work?

A. I enjoy the people and the atmosphere. I love the horses and have always been around them. I don't like when something goes wrong, but there can be excitement in it when the wrong horse comes to the paddock. There was an example recently of a completely wrong horse coming into the paddock; it was an honest mistake. The trainer had four horses running that day and the groom brought the wrong one. Things like that change the routine nature of the day because most of the time, it runs smoothly and there aren't any mistakes.

It is a fun and interesting job. I've had opportunities to do other things. I attended the steward program at the University of Louisville and became steward at a few small tracks. If you are a good horse identifier, though, you tend to keep your job, which is okay as I'd rather be in a "dead-end" job I enjoy than one I don't. Horse identifier is not exactly a springboard to any-thing—there is no natural progression from it to anything else—so you must enjoy doing the job.

Q. What is the most rewarding part of being a horse identifier?

A. Catching a mistake. I don't get joy out of it, but I'm happy to stop a mistake. That's my job.

Q. What is the most challenging part of being a horse identifier?

A. The identification part. My challenge every day is to look at first-time starters and other horses I haven't seen before and make sure no mistakes have been made. You can never assume that if a horse is running, it is the right horse.

Q. What is the biggest achievement of your career?

A. Having a good work ethic. I am helpful to the horsemen and very serious about the job. I take the job with me all the time and think about it a lot.

Q. What is your most memorable moment?

A. I get to work the Kentucky Derby and there is no feeling like when the horses walk in for the Derby. Racing in general in Kentucky is really good. I enjoy being around good horses and good races.

Q. What personal strengths or skills should a person have who is interested in this career?

A. Horse identifiers cannot be meek and mild. They must be assertive so no one will mess with them. I can't let trainers or owners intimidate me. If I see something wrong, I will call the steward no matter what and no matter who tries to talk me out of it. And you have to do it firmly, but nicely at the same time. Most days go by without incident, though.

Q. What advice would you give to someone interested in working as an identifier or in racing?

A. A background in racing is helpful. If you can hook up with someone to learn the job, that is helpful. Often, getting a job is about being in the right place at the right time. If you don't have contacts, you can hang around and try to get a job as a hot walker, then you can look around and see what other jobs interest you. There are a million jobs at the track that people can do, so decide what you want to do and then pursue it.

Horsemen's Bookkeeper

ABOUT THE JOB

Horsemen's bookkeepers handle the records and accounts of the horsemen. ("Horsemen" is a common racing term in racing for the owners, trainers, and jockeys, who may be men or women.) The horsemen' s bookkeepers maintain contact and tax identification records for the horsemen; partnership, syndicate, and lease statements and agreements; and money on account and due. The bookkeepers also receive, maintain, and disburse the purses of each race, and handles jock mount fees, entrance money, and purchase money in claiming races. In addition to strong bookkeeping and accounting skills, the bookkeeper should be organized and have good people skills.

EDUCATION AND TRAINING

A bachelor's degree in bookkeeping or accounting, and experience in racing.

SALARY

Salary is dependent upon the part of the country and track for which you work

RESOURCES

Investigate universities with racing programs, racing publications, area racetracks; also, state racing commissions for information on hiring practices.

Hot Walker

ABOUT THE JOB

Hot walkers cool horses down after races, so they should know how to properly lead horses when horses are appropriately cooled down. Some trainers may also use hot walking machines to supplement human hot walkers.

Hot walking can be a way for people without contacts in racing to enter the racing world. Trainers often need hot walkers for their horses and may hire job seekers hanging around the track in the morning looking for work. People with prior horse experience are picked up first, but even those without a strong horse background can find work as hot walkers when the needs of the trainer are strong enough. Usually hot walkers are paid a small amount per horse.

EDUCATION AND TRAINING
A high school diploma.

SALARY
Hot walkers receive a small amount per horse walked.

RESOURCES
Check out *Thoroughbred Times* and other racing publications for industry contacts. Local racetracks may provide publications with the names and pertinent information on the trainers, owners, and jockeys on their racing circuit.

Jockey

ABOUT THE JOB
Jockeys must be extremely strong, fearless riders, with the ability to break safely from the starting gate and control horses many times their size while moving at speeds of up to 40 miles per hour among a field of other horses. Jockeys in high demand by trainers may ride as many as nine or 10 horses in a day. They confer with trainers on each horse's temperament and behavior, and on race strategy prior to races. Successful jockeys also make themselves familiar with the characteristics of the horses they are racing against, to help them better determine their own strategy in the race. In addition to having excellent riding skills and horse knowledge, successful jockeys are good strategic thinkers and have strong hand-eye coordination and quick reflexes.

Jockeys must maintain rigid diets to keep their weight down, which for many jockeys is one of the toughest—if not the toughest—aspects of their career. Fasting is common among jockeys as they seek to stop their weight from creeping upward or try to drop that final pound or two. The upper weight limit for jockeys is 115 pounds, and they must be a minimum of 16 years old to be licensed. Many jockeys begin their careers by volunteering around the barn or working as grooms and stable hands at the track to get to know trainers and others in the business. Others gain experience and contacts as exercise riders.

EDUCATION AND TRAINING
On-the-job training or attendance at a jockey school is essential. State licensing is required, which involves the recommendation of a trainer and testing.

SALARY

Jockeys are paid a fee per each horse they race, called a jock mount; they also receive a percentage of winning purses. Jock mount fees range from $35 and up. They also typically receive six to 10 percent of the purse for wins and a lower percentage for placing and showing.

RESOURCES

Jockeys' Guild, Inc.
P.O. Box 150
Monrovia, CA 91017

Jockey's Agent

ABOUT THE JOB

Just as many other professional athletes employ agents, so do jockeys. Jockeys' agents represent the interests of the jockeys in negotiations with racehorse trainers and owners. They also try to procure the best mounts and riding fees for the jockeys they represent. Agents coordinate the jockeys' availability to ride and they keep trainers and owners informed about which jockeys are available for specific races. Strong knowledge of the racing industry and the people in the industry as well as good communication, people, and negotiation skills are required to be a jockey's agent. Some agents were once jockeys themselves, or aspiring jockeys, who bypassed the height and weight restrictions for pursuing careers as jockeys. The jockeys they represent pay agents a fee.

EDUCATION AND TRAINING

Extensive experience in the racing industry.

SALARY

Agents receive a fee from the jockeys they represent and their income is determined by the success of their jockey's.

RESOURCES

Check out *Thoroughbred Times* and other racing publications for industry contacts. Local racetracks may provide publications with the names and pertinent information on the trainers, owners, and jockeys on their racing circuit.

Jockey Room Custodian

ABOUT THE JOB

Jockey room custodians are employees of the racetrack who supervise the conduct of the jockeys and their attendants while they are in the jockey room. They are responsible for keeping the jockey room clean and safe and keeping unauthorized people out of the room. Jockey room custodians ensure that the racing silks are there and that all jockeys leaving the room to prepare for mounting up are in the correct colors. (Racehorses are identified by the colored silks the jockeys wear; the silks represent the owner of the horse.)

Room custodians also keep a daily film list, displayed in plain view for the jockeys, as well as a daily program, so that jockeys may have ready access to mounts that may become available.

EDUCATION AND TRAINING

A high school diploma and experience in racing are necessary.

SALARY

Salary is dependent upon the part of the country and track for which you work.

RESOURCES

Racing publications, area racetracks, and state racing commissions for information on hiring practices.

Jockey's Valet

ABOUT THE JOB

A jockey's valet helps the jockey dress for races. He obtains the correct silks, lays out clothes, washes silks, cleans saddles, and shines boots following races. Valets also place entry numbers on saddles, insert weights into saddle pockets, and sometimes saddle horses. They usually assist several jockeys at a time.

EDUCATION AND TRAINING

A high school diploma and experience in racing are important.

Salary

Valets are usually paid by the track. Their salary is dependent upon the part of the country and track for which they work. They may receive a small percentage of their jockeys earnings.

Resources

Thoroughbred Times and other racing publications for industry contacts. Local racetracks may provide publications with the names and information on the trainers, owners, and jockeys on their racing circuit.

Outrider

About the job

Outriders are employees of the racetrack who are responsible for the orderly conduct of racehorses during on-track training sessions and races and for getting horses safely to the gate on time. Each race has at least two outriders: one outrider leads the post parade while the other follows it. During races and training sessions, they catch loose horses. Outriders are highly experienced riders who can control racehorses without getting in the way of training sessions or races. In harness racing, this person may be called a marshall.

Education and experience

A high school diploma; extensive experience with horses and the world of racing are vital.

Salary

Salary is dependent upon the part of the country and track for which you work.

Resources

Check out *Thoroughbred Times* and other racing publications for industry contacts; local racetracks.

Career Spotlight

JOE RIGGS, OUTRIDER

Joe Riggs has chased loose horses and helped ensure safety on the racetrack for more than 30 years. He got his start as an outrider at a small track in Louisville, Kentucky, when the regular outrider broke his leg and the track needed a quick replacement. Joe, who worked as an exercise rider at the time, had access to a pony, so he filled in for the injured outrider. Joe continued his career galloping horses (as many as 12 to 18 in the morning) as his main source of income while also continuing to work as an outrider for extra money. He has worked at tracks throughout Kentucky and Tampa Bay Downs in Florida. Eventually, Joe stopped exercising and went to work full-time as an outrider. Since 1988, he has worked strictly for Keeneland Race Track in Kentucky.

Q. What is a typical day like?

A. I'm at the barn at 5 A.M. to feed my horse, clean his stall, groom, and tack him up. I change into my working/riding clothes and am on the track during exercise hours riding around, helping out exercise riders. We are there to help ensure safety, chase loose horses, help when horses balk, or do anything we can to be of assistance. During the race meet, I lead the horses out during the post parade. Two outriders are in front of the starting gate to help with fractious horses. Then, we are on the track to catch loose horses and help jockeys.

Q. How many hours a week do you usually work?

A. Six days a week, six hours per day. When the race meet is not on, we strictly do morning patrol and take care of the horses we use for that patrol. If the race meet is on, then I'll work 75 hours per week.

Q. What do you enjoy most about your work?

A. I love riding horses. I can't think of anything else I was meant to be doing. I also love the morning sunrise.

Q. What do you like least about the work?

A. Working on snowy days, when I don't have enough warm clothing on.

Q. How long have you ridden?

A. I've never done anything else. We lived near Churchill Downs. When I was 11 or 12 years old, our neighbor, who was a trainer, took his son and me to the track. We walked horses for 50 cents a head before school. That was a lot of money for a young boy back then. I started galloping horses from there.

Q. What other work have you done in racing?

A. I rode in races for six years, won my first and third race. I did pretty well as an apprentice. I hated fighting the weight, though. It takes a special kind of person to be a good rider. I didn't have enough drive to stop eating and maintain that 108-pound frame. I was 114 pounds. That doesn't sound like a lot to lose, but it is when you're trying to take it off an already small frame.

I also did a scene in the 2003 movie *Seabiscuit*. I played a wrangler. We worked about 15 days at Keeneland with the Seabiscuit filmmakers. Filming that movie was a lot of work for the filmmakers—I have to give those people a lot of credit. I've also done some television work, a miniseries in which I played an outrider. I worked with Forrest Tucker, Cheryl Ladd, and Wayne Rogers. I've done five different movies and television shows that were filming in Keeneland or Tampa.

Q. What is the name of your horse?

A. Frog is my ex-racehorse. He wasn't very successful, but he is as good an outrider horse as there ever was. I believe you need to ride a Thoroughbred as an outrider—they'll stay with you longer, run faster.

Q. What is your most memorable moment?

A. I don't know. I've done a lot, caught horses without bridles on, caught riders in trouble. When you can stand and catch a horse with no equipment on his face and a rider on his back, that is something memorable.

Q. What is the most rewarding part of your job?

A. It's hard to say. The majority of time people appreciate what you do. I like that part. I like being there to help. Most of the people there are your friends, anyway.

Q. What advice would you give to someone who wants to work as an outrider?

A. I can't think of a better life for certain people. It doesn't suit all people, though. You have to be dedicated, love horses, and love the life. I look at it like this: most people get up in the morning and go to work; I can get up and go horseback riding. It is a passion for me. I've been doing it for 33 or 34 years.

Q. What personality traits should a person have who is interested in this career?

A. You've got to be a happy, diplomatic person. There are always things that you have to settle. It takes a certain kind of person.

Q. Is there anything else you would like to say about your career?

A. I must have been meant to do it. I can't think of anything else I'd rather be doing. I've truly enjoyed the outriding part of my career. I've caught a lot of horses. It's a great satisfaction to me to be good at what I do. It's been a great ride.

Career Spotlight

JULIET KAGNO, OUTRIDER

Juliet Kagno, or Julie as she is known around the track, is an outrider at Arlington Park International Racecourse in Illinois, and at Tampa Bay Downs in Florida. She has been an outrider for four years, getting her start after stepping in to help when an outrider was injured at Tampa Bay Downs.

At that time, she was racing horses. Julie has also been an exercise rider and pony rider; she has broken yearlings during her career in the racing industry. She has four horses—two Thoroughbreds, a quarter horse and a quarter horse/ Appaloosa cross. All of Julie's horses are kept at the track during meets unless injured; then, they are sent to a farm for lay up. In

between meets, her horses spend their time at the farm. Julie spends many of her nonworking hours on horseback as well. She enjoys pleasure and trail riding when she has the opportunity.

Q. How did you get involved with racing?

A. I rode horses for pleasure and lived near the racetrack as a kid. I got summer jobs hot walking, and then I started ponying and galloping racehorses. Thirteen years later, I started riding races. I started as a jockey after volunteering to ride a horse I had exercised for a long time—the horse came in third. I never thought I'd become a jockey because I like to eat, but I rode races for three-and-a-half years. When a job opened up for an outrider, I stopped racing. In this job, I get a regular, salaried paycheck and I can eat all I want!

Q. What are the specific duties of an outrider?

A. If a horse gets loose, it is the outrider's responsibility to catch him. The outrider takes care of emergencies, ensures horse and rider safety. The responsibilities of the outrider are big.

Q. What is your typical workday like?

A. I'm at the barn at 4:30 A.M. Training hours are from 5:30 A.M. to 10:30 A.M. and I'm out on the track during training hours. Following training, I go back to the barn and put away my morning horse. I use a different horse in the afternoon. I'm out there doing races until 5:15 P.M. or so, then I put the horse away and feed the horses. I'm done about 6:30 P.M. I work seven days a week. Even on dark days, I have to be there to care for my own horses.

Q. What do you enjoy most about your work?

A. The fact that I'm on my own horse. It's a challenge having your own horse that you've trained beneath you. When someone's life is at stake and you catch that loose horse, you know you've done a good job.

Q. What do you like least about it?

A. Sometimes, sitting on a horse for 10 hours a day can be very boring if nothing goes on.

Q. What is most rewarding about your career in racing?

A. As a jockey, it was winning races. As an outrider, it is being proud of training my own horses.

Q. What is the most challenging part of your career?

A. Keeping a good horse underneath you, keeping him sound, having him respond immediately to what you ask.

Q. What is your most memorable moment as a horsewoman?

A. I've loved winning races; also knowing that I rode a really good race even though I wasn't on the best horse. As an outrider, knowing that if I hadn't caught a loose horse someone would have been seriously injured. There was one incident when I stopped a horse whose saddle had slipped back and the rider's foot was wedged in the stirrup. I knew if I missed the horse, the rider would have been hurt. There was no possible way the horse was going to stop without the rider going underneath him.

Q. Was that frightening for you?

A. You don't feel fear at the time. You may feel it later when you replay the scene. When it is happening, you must react instantly; there is no time to panic.

Q. What personal strengths or skills should a person have who is considering this field?

A. The ability to ride horses, of course. They should be hardworking and responsible. They should be levelheaded and able to handle whatever happens, and have the ability to get along with people. With all the people and horses out there, you are a cross between a safety engineer and a traffic cop. You have to be able to tell people when they shouldn't have done something and they may get mad. That is something I'm still working on: getting along better.

Q. What advice would you give to someone interested in working as an outrider, or to someone interested in working in racing?

A. Everybody starts at the bottom walking hots or cleaning stalls. The hot walker walks the horses around the barn, cools them down, and gives them a drink. One way to get started, for someone who doesn't know anyone in racing, is to go to the stable gate early in the morning. You may find trainers looking for hot walkers. When the regular hot walkers don't show up, trainers will take gate people because they need people to walk the horses.

Gain as much riding experience as you can. I was taught to ride English, and as an outrider, I would have liked to know more about riding western. Outriders at most tracks ride western, as it's the most versatile, though English is still the tradition. In western you have a saddle horn to grab onto when you are swinging down and going 30 miles an hour.

Q. Do trainers use hot walking machines?

A. The better tracks don't have machines; the cheaper tracks are more likely to have them, though most trainers still use people to walk horses.

Q. If you could do it over, is there anything you would have done differently to reach your career goal?

A. When I started riding races, I might have gone further sooner if I had had a mentor. It would have helped me greatly if I had hooked up with an older rider.

Q. What has driven you to excel in your career?

A. My own hard work and determination and enjoyment of a challenge. I've always liked challenging myself to succeed.

Paddock, Patrol, and Placing Judges

ABOUT THE JOB

Racing judges include paddock judges, patrol judges, and placing judges. In harness racing, there is also a board of judges. The judges on the board are the top officials at harness racing meets, as stewards are in flat track racing.

Paddock judges are in charge of the paddock area. They are also responsible for supervising the assembly of horses in the paddock no later than 15 minutes before the scheduled post time for each race. These officials maintain security and order in the paddock, ensure the orderly saddling and equipping of horses, and verify that the equipment used is the same as that which has been previously listed to be used. These judges also ensure that all horses are mounted at the same time and leave the paddock for the post in the proper sequence. They also report to the stewards any cruelty to horses and any unusual or illegal activities they may observe. The paddock judges observe how horses behave in the paddock and have the authority to remove horses that behave poorly or that may possibly endanger the safety of other racing participants. The paddock judges maintain a list with the names of these horses and these animals must be schooled (overseen by the judges) in proper paddock behavior before they are allowed to race.

Patrol judges are stationed at various locations along the racetrack to watch for rule violations, lameness in horses, broken equipment, and unusual or illegal behavior by jockeys or drivers. (If the track has adequate video replay equipment, the use of a patrol judge is optional.) Racing commissions may also sometimes require gate judges to be present at the starting gate just prior to the running of races, to ensure that rules are followed.

Placing judges view races from the stands directly above the finish line and determine the order of horses as they cross the line. They are responsible for getting the numbers of the first four horses to cross the line posted on the total board. Placing judges review finish-line photos in disputed races and, once the correct order of the finish has been determined, post the photos in the grandstand and clubhouse areas for viewing. (Sometimes, stewards perform the duties of the placing judge.)

EDUCATION AND TRAINING

Extensive experience in racing, or a four-year equine degree with a racing, administrative, or managerial focus, and an internship in racing are essential.

SALARY

Salary is dependent upon the part of the country and track for which you work.

RESOURCES

Look into universities with racing programs, racing publications, and area racetracks; also check with state racing commissions for information on hiring practices.

Pari-Mutuel Personnel

ABOUT THE JOB

Pari-mutuel personnel manage, take, and place bets and work in the money room, where they are responsible for all money wagered and paid out. Managers also oversee clerks and money room personnel. ("Pari-mutuel" is a French expression meaning "betting among yourselves," rather than against the house.) Pari-mutuel clerks are often hired by racetracks for seasonal work. If you're interested in working in the pari-mutuel arena, you should be good with numbers, well organized, and comfortable handling money.

EDUCATION AND TRAINING

A high school diploma through a college education, depending on the level of responsibility you're seeking, is required. For those interested in managerial or senior-level positions, extensive experience in horse racing or a four-year equine degree with a racing, administrative, or managerial focus is important. An internship in racing is also important and a good way to get your foot in the door.

SALARY

Salary is dependent upon the part of the country, level of responsibility, and track for which you work.

RESOURCES

Investigate universities that have racing programs, racing publications, and area racetracks; also investigate state racing commissions for information on hiring practices.

Pony Rider

ABOUT THE JOB

Pony riders ride next to each racehorse and escort the horses to the starting gate and sometimes to morning training sessions. They may even gallop alongside racehorses during exercise sessions. Pony riders are independent contractors hired by racehorse trainers and they often own two or three ponies that they use as escorts. Pony riders are paid per horse escorted and may work for more than one trainer at a time. Racehorses are not required to be escorted. and whether they are escorted or not is up to the individual trainer.

Pony riders are expert riders who can safely keep sometimes-excitable racehorses from getting away, while also staying out of the way of the action at busy tracks. Some large racing stables may own their own ponies and hire someone to ride them.

EDUCATION AND TRAINING

A high school diploma and strong experience with a variety of horses is essential.

SALARY

Pony riders are paid a fee from the trainer per each horse escorted.

RESOURCES

Thoroughbred Times and other racing publications for industry contacts. Local racetracks may provide publications with the names and pertinent information on the trainers, owners, and jockeys on their racing circuit.

Racehorse Owner

ABOUT THE JOB

Racehorse ownership is not just for the wealthy anymore. There are many different ways to own racehorses, involving various levels of commitment in money and time. Some racehorse owners breed, train, and race their own horses. This method requires more money, time, and knowledge, of course, than buying a horse as part of a partnership or syndicate. In this type of ownership, all costs are shared, which is an increasingly popular path to racehorse ownership. There are also owners who buy one or more horses directly from a breeder, auction, private sale, or claiming race. They often do this with the help of a reliable bloodstock agent.

A person interested in racehorse ownership should consider his own situation. Is he in a suitable financial position? Does he have the knowledge to start a full-time breeding and racing operation or would a racing partnership or syndicate be a better option? Where you live as well as the type of racing and horse breeds you are interested in will also be determining factors. While harness racing is popular throughout the country, the largest followings are in the Midwest and the East, so if you don't live in these regions, consider whether you are willing to relocate. The breed of racehorse you buy will also have an effect on your pocketbook. Buying a quarter horse or Appaloosa for racing is less expensive than investing in a Thoroughbred.

To discover if owning racehorses is right for you, the best thing to do is educate yourself. Talk to trainers, owners, jockeys, and drivers; read racing publications; and contact racing organizations.

EDUCATION AND TRAINING
.A bachelor's degree in an equine field or in business administration is helpful.

SALARY
Income from owning racehorses may be small or large depending on a variety of factors: how many horses you own, whether you are the sole owner or part of a syndicate or partnership, and the successes of your horses, as well as how much money is outgoing for training, breeding, and more.

RESOURCES
Thoroughbred Owners and Breeders Association
P.O. Box 4367
Lexington, KY 40544-4367
www.toba.org

American Quarter Horse Association
P.O. Box 200
Amarillo, TX 79168-0001
www.aqha.com

United States Trotting Association
750 Michigan Ave.
Columbus, OH 43215
www.ustrotting.com

Racehorse Trainer

ABOUT THE JOB

Racehorse trainers are responsible for the training, management, and total well being of horses in their charge. In essence, they are the most important people in a racehorse's life. They evaluate the racehorse's potential; set up feeding and training programs; determine with owners where and when the horse will race based on the animal's abilities; supervise and hire the services of grooms, exercise riders, stable managers, and others involved in the horse's day-to-day care and training; and find the right jockey to ride him. They must also make contacts among racehorse owners to find employment.

Strong riding, horsemanship skills, knowledge of equine behavior and specifically of the breed being trained, and training methods are necessary for this position. Other helpful personal attributes include having good communication skills and a great amount of patience. Trainers in horseracing must pass a licensing examination, verifying they are qualified to work in the profession. The exam includes testing of horse knowledge as well as racing rules and regulations.

EDUCATION AND TRAINING

On-the-job training as an apprentice, participation in clinics, trade school attendance, or college degree in equine studies or science with classes in training methods. Business and marketing classes are also helpful as is experience in racing.

SALARY

In addition to training fees charged per horse, which vary, trainers receive a percentage of winnings for the horses they manage.

RESOURCES

United Thoroughbred Trainers of America
19800 W. Nine Mile Road
Southfield, MI 48075-3960

United States Trotting Association
750 Michigan Ave.
Columbus, OH 43215
www.ustrotting.com

Racing Groom

ABOUT THE JOB

Racing grooms rise early to get horses fed, groomed, tacked up, and their legs wrapped for morning exercise hours. They muck stalls, clean water buckets, bathe horses, and are the primary caretakers to an average of four horses every day. Grooms are an important link between trainers and horses and are invaluable in bringing any problems or illnesses to the trainers' attention.

Working as a racing groom can be rewarding in its own right for horse lovers, in spite of the often seven-day workweeks. Racing grooms have a lot of hands-on time with the horses, get to know each horse's personality well, and often form strong bonds with their equine charges. Working as a groom can also be a way to gain experience in the racing world for aspiring trainers, jockeys, drivers, and others. (Also see entry for "Groom" in Chapter 18.)

EDUCATION AND TRAINING

A high school diploma.

SALARY

$15,000 to $20,000 per year, often with room and board provided. Grooms may receive a small percentage of purses or bonuses tied to their horses' successes.

RESOURCES

Check *Thoroughbred Times* and other racing publications for industry contacts. Local racetracks may provide publications with the names and pertinent information on the trainers, owners, and jockeys on their racing circuit.

Racing Secretary

ABOUT THE JOB

Racing secretaries are senior racing officials who establish the conditions, or criteria under which each race is run, compile and publish condition books, ensure races are filled, and determine and assign handicap weights. Racing secretaries verify the eligibility for racing of all horses stabled at racetracks. They assign stall space and keep records of all horses on the grounds, including arrivals and departures, eligibility documents, and health testing certificates. They publish the official daily program and ensure the accuracy of its information, such as sequence of races and post times, the names of licensed owners, racing colors for each horse, the name of the trainer and jockey, and the weight to be carried.

EDUCATION AND TRAINING

A four-year degree in equine administration or other equine-related degree and extensive experience in official positions in the horseracing industry or as a horseman (owner, trainer, jockey), or a combination of the positions is required.

SALARY

Salary is dependent upon the part of the country and track for which you work.

RESOURCES

Contact universities with racing programs, racing publications, and area racetracks; also state racing commissions for information on hiring practices.

Stable Manager/Foreman

ABOUT THE JOB

Stable managers (or foremen) are hired by the trainers to manage the racing stable. They might also act as assistant trainers. Stable managers oversee racehorse care, including farrier and veterinarian visits, and grooming and feeding; they also supervise grooms and other employees. In-depth knowledge about racing and the needs of racehorses is required.

EDUCATION AND TRAINING

A four-year degree in equine studies or equine administration or similar, with stable management classes, plus experience in horseracing are necessary.

SALARY

Monthly salary plus a percentage of the purse.

RESOURCES

Check *Thoroughbred Times* and other racing publications for industry contacts. Local racetracks may provide publications with the names and pertinent information on the trainers, owners, and jockeys on racing circuits.

Starter

ABOUT THE JOB

Race starters are the track officials responsible for managing the starting gate and starting the race. They are in charge of all horses from the time they leave the paddock until the race begins, and they oversee tack changes or adjustments, withdrawals, or other issues that may occur. Starters make sure that horses enter the gate in the correct sequence and that all horses have a fair and equal start; they report to racing stewards any attempts to take an unfair advantage at the starting gate. Starters have the authority to remove horses from races who are not sufficiently trained in starting gate procedures; they also can require and supervise schooling of these horses. In addition, they observe and assess the ability of jockeys applying for licensing to break from the starting gate and report their assessments to the racing stewards.

Starters should be assertive and have good communication skills. They also need managerial skills to supervise assistant starters who help with the loading of horses into the starting gate.

EDUCATION AND TRAINING

Experience in racing or a four-year equine degree with a racing, administrative, or managerial focus and an internship in racing.

SALARY

Salary is dependent upon the part of the country and track for which you work.

RESOURCES

Universities with racing programs, racing publications, and area racetracks, also state racing commissions for information on hiring practices.

Steward (Judge in Harness Racing)

ABOUT THE JOB

Racing stewards (usually called judges in harness racing) are the highest ranking officials at races. They have authority over all racing officials, track management, and other licensed personnel. They interpret the rules of racing and decide all questions of racing not covered by the rules, resolve disputes, and discipline those in violation of the rules. Stewards are hired either by the state racing commission or by individual racetracks to ensure races are conducted in accordance with the rules of the state. They report to state racing commissions or boards.

Stewards view races to ensure fairness and conduct investigations into alleged violations of racing rules, serve as the final authority on photo finishes, oversee drug testing programs, approve or disapprove equipment changes, and approve licensing of workers. At the end of each race day, stewards file a report to the racing commissions detailing their actions and observations for that day's races. Each race meet has three stewards officiating.

Stewards must have strong managerial skills as well as being assertive. Being a good communicator is also an asset for stewards.

EDUCATION AND TRAINING
A four-year degree plus extensive experience in horseracing as a racing official, jockey/driver, owner, trainer, or some combination of these areas, and accreditation as a racing steward. Accreditation is offered through the *Race Track Industry Program* at Arizona State University and through the University of Louisville in Kentucky.

SALARY
Salary is dependent upon the part of the country and track for which you work.

RESOURCES
Consult state horseracing commissions and individual racetracks.

Timer

ABOUT THE JOB
Timers determine and report the official times of each race. They track the time the first horse crosses the timing beam or track marker at the start of the race until the first horse crosses the finish line. Timers may use both the automatic teletimer and a stopwatch to determine the race time. At the end of a race, the timer posts the official running time on the infield tote board. Timers also maintains written records of fractional and finish times of each race. Strong organization skills and an orientation to detail are important for this position.

EDUCATION AND TRAINING
Get experience in racing or an equine-related degree and internship.

Salary

No information available.

Resources

Check with universities with racing programs, racing publications, and area racetracks; also state racing commissions for information on hiring practices.

Track General Manager

About the job

General managers direct and oversee the day-to-day operations of tracks. They are ultimately responsible for ensuring the smooth operation of all departments at racetracks, allocating human resources, and ensuring compliance with regulatory agencies. Track general managers have excellent leadership, decision-making, and people skills.

Education and training

A minimum four-year degree from a racing industry program other equine field, or business is required. Extensive experience in horseracing and management is important.

Salary

Though salary is dependent upon the size of the track and area of the company, general managers may make from $140,000 to $230,000 per year.

Resources

Check with racetracks and state racing commissions; management organizations.

Official Veterinarian/Racing Veterinarian

About the job

In addition to veterinarians who care for the health of racehorses for individual trainers and owners (see more on veterinarians in Chapter 9, including a career spotlight of equine veterinarian Josh Hill), veterinarians in racing also hold official positions. The official veterinarian is employed by the state racing commission and holds the highest veterinary authority at the racetrack. The official veterinarian implements and oversees drug testing, recommends the removal of horses from races that he deems are unsafe to be raced (or he believes would be inhumane to race), supervises all other veterinarians practicing at the racetrack, and inspects and reports on conditions of horses. A racing veterinarian may also be on hand at race meets to assist the official veterinarian. The racing veterinarian is also employed by the state racing commission and is responsible to the official veterinarian. The racing veterinarian handles many of the hands-on activities, such as being present in the paddock during saddling and on the racetrack during the post parade and at the starting gate until the horses begin running. The racing veterinarian conducts soundness inspections prior to races and inspects any horses that seem to be in distress during or after the race. At smaller tracks the official veterinarian may carry out the duties of the racing veterinarian.

EDUCATION AND EXPERIENCE

Requirements include four years of pre-veterinary study, plus four years of veterinary school and a DVM degree, followed by passing a state licensing exam. Competition to get into veterinary school is intense, as there are only 28 accredited colleges of veterinary medicine in the United States. High school science coursework, an internship or part-time job working with horses, and strong grades in college pre-veterinary studies will increase the chances of being accepted to a school. Experience working in the racing field is required for veterinary official positions in racing, as well as licensing through the state racing commission.

SALARY

According to American Veterinary Medical Association statistics, the mean annual salary for state-employed veterinarians is $69,600.

RESOURCES

American Association of Equine Practitioners
4075 Iron Works Parkway
Lexington, KY 40511-8434
www.aaep.org

American Veterinary Medical Association
1931 N. Meacham Rd. #100
Schaumburg, IL 60173-4360
www.avma.org

CHAPTER 12

Human Health and Well-Being Careers

The educational requirements for careers in this section range from a high school diploma to a doctorate degree, but the common thread running through these jobs is the desire to help people, combined with a strong love of and respect for horses. While a variety of levels of horse experience are required, career seekers interested in these positions should first and foremost enjoy being around people and have strong communication skills.

Many of the jobs profiles in this chapter involve using horses to help heal humans. For example, did you know that speech language specialists use the movement of horses to treat people with impaired neuromuscular function? Or that therapists use horses to help someone with a stress disorder feel more confident? There are many opportunities to help people and gain horse experience.

Mounted Law Enforcement Officer

ABOUT THE JOB

Mounted law enforcement officers work for local, state, and federal public safety agencies as well as special police forces at colleges and universities. They handle crowd and traffic control; patrol parks, campuses, national forests, and city streets; pursue and arrest criminal suspects; and participate in parades and other events. Agencies and police forces have varied requirements for mounted law enforcement personnel, though most law enforcement officers are required to have some experience as field officers before being eligible for a mounted unit. The majority of mounted police officers own and care for their own horses.

Mounted police officers must have experience with horses (if they don't have it going into the police force, they can pursue riding instruction to become eligible), be in good physical shape, and have the characteristics necessary to work in law enforcement such as honesty, good judgment, and courage. They should also enjoy being around people and have good communication skills.

EDUCATION AND TRAINING

A minimum high school diploma (some agencies require a four-year degree in a law enforcement major such as criminal justice), police academy training and police background checks, as well as drug testing are required.

SALARY

The median annual salary for police and sheriff's patrol officers is $39,790.

RESOURCES

Check with the individual law enforcement agency or police department you are interested in for information on mounted units.

Mounted Security Patrol Officer

ABOUT THE JOB

Mounted security patrol officers work for private firms that provide security for special events, commercial projects, ranches, shopping malls, and other businesses. They are not law enforcement officers and do not carry weapons.

Mounted security patrol officers act as eyes and ears and contact law enforcement officers if needed. They also help with crowd and traffic control.

Strong riding skills are required as well as horse ownership or access to a horse. Like mounted police officers, mounted security patrol officers must enjoy being around people and have good communication skills as they are often approached by children and adults who want to talk about and pet the horses. Mounted security officers may be employees of the security service with full benefits or they may be freelance contractors. Requirements for both horses and security officers can be quite specific depending upon the employer.

EDUCATION AND TRAINING
A high school diploma, as well as training and testing through the employer for both horse and rider. Drug testing and background checks may be required. Some states require licensing. Check with the security licensing board for your state to learn more about specific requirements.

SALARY
While there are no data available for salaries of mounted security patrol officers, unmounted security officers receive a median annual income of $20,575, according to PayScale (www.payscale.com).

RESOURCES
Check with local security services or search the Internet under "mounted security patrols" or a similar phrase.

Physical Therapist, Occupational Therapist, Speech-Language Pathologist (Hippotherapy)

ABOUT THE JOB
Physical and occupational therapists and speech-language pathologists use the movement of the horse as a tool to treat people who have impaired neuromuscular function. This approach is called hippotherapy and is used in conjunction with other therapeutic methods. The therapist assesses the movement, gait, and size of individual horses to determine which horse will provide the appropriate amount of sensory stimulation to help each rider most successfully.

Therapists practicing hippotherapy must be licensed in their respective professions of physical or occupational therapy or speech-language pathology. Some therapists are also certified as therapeutic riding instructors; those therapists who are not certified as therapeutic riding instructors work in collaboration with therapeutic riding instructors during therapy sessions as an experienced horse person must be involved in each session. It is important to remember that the goal of hippotherapy is to improve function and mobility, not to teach riding. See the entry for Therapeutic Horsemanship Instructor for more on teaching people with disabilities to ride.

EDUCATION AND TRAINING

An appropriate degree and licensing in the respective health field, with additional training or certification in hippotherapy are necessary. The North American Riding for the Handicapped Association offers workshops as well as certification to experienced, licensed therapists.

SALARY

The general median annual earnings for therapists are as follows. (No specific figures are available for therapists who practice hippotherapy.)

Physical Therapist	$54,810
Occupational Therapist	$49,450
Speech-Language Pathologist	$46,640

RESOURCES

American Hippotherapy Association
North American Riding for the Handicapped Association
P.O. Box 33150
Denver, CO 80233
www.narha.org

Psychotherapist (Equine-Assisted Psychotherapy)

ABOUT THE JOB

Equine-assisted psychotherapy (EAP) is a mental health treatment method that involves horses in therapy. Licensed psychologists and other mental health practitioners use horses as partners to treat clients with a wide range of emotional, behavioral, and learning issues. They use both ground and mounted sessions to help child and adult clients increase self esteem, confidence and feelings of empowerment; improve coping skills and self-control; reduce stress and find physical and emotional balance; follow direction and concentrate better; improve communication skills; and more. As with hippotherapy, the goal of equine-assisted psychotherapy is not to teach riding and, in fact, the majority of sessions are unmounted.

Psychotherapists using equine-assisted psychotherapy may specialize in the field or they may be in a practice that uses a variety of treatment approaches. During EAP sessions, psychotherapists team with therapeutic riding instructors or other horse professionals who are themselves trained in EAP methods.

EDUCATION AND TRAINING
A master's or doctorate degree in psychology, social work, or therapy, plus licensing; additional training or certification in equine-assisted psychotherapy. (The two organizations listed below offer training and/or certification in equine-assisted psychotherapy.)

SALARY
The general median annual salary for psychologists is $48,596; social workers earn a median annual salary of $31,470. No specific figures are available for therapists who practice EAP.

RESOURCES
Equine Assisted Growth and Learning Association (EAGALA)
P.O. Box 993
Santaquin, Utah 84655
www.eagala.org

Equine Facilitated Mental Health Association
North American Riding for the Handicapped Association
P.O. Box 33150
Denver, CO 80233
www.narha.org

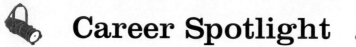

Career Spotlight

LINDA J. MYERS, MA, CCDCIII-E, LPC, NCACI, EQUINE-ASSISTED
PSYCHOTHERAPIST

Linda J. Myers was one of the first 15 therapists to be certified in Equine-Assisted Psychotherapy when she participated in the first certification program in the United States in 1997. Born in Cleveland, Linda has spent her life in Ohio. As a child, she loved riding horses, but she didn't realize a career with them until much later. After obtaining her master's at Kent State University, she pursued counseling. During her career as a psychotherapist and counselor for teens, she experienced many successes over the years, but eventually became discouraged when the lack of insurance support interfered with her ability to successfully treat clients. At that time, Linda was diagnosed with cancer and had to endure exhausting treatments. Her husband suggested she take up horseback riding to help her through this depressing time, and her horse was instrumental in her recovery. In

1997, Linda came across an article about EAP and she knew it was what she wanted to do. She flew out to Utah and went through the EAGALA (Equine Assisted Growth and Learning Association) program to receive her certificate. As a certified Equine-Assisted Psychotherapist, she now helps teens and others heal through horses.

Q. What made you decide to go into this field?

A. I had been a chemical dependency counselor working with adjudicated teens for more than 14 years and had seen some wonderful success in terms of long-term sobriety with my clients. Then, insurance companies were no longer allowing us to send clients to inpatient treatment facilities. Outpatient programs had developed, but we weren't seeing the same kind of success with teens that we had observed through inpatient care. I was discouraged and was actually considering a career move into real estate when I found out that I had cancer and had to take time off work for surgery, treatment, and recovery.

Though my cancer is currently in remission, the process of getting there left me physically exhausted and emotionally depressed. I had a horse as a child and loved to ride, so my husband suggested riding lessons, and I began riding weekly. I went from weekly riding lessons to leasing a horse to buying a horse and boarding him. My horse was instrumental in bringing me out of my depression and helping me through the recovery process. It was after an exhilarating trail ride that I drove home and opened the mailbox to find a copy of *The Counselor* magazine (Nov/Dec, 1997) and an article, "Straight from the Horse's Mouth, The Truth About Equine-Assisted Psychotherapy," written by Greg Kersten and Lynn Thomas. The article talked about using horses in a mental health setting with delinquent youth and how successful they'd been. I spent the next week trying to locate Greg and then flew out to Utah for the first certification program.

I now serve on the board of EAGALA, (Equine Assisted Growth and Learning Association) and have a very active EAP program incorporated into my practice. In fact, within a year of returning from Utah, my practice grew to the point that I was monopolizing the arena in the facility where we boarded my horse. The owner kindly suggested that we find another place to board because her boarders weren't able to get into the arena for riding lessons or to ride their horses.

My husband suggested that we sell our home and buy a farm. We bought an old Amish farm in rural Geauga County, with 15 acres and a century-old home. Before we began work on the house, we gutted the barn and put in box stalls. We built an indoor arena, and an office, waiting room, and bathroom for my clients. The practice is extremely successful and last year we worked with more than 500 people! The horse that was with me when I started the practice, Stoney, (or, "Stone Fox," which is his full name) has had the farm named after him. He is the second horse in the history of the Ohio Animal Hall of Fame to be inducted, and was named EAGALA's Outstanding Professional Horse for 2003.

Q. What does your job involve?

A. I'm really the only therapist here, so I do it all. I have a horse specialist who works with me. I do intake interviews and chemical dependency and mental health assessments in the office and I run a recovery group called Soberspace, which works with the horses on a weekly basis. I also do individual and family counseling and those clients also work with the horses, although not exclusively. In other words, I incorporate office-based counseling with EAP.

Q. How many horses do you have for your program?

A. I currently have three horses that I use on a routine basis for my EAP practice. Two of the horses travel to schools, universities, and a variety of places to provide different programs to students and even other professionals. For instance, Stoney and Okie, two of my geldings, traveled to a farm in Kirtland, Ohio, where they spent an afternoon teaching 40 therapists, teachers, and probation officers how to work with resistant clients.

Q. What type of facilities do you have for the program?

A. I have a barn and four pastures and a 60-by-80-foot indoor arena. I also have a group room in the barn that is heated and well insulated; this is used for family/group/team development sessions.

Q. How did you get your first job in this field?

A. I was already in private practice and had a solid referral source. I slowly began to incorporate EAP into my more traditional, office-based practice.

Q. What did you do prior to your current career?

A. I started out in juvenile court, working as an intake and probation officer. I was working on my master's degree at the time and then transitioned into practice as director of a local agency and as a consultant to various agencies. I eventually went into a full-time private practice. I've been in private practice for more than 24 years.

Q. What is your typical workday like?

A. Unfortunately, I don't really have a "typical" workday. Or maybe that's fortunate. My clients are usually scheduled between 9 A.M. and 5 P.M., with about two nights a week also spent with clients who can't make it during the day. I work with adolescents, so they must have transportation to and from appointments and that's difficult if parents work.

Q. How many hours/days per week do you typically work?

A. I usually work 10 to 12 hours a day, but that's not all spent with the horses. I have reports to write, case notes to file, phone calls to return. I also make home and school visits and about half of my day is spent in the more traditional style of office-based counseling. Sometimes, appointments may start out in the office and end up in the arena.

Q. What happens during a session with a client?

A. That depends on the client and the issue(s) trying to be addressed. Let me give you a brief example. I often work with clients who have sexual abuse issues and so being victimized is common to them. The residual effects of the sexual abuse may present themselves in sexual promiscuity and/or becoming victims in other areas of their lives. Not standing up for themselves and not perceiving themselves as having control over their environments or situations is a common problem. An exercise for clients like this is to have them move the horse forward and backward and around obstacles. They're on the ground working around the horse. They can't touch the horse, bribe the horse (or simulate bribery) and can't use a halter or a lead rope. They're often invited to use only the resources available to them in the arena. Clients struggle hard with this exercise but several things are accomplished: they learn how to gain the respect of the horse and how to maneuver the horse forward, backward, sideways, etc., just by using their body language and learning to read the horse's body language. They learn the basics of a healthy relationship (they can't bully the horse to go where they want him to go, but they also can't take a passive role and expect the job to be done on its own).

I had a six-year-old girl who learned to basically lunge the horse freestyle around the arena just by using body language. She was a sexual abuse victim and knowing that she had control over a 1,000-pound animal and could get him to go where she wanted just by being consistent and using her body language was an extremely empowering lesson for her.

Another example involves my recovering chemical dependency kids who have had a hard time breaking down a large task into smaller tasks. They were all working on a relapse prevention plan and couldn't figure out how to get from where they were now to where they needed to be if they should encounter a situation that was dangerous to their sobriety. So, we had the kids think about how they would teach a horse to kick a ball. They were to come back the next week with the steps broken down and be ready to demonstrate these steps to the rest of the group. They did that and then we divided them into teams and they used the techniques that they thought were most appropriate with the horses. Now, my horses kick a ball on command. The kids learned a lot of valuable lessons in this exercise. With goals based on my clients' issues, I go into the arena with a treatment plan just as I would if I were working with them in the office.

Q. What do you enjoy most about your work?

A. I love working with the horses. Watching my clients get involved in the challenge and the process they go through is wonderful.

Q. What do you like least about your work?

A. I really, really, really hate the bitter cold winters that we have here in Ohio. I personally don't enjoy working with the horses in extreme weather. If the weather is extremely hot, we have the arena to work in that is well ventilated and also shady. But in the winter, the arena is often bitter cold. Now, a real cowboy wouldn't let that bother him, but I definitely use the horses less in the winter than I do in the warmer climates.

Q. What is the most rewarding part of your job?

A. The most rewarding part is when I see the look in peoples' eyes when they finally get it. I love it when an hour in the arena is more productive than six weeks of hourly sessions in the office; when they understand that what they do, how they present themselves, and what they believe in truly does make a difference.

Q. What is the most challenging part of your job?

A. The most challenging part of my job is my work with adjudicated youth, especially the ones who don't want to be here and who make it very difficult for me to work with them.

Q. What is the biggest achievement of your career?

A. The biggest achievement of my career was developing a successful EAP practice at a time when no one knew what it was or how effective a form of treatment it could be. I was fortunate enough to be affiliated with a juvenile court that wanted to find an effective means of working with the youth as much as I did and they had enough faith in me to let me incorporate horses into my practice. Now that we're five to six years into this venture, we've seen recidivism rates drop dramatically, and the Ohio Department of Youth Services suggested that we write the program up as a model program for the state.

Q. What is the most challenging obstacle in your career?

A. The most challenging obstacle would probably be the naysayers—the traditional therapists who won't give this form of therapy a chance—yet.

Q. What advice would you give to someone interested in working in equine-facilitated psychotherapy?

A. Get certified by EAGALA and network with others doing the same, get active, read everything you can get your hands on about therapy (if you're the horse specialist) or horse psychology (if you're the therapist and not very familiar with horses) and go out there and get yourself some experience. It's hard to break old habits, but once you see the power of this form of therapy, you'll never want to go back to what you were doing before.

Q. What personality traits do you believe a person should have who is considering this field?

A. Anyone wanting to do EAP needs to be flexible. As the therapist, I can go out to the arena with a treatment plan in hand and something entirely different may happen. You need to be prepared to take what you're given (in the session) and help the client process it. I think anyone wanting to do EAP has to have a great sense of humor. People wanting to do this form of work can't be afraid of trying new things and they can't always be in control.

Q. Is there anything else you would like to say about your career?

A. It's wonderful! I've never had so much fun doing therapy. I'm in the sunshine; I get to work with my best friends (my three horses and my horse specialist); the wonderful folks at EAGALA who have provided me with a tremendous amount of support surround me. I also have the most wonderful husband that God ever made. He just built us a group room in the barn, my office, and a waiting room. He keeps my arenas groomed, he's incredibly supportive, and I definitely could not have done this without him by my side.

Sports Psychologist

ABOUT THE JOB

Sports psychologists work with both amateur and professional riders and help them achieve peak physical and mental performance. Using imagery, relaxation techniques, concentration training, and other methods, they help riders reach their competitive goals while also seeking to improve the dynamic partnership between the human and equine athletes. Sports psychologists counsel riders in English and western disciplines, jockeys, and harness drivers; they also may work with non-riders involved in equine sports, such as racehorse trainers.

To maintain a thriving practice, most sports psychologists represent athletes in several sports and, if they are licensed psychologists or therapists (as many sports psychologists are), they are also clinical practitioners, who counsel people in areas unrelated to riding or sports psychology. Some sports psychologists are trained in sports science rather than psychology, so they may work in other areas of the sports world or teach to supplement their incomes.

Sports psychologists working with equestrians are not expected to be better riders than their clients, but they should have a working knowledge of riding and horses and be comfortable with asking questions of their clients to improve that knowledge.

EDUCATION AND TRAINING

A doctorate in psychology with additional training in sports psychology and sports sciences, or doctorate in sports sciences or sports psychology with additional training in psychology or counseling psychology is required.

SALARY

The median annual salary for clinical psychologists is $65,000 according to a survey by the American Psychological Association.

RESOURCES

Certification from the Association for the Advancement of Applied Sports Psychology (AAASP)
801 Main St., Suite 010
Louisville, CO 80027
www.aaasponline.org

American Psychological Association
750 First Street, NE
Washington, DC 20002-4242
www.apa.org

Career Spotlight

KATHLEEN ZECHMEISTER, PHD, MFT, PSYCHOTHERAPIST AND
PERFORMANCE ENHANCEMENT CONSULTANT

Kathleen Zechmeister is a licensed psychotherapist and performance enhancement consultant who specializes in the psychology of human performance. She practices in Southern California, where she was born and raised, and has worked in the field of sports psychology since 1986. Kathleen's equestrian clients include athletes involved in horse racing, jumping, dressage, and barrel racing. She also works with runners, golfers, swimmers, cyclists, race car drivers, and volleyball players. In addition to her work in helping athletes excel, Kathleen is a licensed marriage and family therapist who counsels individuals, couples, children, and families. She is a horse person herself and owns a retired 14-year-old Thoroughbred racehorse she uses for pleasure riding, named Yukon Robbery; he is a grandson of Northern Dancer. Other animals that share Kathleen's life include three dogs, two cats, and three birds. She is married with two children, a boy and girl, adopted from Ethiopia.

Q. What does your job in sports psychology involve?

A. My job involves interviewing, testing, and developing performance enhancement programs for individuals and teams trying to improve performance, increase concentration or motivation, develop and complete specific goals, overcome psychological aspects of sports-related injuries, or decrease anxiety. I also serve as an expert witness for attorneys defending athletes suffering negative psychological symptoms from sports-related injuries, e.g., posttraumatic stress disorder.

Q. What is your typical workday like?

A. A typical workday includes meeting with clients, analyzing previously performed tests, completing session notes and treatment plans, and returning telephone calls. I also have to work the business side, such as accounting, updating ledgers, and reviewing potential marketing materials.

Q. How many hours per week do you usually work?

A. Being self-employed, I have the luxury of setting up my own schedule. Most clinicians are comfortable with about six client hours of face-to-face counseling a day and one day off.

Q. What is the most rewarding part of your work?

A. The part of my work that is most rewarding is seeing a client overcome an issue that previously placed limitations on his or her life. Watching a big breakthrough occur that brings happiness into a person's life is a very joyous experience.

Q. What do you like least about the work?

A. I don't think I will ever enjoy insurance paperwork, no matter how easy they make it! I have an individual who does all my billing for me, which helps dramatically.

Q. What do you find most challenging about your work?

A. The most challenging part of being a sports psychologist is when parents bring in their child athletes to "make sure they stay in competition" so they can get a scholarship and the athletes confide that they want to retire from the sport.

Q. What is the biggest achievement in your career?

A. A great accomplishment for me is when I can help an athlete overcome post traumatic stress disorder or overtraining and make it to the Nationals or the Olympics.

Q. What is your biggest obstacle?

A. My biggest obstacle is that some coaches are somewhat reluctant to refer their athletes to sports psychologists/performance enhancement consultants when their athletes clearly are dealing with a psychological challenge versus a technical/physical challenge.

Q. What has driven you to excel?

A. I grew up in a family where we were taught to be the best we could be, whether it was in friendship or marriage, school or the workplace. That strong work ethic, along with a belief in the importance of helping others and obtaining a good education, were, I believe, quite instrumental in directing my career path.

Q. When did you know you wanted to work in sports psychology?

A. When I was working on a master's degree. I originally wanted to pursue experimental psychology, which is the research side of psychology. I had always been interested, though, in working with athletes and one of my professors recommended that I pursue a master's in marriage and family counseling and follow it up with a license so I could practice as a clinician and work with athletes. I took his advice and then, in order to improve my credibility, I pursued a doctorate, which enables me to perform psychological testing and specialize in the performance aspects of sports injuries.

Q. What is your background with horses?

A. I rode as a child at my uncle's farm and on family vacations. My mother's love of horses, especially her love of horseracing, was shared with us growing up. When my son began riding lessons four years ago, I resumed my riding as a way of taking care of my body and soul. As my husband and I continued riding, we decided to invest in a pleasure horse.

I have always loved the strength and sensitivity of horses. As a therapist, I am well aware of their therapeutic benefits in the treatment of depression, anxiety, gang affiliation, prison rehabilitation, and more.

Q. Do you have any other horse industry experience?

A. I'm involved in Thoroughbred horseracing as an owner in a few partnerships and have plans for involvement in the breeding aspect of the Thoroughbred industry.

Q. What is most memorable to you as a horse person?

A. It has been most memorable seeing the loving relationship my son has with horses. This love has helped heal the pain in his life due to having a family member deal with a serious illness.

Q. Is having horse experience necessary to be successful?

A. I believe that in order to work with specific sports as a performance enhancement consultant, an individual needs to have a good understanding of the different dynamics in the sport and of the athlete's physical and psychological challenges.

Q. Are you around horses as part of your job?

A. Only when I'm watching a competition to observe the rider and gain a better understanding of the rider's challenges, or if I'm using horse contact as a form of therapy.

Q. What education and experience do you recommend for someone interested in the field?

A. If you want to be a sports psychologist or work in the field of performance enhancement, it's important to obtain a master's or PhD in counseling, sports psychology and/or clinical psychology. In California, to perform counseling, an individual must obtain a counseling license or obtain a doctorate and then take the clinical psychologist exam. This way, if an athlete has a personal problem, you can legally and ethically counsel him, you don't have to refer out to a clinician, and you can treat the entire athlete. Throughout the education process, work with athletes whenever and however you can.

There is a long-standing feud between the physical education field and the psychology field as to which field should govern sports psychology. There are very few graduate programs in sports psychology and a few doctoral programs. If an individual is interested in the research aspect of sports psychology, then a master's degree or PhD in sports psychology would help land a research and/or teaching position. On the other hand, if you are interested in applied sports psychology, a graduate degree in sports psychology and a doctorate in clinical psychology with an emphasis on sports psychology will provide the educational requirements for taking the exam to become a clinical psychologist in California (check your state for licensing requirements), it will also help you prepare for working one-on-one with athletes in a variety of settings. This education will also provide you the ability to perform testing and interpersonal counseling if necessary.

Q. What personal strengths or skills should a person have who is considering this field?

A. Strengths and skills needed include effective writing and speaking skills, self-motivation, marketing knowledge, and patience to remember that developing a successful private practice requires time and consistent networking, community outreach, and perseverance.

Q. What advice would you give to someone who wants to work with riders as a sports psychologist?

A. Don't let anybody stop you if it's what you want to do. Share your knowledge by writing articles in horse magazines on specific performance enhancement topics. Do consistent advertising to expose your name to riders. Minimally, take some riding lessons and spend time watching horses to become acquainted with them, because riders will be skeptical if you have never ridden and you're offering them advice. Seek out internships with individuals already established in the field.

Q. What do you think the job outlook is for sports psychologists in the horse world?

A. I think the job outlook is positive in riding. The United States Equestrian Team has psychologists to assist the team and there is a greater acceptance, generally, of psychological assistance. There is still a negative stigma attached to jockeys seeking help, much to my dismay, though it is improving a little bit.

Q. In very general terms, what level of income do you believe someone starting out can expect?

A. If a young professional has adequate educational experience and a license, he can expect to receive $75 per hour, starting out.

Q. Is there anything else you'd like to say about your career or life with horses?

A. The more involved I have become with the different equestrian fields, the more respect I've gained for these strong yet fragile, loving yet assertive, playful, and tender creatures.

Therapeutic Horsemanship Instructor

ABOUT THE JOB

Therapeutic horsemanship instructors teach riding and general horsemanship to children and adults with disabilities. Group or private lessons may be in English, western, bareback, or even in specialty areas such as driving or interactive vaulting. All instructors must be highly experienced with horses, have strong communication and teaching skills, be focused on safety, and have a great deal of patience.

Instructors may wear many or few hats, depending on the size of the program. In small programs, instructors recruit and train volunteers, groom and tack up horses, and plan and give lessons. Large programs with many volunteers and staff members might have several riding instructors who focus mainly on planning and giving lessons. While some riding instructors are volunteers, the majority of paid therapeutic riding instructors work in this field part-time.

EDUCATION AND TRAINING

There are several different ways to enter the field: a four-year college degree in therapeutic riding instruction, a degree in equine studies with a minor in therapeutic riding instruction, attendance at a riding instruction program, or volunteering for a therapeutic riding program and working your way up. Certification is available through NARHA and the Certified Horsemanship Association.

SALARY

The average wage for part-time therapeutic riding instructors across the country is approximately $14 per hour, according to a 1998 survey by the North American Riding for the Handicapped Association. Full-time instructors (full-time is defined as 32 hours per week or more) receive an average salary of $21,811 per year.

RESOURCES

North American Riding for the
Handicapped Association
P.O. Box 33150
Denver, CO 80233
www.narha.org

Certified Horsemanship Association
5318 Old Bullard Road
Tyler, TX 75703
www.cha-ahse.org

Career Spotlight

LORRIE RENKER, MASTER THERAPEUTIC RIDING INSTRUCTOR

Lorrie Renker is a master therapeutic riding instructor certified by the North American Riding for the Handicapped Association. Growing up, she was the typical kid who wanted a horse and hung out at the local stable. It was there that she had her first exposure to people with disabilities. The stable owner lost an arm in a machine accident and worked to combine kids with disabilities and horses. As a teenager, Lorrie helped out unofficially with that local riding program, and after high school, moved to Martha's Vineyard, where she worked with young riders at a camp for kids with cerebral palsy. Her formal entry into the world of therapeutic riding came in 1983. After marrying the local blacksmith on Martha's Vineyard, the couple moved to Wisconsin. There, Lorrie co-founded the Three Gaits therapeutic riding program, which began as a pilot program with two borrowed horses and eight riders. She now lives with her husband in New York.

Q. Do you currently work in therapeutic riding?

A. Yes. I am currently self-employed. I conduct workshops for therapeutic riding instructors and interactive vaulting workshops, consult, and develop online educational opportunities for the therapeutic riding industry. I am working on an introduction to therapeutic horsemanship book with a colleague. My focus has been on the education of therapeutic riding instructors. I actively taught therapeutic horsemanship until the fall of 2001.

Q. What does the job as a therapeutic riding instructor involve?

A. Many therapeutic riding instructors working in small programs must do everything. They are kind of a one-man band. Larger centers have more focused positions such as a program director who organizes all the lessons and activities as well as teaching lessons.

Q. How does teaching therapeutic riding differ from teaching general riding?

A. I personally don't think it differs that much. You have to be a knowledgeable horse person, understand horse behavior, people behavior, and know how to teach and what to teach within a systematic progression. Depending on the types of disabilities that you work with, you have to have increased knowledge about characteristics of the particular disabilities in order to safely and effectively teach each individual. For example, if you work with someone who is hypertonic then you need to know the precautions, contraindications, best teaching practices, etc. to be most effective. If anything, a therapeutic riding instructor has to be more knowledgeable than a riding instructor for folks without disabilities.

Q. How does a person become trained as a therapeutic riding instructor?

A. There are different options for training. A person can choose to attend a four-year college and receive a degree in therapeutic riding or perhaps a minor or a concentration. There are several training programs around the country that offer month or longer courses for folks who want to become therapeutic riding instructors. Some of the colleges and training courses are recognized by NARHA as approved training courses and can receive certification through the training course if they meet the requirements. There are also workshops that folks can attend such as a two-day entry-level workshop or a more advanced workshop. Often people who are interested in becoming TR instructors come up through the ranks. They volunteer at a program and then become more involved and start teaching and then decide to pursue certification. Some people choose to be mentored by another instructor. One thing that often happens is that people think teaching therapeutic riding is easier, it is not. The instructor has to be a knowledgeable and safe horseperson first and foremost. The United States does not have a federation that makes things more structured. In many other countries a person must be a recognized riding instructor before they can pursue teaching therapeutic riding.

Q. What is a typical workday like?

A. It depends on the program. The larger programs will have several instructors working full-time. They will have teaching responsibilities, paperwork, lesson planning, progress notes, perhaps working with the horses, etc. Other programs that are small may only operate one day a week and the instructor is it, so they have to get the horses ready, provide training, train the volunteers, teach the lessons, etc.

Q. How many students/classes would typically be taught in one day?

A. Again, it depends on the program and resources of the program. Some programs might have two horses and can only teach two riders at a time. So that would determine the numbers. Large programs might have 40 head of horses and two rings and could teach four to six riders in a class. They might have 200 – 400 riders per week. There is a standard related to how many hours a day a horse can work. Usually six is the upper limit in a class and many instructors prefer to teach no more than four or even private sessions.

Q. How many hours/days per week do you typically work?

A. When I was working full-time in a TR program it was just like any other horse endeavor. Many instructors are part-time and teach their lessons. Often they are paid for the lesson and time to prepare and evaluate. So a good rule of thumb might be two hours for an hour lesson.

Q. What do you enjoy most about the work?

A. To be able to combine both my interests: horses and teaching. It is also dynamic and not static—it is something different all the time.

Q. What do you like least about the work?

A. It is difficult to work with riders who have a progressive disease who will eventually worsen and perhaps have to discontinue riding and may even die. I also don't like the fundraising part of trying to make ends meet.

Q. What is your educational background?

A. I have a degree in elementary education and graduate credits in special education. I attended the Cheff Center therapeutic riding instructor program in Michigan in 1985.

Q. What is the most rewarding part of being a therapeutic riding instructor?

A. The most rewarding part for me has been being able to teach and share the benefits of the horse with people. I think that teaching college students and future riding instructors has been the most rewarding. It means that I will be affecting so many riders by helping produce quality therapeutic riding instructors.

Q. What is the most challenging part of your career?

A. Figuring out how to improve instructional skills of riding instructors who don't seem to have a natural ability for teaching. Also to figure out the best teaching methodology to improve a rider's skills physically and cognitively.

Q. What is the biggest achievement of your career?

A. Receiving the James Brady Professional Achievement award.

Q. What has driven you to excel in your career?

A. I believe in the magic of the horse. I always said that if my horse could talk when I was in high school, I would be in big trouble . . . because I told him everything. He listened and never passed judgment. I think the horse can provide motivation to achieve so much. So many people (disabled and non-disabled) have not had the exposure to animals. I have pursued the education part because I think that is so lacking in the horse industry in general. I have seen so many riding instructors that are not very good because either they do not have the horse knowledge to be able to teach the skills or they don't have the knowledge of how to teach (communication, learning styles, clarity, etc). There is more to teaching riding then standing in the center of the arena and directing traffic. People need to understand and have compassion for the horse as well. There are so many ill-fitting saddles, hurting horses because people are riding poorly or providing training techniques that are abusive. I want to help make a difference. I have happened to choose to do that in the therapeutic riding field because I think people are more open to learning how to teach because the addition of the disability poses an additional challenge.

Q. What combination of education and/or experience do you advise for someone interested in becoming a therapeutic riding instructor?

A. Become a knowledgeable and safe horse person (including competent riding skills). Volunteer at a therapeutic riding program to determine if therapeutic riding is what you want to do (some people decide it is not for them or they may decide to focus in certain areas). Determine what areas you want to work in. If it is therapeutic riding determine what educational opportunities will work best for you (a weekend course, a month course, distance education, four years at college). If you want to be a therapist and provide hippotherapy or psychotherapy, then a four or five (or more) year college degree is mandatory. Teach riding to improve skills. Finding a mentor is ideal. Start by teaching riders without disabilities to become familiar with ring control, riding skill progression, the whats, hows, and whys, lesson planning and evaluation, and problem solving. Then add the disabilities.

Q. What personal advice would you give to someone who wants to pursue a career within the horse industry?

A. Strive to be a caring, safe horseperson. I see so many instructors who don't have the safety ingrained or who are unable to read their horses. So many horses come to TR programs because they are no longer useful in their previous lives and often it seems like many of the problems may have been able to be prevented with correct riding and attention to the horse's needs. Learn as much as you can about many different areas related to horses. Know how to fit a saddle so the horse won't hurt because of poor saddle fit. Know how to use training aids to not restrict horse's natural movement and cause issues later on. Realize that the horse is a part of the equation and should be treated with respect and understanding.

If someone is pursuing a teaching career, learn how to teach. I don't mean standing in the middle of the arena and shouting out directions like a traffic cop. Learn how to clearly teach the hows of riding—how to do something, not just to do it. Add the whys to add meaning. Understand progression. Develop an eye for body alignment. Be a detective and a problem solver.

Q. If you could do it over, is there anything you would have done differently to reach your career goal?

A. I would have finished my master's degree and perhaps pursued a doctorate to help give credibility to the profession.

Q. What do you think the future outlook is for therapeutic riding instruction?

A. I think it has a good future outlook. I also think that therapeutic riding will affect the teaching of riding in general. In order to teach people with challenges, the riding instructor has to increase knowledge of how to teach and that knowledge can be helpful in improving the teaching skills of all riding instructors.

Q. Is there anything else you would like to say about your career?

A. It has been very rewarding to be able to combine horses and teaching (my two loves) to affect the lives of persons with disabilities as well as those instructors who teach riders with disabilities.

I have also enjoyed working with the national association (NARHA) as it has given me the opportunity to meet lots and lots of great people across the country and across the world. The input of so many different people with so many different backgrounds has been enlightening and stimulating. There are a lot of great people working in this field. It has helped keep my mind open and accepting to new ideas and methods.

Therapeutic Riding Program Director

ABOUT THE JOB
Larger therapeutic riding programs have program directors who run the day-to-day activities of the program. They handle public relations and fund-raising, recruit volunteers, organize lessons and other activities, manage the budget, and, depending on their backgrounds, may also teach riding.

In addition to the skills discussed in the description of the therapeutic horsemanship instructor, directors of therapeutic riding programs must have strong management, communication, organizational, and business skills.

EDUCATION AND TRAINING
Important are a degree in business, equine studies, or other area, as well as experience working with the disabled, managing a riding program, or working with nonprofit organizations.

SALARY
No information available.

RESOURCES
North American Riding for the Handicapped Association (NARHA)
P.O. Box 33150
Denver, CO 80233
www.narha.org

Certified Horsemanship Association
5318 Old Bullard Road
Tyler, TX 75703
www.cha-ahse.org

CHAPTER 13

Industry Service Careers

— — —

Wherever you find horses, you'll find horse owners who need a variety of equine-related services. Businesses that cater to the horse industry offer everything from laundering horse clothes to restoring tack and carriages to caring for horses when owners are out of town. Most of these careers involve running your own small business, so being organized and having marketing and business administration skills is important to your success. Many of these businesses find customers by setting up booths and advertising at horse shows, advertising over the Internet, and distributing information to tack shops and area stables. Word of mouth in the equestrian community is also a way of gaining business, so having an excellent reputation is essential.

Blanket Cleaning Service Operator

ABOUT THE JOB

Blanket cleaning services clean and repair blankets and other horse clothes. The spring and summer months are especially busy times for these service providers. The blankets come off and are ready for cleaning after they've kept the horses warm during the fall and winter. Blanket cleaning services may pick up blankets for cleaning and repair, provide walk-in service, accept dirty and torn blankets through the mail, or use a combination of these methods to accommodate customers. Because it can be difficult to make a full-time living by exclusively cleaning and repairing blankets and other horse clothes (especially during the slower cold-weather periods), many businesses offer other services such as making stall curtains and banners for shows, embroidery, tack repair, boot fitting, and clipper sharpening. Some blanket cleaning service owners may also work in jobs outside the horse industry.

Running a blanket cleaning service takes business and marketing skills. Horse experience is not required but is helpful to know how to find customers and market the service.

EDUCATION AND TRAINING

A high school diploma and on-the-job training; sewing and business skills; a college degree in business, or college-level courses in business administration and management and marketing are helpful.

SALARY

Blanket cleaning services charge per item, with fees dependent on the size and weight of the item and sometimes the condition. Some blanket cleaning services charge $5 to $10 for saddle pad cleaning, $10 to $25 for blankets, and $5 to $20 for blanket repairs depending upon the severity of the damage.

RESOURCES

Check with local barns and farms, tack and feed stores, horse publications, and the Internet.

Career Spotlight

KATHLEEN CONKLIN, HORSE BLANKET CLEANING AND REPAIR

Kathleen Conklin started her blanket cleaning and repair business 25 years ago when she had trouble finding such a service for her own horses. In addition to cleaning and repairing blankets, Kathleen combined her creative skills as a seamstress and her knowledge of horses and expanded her business to include making stall drapes, valances, carriage covers, customized banners, and custom equipment for the mounted police. She also is a desktop publisher and works part-time for the state government. Kathleen grew up near the Hudson River in New York State, not far from where she currently lives, and majored in fine arts in college. For many years, Kathleen competed in the hunter/jumper world and enjoyed fox hunting. When her 10-year-old Belgian/saddlebred-cross mare developed a breathing disorder, Kathleen decided to make a change. She searched for and found the perfect mule—John Henry—to replace her horse. Her current passion now involves competing in combined driving and pleasure driving. John Henry has won numerous awards and achieved many mule firsts in driving competitions. His competition successes influenced the American Horse Show Association, now U.S. Equestrian, to admit mules in all levels of combined driving after a 50-year ban. Not only are Kathleen and John Henry well recognized in the driving world, but John Henry also has his own mule advice column in *The Brayer*, called, "Ask John Henry."

Q. What made you decide to go into the field of blanket cleaning and repair?

A. Necessity and convenience. I couldn't find anyone to do blanket cleaning and repair and I was a competent seamstress and horse person who understood the requirements involved in horse gear.

Q. How many people does your service employ?

A. Just me.

Q. What is your job?

A. I clean and repair all kinds of horse blankets. I also make stall drapes, trunk covers, mounted police saddle pads, barn banners, and carriage covers.

Q. What is your typical workday like?

A. I work at my state job two days a week and do the blanket business the rest of the week. As with most home-based businesses, I have no set hours and am able to work it in between other things, like going to the barn, a lesson, or a competition.

Q. How many hours/days per week do you typically work?

A. It varies according to the workload. Usually, I am slow in the middle of winter and work lots of hours in the spring and fall. I just started to make carriage covers and that seems to fill out the slow periods in my schedule.

Q. What do you enjoy most about your work?

A. I really like to sew and I also like the ability to walk away from it for a while when I'm tired, but most of all, I like the people I deal with. It is fun meeting horse people from lots of different disciplines.

Q. What do you like least about your work?

A. Well . . . my husband has a fit when I get bags of blankets that have barn mice in them! I can always tell because my Jack Russell terriers go on the hunt in the basement where I work . . . a sure sign of a new mouse!

Q. What is your overall background with horses?

A. I started out, and competed for years, in the hunter/jumper world—both in U.S. Equestrian A-rated shows and quarter horse A-rated shows. I fox hunted for 13 years and in the last six, I have been competing John Henry in combined driving and pleasure driving all up and down the East Coast.

Q. How did you get involved with mules?

A. I had horses for about 20 years and wanted a new challenge. I had met a pair of mules owned by a local woman many years before. They were wonderful animals, and I always kept it in the back of my mind that maybe, someday, I would get a mule. Mules are very rewarding animals to own—mules want to be dogs and horses want to be cats!

Q. What is your most memorable moment in the horse industry?

A. Another part of my business is making mounted police saddle pads and I have designed and made pads for Washington, D.C. Metro Police and the U.S. Department of Justice Border Patrol in California, among many. The most memorable and sad moment was when a police department from California called me for a rush order of mounted police saddle pads because they just had an officer killed in the line of duty and needed them for the funeral. Needless to say, I got them out in time, but it was a sad deadline to keep.

Q. What is the most rewarding part of your job?

A. I actually like knowing that I can save owners money by repairing their horse blankets. If blankets are cleaned and repaired at least once a year, they really can last a long time.

Q. What is the most challenging part of your job?

A. I think that the most challenging part of my job is the design and creation of all the banners I make. Each one is different and has to reflect the interests of the person who ordered it.

Q. What advice would you give to someone interested in working in blanket repair and cleaning?

A. Start small. Do all your own cleaning and repair and then expand to your horse friends and barn friends. From there, you will naturally get word-of-mouth advertising.

Q. What education and/or experience do you recommend for someone interested in working in this field?

A. Know how to sew; know about horse blankets; buy industrial sewing and washing machines; and make sure horse hair and dirt don't offend you!

Q. What personality traits do you believe a person should have who is considering this field?

A. I think that it is important NOT to be a neat freak because it is impossible to have dirty horse blankets all around and also be super neat.

Carriage Builder/Restorer/Dealer

ABOUT THE JOB

People involved in the carriage trade restore carriages, build and sell carriages, buy old or used carriages, restore carriages for resale, or act as sales agents between carriage buyers and sellers. Some carriage dealers build carriages to order, while others build carriages and keep them in stock; others trade in and restore antique and used carriages. Dealers sell carriages to carriage tour operators, pleasure drivers, and driving class participants. They may participate in some or all of these activities as a part-time hobby or business, or go into it as a full-time operation. What successful people in the carriage trade have in common is a deep interest in history and a love for the beauty and craftsmanship of carriages.

To learn more about carriages and carriage building, visit the Web sites for The Carriage Museum of America Library and The Carriage Association of America. Both offer books and magazines about carriages and driving. Also, visit your local library, surf the Internet, or visit a carriage builder or carriage museum in your area.

EDUCATION AND TRAINING

A high school diploma. To truly appreciate the craft, seek training in woodworking, carpentry, wheelrighting, and smithery; an apprenticeship with a carriage builder; and marketing or business classes are helpful as well.

SALARY

Carriage builders charge in the hundreds to thousands of dollars for carriages. The number of carriages you build and repair minus your expenses will determine how much you earn at this trade.

RESOURCES

The Carriage Association of America
177 Pointers - Auburn Road
Salem, NY 08079
www.caaonline.com

Carriage Museum of America Library
P.O. Box 417
Bird-in-Hand, PA 17505
www.carriagemuseumlibrary.org

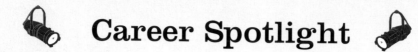

Career Spotlight

Bill Twigg, Carriage Builder and Wheelwright

Bill Twigg, owner of Moscow Carriage Co. in Idaho has built and restored horse carriages and wooden wheels for 21 years. His work started as a hobby after he met Mel DeWitt, who built wheels and carriages as a retirement hobby and

became Bill's mentor. Bill learned what he could from Mel and then added to his own knowledge by reading, experimenting, and learning from other craftsmen. After two years of working at his hobby, Bill quit his day job to pursue his craft full-time. A few years later, Moscow Carriage Company was born.

Q. What made you start Moscow Carriage Company?

A. My wife and I discussed the idea of starting Moscow Carriage and decided that it just was the right thing to do.

Q. What does your job involve?

A. I build new and repair old wooden wheels; build new and repair old carriages, wagons, and sleighs; manufacture wheelwright equipment; and teach wheelrighting and other related skills. These things involve design work, woodwork, metalwork, painting, upholstering, and pin striping.

Q. What is your typical workday like?

A. I typically start the day around 7:00 A.M., catching up on phone calls, e-mail, and paperwork. Then, I'm off to the shop to work on whatever job or jobs I currently have. (For example, my next jobs will be repairing wheels and starting restoration work on a sleigh.) Phone calls and drop-in visitors are common throughout the day. Somewhere in the 4:00 P.M. to 7:00 P.M. range, I quit for the day.

Q. How many hours per week do you usually work?

A. I put in between 40 and 60 hours a week and hope to charge out at least 30 of those hours.

Q. What do you enjoy most about your work?

A. Working with my hands. I enjoy starting with a customer's idea, designing the carriage, and then building it.

Q. What do you like least about your work?

A. Paperwork.

Q. What is the most rewarding part of your job?

A. Hearing from satisfied customers after years of using the carriage I built for them.

Q. What is the most challenging part of your job?

A. Dealing with myself. My business treats me much better than I treat it.

Q. What is your educational background?

A. I have a bachelor's of science degree in forestry from the University of Idaho.

Q. What is your overall background with horses?

A. Not much. I've ridden about 30 miles and driven about 3,000 miles.

Q. Do you have any horses?

A. I don't have any horses at this time. The horses I've had in the past were Morgan/Percheron crosses.

Q. What advice would you give to someone interested in working as a wheelwright or building and restoring carriages?

A. Learn to do the work correctly, learn to deal honestly and fairly with customers and suppliers, recognize that it will not make you wealthy, and that it is work.

Q. How high is the demand for wheelwright and carriage building and restoration services?

A. I don't know how to answer this question other than to say that I steadily have from three to six months of work waiting for me. My orders come in from all over the United States and parts of Canada.

Q. What education and experience do you recommend for someone interested in working in these fields?

A. Generally, gain experience working with your hands and have an aptitude for mechanics. Get training in the specific skills of wheelrighting, woodworking, welding, forging, upholstery, and painting.

Clipper Sharpening Service Operator

ABOUT THE JOB

A clipper sharpening service keeps the blades of clippers sharp which, in turn, keep your horses looking good. This business comes in a variety of forms: it may be a one- or two-person mobile truck that visits barns and farms and performs sharpening on-site, or it may be part of a larger business, such as a tack store or blanket cleaning business, that offers several services and products to the horse industry. Some clipper sharpening services specialize in sharpening and repair only, sharpening knives, scissors, garden tools, chain saws, and other items for use by humans or on animals.

To start a clipper sharpening service for horses, it's important to have an idea of the demand in your area for such a service. If you prefer to visit barns and farms to sharpen on-site, be sure there is enough demand within reasonable driving vicinity to make your investment in a truck and equipment worthwhile. As an alternative, starting a business offering other horse products and services in addition to clipper sharpening, or one including sharpening of items for other industries, will help ensure more demand for your business and keep money coming in during slow periods. Many specialized sharpening services accept blade and clipper shipments through the mail and advertise this service over the Internet, potentially bringing in clients from throughout the country.

EDUCATION AND TRAINING

A high school diploma and on-the-job training as well as business and marketing skills and/or college courses in business management and marketing are necessary.

SALARY

The income you make from a clipper sharpening service will depend on how many blades you sharpen, minus your expenses. The amount of business you get will be determined by the demand in your area, your marketing ability, and your attention to customer service, as well as any other products or services you offer. General prices for clipper sharpening range from $3 to $8 per set of blades.

RESOURCES

Consult local barns and farms, tack and feed stores, horse publications, the Internet, and advertising.

Custom Embroidery Service Operator

ABOUT THE JOB

Custom embroidery services create personalized products for horses and riders. They embroider farm logos, horse breeds, organization names, and other designs onto jackets, caps, polo shirts, sweatshirts, and other clothing items. Embroidery services provide stock designs that can be customized with colors and lettering styles or customers may provide their own designs. Embroidery service operators sometimes work with equine artists to develop stock designs for customers; they may sell clothing items to be embroidered, but may also embroider items customers provide. As with many other horse industry services, custom embroidery services may also supply other services, such as engraving and leather working.

Starting a custom embroidery service requires an investment in embroidery machines, threads, clothing, and supplies. Business and marketing skills are important, as well as an understanding of the types of designs and clothing horse people use and wear. Direct horse experience is not required but is helpful for finding customers and marketing the service. Many equine embroidery services set up booths at horse shows and expos and other events where horse people gather.

EDUCATION AND TRAINING

A high school diploma and on-the-job training are necessary.

SALARY

Prices charged for embroidery depend upon the type or work being done. Your salary will depend upon the amount of work you take in, minus expenses.

RESOURCES

Horse shows and events, equine expos, barns and farms, tack and feed stores, horse publications, the Internet, and advertising.

Custom Engraver

ABOUT THE JOB

Custom engraving services supply horse owners with personalized stall signs, halter and bridle nameplates, plaques, and license plate frames. Some engravers also sell horse show trophies and ribbons, and provide engraving for trophies. As with many other horse industry services, custom engravers may also supply other services and products such as embroidery and embroidered products and leather goods.

Starting an engraving service requires an initial investment in engraving machinery as well as brass, metal and plastic plates; signs, trophies, and other items to be engraved. Horse experience is not required but is helpful for finding customers and marketing the service. Some engravers set up booths at horse shows and expos and other events where horse people gather. Business and marketing skills are required to be successful.

Education and training
A high school diploma and on-the-job training.

Salary
Prices charged for engraving depend on the type or work being done. Your salary will depend upon the amount of work you take in, minus expenses.

Resources
Horse shows and events, equine expos, barns and farms, tack and feed stores, horse publications, the Internet for contacts, and advertising.

Horse or Farm Sitter

About the job
Horse and farm sitters take over the duties of the farm or stable, including care of the horses and property, when the owner or farm manager is away. They may stay on-site at the property or visit one or more times daily, depending on the size of the operation and personal preference of the farm manager. In addition to daily horse care (including feeding, watering, cleaning stalls and turn-outs, and sometimes lunging and exercising) sitters may also care for household pets and other animals, bring in mail, and perform other services that the farm owner or manager requests (an additional fee may be charged for these extra services). Horse sitters may charge by the number of visits made per day, the number of horses cared for, or, if they are spending a long period of time at the farm, a flat fee for that time based on the duties involved.

Being dependable is of the utmost importance in this position, as are people skills and the flexibility to work unusual hours. As self-employed business people, networking and marketing skills are also important. Strong horse experience is necessary and horse sitters must be able to deal with a wide variety of equine personalities, recognize signs of any potential health problems, and gain the confidence of horse owners.

EDUCATION AND TRAINING

A high school diploma is important.

SALARY

Horse sitters charge an average of $15 or more per visit, depending on the number of horses and the services requested.

RESOURCES

Pet Sitters International
201 East King Street
King, NC 27021-9161
www.petsit.com

Saddle Fitter

ABOUT THE JOB

A poorly fitted saddle can be uncomfortable for a horse and cause performance problems for both horse and rider. Saddle fitters try to make horses more comfortable by advising horse owners on correct saddle and saddle pad fit, through clinics or individual consultations with horse owners. Also, they may have booths at horse expositions that educate horse owners on correct fit or they may hold private clinics for horse clubs and groups. People involved in saddle fitting may work in a variety of other areas in the horse industry. For example, they might be employees of tack stores or saddlers; they may be involved in the sale of a particular type or style of saddle; they may be trainers doing saddle fittings as an adjunct to their horse training careers; or they may be equine consultants who offer their expertise in a variety of areas, such as horse appraisal, stable management, and advising.

Saddle fitters must be very experienced with horses and familiar with horse anatomy in order to recognize fitting problems.

EDUCATION AND TRAINING

A high school diploma and certification as a saddle fitter are required. Two organizations that offer certification are listed under resources below. People with a variety of educational backgrounds work in saddle fitting, but horse experience is key.

SALARY

A standard saddle fitter charges $75 for a full evaluation. Initial evaluations generally take about one hour. Saddle fitters also charge for travel time, up to approximately $30. The amount you can expect to make will depend on the demand in your area, your expertise, and marketing skills, minus expenses.

RESOURCES

Master Saddlers Association
2698 Jennings Chapel Road
Woodbine, MD 21797
www.mastersaddlers.com

Animal Dynamics
9791 NW 160th Street
Reddick, FL 32686
www.animaldynamics.com/seminars/sfitdetails.html

Career Spotlight

SANDY PANEK, MASTER SADDLERS ASSOCIATION CERTIFIED SADDLE FITTER (MSA CSF)

Sandy Panek has been working as a certified saddle fitter for over five years, in addition to being a saddlery sales agent. Prior to finding her specialty working in the horse industry, she earned a B.S. in accounting from George Mason University in Virginia, and was beginning a career in finance and accounting when, a few years later, she realized her personality was more suited to sales, service, and education. Sandy then found greater satisfaction as a successful sales representative for a major wine wholesaler.

Sandy grew up loving horses, but only had sporadic occasions to ride them, including western riding lessons when she was eight years old. It wasn't until she was in her twenties that she actually began riding regularly and got her first horse, a Thoroughbred named Rio. While trying to fit a dressage saddle to Rio, Sandy realized she had many unanswered questions about properly fitting saddles. In her research, she determined that there were no fitting standards in the United States, as there were in Great Britain and Europe. In her quest to learn more, she eventually trained in England with the senior lecturer at The Society of Master Saddlers. She now loves her career, sharing her expertise on properly fitting saddles with riders and horses, and thus creating an ultimate riding experience for the two.

Q. What does your job involve?

A. I wear two hats in my job. The first hat is a Master Saddlers Association Certified Saddle Fitter (MSA CSF). Using a standardized 10-step approach, my job involves evaluating and assessing the fit of any saddle for both horse and rider (more aptly put, I fit "both sides of the saddle"). I also make adjustments to the saddle's wool-flocked panels, directly on-site, to improve fit. My second hat is as Direct Sales Agent in Virginia, for County Saddlery, a British manufacturer of world-class saddles.

Q. What is your typical workday like?

A. Most of the time, I drive from stable to stable to evaluate, adjust, or fit a new or used saddle. No two appointments are alike. Each appointment takes about an hour, sometimes more. Some cases are more complicated than others; regardless, I must pay close attention to the entire history of the particular horse being assessed. This requires a lot of mental energy. Obviously, I come home pretty dusty and dirty at the end of the day.

I also lecture at saddle fitting seminars and perform clinics for various equine groups. I spend time at horse shows, usually with a vendor booth, so I can introduce my service to those passing by. I have office days (especially when inclement weather hits) when I sit tethered to the computer updating clients' files, writing letters, and responding to e-mails. I also spend a lot of time on the phone, providing telephone consultations and following up with clients to ensure their satisfaction.

Q. How many hours/days per week do you typically work?

A. I spend 30 to 50 hours per week, depending on the season. If I travel away from home, I can spend 14 hours in one day performing saddle fittings. I work on my business almost every day in some fashion.

Q. What do you enjoy most about your work?

A. I love meeting my clients and their horses. This aspect of my job is truly rewarding. Without question, all my clients love their horses dearly and want the best for them. If saddle fit is the issue (the issue may be veterinary or training), I truly enjoy witnessing, within minutes, a happier horse and rider because I have readjusted or properly fit the saddle. It is priceless to hear someone say, "Thanks so much, my horse and I feel so much better!"

Q. What do you like least about your work?

A. Scheduling. Since travel to a particular area involves logistics and long distances, I try to minimize the travel charges to my clients by seeing everyone in the same area on the same day. Invariably, someone will have a scheduling conflict, which results in a lot of going back and forth about days and times suitable to all.

Q. What made you decide to go into this field?

A. In 1996, while working as a wine sales representative, I was trying to fit a dressage saddle to my Thoroughbred, Rio (notice the word "trying"). I visited as many tack shops as practical, lugging saddles back and forth to the barn. I am sure my barn mates thought I was a bit obsessive. Although tack store personnel tried to be helpful, I kept asking the same questions: How do I know when my saddle fits properly? What standards exist for this task? It became clear to me that such standards had not been clearly defined or made public in the equestrian community, at least in the U.S.

After some research, I discovered that the British Society of Master Saddlers (SMS) had a "Qualified Saddle Fitters" course. In Great Britain and Europe, it is a bona fide equine profession. No one across the ocean purchases a saddle unless a professional saddle fitter fits it. I immediately applied for the course. Unfortunately, I was ineligible to participate, because you need to be a member of the SMS and also a resident of the U.K. in order to be eligible. I was disappointed, but remained relentless in my quest. At one point, I was labeled the "aggressive American woman." My determination paid off, and I was able to train with the Senior Lecturer of the SMS course by travelling to Kent, England, for a few weeks. I returned to the U.S. with more knowledge and began working with a local tack shop in a synergistic way. I set up appointments with clients, visited them with a truckload of various makes and models of saddles, and thus my saddle-fitting career was born. At this point, I thought I knew a lot, but in actuality, my knowledge was limited compared to my knowledge and expertise now. True expertise comes from actual experience over a long period of time.

Q. What are the names, ages, and breeds of your horse(s)?

A. Zesty Session is my 14-year-old, 16.2 hh gray, off-the-track Thoroughbred mare. She used to be a Training Level event horse. Now she has a dressage career with me. Her career path is slow because I have a lot to learn, and I want to make sure I learn the basics extremely well. There is a lot to Training Level dressage, if you want to do it properly. "Properly"—for me—means riding harmoniously no matter what. Just recently, I rescued an emaciated 26-year-old, 14.3 hh gray Arabian gelding named Trigger (I call him "Twigger" affectionately) who now serves as Zesty's companion and a trail horse for my friends. He rules the barn, and is extremely feisty for a senior horse.

Q. What is your most memorable moment as a horsewoman?

A. I have had memorable moments when I have "thought it" and my horse has "done it."

Q. What is the most rewarding part of being a saddle fitter?

A. As a MSA Certified Saddle Fitter, I adhere to a very high standard. The definition of a properly fitted saddle is much more complex than what it appears to be on the surface. Because of this—to do it well—a great deal of intellect and expertise is required. I take pride in doing my job well, and this I find rewarding. The other, more important reward for me is that a properly fitted saddle will improve the horse's performance on the micro and macro level, without a doubt. I know this as fact now, having fit and adjusted hundreds of saddles to horses and riders. My service is of bona fide value to the horse and rider combination.

Q. What is the most challenging part of being a saddle fitter?

A. Any career has its challenges. As a saddle fitter, here are some of mine and how I respond to them:

1) A saddle fitter cannot make any saddle fit. I cannot create a silk purse out of a sow's ear. Unfortunately, some clients don't understand this. Before an appointment, I always communicate to the client what she can expect realistically from my service. For example, with a 25-year-old saddle, we will be very limited in what we can achieve, especially if she wants the best for her horse.

2) Some horse-and-rider combinations have other issues beyond saddle fit. These can be obvious or less so. In these situations, all equine professionals must be involved in order to achieve the correct resolution, especially if there is a veterinary and/or training concern. In cases like this, I insist that such other professionals be involved when I am engaged with such clients.

3) Changing the perception that saddle fitting can be performed successfully by "do-it-yourselfers" or that it is not such a big deal. I have changed this perception for some by writing highly technical articles addressing the less obvious saddle-fit issues.

Q. What is the biggest achievement of your career?

A. Starting this business on my own, sticking to it, and succeeding in spite of the naysayers. When I began, I had some people express their doubts about my direction. They obviously did not understand how complex and involved saddle fitting could be. I think some of them have a different viewpoint now.

Q. What is the most challenging obstacle in your career?

A. When I began this profession, I thought it would be a lot easier, technically, in the first few years. Without question, the learning curve during this time was extremely steep. I became professionally challenged because I wanted to be perfect. I then understood the reality: all saddle-fit situations are unique because of the infinite number of horse-and-rider variables. Now, almost six years later, although I know more because of my experience, I realize there will always be new problems presented to me, and I will always need to work harder to resolve them. The obstacle is no longer such, but has become a realization.

Q. What has driven you to excel in your career?

A. I am driven by the fact that there is so much to learn; I also have a strong desire to do the best job humanly possible. I am, admittedly, compulsively obsessed with getting it right. I sometimes wake up in the middle of the night thinking about saddle fit. And, I care deeply about my clients and the well-being of their horses.

Q. What education and/or experience do you recommend for someone interested in saddle fitting?

A. First, they have to love the equestrian world, both on the human and equine level. Second, they should apprentice or work with another professional for a time to determine whether they would actually enjoy performing this role, day in and day out. Third, if they decide that this is the direction they want to follow, they should get professional training. I would say they should practice for about six months to a year before applying for certification.

Q. What personal strengths or skills should a person have who is considering this field?

A. They need to have patience, the ability to communicate extremely well; a high energy level, both physically and mentally; technical ability to determine static and dynamic saddle-fit issues; technical ability to recommend or perform the solutions to such issues; adherence to a very high standard and the tenacity to get it right; and diplomacy.

Q. If you could do it over, is there anything you would have done differently to reach your career goal?

A. I would have done it sooner!

Q. What do you think the job outlook is for saddle fitters?

A. I think it is good, although some non-believers present an obstacle. Not every equestrian has a saddle fitter, like they do a farrier. However, this is changing.

Q. How long does it take to build a successful saddle fitting business?

A. In this business, you are developing a client base. This takes time. Some prospects become clients immediately, while others take years. The main thing is to continue to do your job well, as there will be different types of hiccups along the road for various and unforeseen reasons. It took about three years before I felt as if I had arrived.

Q. Is there anything else you would like to say about your career or your life with horses?

A. I love my career profoundly. I am so happy I chose to do this.

Saddle Maker/Leathercrafter

About the job

Saddle makers/leathercrafters make and repair saddles, harnesses, and other custom tack for equestrians. They may also fit saddles and make, fit, and repair boots. Some saddlers work for tack stores while others operate their own small businesses. Independently employed saddle makers may handcraft other leather products as well, including belts, chaps, holsters, and saddle-bags to bring money into the business. Some saddle makers also offer classes in their craft, during which they teach students the basics of stamping and tooling and allow them to work on crafting their first saddles.

Starting a saddle making and leather working business requires an investment in time in order to adequately learn the trade, which can involve several years of apprenticeship and practice. It also will take a financial investment to purchase tools and leather. In addition, marketing and advertising skills are important to get the word out about your business. Some saddle makers and leather workers set up booths at horse shows, expos, and other events to help them find customers and practice nontraditional methods of advertising. Some may rely only on word of mouth in the horse community to gain business.

Education and training

A high school diploma, plus an apprenticeship with a saddle craftsman are requisite. (Saddle making schools that teach the basics are valuable, but master saddle makers recommend an apprenticeship even if you attend a school.) Trade schools also offer classes in leather working and boot and shoe making.

Salary

The salary range is $14,000 to $30,000 per year.

Resources

Saddle Harness Allied Trades Association
1101 Broad St.
Oriental, NC 28571
www.proleptic.net

CHAPTER 14

Industry Support Careers

People who support the horse industry and are vital to its smooth functioning include insurance professionals, accountants, lawyers, appraisers, clerical workers, and more. Though these positions may not usually involve working directly with horses, they do provide the opportunity to be an important part of the horse industry, and may require a strong knowledge of the horse industry and its ins and outs. Many of the jobs are highly skilled and require advanced degrees of education.

The major benefit of a support position is the regular salary and the chance to incorporate your love for horses into a business-related position.

Accountant

ABOUT THE JOB

Accountants work directly for horse associations and businesses, or public accounting firms. They also may be self-employed businesspeople whose services support farms and other horse operations. Accountants employed by public accounting firms usually do not specialize in equine-related business; instead, they support a variety of industries. As employees, they work fairly regular hours and are responsible for the financial management of the association or business that employs them. Even self-employed accountants may not be able to deal with equine businesses exclusively, often diversifying into other industries to make a full-time salary. Public and self-employed accountants consult with start-up businesses on preparing business plans, setting up accounting systems, keeping financial records, and selecting financial software. They offer tax-planning services, do bookkeeping, prepare income tax returns and financial statements, and keep clients up-to-date on changes in tax laws.

Good communication skills are essential for accountants. Marketing and networking know-how are important for the self-employed. Advertising in horse publications, marketing their services to equine associations and businesses, and networking at barns and horse events are some of the ways that equine accountants obtain business. Horse experience is not necessary, though it may make you more familiar with the issues your clients face and better able to communicate with them about those issues.

EDUCATION AND TRAINING

A four-year degree in accounting and certification as a Certified Public Accountant. It is a good idea to begin your career with a large public accounting firm to gain experience before striking out on your own.

SALARY

The median annual salary for accountants is $45,380.

RESOURCES

American Institute of Certified Public Accountants
1211 Avenue of the Americas
New York, NY 10036-8775
www.aicpa.org

Career Spotlight

CAROLYN MILLER, CERTIFIED PUBLIC ACCOUNTANT AND HORSE BREEDER

Carolyn Miller is a certified public accountant who works almost exclusively with horse industry clients; she is also a breeder of quarter horses. Carolyn has combined these two careers for more than 11 years. She lives on a Texas ranch with her husband, a blacksmith, and their young daughter, who has already developed a love for horses as well as other animals. Carolyn's breeding program includes approximately 15 horses. She also has two horses that are not part of the program—a quarter horse gelding that Carolyn shows in reined cowhorse events and a miniature horse for her daughter. Carolyn has shown reining horses for 10 years and has placed with her horse in such events as the Quarter Horse Congress and the National Reining Horse Association Futurity Show. She was born in Yuma, Arizona, but grew up in Montreal, Quebec, where she spent her childhood dreaming about a moving to a farm where she could have horses. The move didn't happen until she was an adult, but as a child, she took riding lessons and hung out at the local stable as much as her mother allowed and, eventually, she got her own horse.

Q. What is your overall background with horses?

A. I was born with a love for horses. Where it came from, I have no idea because no one in my family had anything to do with them. Every Christmas, the first item on my list was a horse. I started taking riding lessons at age five. At 12, I was lucky enough to get a horse of my own, a sorrel quarter horse mare. Mom thought this would be a wise strategy to keep me away from the trouble that seems to find teenagers. The mare wasn't exactly an ideal horse for a girl of 12, but I loved her anyway. I can remember her taking off with me on trail rides, galloping as fast as she could go, before heading back to the barn. There was no stopping her, but that never daunted me! Since then, I have had a variety of horses, all quarter horses. Our love for horses has brought us to Texas, to pursue our riding and breeding activities without fighting the bitter cold of the North.

Q. What made you decide to become an equine accountant?

A. I was in college and had no idea what I wanted to do for a living other than work with horses. I had observed that most people who went to work at stables didn't progress very far, and they always worked for someone else. I knew I wanted to be the owner of the stable, not an employee. I decided to take some courses that would help me run my own business. Well, I took my first accounting course and received a grade of 100 percent. That was a turning point for me. I had found my niche. When I began my practice, I decided to focus on equine businesses since I already had the horse industry knowledge and liked working with horse people.

Q. What does your work as an equine accountant involve?

A. I work about 40 hours a week. I don't keep a 9 to 5 schedule, but accommodate my clients—and myself—with flexible hours. If it is nice out, I ride before hitting the books. I don't really specialize in a particular area of the horse industry, but because I raise reining and working cowhorses, I have many contacts within this sector of the industry and that's where many of my clients come from. I also have many clients who are backyard breeders, because this group often needs help developing business plans and setting up their books. Income tax rules are the same whether you are showing Arabian horses or USET show jumpers.

As an equine accountant, I prepare income taxes at tax time. The rest of the year, I help horse owners start up new business ventures by preparing business plans, choosing the appropriate organizational forms for their businesses, selecting business software, and setting up accounting systems. I also help clients select horse management software. I do bookkeeping, prepare financial statements, prepare loan applications, and offer tax-planning services.

As a tax advisor, I must stay current with tax laws and be aware of any changes that affect my clients. If a law changes that will benefit my customers, I like to inform them personally so they can plan their affairs to best take advantage of the changes.

Q. Is it necessary to have direct horse experience to go into equine accounting?

A. I don't feel it is absolutely necessary to have direct horse experience to go into this field, but it sure does help. My clients come to me because I'm knowledgeable about the industry. I understand the lingo and how things work. A person could acquire this knowledge without actually working with horses, but it would probably be more difficult relating to customers. I think what sets me apart from the generic accountant is the fact that I am a horsewoman, and an active member of the horse industry. Having direct horse experience helps me be aware of issues a horse business owner will need to face. Many of my customers are large ranch owners, and they like that they can talk to me as a horse person. I understand the terminology and can relate to their situations.

Q. What personal strengths or skills should someone have who is considering this field?

A. One of the less obvious strengths is communication skill. Many of my customers have expressed that they like using me because I talk to them in a language they can understand and I don't use accountant "mumbo-jumbo." I am an advisor to my clients and have to be able to advise them on whether or not to take a specific action and I must be able to explain why.

And, of course, to get your CPA certificate, you need to have a mind that is good with figures. If you don't like figures, don't consider this field.

Q. What do you think the job outlook is for equine accountants?

A. I don't really think there is a "job market" out there for equine accountants. I have never seen an ad in the newspaper looking for equine accountants to hire. On the other hand, I do think there is a demand for equine accountants in the industry. It is an industry where you have to promote yourself; if you can show your potential customers how you can benefit them, they will come to you.

Q. How did you become interested in breeding horses?

A. I raised my first foal when I was 18 years old. I started actively breeding quarter horses when my husband and I purchased an 80-acre farm in Lanark, Ontario, 11 years ago. Because I had always enjoyed raising foals, it seemed only natural that we would start breeding horses. My husband had a nice stallion, Tuff Joe Sugar, who we still have today.

Q. How did your background prepare you to become a breeder?

A. I had the knowledge to choose nice mares to start our breeding program. We didn't have lots of money to spend on mares, so we chose mares that looked the part but didn't have the fancy pedigrees. Over time, we have steadily improved the quality of our broodmares.

Q. What does the day-to-day involvement in the breeding program entail?

A. On a day-to-day basis, we care for the horses, which entails feeding, cleaning, grooming, maintaining a herd health program, and facility maintenance. We also train and show the offspring, which is the most time-consuming aspect of the business.

Q. How does your experience as a breeder benefit your accounting work and vice versa?

A. My horse industry knowledge helps me advise clients on their horse businesses. I can help people write realistic business plans because I know what is plausible and attainable and what is not. My experience as an equine accountant lets me see what is hot in the business and what is not. I can see what breeding programs are successful, and whose are not.

Q. What is your most rewarding moment as an equine accountant? As a horse breeder?

A. As an accountant, it has to be a client winning a case in which I testified against the IRS as an expert witness. The IRS had challenged my client's expectation of a profit with his horse business and wanted to treat it as a hobby. I helped my client prove that he did indeed have a legitimate horse business.

I can't say I have one most memorable moment as a breeder, though there are many small moments. We currently have in training the best three-year-old horse we have ever owned. We've raised her from day one. Last week, a notable trainer was here to have his tax return prepared and asked us to price her because he liked her. She is not for sale!

Q. What have been your most challenging moments?

A. As an equine accountant, I think my biggest challenge is one I face almost every day, and that is convincing many of my clients to keep better books. Horse people are notoriously poor bookkeepers. They'd rather be outside riding or in the barn than inside doing books.

The most challenging part of being a horse breeder is keeping faith in your program. Sometimes, it seems that everything else is hot and it's tempting to jump ship and buy into another program. Horse breeding is not usually a business with short-term rewards, unless you're extremely lucky, so you have to stick with it for some time before you attain success. We have been breeding for over 10 years and only just now have we gotten to the point where we like all the horses we are raising.

Q. What is your biggest achievement?

A. My biggest achievement is obtaining a strong reputation as a good equine accountant. Most of my business comes by word of mouth, so it's important that my clients speak well of me.

Q. What do you like most about your work?

A. Believe it or not, being an equine accountant is quite an interesting occupation. Tax laws are always changing, so I must keep abreast of the changes throughout the year. I have an interesting mix of clients and enjoy working and learning about their businesses.

Q. What do you like least about your work?

A. I don't like the seasonal aspect. From January through April, I have double the workload over the rest of the year. I also don't like the fact that because I'm working from home, my customers call me during all hours of the day.

Q. What advice would you give to someone who wants to become an equine accountant? A horse breeder?

A. For someone who wants to be an equine accountant, she needs to go to college, get her CPA certificate and then work for a Certified Public Accounting firm to gain experience. She should choose a firm that has a large base of farm tax clients. I also can't emphasize enough how valuable it is to have good bookkeeping knowledge.

The best thing someone can do if she wants to become a horse breeder is to go to school and learn a profession that will enable her to afford becoming a horse breeder or work for a breeding farm for a while to learn all about the breeding process.

Q. Is there anything else you would like to say?

A. I'm happy doing what I do. I know I could earn a lot more money working for a big CPA firm in the city, but I wouldn't be happy. My family and horses come before anything else, as they are what are truly important to me.

Appraiser

ABOUT THE JOB

Equine appraisers assess a horse's value to be used by attorneys, insurance companies, breed associations, and buyers and sellers of horses. They may specialize in a particular breed or type of horse, or offer appraisal services for a variety of horse types and breeds, depending on their knowledge and preference. Appraisers are experts in the horse world, typically having years of experience as trainers, judges, horse owners, or breeders, or they have worked in other facets of the horse industry. Some appraisers work part-time in the field and may also work in other horse-related jobs; other appraisers pursue the field full-time. According to the American Society of Equine Appraisers (ASEA), this is a growing field, with most regions of the country in need of qualified appraisers.

Because equine appraisers are self-employed, skills in networking, marketing, and business are necessary in addition to horse expertise. The ASEA offers certification in the field of horse appraising. Check with them for more information (see contact information below).

EDUCATION AND TRAINING

No advanced education is required. However, business studies can be a plus as equine appraisers are self-employed, and an equine degree can be helpful.

SALARY

While there is no average salary data available for this career, the American Society of Equine Appraisers reports that the earnings can be high. Part-time appraisers may earn from $5,000 to $50, 000 per year, depending on how many appraisals they do. Full-time appraisers can command more than $100,000 per year.

RESOURCES

American Society of Equine Appraisers
1126 Eastland Dr. N., Suite. 100
P.O. Box 186
Twin Falls, ID 83303-0186
www.equineappraiser.com

Administrative/Clerical/Secretarial Worker

ABOUT THE JOB

Administrative, clerical, and secretarial workers provide day-to-day support operations for horse associations, product manufacturers, equine travel agencies, humane and rescue organizations, advertising agencies, insurance companies, breeding farms, and just about every other horse-related operation. Positions include word processor, administrative assistant, breed registrar, pedigree researcher, secretary, bookkeeper, human resources assistant, data entry specialist, receptionist, office manager, executive assistant, and sales assistant. Most of these positions require strong computer skills and software knowledge and familiarity with various types of office equipment. Good interpersonal, organizational, and telephone skills are also important. Higher-level positions may require workers to do more advanced work, such as purchasing, facilities management, office staff supervision, employee training, research, and coordination of travel arrangements. Administrative personnel who assist veterinarians, researchers, and others involved in technical arenas must have more specialized knowledge of job-specific terminology and procedures.

Horse knowledge is often not required, though it may be in some instances, depending on the particular employer and position. To find employment, contact horse-related businesses and associations or an equine-industry job search service.

EDUCATION AND TRAINING

The required education and training can range from a high school diploma with on-the-job training to a bachelor's degree with professional certification. The level of education and training is dependent upon the position. Business schools, vocational and technical institutes, and community colleges offer programs in office administration.

The International Association of Administrative Professionals (see address below) offers testing of and certification for entry-level office skills and provides certified professional designations to qualified experienced secretaries and administrative assistants.

SALARY

The following are the median annual salaries for various administrative and clerical positions:

General Office Clerk	$21,780
Word Processor	$26,000
Bookkeeping, Auditing and Accounting Clerks	$26,540
Executive Secretaries and Administrative Assistants	$32,380
Office Manager	$37,990

Additionally, salaries for farm office workers run an average of $23,794.80 annually, according to a survey by Equistaff, an online job placement agency for the horse industry. Seventy-five percent of people polled received traditional benefits, such as medical and dental insurance; 50 percent reported additional benefits, such as riding when the workday is done, free boarding of horses, or use of vehicle; 60 percent received housing or a housing allowance. Most farm office helpers work the traditional 40-hour week. Duties include bookkeeping, human resources, contacting clients, pedigree research, answering phones, and typing contracts.

Resources
International Association of Administrative Professionals
10502 NW Ambassador Dr.
P.O. Box 20404
Kansas City, MO 64195-0404
www.iaap-hq.org

Expert Witness

About the job
Expert witnesses provide specialized advice and insight into their area of the horse world. Principally used by lawyers, they are called upon when an expert's opinion is needed. They may consult on horse-related cases in any number of ways: educating the attorney, evaluating the strength of a case, assisting in developing the case, and providing written statements of their findings to be used in negotiations. When the case goes to trial, which the majority do not, the expert witness may be called upon to testify in court. People who work in this field usually do so as part of another horse-related career.

Individuals wanting to use their horse expertise as an expert witness should know how to conduct research, have knowledge of the laws regarding horses, and be able to confidently make professional judgments. To get started, contact equine attorneys in your area or register with an expert witness service.

EDUCATION AND TRAINING

The education you receive will depend on your area of expertise and may or may not involve higher education.

SALARY

Expert witnesses normally charge by the hour; fees usually start at $100 and go up from there.

RESOURCES

Contact equine attorneys in your area or register with expert witness services.

Human Resources Specialist/Manager

ABOUT THE JOB

Human resources professionals recruit, hire, and train employees for the horse industry. They work for equine businesses, breeding farms, associations, government agencies, and equine employment services. HR professionals are responsible for administering benefit programs, developing wage and salary scales, implementing payroll, and taking care of employee relations. People in this profession have strong communication and administrative skills, work well with others, are familiar with labor laws, and know how to operate computers and other office equipment.

EDUCATION AND TRAINING

A four-year degree in human resource management, personnel administration, business, or an equine area is necessary.

SALARY

The following are the median annual salaries for different human resources positions:

Human Resources Specialists:

Employment, recruitment, and placement	$36,480
Training and development	$40,830
Compensation, benefits, and job analysis	$41,660
Human Resources Manager	$59,000

RESOURCES

Contact equine businesses and associations for job openings.

Insurance Claims Representative

ABOUT THE JOB

Claims representatives, including adjusters, examiners, and investigators, work directly for equine insurance companies or for independent contracting firms. They investigate policyholder claims, negotiate settlements, review adjuster reports, and authorize payments. Claims representatives must protect the company from false or inflated claims while also settling legitimate claims fairly. Claims adjusters determine whether a claim is valid and recommend a settlement. (In life and health insurance companies, claims examiners are the same as claims adjusters.) Insurance investigators handle claims in which fraudulent or criminal activity is suspected such as arson, staged accidents, or unnecessary medical treatments. They take statements from claimants and witnesses, and search databases for prior fraudulent activity. They also may perform surveillance work and act as expert witnesses in court cases.

Claims adjusters and investigators spend much of their time traveling and actively investigating claims. Examiners, on the other hand, spend most of their time in the office and work more traditional hours than their investigative counterparts.

Equine claims representatives should have horse knowledge to effectively investigate claims.

EDUCATION AND TRAINING

For adjusters and examiners, a four-year degree in business or an equine degree with business classes. About a third of the states in America require independent adjusters to be licensed. Licensing requirements vary among states. However, adjusters working directly for an employer are usually licensed under the employer's license.

Insurance companies often hire former private investigators and law enforcement officers as insurance investigators. Also, a four-year degree in a law enforcement field may be beneficial.

SALARY

The median annual salary for claims representatives is $42,440.

RESOURCES

Occupational information about these positions is available from many local insurance offices and insurance companies. The department of insurance for each state provides licensing requirements for adjusters and investigators.

Insurance Underwriter

ABOUT THE JOB
Underwriters evaluate insurance applications to determine the risk involved in issuing a policy. They decide whether to accept or reject an application and determine the appropriate premium rate for each policy. Much of the underwriter's time is spent dealing with agents and other insurance professionals. Underwriters also spend time on computers, using software programs to help them analyze information in insurance applications and accessing database records via the Internet. Therefore, a high degree of computer proficiency is required for this job. Underwriters should have good judgment and decision-making skills, be attentive to detail and know how to work with people. Horse experience is not required.

EDUCATION AND TRAINING
A four-year degree in business, communications, or an equine-related program is required. Courses in accounting and business law are also helpful.

SALARY
Median annual earnings for this position are $44,060.

RESOURCES
The American Institute for Chartered Property and Casualty Underwriters
720 Providence Rd.
P.O. Box 3016
Malvern, PA 19355-0716
www.aicpcu.org

Insurance Information Institute
110 William St.
New York, NY 10038
www.iii.org

Lawyer

ABOUT THE JOB

Equine lawyers advise businesses on insurance, liability, and other legal matters. They draft contracts and releases, arbitrate disputes, defend clients from lawsuits, and help new business owners set up contracts and liability releases. Lawyers specializing in equine law usually have clients across different industries, as the market often doesn't allow for them to practice in the horse industry exclusively. Horse-industry clients include breeders, riding schools, boarding stables, trainers, insurance companies, product manufacturers, associations, horse owners, and other horse-related businesses.

Three out of four lawyers are in private practice either in a law firm or on their own. The hours can be long and irregular, with more than half of the lawyers' working weeks that are longer than 40 hours. Lawyers spend most of their workdays in the office, in court, or meeting with clients in various locations. Good communication, organizational, and writing skills are important. Trial lawyers should be assertive and have strong public speaking skills.

While horse experience is not required to practice equine law, it is extremely helpful in understanding the industry and being able to communicate with clients.

EDUCATION AND TRAINING

A four-year degree plus doctor of jurisprudence degree is essential. Passage of the state bar exam is required.

SALARY

The median annual salary for lawyers is $88,280.

RESOURCES

Information Services
American Bar Association
750 North Lake Shore Drive
Chicago, IL 60611
www.abanet.org

Association of American Law Schools
1201 Connecticut Avenue NW, Suite 800
Washington, DC 20036-2605

Career Spotlight

JULIE I. FERSHTMAN, EQUINE ATTORNEY

Julie I. Fershtman has been an attorney for 17 years and a specialist in equine law for 10. Her law practice crosses many horse breeds and disciplines and her clients include boarding and breeding stables, national clinicians and competitors, trainers, insurance companies, individual horse owners, associations, product manufacturers, and show managers.

Though Julie advises a large number of horse industry clients (about 75 percent of her practice involves equine law), she continues to practice law in other industries. The desire to educate horse owners to avoid or lessen disputes is one of the things that has driven Julie to excel in her field. In 1998, the American Riding Instructors Association presented her with an Outstanding Achievement award for her service to the equine industry. The Certified Horsemanship Association honored her with its prestigious Partner in Safety Award one year earlier. She was also named by the American Bar Association's Barrister Magazine as one of "21 Young Lawyers Leading the Nation into the 21st Century" and is listed in Who's Who in American Law and The Bar Register of Preeminent Lawyers (2001 edition). Julie, who was born in Detroit, Michigan, also writes a column on equine law that appears in several magazines.

Q. What is your personal background with horses?

A. I have ridden horses since I was seven years old. I owned my first horse at the age of 10. In 1992, when I showed horses very extensively on a state and regional level, I became a state champion and was a finalist at the world's largest single breed horse show. Presently, I own no horses. However, I am looking forward to buying a horse or pony some day for my daughter.

Q. How did you decide to specialize in equine law?

A. After seven years as a lawyer, I became curious about how the law affected horse ownership and horse businesses. To learn the law, I spent numerous weekends researching it in libraries. I organized what I found and began to write about it. Slowly I developed a client base.

Q. What does your job involve?

A. Drafting contracts (releases, breeding, boarding, sales, leases, training, etc.), advising businesses and insurers on various matters and disputes, litigating cases through the court system or arbitrating disputes, consulting with people and lawyers who need assistance on specific projects.

Q. Is it necessary to have direct horse experience to go into the field?

A. It is a definite plus to have horse experience because through the experience you understand the way the industry operates and, of course, you have a very firm grasp of the terminology. I strongly believe that a lawyer who understands the terminology costs less than one who does not because the former is up to speed on the issues while the latter must learn a great deal (and, of course, charge the client to learn).

Believe it or not, years ago, I was once hired to explain to a well-intentioned lawyer the difference between a Paint and an Appaloosa. "But they both have spots!" he kept declaring.

Q. Do you ever have direct contact with horses as part of your job?

A. Interestingly, yes. In a few cases I've handled there were horse inspections and I had to be present right near the horse. Sometimes I have appointments with clients at major horse shows, which is always fun for me.

Q. What strengths or skills should someone have who is considering this field?

A. It depends on the type of law practice the person envisions having. Those who plan to focus on drafting complex contracts and who do not want to become trial lawyers do not need the type of communication and public speaking skills that trial lawyers need. For any lawyer, though, the ability to communicate effectively is a must. Good organizational skills are a must.

Q. In which publications does your column appear?

A. I have written a column on equine law since 1992. At one time the column appeared in any given month in 75 different publications. Now, about 25 publications and Web sites nationwide have been running the column. In addition to the monthly column, I occasionally write articles for magazines that include *EQUUS*, *Horse Illustrated*, *Horse and Rider*, and others. In addition, I've written two books: *Equine Law & Horse Sense* (1996) and *More Equine Law & Horse Sense*, (Horses and the Law Publishing, 2000).

Q. What, or who, inspired you to become an attorney?

A. As a child, I saw a lawyer on television giving practical advice to people and found this fascinating. Also, my father was an attorney. Just about every job I have ever held since I was old enough to work has been in a law office.

Q. What is your most memorable moment as an equine attorney?

A. There have been several. Winning a case in court for my clients is always a memorable moment. In particular, in 1995, I defended a case on behalf of a riding stable that was accused of negligently causing a customer to be injured when a horse reared up and fell on her. The stable had a liability release, which the rider signed. Fortunately, the rider was not seriously injured, but sued nonetheless. Even though an attorney had drafted the stable's release, the stable was convinced that the release was "not worth the paper it was written on." The plaintiff's attorney held the same sentiment. Yet, through persistence, a careful strategy, and research, I won the case for my clients. The release was enforced and the case dismissed.

Q. What is your most challenging moment as an equine attorney?

A. Handling cases involving serious personal injuries. For example, I assisted in a case from California where a rider suffered a serious head injury during a lesson. This injury transformed a beautiful 47-year-old woman and mother of teenage daughters into an institutionalized individual with a mental capacity of probably a four year old. Also, I personally defended a lawsuit involving a wonderful 16-year-old girl who is now confined to a wheelchair after a horse reared up and fell on her. Both of these cases involved truly freak accidents. Even though my job, as defense counsel, is somewhat to serve as a roadblock to these cases' success, I, like any normal human being, cannot help but be tremendously moved when learning of these tragedies.

Q. What do you believe is the biggest achievement of your career?

A. Developing a good client base, having two books that have combined sales of over 11,000 copies, and being entrusted to handle cases and legal matters around the country.

Q. What has driven you to excel in your career?

A. The desire to educate the industry to avoid disputes, and the desire to merge an interest in horses with a career.

Q. What do you like most about your job?

A. I love the ability to combine a personal interest with my profession. For many lawyers, this is a dream come true.

Q. What do you like least about your job?

A. The negative is that very often, equine industry matters are rush matters that need immediate attention. Examples: someone wants to see a horse *today* and needs the contract done now, or someone wants an immediate lawsuit filed to block a disputed sale. Consequently, you need to work under pressure and the hours can sometimes be very long.

CHAPTER 15

Marketing and Sales Careers

— — —

Individuals interested in jobs in sales and marketing must have outgoing personalities, confidence, the patience to deal with difficult people, good communication and presentation skills, and genuine enthusiasm for the product or service being marketed or sold. A strong orientation in customer service, attention to detail, and good follow-through are also necessary. Some positions require a high degree of horse experience, while others require little.

Marketing and sales positions offer good pay and more regulated hours. There are also many good opportunities for horse enthusiasts who have an entrepreneurial spirit and enjoy working with people.

Advertising Sales Representative

ABOUT THE JOB

Advertising sales representatives sell space in horse publications, event programs and prize lists, and on radio, television, and the Internet to product manufacturers and retailers, event operators, and other businesses and organizations. They handle a particular geographical territory or category and spend their time on the road meeting with advertisers and pursuing new leads. They attend shows, horse expos, and other industry events, and they work on the telephone, the computer, or in the office doing paperwork. When not actually contacting advertisers, sales representatives may be found preparing sales presentations and cost estimates to present to advertisers.

Many advertising sales representatives work out of their own homes rather than in their employers' offices. Being assertive and persistent, having good communication and people skills, and an enthusiastic personality are all qualities of successful salespeople. While direct horse experience is usually not required for this type of position, an understanding of the target market audience is important.

EDUCATION AND TRAINING

A four-year degree in marketing, business, or advertising is requisite.

SALARY

Advertising sales representatives usually work on commission, although the employer may provide a base salary in addition to the commission. The median annual salary for advertising sales representatives is $36,560; sales representatives working in television and on large-circulation magazines may earn considerably more.

RESOURCES

American Horse Publications
49 Spinnaker Circle
South Daytona, Fl 32119
www.americanhorsepubs.org

Auctioneer

Auctioneers arrange the sale of horses at auctions. They must have flexible personalities and be organized enough to handle a variety of duties that go beyond bid calling. Some additional duties include locating a facility, acquiring horses, marketing, advertising, developing contracts, registering bidders, and collecting payments. Livestock auctioneers must know how to make a horse appear at his best; recognize conformation, value, and performance; and understand horse pedigrees.

Auctioneers should be comfortable in front of a large audience and have good public speaking skills, as well as enthusiasm and the energy to deal with a variety of people for long hours. Many auctioneers start out as part-timers while also holding down other jobs. Horse auctions offer other jobs besides auctioneer, including auction sales manager, auction clerk, bid caller, ring assistant, and cashier.

EDUCATION AND TRAINING

It is necessary to have horse experience in order to understand the market. According to the National Auctioneers Association, many auctioneers grew up in auction families. If you didn't, attending an auction trade school or college program, or serving as an apprentice are two ways to become an auctioneer. Some states require licensing of auctioneers, which may determine the type of education required. Check with your state government for any licensing regulations.

SALARY

Approximately $150 a day and up.

RESOURCES

World Wide College of Engineering
P.O. Box 949, Dept. WHD
Mason City, Iowa 50402-0949
www.worldwidecollegeofauctioneering.com

National Auctioneers Association
8880 Ballentine
Overland Park, Kansas 66214
www.auctioneers.org

Circulation Manager/Personnel

ABOUT THE JOB

Circulation managers and personnel acquire new readers for horse publications and renew current readers. Many different methods and media are used, the most popular being a direct mail campaign. (Using lists that are carefully selected by circulation personnel, offers are mailed to potential subscribers.) Other methods of finding readers include television, promotions, sweepstakes, and online advertising. Circulation personnel also coordinate renewal and billing for their publications, manage customer service, and oversee fulfillment houses. Circulation is a very numbers-driven business and circulation personnel spend a significant amount of time analyzing reports on circulation data, profiling customers, and monitoring sales trends.

Strong analytical capability, communication and organizational skills, and attention to detail are important for success in this field.

EDUCATION AND TRAINING

A four-year degree in business or marketing is requisite.

SALARY

The mean annual salary for this occupation is $25,000 to $35,000.

RESOURCES

American Horse Publications
49 Spinnaker Circle
South Daytona, FL 32119
www.americanhorsepubs.org

Magazine Publishers of America
919 Third Ave., 22nd Floor
New York, NY 10022
www.magazine.org

Feed/Tack Store Owner

ABOUT THE JOB

Feed dealers stock feed for ahorses and livestock and must be knowledgeable enough to help customers with various feed options. Tack store owners sell saddles, bridles, blankets, grooming supplies, riding clothes, helmets and many other rider- and horse-related products. Tack stores may sell both English and western tack and clothing or specialize in one style or the other depending upon the demand for the particular riding style in their area of the country and the owners' personal preferences. Some stores deal in both horse feed and tack.

Store owners must have enough horse experience to understand their customers' needs and help them select appropriate tack and other products. People who wish to sell feed, tack, and other horse-related products must have enough capital to start their own business as well as the skill to ensure the business is profitable. Some of the major costs of running the business will include buying or leasing a location, purchasing inventory and insurance, paying salaries, and advertising and marketing. People skills, marketing know-how, and the ability to be on top of the latest horse industry trends are important for store owners. Organizational, accounting, inventory control, and supervisory skills are also important, as is the ability to select responsible employees with good customer-service skills.

Many horse-supply stores also offer their products for sale over the Internet and through catalogs. Deciding whether to broaden the business to include mail order as well as walk-in customers is also an important consideration for store owners. Visiting local tack and feed stores and reviewing catalogs and Web sites will help you decide if a career in this area is the right one for you.

EDUCATION AND TRAINING

A bachelor's degree in business or marketing or classes in agriculture, agribusiness, equine studies, or business are helpful.

SALARY

Incomes vary throughout the country. The income you can expect from owning a feed and tack store will depend on the demand in your area, your marketing ability and customer service skills, minus your expenses.

RESOURCES

American Feed Industry Association
1501 Wilson Blvd., Suite1100

Arlington, VA 22209
www.afia.org

Western-English Trade Association
451 E. 58th Ave., #4323
Denver, CO 80216-8468
www.waema.org

Saddle, Harness and Allied Trades Association
1101 Broad Street
Oriental, NC 28571
www.proleptic.net

Tack n' Togs
12400 Whitewater Drive, Suite 160
Minnetonka, MS 55343
www.tacntogs.com

Career Spotlight

MARK RAISBECK, TACK STORE OWNER

Mark Raisbeck owns Charlotte's Saddlery in Houston with his twin brother, Tim. The two took over running the store, which has two locations, after their mother, for whom the store is named, passed away in 1995. Charlotte Raisbeck started Charlotte's Saddlery in 1977 after recognizing the need for a saddlery and tack store for English riders in the area. About 10 years ago, the store expanded its product line to include Western tack and clothing. Mark, born and raised in Kansas City, Missouri, came to work at the store after graduating from Iowa State University in 1979, where he studied animal science and farm management.

Q. What does your job involve?

A. It involves everything from accounting, finances and people management to product development. This includes buying, advertising, merchandising and promoting, and selling new lines of equipment and clothing. I also like interacting with our customers, which falls under customer and public relations. I also do window displays!

Q. What is your typical workday like?

A. From 8:00 A.M. to 10:00 A.M. I do paperwork and accounting, from 10 A.M. to noon its inventory management and filling customer orders, and from noon to 6 P.M. I work on customer relations, product development, and merchandising.

Q. How many hours/days per week do you typically work?

A. I work 10 hours a day five to seven days a week depending on the time of year.

Q. What do you enjoy most about your work?

A. Interacting with our customers and helping them with their needs. It is sometimes challenging and always fun to help them make the most of their horse experience.

Q. What do you like least about your work?

A. The amount of paperwork and forms, both government and otherwise, that are required to run a business.

Q. What other horse industry experience do you have?

A. I worked a mobile tack shop for the first five years upon entering the business. This gave me a very broad background about showing, training, and caring for horses.

Q. What is your overall background with horses?

A. My family owned and showed horses as I was growing up. My mother, Charlotte, showed saddlebreds and my sister Arabians and Thoroughbreds.

Q. What is your most memorable moment in the horse industry?

A. Every year at our annual tent sale, we donate thousands of dollars worth of merchandise and gift certificates to hundreds of customers who have supported us through the years. We donate to many organizations throughout the year, but this one weekend is the most exciting.

Q. What is the most rewarding part of owning a tack store?

A. I enjoy the challenge of building a family business and being involved with its development at every level of the organization.

Q. What is the most challenging part of owning a tack store?

A. This would be a toss up between finding good, knowledgeable personnel to work for you versus managing the inventory product lines as it relates to the ever-changing customer base.

Q. What is the biggest achievement of your career?

A. Building a successful business, which allows me to give back to our horse community and help promote the growth of equestrian sports as a whole.

Q. What is the most challenging obstacle in your career?

A. Trying to successfully predict the ever-changing consumer.

Q. What advice would you give to someone interested in owning a tack store?

A. Build good, strong relationships with your customers and a healthy business will develop around this foundation. Be open to suggestions and listen. Also, have a love or interest in horses and related activities.

Q. What education and/or experience do you advise for someone interested in owning a tack store?

A. Have a business, finance, advertising, and marketing background and, above all, good people skills.

Q. What personal strengths or skills do you believe a person considering this field should have?

A. Be motivated, self-starting, energetic, organized and a good communicator.

Q. What professional or horse-related associations or organizations do you belong to?

A. I help promote several organizations including Arabian Horse Committee at the Houston Livestock Show and Rodeo, Houston Dressage Association, Texas Hunter/Jumper Association, Greater Houston Combined Training Association and SIRE-Therapeutic Riding Program.

Q. Is there anything else you would like to say about your career in the horse industry?

A. This career provides the opportunity to meet a variety of people who love animals. It is a truly unique industry unlike most others, involving specialized equipment and apparel manufactured from around the world and carried by a small number of stores in this country. The industry is small and most everyone knows everyone else. I would like to see the sport of horses gain popularity and recognition, but the expense of owning horses works against the growth of the industry. It's truly a fun and enjoyable sport to be involved in at many different levels.

Feed/Tack Store Staff Person

ABOUT THE JOB

Working in a feed or tack store is a good way to gain experience in the industry while getting to know the horse community. Hands-on experience with livestock and horses may or may not be required, depending upon the employer and the job itself, but knowledge of the products you sell and what they are used for is important. Strong communication skills, patience, and a pleasant personality are important for people working in retail sales. Being organized and good with numbers is important, as you'll have to count money and balance the cash register. Working hours may be full-time or part-time and may include weekends and evenings.

EDUCATION AND TRAINING

High school attendance or diploma is necessary.

SALARY

The starting salary is typically minimum wage.

RESOURCES

Check with stores in your area for employment opportunities, equine employment agencies, publications and Web sites.

Horse Sales/Trading

ABOUT THE JOB

People involved in horse sales may act as agents who assist buyers in finding the right horse and then arrange sales for a percentage of the sales price. Or, they may buy horses and resell the animals at higher prices. Sales agents may find customers among riding students, boarders, and breeders. Many people who engage in horse sales do this as an adjunct to another job within the horse industry. Trainers, riding instructors, and boarding stable operators may supplement their income by acting as sales or trading agents when they buy, train, and resell horses. Some traders also buy and sell saddles, trailers, carriages, and other horse-related items.

To be successful as a sales agent or trader, you need strong horse handling skills as well as familiarity with horse conformation, anatomy, breed characteristics, and pedigree. Knowledge of the overall horse market and how it works is also important. Traders sell horses via competition sales, auctions, the Internet, published media, horse expos, and word of mouth. Marketing and networking expertise are necessary to get the word out about the business, as are good negotiating skills.

EDUCATION AND TRAINING
A college education is not required; however, equine studies and business or marketing classes are helpful.

SALARY
Ten percent of the sale price for each horse is a standard fee for sales agents. Traders earn the difference between the buying and selling cost, minus any expenses incurred while the horse is under their care. Expenses could include feed, training aids, boarding costs, and veterinary care.

RESOURCES
Contact horse people in your area, local and regional horse directories, and publications.

Insurance Sales Agent

ABOUT THE JOB
Equine insurance agents specialize in providing insurance to individual horse owners and horse businesses. They insure against horse loss, injury, lawsuits, fire, and other disasters. Agents may be employed by one agency or they may operate as independent business people, representing several companies and placing policies directly with the company that best serves their clients' needs. Agents spend their time meeting with clients at horse events, barns, and farms—they also work at the office making calls and doing computer and paperwork. Sometimes their cars often double as offices. Agents usually determine their own working hours, often scheduling appointments on weekends and in the evening for the convenience of their clients.

A high degree of self-motivation is necessary to be successful in this field, as agents work on a commission basis. Marketing and networking skills are important for building a client base. Experience with horses is desirable, since it allows you to better understand customer needs and concerns, and will be beneficial for networking and marketing your services. Also, insurers sometimes prefer to hire individuals with technical expertise in the market they are targeting.

EDUCATION AND TRAINING

A four-year degree in business, economics, or an equine-related field, or experience in sales, business, or finance is essential. State licensing is required.

SALARY

The median annual salary is $38,750.

RESOURCES

To make contacts in the industry, visit horse shows, expos, rodeos, and other places where horse people convene. Occupational information about insurance sales agents is available from many local insurance offices. The department of insurance for each state provides licensing requirements. Other resources include:

Independent Insurance Agents and Brokers of America
127 South Peyton Street
Alexandria, VA 22314
www.independentagent.com

Insurance Vocational Education Student Training (InVEST)
127 S. Peyton St.
Alexandria, VA 22314
www.investprogram.org

Career Spotlight

JORENE MIZE, INSURANCE BROKER

Jorene Mize has been in the insurance business for over 40 years and has spent the last five years specializing in equine insurance. After many years of working in the general insurance industry, Jorene finally found a niche for herself in equine insurance and started her own successful business with the support of her family. Because of her daughter's love of horses, Jorene has become a western pleasure rider herself and has a 9-year-old Red Dun named Kate, after Katharine Hepburn. Although her family started out with only one leased horse for her daughter, now they own 14 quarter horses and a jackass named Radar; all are cared for and trained by her daughter in Lancaster, California.

Q. How long have you worked in insurance?

A. 40-plus years.

Q. What did it take to start your own business?

A. I had always worked successfully for insurance agencies owned by others, but, although I loved helping my clients, I had some unsatisfying experiences in these agencies. My daughter and son convinced me to take my accounts and open my own office out of my home. I followed the example of my daughter, who had taken what she loved—horses—and created her own boarding and training business. I took what I loved and built my own business helping people with insurance. My son did my Web site, and my daughter provided moral support to keep me going while trying to make ends meet. I started with a small room with one desk, a printer, a computer, and a file cabinet. And for the first year and a half, it was a struggle—more than I'd bargained for, actually. It was enough of a struggle that I considered going back to work for others. But as the Web site progressed, and really began to take off, the business went from being in the red to being in the black. Now, I have an entirely separate office building with three desks, three computers, four file cabinets and so much work that now my daughter is working with me!

Q. What did you do prior to your current career?

A. Prior to specializing in equine insurance, I wrote all types of insurance: home, auto, commercial. I have worked as an insurance agent since graduating from high school (many years ago).

Q. What does your job involve?

A. I continuously keep updated on the current markets for equine insurance. I speak with clients on the phone, explaining coverages, and I e-mail quotes. In dealing with the insurance companies, I'm particular about giving them the accurate information they need in a timely manner. Mostly, I enjoy finding ways for people to meet their insurance needs. I've found that I like horse people and I like being able to help them.

Q. What is your typical workday like?

A. In the morning, I check my e-mail and respond to quote requests for insurance on horse mortality, horse trailer, guided trail ride, pony ride, farm and ranch, and horse training and riding instruction. Then, I begin processing new business by doing applications, faxing companies for quotes, faxing applications to prospective customers, returning customers' phone calls, rating, mailing policies, invoicing, and answering more e-mails. I typically receive 20 to 40 quote requests daily on the Internet.

Q. How many hours/days per week do you usually work?

A. Anywhere from 10 to 12 hours a day and usually four or five hours on Saturday and Sunday. However, now that my daughter is working full-time with me, I will probably be able to cut down to seven or eight hours a day. And, I would have to work even more hours if it weren't for my son. He has streamlined and automated some of my online quoting and application processes, which has probably cut my time in half.

Q. What percentage of your business is devoted to equine insurance?

A. Sixty percent.

Q. What other types of insurance do you sell?

A. Home and commercial.

Q. What do you enjoy most about your work?

A. Equine people have been the absolute best to work with. They are appreciative of the service we give them and are not just shopping for the best deal, even though we always try to find the best rates possible.

Q. What do you like least about your work?

A. The paperwork. It never ends!

Q. What is your educational background?

A. High school and insurance courses.

Q. When did you know you wanted to go into insurance sales?

A. In my senior year of high school, an insurance agent in my hometown, Fairbanks, Alaska, needed a secretary. I had the first appointment and he was such a sweet man who couldn't say no to anyone, so he hired me.

Q. What is your background with horses?

A. My daughter has been involved with horses since she was 11. I would take her to a ranch every weekend where she would work with the horses. Then, we leased her a horse. Now, we have 14 of our own. Since she takes care of all the horses, trains, and gives lessons, I continuously learn from her.

Q. In what discipline do you ride?

A. I ride western for pleasure.

Q. What is your most memorable moment working in the horse world?

A. Seeing the foals born. As far as insurance goes, there are a lot of great moments, especially when clients thank me for talking them into equine medical insurance. When something terrible happens to their horse, they then have coverage and they don't have to worry about how they'll pay for it.

Q. Is having horse experience necessary to be successful working in equine insurance?

A. I feel it is because that's what helps me understand the illnesses of horses, the various breeds, and uses.

Q. What is the most rewarding part of selling equine insurance?

A. I appreciate the people who are thankful that this type of insurance is available at a fairly inexpensive price; it gives them peace of mind.

Q. What is the most challenging part of working in equine insurance?

A. Trying to find companies to write trail ride insurance.

Q. What is the most challenging obstacle in your career?

A. Opening my own business.

Q. What has driven you to excel in your career?

A. My family.

Q. What education and/or experience do you recommend for someone interested in an insurance career?

A. Pick a specialty that you are really interested in and specialize in selling that kind of insurance. Really know the coverages so you can properly advise the clients on what is worthwhile to purchase as opposed to what they don't really need.

Q. What personal strengths or skills do you believe a person should have who is considering this field?

A. Good conversation skills and product knowledge.

Q. What advice would you give to someone who wants to specialize in equine insurance?

A. Work for a reputable agency or company and learn all you can about insurance. Get as much one-on-one experience with horses or veterinarians to gain knowledge of horses.

Q. If you could do it over, is there anything you would have done differently to reach your career goal?

A. Yes. I would have opened my own office MUCH, MUCH earlier in life.

Q. What do you think the job outlook is for equine insurance agents?

A. I think it is quite good as there are only a few agents who actually specialize in equine insurance. I find that being licensed in 40 states, it is amazing how much business I write. Clients tell me they cannot find anyone in their state who writes equine business, or if they do, those agents don't know enough about the product.

Q. In very general terms, what income do you believe someone in your field can expect starting out?

A. If they go to work for an agency, they would probably start out at around $30,000 a year; and if they work on commission, it could be up to $60,000 or more a year.

Marketing Specialist or Manager

ABOUT THE JOB

Marketing specialists and managers develop and implement plans to sell products or services and to promote the organizational interests of horse industry manufacturers and other businesses, associations, and event operators. Product and brand managers focus on all promotional and marketing programs related to a specific product group or brand. Market research analysts evaluate the customer market and conduct consumer research studies to determine what the demand is for a specific product or service.

Marketing personnel may work directly for equine organizations and businesses, or for agencies specializing in marketing and promotions. They may also be self-employed. Individuals employed by agencies supporting the horse industry must be prepared to support other industries as well because most agencies diversify across several industries. Marketing personnel work closely with sales, advertising, and public relations organizations to implement overall marketing strategy, and may travel frequently to meet with customers and attend industry events. Strong communication and creative skills are necessary to work in this field.

EDUCATION AND TRAINING

A four-year degree in marketing or business is requisite. Internships in the marketing field are also recommended. Certification is available for marketing professionals through the American Marketing Association.

SALARY

The median annual salary for marketing managers is $71,240, according to the U.S. Bureau of Labor Statistics. The median annual salary for marketing specialists is $37,200, according to the 2000 Compensation in the Marketing & Sales Field survey, by Abbott, Langer & Associates Inc., for the American Marketing Association. Market research analysts earn an annual median salary of $58,000 and product and brand managers earn $65,000.

RESOURCES

American Marketing Association
311 South Wacker Drive, Suite 5800
Chicago, IL 60606-2266
www.marketingpower.com

Career Spotlight

LANIER CORDELL, MARKETING CONSULTANT

Lanier Cordell has worked in the marketing field for 27 years, 15 of which have been spent in the horse industry. She is the marketing representative for the equine studies program at Virginia Intermont College and the marketing and public relations officer for the Intercollegiate-Interscholastic Dressage Association (IDA). She serves approximately 15 other horse business accounts and several nonhorse clients. Prior to her current position, Lanier worked in public relations. Though Lanier herself does not ride, she is surrounded by a family of hands-on horse people: her daughter is a riding instructor, her son is a farrier, her son-in-law is an equine veterinarian, and the youngest member of the family, Lanier's granddaughter, is a "pony girl." Lanier grew up in New Orleans and still lives in Louisiana. When not supporting the horse industry through her marketing efforts, she enjoys distance bicycling and sailing.

Q. What is your job?

A. I help people and businesses determine how best to generate interest in their product or service.

Q. What is your typical workday like?

A. I spend the majority of time writing copy, designing logos, brochures, ads, newsletters, and more. I also speak with media representatives such as editors, writers, and ad sales representatives, and consult with clients, printers, layout artists, graphic artists, and manufacturers.

Q. How many hours per week do you typically work?

A. Forty-five or more.

Q. What do you enjoy most about your work?

A. I enjoy the creative aspects and really helping people.

Q. What do you like least about your work?

A. Billing.

Q. What is your educational background?

A. I grew up in businesses owned by my parents. I studied art and writing, and I went to college for two years studying fine arts.

Q. When did you know you wanted to go into marketing within the horse industry?

A. When I saw how poorly my daughter's excellent trainer marketed herself.

Q. How did you become involved with the IDA?

A. When the decision was made to make the organization a national one, I was asked to take the reins and get it moving forward. Eddie Federwisch, who asked me to help out, knows from our long association that I am a neurotic detail person and that I have helped form other organizations. So Beth Beukema, president of IDA, and I got the bylaws done and I worked with all the necessary people and handled compromises when conflicts arose. I did and continue to do a lot of the detail work that others don't have the time or inclination to do.

Q. What sparked your interest in horses?

A. My children both loved horses and riding.

Q. In what discipline do you ride?

A. I don't, but if I were to start, I'd do dressage. I like the attention to detail and the sense that you are competing more against yourself than others.

Q. What is your most memorable moment in the industry?

A. I'd have to say that the most memorable moment was learning that we had tripled the enrollment in Virginia Intermont College's equine studies program in just two years. I began working with Virginia Intermont during my daughter's freshman year there. The number of students in the equine studies program had dwindled from more than 100 to less than 40. I wanted to do everything I could to assure that, by the time she graduated, the school had a reputation for graduating the best and most qualified horse professionals in the country. Fortunately, Eddie Federwisch was hired as program director at the beginning of my daughter's second semester. He shared my goals for the program and we have worked together ever since.

Q. Is having horse experience necessary to be successful in your field?

A. Actual riding experience may not be necessary, but it is imperative that you have a deep understanding of the industry and the people who populate it.

Q. Do you have direct contact with horses as part of your job?

A. The only direct contact with horses I have is when I take photos for clients for promotional or public relations purposes. I would estimate that it consists of less than 5 percent of my time.

Q. What is the most rewarding aspect of working in the horse industry?

A. I really think that interacting with horses is an invaluable experience for any human being and I love helping to expand such opportunities.

Q. What is the most challenging part of your job?

A. Dealing with clients who have limited understanding of marketing and with those folks who feel that just because they can write a grocery list, they can also write effective marketing and advertising copy.

Q. What is the biggest achievement of your career?

A. The growth of Virginia Intermont College's equine studies program and the existence of the Intercollegiate-Interscolastic Dressage Association.

Q. What is the most challenging obstacle in your career?

A. Dealing with extremely small marketing budgets.

Q. What has driven you to excel in your career?

A. I think the horse industry is invaluable to the human race and I want to see it survive and thrive.

Q. What education and experience do you recommend for someone interested in a marketing career?

A. A college degree in marketing is helpful, but understanding people and what motivates them is even more valuable. I think that once you have your degree, you should work with folks with extremely small budgets; it forces you to be more creative and develops your problem-solving skills.

Q. What advice would you give to someone who wants to work in the marketing field within the horse industry?

A. Be prepared to work hard with very small budgets.

Q. What personal strengths or skills should a person have who is considering this field?

A. Creativity, writing skills, and a devotion to solving problems.

Q. What do you think the job outlook is for marketing professionals in the horse industry?

A. Like any industry, growth in marketing opportunities is dependent upon overall growth in the industry. Of course, it is rather like the chicken or the egg: effective marketing increases demand, which helps the industry grow, which increases marketing opportunities.

Q. Is there anything else you would like to say about your career?

A. I think that despite the few bad apples you come across, the horse industry is really great. I think that the present movement towards greater professionalism and ethics will only improve things.

Real Estate Agent/Broker

About the Job

Real estate agents and brokers specialize in the buying and selling of ranches, farms, dude and guest ranches, and other commercial and residential horse properties; they also help horse lovers relocate or start businesses. Many agents who specialize in horse properties are horse lovers themselves who have found a way to combine their love of horses with their talent for property sales. To be a success in this competitive field, it is important to have the flexibility to meet with clients on their time, good communication skills, enthusiasm, honesty, and professionalism.

Agents are usually self-employed and work for licensed real estate brokers on a contract basis. Self-employment dictates that agents also have good organizational and business skills because they must manage their budgets to provide for their own insurance and retirement savings. Agents receive a commission on the properties they sell.

Education and Training

A bachelor's degree in real estate or instruction at a specialty school is essential. All states require real estate agents and brokers to be licensed. Most states require between 30 and 90 hours of classroom instruction for agents, and additional training plus experience for brokers. Contact local real estate organizations or your state's commission or board for additional licensing information.

Salary

The median annual salary for real estate sales agents is $27,640; the median for real estate brokers is $47,690.

Resources

National Association of REALTORS
30700 Russell Ranch Road
Westlake Village, CA 91362
www.realtor.org

Career Spotlight

JANET INGOLD, REAL ESTATE BROKER

Janet Zachman Ingold is a licensed real estate broker and Missouri real estate salesperson who specializes in the buying and selling of horse properties. She has been in the field for approximately four years. Prior to her career in real estate, Janet worked in nursing homes as a physical therapy assistant and wound care specialist. In addition to being an accomplished real estate agent who, in her first year in the field, was awarded Rookie of the Year, Newcomer of the Year, and third top real estate agent honors, she is also an accomplished horsewoman. Janet has two horses, Jack, a 9-year-old quarter horse gelding, and Sweetie, a 9-year-old quarter horse mare belonging to her eldest daughter. Janet was born and raised in Kansas, and spent much of her time as a child at her family's weekend retreat, a cattle ranch not too far from their home.

Q. What is your typical workday like?

A. My workday varies, but it starts at about 6 A.M. when I check and send e-mails to clients or people involved in transactions. I may also send out the morning list of new properties on the market that may fit my buyers' needs. Then I am off to drop the kids at school and day-care. Typically by 9 A.M., I am at the office or back at my home office to finish the day. Some days I spend doing paperwork, making sure everything is turned in and client records are up-to-date. Other days may be spent showing buyers property, writing up a listing or just running general errands that need to be done. I am on call seven days a week, though I do try to make time for the family and myself. Some weeks are busier than others, so it really depends on the week and time of year. For the most part, holidays and wintertime are slower, so I do get some down time. I can work on marketing materials or use it for family and myself.

Q. What ratio of horse properties to nonhorse properties do you handle, on average?

A. I get a pretty even split on horse properties to residential sales, due in part to the buyers who are usually moving to the country from town and vice versa.

Q. Is having horse experience necessary to be successful in helping clients buy and sell horse properties?

A. Definitely! It is important to know what your clients are saying and to understand what they are looking for. Also, knowing different types of barn builders and their ability, and knowing farriers and veterinarians in the area to refer clients to is so important. I look at a lot of properties on the market and know what is available, so I can answer questions about almost any horse property out there. You also need to know about schools for the kids, local trainers and boarding facilities, horse show circuits for the particular breed, and most importantly, county regulations for land use.

Q. What do you enjoy most about your work?

A. Meeting people. In this job, you get the opportunity to work with so many different folks. Each one is different and unique in his own special way. I have developed wonderful friendships with lots of them—from a show buddy, trail riding friend, or even the head nurse of the maternity floor who held my hand and was there the entire time I delivered my last child—it is awesome the kinds of relationships I have developed working in real estate.

Q. What do you like least about your work?

A. Calls on holidays.

Q. What education and experience do you recommend for someone interested in a real estate career?

A. Statistics say that 80 percent of people who get into real estate fail within the first three years. So, my best advice is to educate yourself as to what this profession requires. Know what your inspectors look for and ask lots of questions. (For example, rural properties have septic systems, so I went to the Pumper Show in Nashville for five days to learn about septic systems). Know how a house is built and the building code requirements for your state or county (they do vary by county). Know about surveying land, the process, and the cost. If you specialize in new homes or choose to sell land, you should know what you are talking about. Get to know a lot of people in the horse industry, from barn builders to veterinarians. My associates rely on me to answer questions about horse properties or rural properties, but in the same vein, I ask them questions about their areas of specialty. If you don't know the answer, admit it, and go get the answer!

Q. What personal strengths or skills do you believe a person should have who is considering this field?

A. People skills. If you are shy or timid about knocking on peoples' doors, you'd better look elsewhere for a career. This job requires that you market yourself hard at all times. Whether you are standing in line at the grocery store or eating at a restaurant, you have to be prepared to speak up and let people know that you are in real estate. Also, this is a very difficult career to do part-time. Plan on dedicating your life to the business the first couple of years, to developing relationships and getting your name out there. An understanding family is important, since the job sometimes requires long days and weekends.

Q. What advice would you give to someone who wants to specialize in horse properties?

A. Know horse people and horses. People searching for horse properties do not want an agent who doesn't know anything about horses or who doesn't understand what they need in a horse-related property. Being involved in your community's horse shows is the best way to make good contacts. Everyone on the circuit or in my area who has horses is on my mailing list.

Q. What do you think the job outlook is for agents specializing in horse properties?

A. For the most part, we are a small and exclusive group. You just have to market yourself really well in this area so your name gets out and other agents are aware of your specialty.

Q. In general terms, what starting income do you believe someone in your field can expect?

A. It is really hard to say. It depends on the area in which you live and how strong the market is. You spend a good portion of your income on marketing yourself and your properties (from advertising in magazines to monthly mailers), so anticipate at least 20 percent of your income going towards marketing. If you are in an average real estate market, as I am, the typical rural property can sell from around $200,000 to $500,000. The best answer I can give is around $70,000-plus a year.

Q. If you could do it over, is there anything you would have done differently to reach your career goal?

A. Not really, except hiring an assistant from the beginning to help with all the paperwork and marketing materials.

Q. How long have you ridden?

A. I started riding before I was five, but my first pony was given to me on my fifth birthday. Her name was Mary Sue. We kept her in the backyard of our suburban home for about a week. I rode her every morning in my pajamas. From there, I was hooked. I continued to ride from that point on at the farm. Our ranch manager always had a new horse for me to ride just about every week. He loved to buy and sell horses at the auction and I was the first one on them when they were brought home. I would disappear for hours. I knew my parents were concerned, but I always came home in one piece.

Q. In what disciplines do you ride?

A. I used to ride western and English. These days, with my girls just starting to show, we pretty much stick to western and halter classes. We compete in halter, showmanship, lead-line for my 4-year-old, horsemanship, pleasure, and trail. I also train horses, give lessons, judge occasionally, and show horses.

Q. What is your most memorable moment as a horsewoman?

A. Showing my nationally ranked gelding to top ten in the nation in hunt-seat equitation and competing at the Youth AQHA World Show in western riding. The other memorable moment was when my horse Skip fell on me at a show in Oklahoma, and broke my foot. I went to the emergency room, got a temporary cast put on, and returned the next day to show. I placed second in horsemanship and watched the judge's jaw drop to the floor when he saw me get off the horse and hop away on crutches—he never knew.

Q. Is there anything else you would like to say about your career or your life with horses?

A. Professionally, I was told that being a specialist in horse properties wouldn't be a wise idea, but it was something I felt I could succeed at. I am gaining lots of respect from my peers and getting a name in my area for being the one to call. It was a huge leap of faith and it worked for me. As far as the horses, I wouldn't trade them for the world! They are my escape from my hectic life. My family and I enjoy the horses, so it is my time to relax and spend time with my family.

Sales Manager

ABOUT THE JOB

Sales managers direct the sales programs for their companies. They supervise sales staff by managing day-to-day activities and advising staff on how to improve their performance. They set sales policies and goals, assign sales territories, analyze market trends, monitor the preferences of customers, determine inventory numbers, and establish training programs. Strong analytical, coordination, management, and marketing skills are important for sales managers. Horse experience is often not required.

EDUCATION AND TRAINING

A four-year degree in business or marketing is essential.

SALARY

The median annual salary is $68,520.

RESOURCES

Western-English Trade Association
451 E. 58th Ave., #4323
Denver, CO 80216-8468
www.wetaonline.org

Sales and Marketing Executives International, Inc.
PO BOX 1390
SUMAS WA 98295-1390
www.smei.org

Sales Representative

ABOUT THE JOB

Sales representatives work for manufacturers selling their products to businesses, retail outlets, and large farms and ranches. Sales representatives are employees of a particular manufacturer, whereas independent business people—called manufacturers' sales representatives or sometimes manufacturers' agents—represent the product lines of several companies. Both company and independent sales reps spend much of their time traveling within the sales territories they cover to visit different accounts. They also travel to horse expos, shows, and other horse-related events to represent their employers' product lines. Sales representatives working directly for manufacturers are usually paid a base salary plus commission; manufacturers' sales representatives are paid strictly on commission. Sales reps should be assertive and have strong people and communication skills; independent sales representatives need to know how to manage their own businesses.

The level of horse experience required often depends on the wishes of the employer or product manufacturer. Some employers prefer to hire horse people, while others hire nonhorse people with strong sales background. Either way, manufacturers' sales representatives should have a thorough understanding of their product lines.

EDUCATION AND TRAINING
A minimum of high school and sales experience in a part-time or summer job, or a four-year degree with emphasis in marketing, business, agricultural, or equine fields is important.

SALARY
The median annual salary is $40,340 for sales representatives.

RESOURCES
Western-English Trade Association
451 E. 58th Ave., #4323
Denver, CO 80216-8468
www.wetaonline.org

Manufacturers' Agents National Association
P.O. Box 3467
Laguna Hills, CA 92654-3467
www.manaonline.org

Manufacturers' Representatives Educational Research Foundation
P.O. Box 247
Geneva, IL 60134
www.mrerf.org

Trade Show Manager

ABOUT THE JOB

Trade show managers plan and manage trade shows and expos for sponsoring organizations. They identify show locations; handle administrative tasks, such as budgeting and acquiring permits; rent out exhibit space; arrange for clinicians, speakers, and events; coordinate product and promotional giveaways; and oversee set up and tear down of booths. This position requires frequent travel to show sites. Trade show managers work with vendors as well as marketing and public relations personnel to ensure participation in promotional functions. This requires good communication skills. Excellent management and organizational skills are also necessary. Horse experience may or may not be required.

Visit horse expositions and trade shows to make contacts. You can find them advertised in horse publications or on the Internet. The Web site listed below also offers a trade show search capability and lists job openings for trade show professionals.

EDUCATION AND TRAINING

A four-year degree in marketing or business, with training in event management is required.

SALARY

The median annual salary for trade show coordinators is $31,000 according to PayScale (www.payscale.com).

RESOURCES

International Association for Exhibition Management
P.O. Box 802425
Dallas, TX 75380-2425
www.iaem.org

Trailer Sales Representative

ABOUT THE JOB

Trailer sales representatives help horse owners transport their animals by recommending the best trailer for their specific needs. They work directly for trailer manufacturers in dealerships and sell to the public, or they act as sales agents and purchase trailers for resale to horse owners. Good people skills, sales expertise, and some familiarity with or interest in horses are necessary to succeed in this field. Self-employed sales agents should have business skills as well.

Trailer sales representatives working for manufacturers are often paid on a commission basis. This may be straight commission, following a salaried training period, or a combination of commission and salary.

EDUCATION AND TRAINING
A high school diploma, sales experience, or on-the-job training is important.

SALARY
No information available.

RESOURCES
National Association of Trailer Manufacturers
2951 SW Wanamaker Dr.
Topeka, KS 66614-5320
www.natm.com

CHAPTER 16

Manufacturing and Production Careers

- - -

Thousands of positions are available in horse products and feed manufacturing. While many people may not immediately think of working for a manufacturer when they consider a horse industry career, the opportunities for advancement and to make a difference in the horse world—with both horses and horse people—are numerous. Companies are always pushing the envelope to make new and better products for equestrians and horses. Likewise, research to improve feed, supplements, and drugs for healthier, happier horses keeps scientists, technicians, and other personnel busy in the lab and on the cutting edge of scientific technology.

Fashion Designer

ABOUT THE JOB

Fashion designers create or modify designs of men's, women's, and children's clothing for the equestrian market, across equine disciplines. They work for clothing and pattern manufacturers and wholesale clothing distributors, designing clothes for riding and for wearing around the barn. Designers should be knowledgeable about the latest apparel trends and able to communicate their ideas verbally, in writing, and visually through sketches and computer-aided design. An eye for color, awareness of costs, and understanding of fabrics and production processes are important.

This field is very competitive, so it is critical that designers have a portfolio that illustrates their best work when approaching potential employers. Even so, many aspiring fashion designers are initially hired as assistants or sample makers, and work their way up. While equine fashion designers do not need to ride or have in-depth horse knowledge, they should understand the equestrian market, its needs, and its tastes. Some designers who have the vision for the perfect equestrian clothing start their own companies; this requires business skills as well as strong knowledge of the market and its trends.

EDUCATION AND TRAINING

You will need a four-year degree in fashion design from a college or university, or completion of a fashion design specialty school certificate program; knowledge of the horse industry and the needs of equestrians.

SALARY

Fashion designers earn a median annual salary of $49,530.

RESOURCES

National Institute of Schools
of Art & Design
11250 Roger Bacon Dr., Suite 21
Reston, VA 20190
www.arts-accredit.org

Western and English Manufacturers
Association
451 E. 58th Ave., #4323
Denver, CO 80216-1411
www.waema.org

Career Spotlight

JULIE HOWE, CO-OWNER, EQUINE ATHLETICS (EA)

Julie Howe and her partner, Lori Schoenenberger, began their Equine Athletics apparel business in 1999, in an effort to revolutionize riding wear. Focusing on riders and their needs as athletes, Julie and Lori were instrumental in influencing the equestrian apparel industry to focus on more sport-oriented riding apparel. With the introduction of microfiber fabrics, stretch mesh lining, creative designs, and hip colors, along with their creative

communications campaigns featuring talented young riders, Julie and Lori have helped bring about a change in the industry. Stretch hunt coats and shirts are now industry standard. In addition to being a trendsetter in the apparel industry, Equine Athletics is prominent in investing in the future of equestrian sports. A percentage of every sale of Equine Athletics apparel goes to its Young Riders Fund, which provides young riders who compete with financial support. The company also supports the Intercollegiate Horse Show Association and the North American Riding for the Handicapped Association, as well as a non-profit organization that provides worldwide medical care for working horses and donkeys, and one that offers wild horse protection.

Q. What made you decide to start your own equine athletic apparel business?

A. Being a competitive rider, I was disappointed in the choices available to riding athletes. Although I respect the traditional look of the sport, I felt there could be some innovations made to the overall design of some of the show apparel items.

Q. How did you start your business?

A. I had just returned from living overseas for a number of years and wanted to get back into working full-time. I met my future business and riding partner, Lori Schoenenberger, while living in Asia, and she and I had talked about what business we may be able to do together. I was very interested in starting my own business and felt I should start with something we were both passionate about. I've always been interested in textiles, especially athletically oriented fabrics. My desire to see more options in the riding arena seemed the perfect catalyst for starting some research. Lori and I researched fabrics and decided upon some initial products to test-market.

Q. How many people does your business employ?

A. It's actually just Lori and myself, with some help from my niece, Sara Green. Lori handles the art department and I do the design work, fabric sourcing and all the other day-to-day running of the office. We now have a distributor, Thornhill Enterprises, which takes care of sales and warehousing of the inventory.

Q. What does your job involve?

A. Since Lori and I are both very marketing-oriented, a big part of what we do is work on ad campaigns and marketing materials. However, the biggest aspect of my day revolves around coming up with new fabrics. We are constantly searching for new athletic fabrics and working to improve current designs. We have fabrics milled ourselves, which give us a lot of control on the fiber content so we're always trying to make things better and more practical.

Q. What did you do prior to your current career?

A. I've worked extensively in inventory management and purchasing, but in totally unrelated fields.

Q. What is your typical workday like?

A. My typical workday consists of working with my manufacturing broker on fabric sourcing, new designs, and coordinating advertising in equestrian publications. I also do all the purchasing for our distributor as well as deal with their customers who have questions about our products. I get a lot of e-mail inquires from both consumers and retail stores, so I do a lot of correspondence.

Q. How many hours per day do you typically work?

A. My work schedule varies a lot. It all depends on the time of year and whether or not we've got new fabrics and designs in the works. A typical workday for me is between seven and nine hours. If we're working on trade show preparation, it might be more like 10 hours per day, plus weekends as well. I also am able to do a lot from my home, which makes for a lot of flexibility.

Q. What do you enjoy most about your work?

A. I like the creative process. I like searching for new fabrics that will work well in the equestrian apparel industry. Although we're a small but growing company we work really hard on how we can be more innovative. The other aspect of my job that's particularly rewarding is the brand building process. We're very consistent with our image and look, and our photography style is unique.

Q. What do you like least about your work?

A. Not being able to grow faster. Since our launch, we've tried to take things slowly and keep them manageable. However, it's frustrating when you have a lot of concepts but not enough resources to get them done quickly. Now that we have a distributor, it has freed up a lot of time previously spent on shipping orders, etc., so we can now expect a breakout year.

Q. What is your educational background?

A. I didn't have the opportunity for a college degree, so I always refer to the creation of Equine Athletics as my education. To be honest, I've had to deal with just about every aspect of business—from accounting to marketing—in order to get this off the ground. I look at the knowledge I've gained as invaluable and about as well rounded as you can get.

Q. Where were you born and raised? What is your background with horses?

A. I was born in Illinois, and spent most of childhood begging my parents for a horse. When I was finally able to take lessons, there was really no going back. My poor folks were stuck with a horse-crazy kid. Looking back, it had to be frustrating for them as they weren't horse people themselves. I participated in a lot of western shows, mostly pleasure, and speed classes like barrel racing, with some English pleasure classes. I didn't actually enter into the discipline of show jumping until late in life. I was about 32 at the time. I was living in Asia at the time and got hooked. When I returned to the States, I had an English Thoroughbred called Bo Biddley, who was a saint! We did very well in the West Coast Amateur classes for a couple of years. After that, I started this business and the rest is history. Unfortunately, I don't currently have a horse and I don't have time to compete. However, I'm exploring the possibility of getting back into riding from a "jumping for pleasure" standpoint.

Q. What is your most memorable moment working in the horse world?

A. Seeing our first ad in print. It wasn't quite real until that point.

Q. What is the most rewarding part of your job?

A. I would have to say working with organizations on a sponsorship basis. We've worked with the IHSA (Intercollegiate Horse Show Association) for the past two years and it's always a pleasure seeing riders at the grassroots level who really appreciate our sponsorship. We've also worked closely with the North American Young Riders Championship teams who we've outfitted for the last few years. It's thrilling to see these young riders work toward making it into the Grand Prix ring. They're all very hard workers and dedicated to the sport.

Q. What is the most challenging obstacle in your career?

A. Making a name for us in a market that's really quite small and fractured. There's a lot of competition so we're always looking for creative ways to get our products noticed. We knew when we started in 1999, that the idea of more sport-oriented riding wear was inevitable and that we had to work really hard to get our message across. Now, it's industry-standard and all the major companies have introduced their versions of high-tech designs. Fortunately for us, it took a while for the others to really catch on, which gave us some time to get a foothold. We're a small, growing company. Our biggest challenge is competing with the big guys who have deeper pockets It's a daily challenge to think outside the box and stay in the game.

Q. What is the biggest achievement of your career?

A. Helping to bring about a more forward-thinking philosophy to the sport. There have been very few changes in the English equestrian market. I believe we've helped bring to equestrian competitors the message of thinking like an athlete. We've managed to give riders more of a choice. I'm really proud of that.

Q. What advice would you give to people who want to start their own apparel business?

A. I would tell anyone interested in the clothing business to be prepared for a lot of challenging work. Apparel is a tough business, especially in a niche market like this.

In addition, I would tell them to look to high-tech designs/fabrics and/or innovative designs. Don't be afraid to challenge the old guard and introduce something that's unique.

Q. What education and/or experience do you recommend for someone interested in the equine apparel business?

A. Although it's most certainly a plus to have a textile/design background, it isn't always necessary. If you have good ideas and concepts and are willing to seek out people who can help you, then you can make it work. A good business plan is essential, as are realistic and practical expectations.

Q. What personal strengths or skills should a person have who is considering this field?

A. A person entering into this business needs to be tough-minded, persistent, and optimistic. If you're not an optimist, you probably won't do well. You have to be passionate about what you're doing and keep focused on your goals. A disciplined, straightforward, and outgoing personality is really key in my opinion.

Q. If you could do it over, is there anything you would have done differently to reach your career goal?

A. I don't entertain a "what if" attitude. Overall, I think we've done what we set out to do and have absolutely kept to our original ideals and philosophy. We've grown slowly but steadily and now have a recognizable brand in the industry. That was our goal and we're still alive and kickin'.

Feed Mill Specialist

ABOUT THE JOB

Feed mill specialists are responsible for the operation of feed mills and the formulation of feed for horses. Working as a feed mill specialist could involve anything from designing the feed mill, purchasing feed ingredients, and managing storage to formulating feed under the direction of nutritionists, evaluating feed quality, overseeing maintenance of equipment, and supervising workers. Feed mill specialists should be knowledgeable about agricultural engineering methods; they should also be familiar with agricultural processing equipment and production and management processes. Additionally, familiarity with horses and equine nutritional concerns is important.

EDUCATION AND TRAINING

A four-year degree in agriculture or equine nutrition with additional classes or a minor in feed milling. (North Carolina State University in Raleigh offers a feed milling minor. Information is available on its Web site at www.ncsu.edu.)

SALARY

Information not available.

RESOURCES

American Feed Industry Association
1501 Wilson Blvd., Suite 1100
Arlington, VA 22209
www.afia.org

Manufacturer

ABOUT THE JOB

Many of the manufacturers of horse and feed products started out as regular horse owners who began their businesses after recognizing a need for a new or better product. Whether producing clothes for riders, nutritional supplements for horses, or any of thousands of other potential products, it is important to determine if there is a market for the product; so most manufacturers will typically prepare a detailed business plan. Manufacturers work with designers, engineers, researchers, and others to develop a product. They also must perform test marketing; oversee production, distribution, marketing, and advertising of their product; manage employees; and work with regulatory agencies, among their many duties.

Aspiring manufacturers need to have superior leadership, planning, organizational, and communications skills. Horse experience and knowledge of the equine industry are necessary to help determine the need for your product; these skills will also give you a head start in your marketing and networking efforts.

EDUCATION AND TRAINING
A degree in business, agribusiness, equine studies, or animal science, with a business focus recommended for the latter two areas.

SALARY
Salaries vary widely. The salary you can expect depends upon the product you manufacture and the demand for that product as well as the costs involved in producing it.

RESOURCES
Western English Trade Association
451 East 58th Avenue #4323
Denver, Colorado 80216-8468
www.waema.org

American Feed Industry Association
1501 Wilson Blvd., Suite 1100
Arlington, VA 22209
www.afia.org

Product Designer

ABOUT THE JOB
Designers create the products that are sold to horse lovers, which can include clothing for horses and people, equine-related gift items, tack, horse trailers, toys, and much more. Designers also alter existing products, with

the aim toward product improvement. Many designers are salaried employees of manufacturing and development companies, while others are freelancers who work for a variety of clients within the horse industry. Successful designers are creative and not afraid to ask questions of employers or clients. Designers take into account such things as size, shape, color, weight, materials, safety, fit, and ease of use. They then develop sketches, prototypes, or computer simulations of the product. Aspiring designers should put together a portfolio of their best work.

EDUCATION AND TRAINING
Depending on the product, on-the-job-training or a bachelor's degree in art and design, with a minor in an equine field is important.

SALARY
The annual median salary for commercial and industrial designers is $50,000.

RESOURCES
Western English Trade Association
451 East 58th Avenue #4323
Denver, Colorado 80216-8468
www.waemia.org

National Association of Schools of Art and Design
11250 Roger Bacon Dr., Suite 21
Reston, VA 20190
www.arts-accredit.org/nasad/default.htm

Industrial Designers Society of America
45195 Business Court, Suite 250
Dulles, VA 20166
www.idsa.org

Product Researcher

ABOUT THE JOB
In addition to scientific and technical researchers who spend the majority of their time in laboratories developing new products, feed, or supplements, or

enhancing existing ones (see Chapter 17), other researchers go out of the lab to talk to members of the horse industry (horse owners, business owners, and veterinarians) about their needs. Product (or field) researchers may meet with people face-to-face, talk over the telephone or via e-mail, or they may conduct written surveys. Excellent communication skills and horse knowledge are required.

EDUCATION AND TRAINING
A four-year degree in marketing, equine studies, or science, with training in market research is key.

SALARY
Starting salary ranges from $35,000–45,000.

RESOURCES
Western English Trade Association
451 East 58th Avenue #4323
Denver, Colorado 80216-8468
www.waema.org

Production Engineer

ABOUT THE JOB
Production engineers move horse-related products from design concept to finished goods. They determine what machines are used to manufacture products, develop production schedules, ensure that material inventories are maintained, determine what the production sequence will be, and monitor production to ensure that it stays on schedule. Production engineers must also have an eye on quality and work with quality personnel to ensure that the products being developed are up to standards. They identify problems that may occur, devise plans to fix problems, and implement solutions. Production engineers spend time in their offices planning, analyzing production data, and reporting on progress to management, in addition to visiting the production floor to ensure work is progressing smoothly.

Horse experience is not required for production engineers. Excellent organizational, planning, and coordinating skills are necessary.

EDUCATION AND TRAINING
A four-year or master's degree in industrial technology, industrial engineering, or business administration.

SALARY
The median annual salary for production managers is $61,660.

RESOURCES
Western English Trade Association
451 East 58th Avenue #4323
Denver, Colorado 80216-8468
www.waema.org

Quality Control Inspector

ABOUT THE JOB
Quality control inspectors have the very important job of monitoring the quality of horse feed and horse-related products. At feed mills, trained inspectors review incoming feed ingredients for moisture, bad odor, color, texture, deterioration, and other variables prior to unloading. They also review feed after it is mixed to ensure quality. (If feed lots are found to be unacceptable, inspectors can send the truck away with the refused feed ingredients.) For horse-related products, inspectors use different methods such as sight and touch to look for tears, bubbles, and other defects. They may also verify dimensions, color, texture, weight, and strength.

Inspectors compute the number of defects and other statistical measurements and report on them. Depending on the number of different items being produced by a manufacturer, a quality control inspector may be responsible for looking at a variety of items or only one. Horse experience may or may not be required, depending on the company and product being inspected.

EDUCATION AND TRAINING
On-the-job training or a four-year degree in a production-related or equine field for product inspectors is required; a four-year degree in nutrition, agriculture, or animal science is required for feed inspectors.

SALARY

The median annual salary for a quality assurance inspector is $37,500, according to PayScale (www.payscale.com).

RESOURCES

American Feed Industry Association
1501 Wilson Blvd., Suite 1100
Arlington, VA 22209
www.afia.org

Western-English Trade Association
451 East 58th Avenue #4323
Denver, Colorado 80216-8468
www.wetaonline.org

American Society for Quality
600 North Plankinton Ave.
Milwaukee, WI 53203
www.asq.org

Regulatory Agency Personnel

ABOUT THE JOB

The U.S. Food and Drug Administration's Center for Veterinary Medicine regulates the development of animal feed, drugs, and supplements. The federal agency employs a variety of workers to ensure that these products are safe for horses and other animals. Types of personnel the agency hires include veterinarians, animal scientists, chemists, computer specialists, biologists and microbiologists, engineers, pharmacologists, toxicologists, statisticians, physiologists, administrators, information technologists, communications personnel, medical officers, and consumer safety officers. The USDA and other government and state regulatory agencies also offer employment in similar positions.

EDUCATION AND TRAINING

Requirements will vary from a four-year degree to a veterinary or other doctoral degree; a civil service exam is required.

SALARY

Salaries vary, depending on the position. The FDA Web site provides salary tables at www.opm.gov/oca/payrates/index.htm.

RESOURCES

United States Food and Drug Administration

7519 Standish Place. HFV-12

Rockville, MD 20855

www.fda.gov/cvm

Regulatory Compliance Specialist

ABOUT THE JOB

Regulatory compliance specialists are experts on government rules and regulations as well as internal safety controls regarding the manufacture and production of animal feed, drugs, and supplements. They ensure that their companies fulfill regulatory requirements, such as correct labeling of feed, drugs, and supplements, and utilize proper production practices. They handle registration of new products in compliance with state requirements, handle regulatory correspondence, and interpret all regulatory questions. Some companies hire regulatory compliance specialists as consultants to help them achieve licensing and to set up their regulatory departments and processes.

Horse expertise is not required, but excellent organizational, analytical, and interpersonal skills are important.

EDUCATION AND TRAINING

A four-year or advanced degree in scientific discipline such as pharmacology, chemistry, animal science, or other related area; in-depth knowledge of the Food and Drug Administration, United States Department of Agriculture, and state regulatory requirements.

SALARY

The median annual salary for regulatory compliance specialists is $40,500, according to PayScale (www.payscale.com).

RESOURCES

To gain knowledge of government regulations, visit Web sites for the Food and Drug Administration, United States Department of Agriculture, Occupational Safety and Health Administration, and other regulatory agencies.

American Feed Industry Association
1501 Wilson Blvd., Suite 1100
Arlington, VA 22209
www.afia.org

Wholesale Distributor

ABOUT THE JOB

Wholesale distributors purchase horse products and feed in large quantities from manufacturers for resale to retailers, feedlots, and veterinarians. Some distributors may also sell directly to horse owners and farms. Careers with wholesale distribution companies are available in a wide variety of areas, including sales, marketing, human resources, and computer services. Owners and top-level managers of distributors must understand the market; people working directly with customers, such as sales representatives and customer service personnel, should be able to speak the language of the people to whom they sell. Requirements for horse experience will vary.

EDUCATION AND TRAINING

Generally, a four-year degree is required, except for clerical and labor positions. The degree may be in business, marketing, agriculture, equine studies, animal science, or some other area, such as information systems, depending on your area of interest.

SALARY

Salaries vary by position.

RESOURCES

American Veterinary Distributors Association
2105 Laurel Bush Road, Suite. 200
Bel Air, MD 21015
www.avda.net

National Association of Wholesale Distributors
1725 K St. NW
Washington, D.C. 20006-1419
www.naw.org
(for associations representing various industries)

Other Product and Feed Production Staff

ABOUT THE JOB
Other workers involved in the manufacturing and production of horse-related products are production line and feed mill workers who operate the equipment that builds the product or produces the feed; truck drivers who move supplies and finished products; warehouse staff who bring supplies and products in and out of inventory; administrative and clerical workers; marketing and public relations personnel; nutritionists and other researchers; and scientists and purchasing agents.

EDUCATION AND TRAINING
Education requirements vary, depending on career, from high school diploma to doctoral degree.

SALARY
Varies according to position.

RESOURCES
American Feed Industry Association
1501 Wilson Blvd., Suite 1100
Arlington, VA 22209
www.afia.org

Western-English Trade Association
451 East 58th Avenue #4323
Denver, Colorado 80216-8468
www.wetaonline.org

CHAPTER 17

Research and Education Careers

— — —

Peaple who go into careers in research are characterized by their curiosity about the way things work and the desire to share their findings with others; they work toward the goal of improved horse and animal health. Educators, such as university professors and state extension office personnel, seek to teach the next generation of researchers, veterinarians, and trainers as well as facilitate better day-to-day understanding and care of horses. The majority of these careers require a high degree of education in the form of advanced professional or research degrees.

Opportunities exist both in and out of the classroom, and there are often excellent benefits or tenure tracks offered.

Animal Behaviorist

ABOUT THE JOB

Animal behaviorists are involved in studying the causes, functions, development, and evolution of horse behavior to better understand horses and improve their care, treatment, and health. They often work in university and college settings performing research and disseminating information on their latest findings to veterinarians, trainers, and horse owners; they teach in veterinary schools and animal and equine science programs; and some are employed by government and private industries to assist in health-related research. There are also animal behaviorists who work directly with horse owners and trainers to solve problems in horses such as cribbing, aggression, and separation anxiety.

Some of the fields in animal behavior include ethology, comparative psychology, and behavioral ecology. Although these fields overlap, ethologists and psychologists are interested in the regulation and functions of behavior while behavioral ecologists focus on the relation between behavior patterns and social and environmental conditions. Like other researchers in the animal world, travel may be required to symposiums and other events to listen to or present papers and research findings.

EDUCATION AND TRAINING

A DVM degree with board certification in veterinary behavior and/or or master's or PhD in a behavioral or biological science, with an emphasis on animal behavior is requisite. The Animal Behavior Society offers two levels of certification as an animal behaviorist, depending on the candidate's education and experience.

SALARY

According to the American Veterinary Medical Association, the mean annual salary for veterinarians working for colleges and universities is $83,059; for the federal government, it's $80,479; and for the state or local government, it's $69,549.

RESOURCES

Animal Behavior Society
Indiana University

2611 East 10th Street #170
Bloomington, IN 47408-2603
www.animalbehavior.org

American Veterinary Society of Animal Behavior
www.avma.org/avsab

Blood Typing Lab Technician

ABOUT THE JOB
Blood typing lab technicians work for laboratories that verify the parentage of purebred horses for breed registries and horse owners. Blood typing consists of testing genetic differences for nearly 40 different factors, including red cell antigens and serum proteins. Blood typing is also used in paternity testing, to identify horses in drug-testing cases, or in cases where horses may have been switched (such as in horse racing).

Blood typing lab technicians work under the supervision of veterinarians; their hours are fairly regular and they do not have horse contact as their time is spent indoors in laboratories looking at blood samples. They may also be involved in DNA testing of blood and hair, color testing, and genetic and other research.

EDUCATION AND TRAINING
A two- or four-year degree in an accredited veterinary technician/technologist program and training in blood typing are essential.

SALARY
The most recent survey of its members from the North American Veterinary Technician Association gives these average salaries in the following areas for veterinary technicians/technologists:

University/college	$30,512
Diagnostic/research	$37,410

RESOURCES
North American Veterinary Technician Association
P.O. Box 224
Battle Ground, IN 47920
www.navta.net

High School Agriculture Teacher

ABOUT THE JOB

Some high schools offer agriculture programs; in such programs, the teacher instructs students on a variety of agricultural topics, which may include equine science. Also, high school agriculture teachers may connect students to the National FFA organization and its programs and events, sometimes receiving a stipend for their involvement as FFA advisors. In addition to classroom teaching duties, agriculture teachers may accompany students on field trips, assist students in choosing colleges, and offer leadership to students on extracurricular agriculture-related projects. Teachers also meet with parents to discuss student academic progress and attend education conferences and workshops.

A rewarding benefit of teaching in high school is watching students gain an appreciation for knowledge and learning as well as potentially take an interest in an agricultural career. High school students considering a career as an agriculture teacher should talk to teachers in their own schools about the profession.

EDUCATION AND TRAINING

Educational requirements vary by state, however all states require at least a bachelor's degree with a vocational teaching endorsement in agriculture; some states require a master's degree. Licensing is required for all public school teachers.

SALARY

Median annual earnings of kindergarten, elementary, middle, and high school teachers range from $37,610 to $42,080. According to the American Federation of Teachers, beginning teachers with a bachelor's degree earned an average of $27,989 in the 1999-2000 school year. Private school teachers generally earn less than public school teachers.

RESOURCES

Recruiting New Teachers, Inc.
385 Concord Ave., Suite 103
Belmont, MA 02478
www.rnt.org

American Federation of Teachers
555 New Jersey Ave N.W.
Washington, D.C. 20001
www.aft.org

National Education Association
1201 16th St. N.W.
Washington, D.C. 20036-3290
www.nea.org

Librarian/Museum Curator

ABOUT THE JOB

Librarians and curators work for museums and libraries seeking to inform and educate the public, researchers, equine health professionals, and others about some area of the horse industry. Librarians and curators acquire, exhibit, and maintain collections at research, breed and sport, racing, rodeo, carriage, and other specialty libraries and museums. Curators work with books, artifacts, memorabilia, and photographs on a daily basis.

An interest in preserving history, a healthy curiosity, and strong people and computer skills are important. Librarians and curators usually work standard hours. Travel is sometimes required to review possible acquisitions or to visit educational and equine industry events. An understanding of the language of the industry is critical. Horse experience is helpful, though not required, in finding positions in this competitive area.

Others who work for libraries and museums include visitor services, security, gift shop, clerical, administrative, marketing and public relations employees. See the appendices for a list of equine libraries. General information on becoming a librarian or curator is available from the organizations listed below.

EDUCATION AND TRAINING

A Master of Library Science (MLS), art history, or museum studies is required. Note that while many colleges and universities offer MLS programs, many employers prefer graduates of schools accredited by the American Library Association. Contact the association for information on accredited schools.

SALARY

The median annual salary for librarians is $41,700. The median annual salary for museum curators, archivists, and technicians is $31,460.

RESOURCES

American Library Association
Office for Human Resource Development and Recruitment
50 East Huron St.
Chicago, IL 60611
www.ala.org

Special Libraries Association
1700 Eighteenth St., N.W.
Washington, D.C. 20009-2514
www.sla.org

American Association of Museums
1575 Eye St. NW, Suite 400
Washington, D.C. 20005
www.aam-us.org

Nutritionist

ABOUT THE JOB

Equine nutritionists work to improve horse health through better nutrition. They are employed in research and feed production for feed manufacturers, conduct research and teach at universities, and act as self-employed consultants for feed companies and farms. Nutritionists who are engaged primarily in research conduct experiments, analyze data, and spend much of their time in laboratories using computer analysis to help them in their work. Some travel to symposiums and other events may be required.

In addition to teaching, nutritionists in veterinary programs at universities and colleges also publish articles in academic journals as part of their job. They prepare lesson plans, lecture, and work with students in laboratory settings.

A general knowledge of horse behavior is useful for nutritionists, although horsemanship skills are not required.

EDUCATION AND TRAINING
A DVM with further studies in equine nutrition, or board certification in veterinary nutrition, and/or, PhD in equine nutrition is required.

SALARY
The mean annual salary for veterinarians working for colleges and universities is $83,059 according to the American Veterinary Medical Association; equine veterinarians in private practice earn $108,405.

RESOURCES
American College of Veterinary Nutrition
6 North Pennell Road
Media, PA 19063 www.acvn.org

American Feed Industry Association
1501 Wilson Blvd., Suite 1100
Arlington, VA 22209
www.afia.org

Reproductive Physiology Specialist

ABOUT THE JOB
As the name implies, the goal of a reproductive physiology specialist is to improve the reproductive process in horses. Professionals in this area work in laboratory settings performing research, teach at universities, manage breeding operations, and consult with horse owners on breeding problems. Reproductive physiology specialists manage reproductive disorders, improve artificial insemination and embryo transfer procedures, and study the effects of the environment on equine reproduction, among other duties.

In addition to reproductive laboratory work, researchers in the field attend symposiums, where they listen to or present research findings. University professors plan lessons, lecture, and oversee student projects. They are also required to publish articles in academic journals.

EDUCATION AND TRAINING
A DVM degree with a PhD in reproductive physiology.

SALARY

According to the American Veterinary Medical Association, equine veterinarians in private practice earn an average mean income of $108,405 per year; veterinarians in college or university settings earn an average of $83,059 per year; those working for the federal government earn approximately $80,479 per year; veterinarians working for state and local government earn an average of $69,549 per year.

RESOURCES

American Association of Equine Practitioners
4075 Iron Works Pike
Lexington, KY 40511
www.aaep.org

American Veterinary Medical Association
1931 Meacham Road, Suite 100
Schaumburg, IL 60173
www.avma.org

Research Chemist

ABOUT THE JOB

In an effort to improve horse health, research chemists study the behavior of chemicals and chemical compounds. They assist in the development of veterinary pharmaceuticals and work in other facets of veterinary research. They also conduct research for feed manufacturers to improve the quality of feed for horses and other animals. Research chemists work in university settings, the government, and in the private sector. They are indoors in laboratory settings most of the time and must be detail-oriented and enjoy working on their own. They write reports on their experiments, disseminate information to other researchers, and publish in scholarly journals. Chemists working in university settings may combine teaching and research.

EDUCATION AND TRAINING

A PhD in biochemistry or a DVM degree, with advanced training in chemistry is requisite.

SALARY

According to the American Veterinary Medical Association, the mean annual salary for veterinarians working for colleges and universities is $75,984; for private industry it is $109,941; and for the federal government it is $68,153. According to the 2002 salary survey by the American Chemical Society, the median annual salary for their members who hold a PhD is $85,200.

RESOURCES

American Association of Equine Practitioners
4075 Iron Works Pkwy.
Lexington, KY 40511-8434
www.aaep.org

American Chemical Society
Education Division
1155 16th St., N.W.
Washington, D.C. 20036
www.acs.org

Research Scientist

ABOUT THE JOB

In addition to the research positions discussed in separate descriptions, other scientists who conduct research into equine health and disease prevention include geneticists, cellular and molecular biologists, equine physiologists, biotechnologists, and agricultural scientists. These researchers work primarily in laboratory settings and will have various amounts of direct horse exposure, depending upon their area of research. Many of these scientists combine research with teaching in universities and colleges. They write about their findings in veterinary and scientific journals and present papers to their colleagues at professional symposiums.

EDUCATION AND TRAINING

A DVM degree is required, with specialized training in an area of expertise and/or a PhD in a specialty area.

SALARY

According to the American Veterinary Medical Association, the mean annual salary for veterinarians working for colleges and universities is $83,059; for the federal government it is $80,479; and for the state and local government it is $69,549.

RESOURCES

American Association of Equine Practitioners
4075 Iron Works Pike
Lexington, KY 40511
www.aaep.org

American Veterinary Medical
Association
1931 Meacham Road, Suite 100
Schaumburg, IL 60173
www.avma.org

State Extension Positions

ABOUT THE JOB

Extension horse specialists are part of an educational network that includes the U.S. Department of Agriculture, land-grant universities, and city and county organizations. Every state has at least one land-grant university or college. Each land-grant school employs a state extension specialist who administers the overall state extension program for all areas, including horses. Extension horse specialists provide information, advice, and educational programs to horse organizations and individual horse owners based on the latest ideas and research presented by land-grant universities and other agricultural organizations. They may also be involved in the planning of equine events in their state.

Below the extension horse specialists are extension and agricultural agents at county and local levels. These agents provide leadership for extension system programs and may work with and provide information to local and county horse owners and horse groups. Agricultural and extension specialists at the county and local level usually work on nonhorse programs as well. County extension agents also work as 4-H youth agents and may be involved in administering or leading the local 4-H horse program.

Leadership ability, communication skills, an interest in young people, and a desire to educate are important for these positions.

EDUCATION AND TRAINING

A four-year degree or higher from a land-grant university in agriculture, animal science, or equine studies is ideal. Higher-level positions, such as extension horse specialist and state extension specialist, often require advanced degrees.

SALARY

No information available.

RESOURCES

United States Department of Agriculture
Cooperative State Research, Education and Extension Service
1400 Independence Ave., S.W. Stop 2201
Washington, D.C. 20250-2201
www.reeusda.gov

Statistician

ABOUT THE JOB

Statisticians are employed in research settings and work with veterinarians, nutritionists, chemists, veterinary pharmacologists, and manufacturers seeking to improve horse health and develop improved horse products. They work for the United States Department of Agriculture, in schools, and in the private sector. Statisticians assist in research by applying their mathematical knowledge to design scientific experiments; collect, process, and analyze data; and evaluate results. Statisticians must be quick studies to become familiar with the area they are working in, whether it is developing new veterinary drugs or an improved feed for horses. Statisticians also write formal papers and reports about the work of the research teams in which they are involved.

Computer expertise is recommended, as well as communication skills strong enough to explain complex technical concepts.

EDUCATION AND TRAINING

A master's or doctorate in statistics or mathematics is required.

SALARY
The median annual salary for statisticians is $51,990.

RESOURCES
American Statistical Association
1429 Duke Street
Alexandria, VA 22314
www.amstat.org

Trade or Specialty School Instructor

ABOUT THE JOB
This kind of instructor teaches a particular trade or skill that does not require a college degree, such as farriery, equine massage, photography, veterinary assisting, riding instruction, or horse packing. Instructors at trade and specialty schools are often those who have practiced in the trade they are teaching; they may still work in the field and teach part-time as an adjunct to their careers. Hands-on instruction is a large part of teaching in a trade or specialty school; vocational skills as well as academic learning may be emphasized. Horse contact may be daily or not at all, depending on the subject being taught.

EDUCATION AND TRAINING
Depending on the trade or specialty being taught, expertise in the field and/or a degree as well as licensing or certification is required.

SALARY
Salaries vary widely by trade/specialty, region of the country, instructor credentials, and experience.

RESOURCES
See the appendices for a listing of trade and specialty schools. Also, check bulletin boards at feed and tack stores and stables for names of schools; or, try an Internet search for your area of interest.

Career Spotlight

BOB SMITH, FARRIER AND TRADE SCHOOL INSTRUCTOR

Bob Smith is owner and head instructor of Pacific Coast Horseshoeing School in Sacramento. He founded the school in 1991, and has received many accolades for his teaching work since that time. The American Farrier's Association presented Bob with its Outstanding Farrier Educator award in 1997. A year later, the California State Department of Consumer Affairs recognized Pacific Coast Horseshoeing School as one of 1998's top 12 vocational schools in California. Bob has also been recognized by the Western States Farrier's Association, the Farrier's Association of Washington State, and the Nevada Professional Farrier's Association for outstanding farrier education. His school is the farrier for more than 270 horses at University of California, Davis, in addition to other accounts with rental operations and private horse owners. Bob's school is also the farrier for the hooved animals at the San Francisco Zoo.

Prior to making the decision to teach the trade of horseshoeing, Bob operated a successful farrier practice. He was the farrier for Grand Prix jumpers on the professional circuit; medal-winning dressage horses; winners of snaffle bit futurities in Reno, Oregon, and Idaho; cutting horses competing at Fort Worth, Texas; endurance horses competing in the Tevis Cup 100-mile race; and many trail and pleasure horses.

Although Bob does not currently have his own horse, his wife Krissy owns and shows cutting horses.

Q. What made you decide to leave your farrier practice and open a school?

A. The decision to open a school and leave a lucrative practice was an evolution. As a farrier, I would frequently get calls from young men and women just starting out in the industry. They would ride along with me for several weeks, and I was amazed at how little they knew about shoeing, particularly, how naïve they were about running a small business.

Most of the new guys who rode with me had instructors at their schools who had just graduated the same course and had never worked as farriers. I believed then, and still do, that unless you have successfully run a farrier business that supported your family and made your mortgage payments, you are not qualified to teach. The only thing a student teacher can teach is how to nail a shoe on a foot and that is inadequate training in today's equestrian market. When these new guys left me after a few weeks of observation, they would always say that they wished I had a school. This comment planted the seed that gradually sprouted the school. My initial plan was to open a school and run it for five years, then hire instructors and go back to doing what I like to do: shoe. But I found that I really enjoyed teaching and now I have only a small clientele of therapeutic shoeings. For the first two-and-a-half years I continued working my shoeing practice evenings and weekends.

Q. What made you decide to become a farrier and how long did you practice?

A. I started shoeing in 1974, to finance my way through California State University, Sacramento, and hopefully, law school. I graduated the university with a bachelor's degree in criminal justice, but had fallen in love with shoeing and the shoeing life and I never went to law school. I did graduate work in farrier science at Sul Ross University, in Alpine, Texas; I worked under Doug Butler, PhD.

Q. You have cared for the feet of a wide variety of horses, but what was your area of expertise?

A. Over the years, I gravitated toward upper-level dressage horses. I enjoyed the animals, clients, and the challenge of shoeing to perfect movement.

Q. Have you worked in any other areas of the horse industry?

A. The usual—cleaning stalls, fixing fences, and riding colts—when I was young. Nothing full-time or professional.

Q. What does your current job involve?

A. I oversee the school full-time. I have several part-time instructors. I teach, pay bills, answer the phone, sweep the floor, pretty much everything that needs to be done.

Q. What is your typical workday like?

A. I get up around 5 A.M. and get into the classroom/office around 5:30. I answer e-mails from prospective students as well as e-mail questions from past students. They send digital pictures of problems and I respond. It's sort of a continuing education/support program. I pay bills, and do general paperwork for the school. Students start arriving around 7:30 A.M. for an 8 A.M. start time. My lecture lasts one-and-a-half hours. Then, horses are either coming into the school or we go to various horse facilities to shoe and trim. The afternoons are usually spent in forge work. Each day is a little different, depending upon where we are in the program.

Q. How many hours a day do you usually work?

A. Twelve to 14 hours a day on weekdays and I always spend a couple of hours in the early mornings on weekends.

Q. What do you enjoy most about teaching?

A. I enjoy being a positive influence on so many lives. It's a tremendous rush, having students call several years after they graduate to tell me that their shoeing practice is so successful that life is good—so good that they are buying a home. It is amazing to watch the progression from the first day to graduation day, to watch their confidence and skills grow as they realize that they do have control over their future.

Q. What do you like least about teaching?

A. For some, their only success in life is their constant failure. They assume that if they continue changing professions, they will find that elusive "happy place." It is hard to watch people, who are unable to self-assess, struggle with the same demons that have plagued them throughout their lives and not be able to make a positive contribution.

Q. How many students, on average, are in the program at any one time?

A. Class size averages around 14. Students start and finish together. I do not have new students entering the program every week. To produce a quality student, each day has to be a step up, not a revisit of old material to accommodate the new student.

Q. How did you get the job of maintaining the feet of the animals at the San Francisco Zoo?

A. In the late '70s, I had an opportunity to work on an elephant that was giving rides at grand openings and parades. I researched information on exotics and found the work fascinating. The veterinarian I worked with had a mixed veterinarian practice treating horses, cats, and dogs, but his specialty was zoo animals and he was waiting for an opening at a large zoo. He took a job at a small zoo back east and he would regularly consult with me about ongoing hoof problems. Fifteen years ago, he took over the position as the head veterinarian at the San Francisco Zoo and called me in. Through his contacts, I also consult at the Oakland Zoo. I have had the pleasure of working on musk ox, giraffes, elephants, gazelles, wildebeest, and zebras. The zoos allow me to bring my students, so the work doubles as an educational experience.

Q. What is your overall background with horses?

A. Prior to shoeing, personal ownership.

Q. What is the most memorable moment in your career?

A. There have been many memorable moments. Perhaps the most memorable student was a young man who had dropped out of high school to support his pregnant girlfriend (whom he married after graduating from shoeing school.) What a long row to hoe. After five years, I received a call from him as he was leaving a title company—he had just signed the paperwork to buy a home in the San Francisco Bay area, his wife was pregnant with number two, and, tearfully, he thanked me for helping him achieve a successful shoeing practice.

Q. What is the most challenging part of your job?

A. Getting students to leave their baggage behind and have confidence in themselves; to help them believe in themselves and in what we have taught them so they can prosper. There is no apprenticeship program. My students have to graduate, go home, and develop their own clientele. My job is to not only teach them how to shoe horses but how to be successfully self-employed.

Q. What advice would you give to someone interested in being a farrier?

A. Shoeing horses is hard, physical work and you have to love it to be successful. I tell my students that the man at the top of the mountain didn't fall there: it takes hard work, dedication, and sacrifice.

Q. What advice would you give to someone who wants to teach shoeing?

A. As a horseshoeing instructor, be a successful farrier first, have a strong desire to help people succeed, and establish in your mind and heart that you enjoy teaching.

Q. What education and experience do you recommend for people interested in working in this field?

A. This one is kind of tricky. The one thing that I can't teach in a shoeing program is horsemanship. Everything else I can handle. I would advise someone interested in this field to expose himself to as many horses and as much ground handling as possible. Also, don't smoke and get in good physical condition.

Q. What personality traits should a person have who is considering this field?

A. The same as people in general: good, sound, moral core beliefs, respect for others and animals, and confidence that you can achieve anything in life you desire with enough hard work, dedication, and sacrifice.

Q. What else would you like to say about your career?

A. Farriers are not regulated by any government agency. We are the last bastions of free enterprise left in America. Shoeing horses is the most freedom anyone can experience while making a six-figure income. To have total control over your life and your success is the essence of living in a free society.

University and College Teachers

ABOUT THE JOB

University and college teachers instruct those studying for associate to doctorate degrees. They work in college or university equine and agricultural programs and for veterinary schools. Their classes may be large lectures or smaller seminars; they may oversee laboratory study or perform research in their academic areas. A growing area of responsibility for teachers in the Internet age is preparing and teaching online classes as well as answering large amounts of e-mail from students, so computer and Web skills are necessary. Some teachers oversee student horse clubs and activities and most faculty members also serve on academic or administrative committees that address departmental matters, academic issues, budgets, and other concerns. The amount of time spent working directly with horses will vary, depending upon the teacher's area of specialty. Some will have no direct horse contact while others will spend a significant amount of time working with horses in hands-on settings.

There are generally four positions for four-year college and university faculty that are considered tenure-track positions: instructor, assistant professor, associate professor, and professor. Most new teachers are hired as instructors or assistant professors and move up from there. It takes about seven years to gain tenure following a review of the professor's teaching, research, and overall contributions to the school; a doctorate degree is usually required. (Full professors usually spend a greater amount of their time conducting research than assistant professors and instructors.) Schools may also hire adjunct faculty who teach on a part-time basis while working in other horse careers, and lecturers who are not on the tenure track.

Working hours are flexible but can be irregular, with some faculty teaching evening and weekend classes. Most schools require teachers to work nine months of the year; summer months may be spent teaching additional courses, conducting research, writing, or pursuing other interests.

EDUCATION AND TRAINING

A DVM degree or PhD in equine or animal science, animal nutrition, agriculture, animal behavior, equine physiology, or related fields or a master's degree is required. Professors interested in advancing to a position of dean usually have a doctorate degree.

SALARY

The median annual salary for all post-secondary teachers is $46,330, according to the U.S. Bureau of Labor Statistics. A 1999-2000 survey by the American Association of University Professors broke down the average salaries by rank:

Instructors:	$34,700
Lecturers:	$38,100
Assistant Professor:	$45,600
Associate Professor:	$55,300
Professor:	$76,200

RESOURCES

Investigate land-grant universities, veterinary schools, and other schools with equine or agricultural programs; equine associations related to the academic area of specialty.

Association of American Colleges and Universities
Preparing Future Faculty Program
1818 R. St. NW
Washington, D.C. 20009
www.aacu-edu.org

Career Spotlight

EDDIE FEDERWISCH, DIRECTOR OF EQUINE STUDIES, VIRGINIA
INTERMONT COLLEGE

Eddie Federwisch is the Director of Equine Studies at Virginia Intermont
College. Devoted to the horse industry for 23 years, Eddie has an extensive
background in teaching, schooling,
and show management. Growing
up in Dallas and Atlanta, Eddie
always liked horses and has been
riding them since he was 10 years
old. His discipline is in hunters and
he has a 17-hand, 10 year-old
Hanoverian-thoroughbred cross
named Rushman. Although Eddie's
dedication to the horse world con-
sumes most of his time, he also
enjoys traveling.

Q. How long have you worked in your current position?

A. Nine years.

Q. What did you do prior to your current position?

A. I ran my own training barn and lesson program.

Q. What does your job involve?

A. I teach lessons in hunt-seat and equitation, from beginners through
advanced. I also administer the program; develop curriculum; hire and manage employees; plan and run shows; work with the administration in determining program goals; coach an intercollegiate team; oversee barn
management; take students to horse shows; assist with fund-raising projects;

help admissions in recruiting new students; and market the program and our school-hosted shows.

Q. What is your typical workday like?

A. There is no such thing as a typical day. When you run a program this size, things change on a daily basis. Also, the school calendar determines what has to be done and when. For example, when school is in session, I spend more time working with prospective students. When the IHSA show season is in full swing, I spend more time coaching the team and taking them to horse shows.

Q. How many hours/days per week do you typically work?

A. Over 50 hours a week when school is in session. During the summer months, less.

Q. What do you enjoy most about your work?

A. Planning big events and horse shows.

Q. What do you like least about your work?

A. Trying to build a consensus with the various parties—students, admissions, faculty, and administration.

Q. What is your educational background?

A. Bachelor's in journalism and business management.

Q. When did you know you wanted to direct an equestrian program?

A. I didn't know. I was an instructor at the college when the opportunity presented itself.

Q. How did you go about finding your current job?

A. I was called to come and teach. Then, when the directorship came open, they asked me to take it.

Q. What is your most memorable moment as a horseperson?

A. There are too many to make a single choice.

Q. What is the most challenging part of your job?

A. Dealing with people.

Q. What is the biggest achievement of your career?

A. With the help of many people, taking a program that was in really bad shape and turning it around, making it successful.

Q. What is the most challenging obstacle in your career?

A. Trying to keep numerous people with varying opinions and goals on the same course.

Q. What has driven you to excel in your career?

A. A passion for excellence.

Q. What education and/or experience do you recommend for someone interested in managing an equestrian program?

A. I definitely believe you need a degree in equine studies with lots of classes in psychology and lots of practical experience.

Q. What personal strengths or skills should a person have who is considering this field?

A. Patience, enthusiasm, diplomacy, and a strong work ethic.

Q. If you could do it over, is there anything you would have done differently to reach your career goal?

A. No.

Q. Is there anything else you would like to say about your career or your life with horses?

A. You have to have experience, discipline, a good resume, and experience, along with a strong education, and lots of contacts. This business is a whole lot easier if you are honest and have integrity.

Veterinary Pharmacologist

ABOUT THE JOB

Veterinary pharmacologists develop and test new veterinary drugs, perform research to determine the effects of drugs on horses, consult with veterinarians on drug therapies, and teach. They work in veterinary schools, for government agencies such as the U.S. Food and Drug Administration, and for pharmaceutical companies. They often combine teaching and research.

In addition to scientific skills, pharmacology researchers working in universities are often involved in obtaining funds for continuing research and education, so they should be well organized, persistent, and have good communication skills. Professionals in the field recommend that anyone interested in becoming a pharmacologist try to observe others working in the field before making the commitment of time and education. As most of the pharmacologist's time is spent in a laboratory or classroom, horsemanship skills are not required.

EDUCATION AND TRAINING

A DVM degree with advanced training, or board certification in pharmacology or a PhD in pharmacology is requisite.

SALARY

According to the American Veterinary Medical Association, the mean annual salary for veterinarians working for colleges and universities is $75,984; for private industry it is $109,941; and for the federal government it is $68,153.

RESOURCES

American College of Veterinary Clinical Pharmacology
Department of Veterinary Physiology and Pharmacology
College of Veterinary Medicine
Texas A&M University
College Station, TX 77843-4466
www.acvcp.org

CHAPTER 18

Horse Recreation Careers

Recreational riding takes shape in many forms and is the largest and fastest growing segment of the horse industry. Every year, millions of people visit dude and guest ranches, send their children to summer horse camps, pack into the wilderness on horseback, spend untold hours trail riding on their own horses, rent horses for an hour or two through hack stables, increase their riding skills by taking lessons, and play polo at private and college clubs. The recreational riding industry offers many positions in a variety of career areas. Almost all of these positions involve daily hands-on horse contact and most of them require a high level of expertise with horses. Some jobs are strictly seasonal, and while they many not be career positions in and of themselves, they are good ways to gain solid experience working in the horse industry.

Because recreational riding is the largest sector of the industry, several positions that you might find in other areas of the horse world—such as groom, stable hand, riding instructor, barn manager—are included here as a catchall location. Read the descriptions below, which refer to other segments of the industry in which these positions are also found.

Boarding Stable Owner/Operator

ABOUT THE JOB

Owning a boarding stable can be a full-time occupation or a part-time venture, depending on the size of the facility, number of horses, and types of services offered. Sometimes, people with a few available stalls in their own barns rent those out to make a little extra money; while others may buy or lease land to start their own full-scale boarding operations. In any case, strong horse knowledge, business and stable management skills, and a willingness to work long hours are essential. Boarding stable operators must also have good people skills to deal effectively with horse owners and employees. Some boarding stables also offer riding instruction, training, horse rentals, and other services in addition to basic horse keep and care.

EDUCATION AND TRAINING

A high school diploma or higher is necessary. A degree in business administration or equine studies is helpful.

SALARY

Boarding rates vary widely, depending on location and services offered. Consider all your expenses, such as feed, insurance costs, supplies, salaries, mortgage or leasing costs, and maintenance. Then, take into account what the market in your area will bear before setting a per-stall rate. You must also decide if you will charge extra for such services as turning out, blanketing, and trailering, or if these services will be included in your standard boarding fee.

RESOURCES

Stable Management Magazine
45 Main Street North
Woodbury, CT 06798
www.stable-management.com

Carriage Driver

ABOUT THE JOB

Carriage drivers work for companies that provide carriage rides to the public. They ferry clients on city tours and for such occasions as weddings, parades, and proposals. Single horses or teams of two or more horses, depending on the style of carriage, pull carriages. Drivers are responsible for grooming and tacking up the horses and may be required to clean the carriages and provide day-to-day horse care. City licensing is required for carriage drivers and licensing requirements vary from city to city. The minimum age for drivers is 18 and may be higher in some states.

Carriage ride companies look for drivers who are professional in appearance, and have good communication skills and outgoing personalities. Horse experience is necessary. Previous driving experience may or may not be required (though it is a plus), depending on the hiring company. All drivers are required to undergo training on the carriages, which is provided by the company that employs them.

EDUCATION AND TRAINING

A high school diploma. To gain driving experience before approaching a company, attend a driving school, which can be found on the Internet by typing "carriage driving schools;" through the Carriage Operators of North America Web site (see below); or by talking to horse people in your area.

SALARY

Salaries vary among companies and areas of the country. Drivers are often paid on a percentage basis of each fare, generally 30 to 50 percent.

RESOURCES

Carriage Operators of North America
www.cona.org

Carriage Ride Owner/Operator

ABOUT THE JOB

If you wish to own a carriage driving business, research the rules and regulations surrounding horse-drawn carriages in your city before making the major financial investment of buying or leasing horses and carriages and buying or renting a place to keep them during nonworking hours. Most cities require licensing and permits for animal-drawn vehicles, while some do not allow them at all. City rules govern the safety and suitability of carriages and driving equipment, the routes the carriages can take, how long horses may work in one day, the health of horses, insurance required, and the hours horses may not be on the streets (often traffic rush hours).

As with all hands-on horse businesses, horse experience, marketing expertise, and business skills are required for success. Supervisory skills are necessary if you hire other drivers; if you will be driving along with your staff of drivers, then driving experience is also required.

EDUCATION AND TRAINING
A degree in business or marketing is helpful.

SALARY
Income is based upon the rates you charge, minus your expenses. Rates will vary, depending on the types of driving services offered and your geographical location. Expenses may include repayment of loans for start-up costs, such as buying horses, carriages and harnesses, boarding rent or a mortgage payment on horse property, veterinary care, insurance, salaries, and trailering.

RESOURCES
Carriage Operators of North America
www.cona.org

Dude or Guest Ranch Owner/Operator

ABOUT THE JOB
Becoming a dude ranch owner requires a major financial investment. The cost of buying an existing ranch or starting a new ranch can range from the high six figures into the millions of dollars. Add to that the additional cost of buying or leasing horses and other start-up costs and it can take years to turn a profit. According to the Dude Rancher's Association Web site, it takes most new ranch owners five to seven years from the time they start their operations before they begin to break even. Nevertheless, dude ranching is becoming more popular for those willing to make the commitment of time and money.

Strong business, public relations, and customer service skills are essential to make it in dude ranching, as is horse experience. Dude ranch owners must also have good people management skills to supervise such employees as cooks, wranglers, housekeepers, ranch hands, naturalists, and counselors.

EDUCATION AND TRAINING

A high school diploma is required. A degree in business administration or equine studies is helpful. The Dude Rancher's Association offers a three-day seminar on starting a dude ranch.

SALARY

As mentioned above, dude ranch owners often run in the red for several years before they even begin to break even. While there are no specific figures available as to how much money you can expect to make owning a dude ranch, how well the dude ranch does and consequently the profit you can expect, will depend upon your business, marketing, and customer relations skills as well as factors outside your control, such as the state of the economy and the travel industry overall.

RESOURCES

Dude Rancher's Association
P.O. Box 2307
Cody, Wyoming 82414
www.duderanch.org

Dude/Guest Ranch Worker

ABOUT THE JOB

Dude and guest ranches employ many people in a variety of positions. Jobs are usually seasonal, typically from April or May through September or October, though some ranches also have winter seasons. Employment at a dude or guest ranch is hard work and involves long hours—six-day workweeks are the standard and participation in evening guest activities is often required.

In addition to the hands-on horse jobs, such as wrangler or riding instructor, dude and guest ranches need ranch hands (sometimes called maintenance workers), photographers, cooks, wait staff, bartenders, tour guides, naturalists, cleaning people, children's counselors, and others to ensure that guests have a positive experience at the ranch. Some of these positions may involve riding, but the majority do not.

People wanting to work for dude and guest ranches must have an enthusiastic attitude, excellent people skills, and a willingness to pitch in wherever and whenever help is needed. A neat and clean appearance is expected and some ranches have very specific guidelines as to dress, makeup, facial hair, and hairstyle. While ranch owners want employees to enjoy their time at the ranch, employees are there to work, not to vacation.

EDUCATION AND TRAINING

A high school diploma or higher is required, depending on the position.

SALARY

Compensation typically includes a seasonal, monthly, or weekly salary, room (often shared—sometimes between several people), and board. It may also include an end-of-season bonus or share of tips. A sample salary is $2,000 for a camp counselor for the summer camp season.

RESOURCES

Dude Rancher's Association
P.O. Box 2307
Cody, Wyoming 82414
www.duderanch.org

Fox Hunt Huntsman

ABOUT THE JOB

Professional huntsmen (term used to refer to either males or females) are hired by hunt clubs to hunt the hounds. During the actual hunts, they train and command the hounds, which are usually owned by the hunt club or a hunt committee. The huntsmen maintain jumps throughout the hunt territory and help ensure that everything runs smoothly with the landowners over whose lands the hunt crosses. The huntsmen report to the Master of Hounds, who is the appointed or elected leader of the hunt club. While there are more than 170 hunt clubs in the United States, not all of them use paid, professional huntsmen. Sometimes, the Master of Hounds or another member of the club may also act as huntsmen. Professional huntsmen may go out on several hunts a week. They are also involved in breeding and in the day-to-day care of the hounds. Excellent horsemanship skills, expertise in breeding and training hounds, and physical stamina are required.

EDUCATION AND TRAINING
A strong background in fox hunting, its strict rules, and protocols are required. Apprenticeship in the field. For more, contact hunt clubs in your area. Clubs can be found through the Masters of Foxhounds Web site (see below).

SALARY
No information available.

RESOURCES
Masters of Foxhounds Association of America
P.O. Box 363
Millwood, VA 22646
www.mfha.com

Fox Hunt Whipper-In

ABOUT THE JOB
Whippers-in help the huntsmen control the hounds by riding on the sides or outskirts of the hunt to keep the hounds from venturing into roads, onto train tracks, or onto land where the hunt is not permitted to go. Excellent horsemanship skills, experience with hounds, and physical stamina are required.

EDUCATION AND TRAINING
A strong background in fox hunting and its strict rules and protocols is required.

SALARY
No information available.

RESOURCES
Masters of Foxhounds Association of America
P.O. Box 363
Millwood, VA 22646
www.mfha.com

Groom

About the Job

Grooms are responsible for the day-to-day well-being of the horses under their care. They work for boarding facilities, training and riding stables, racetracks, breeding farms, polo and hunt clubs, riding schools, and at shows and rodeos. Grooms feed, water, groom, and trim horses; braid manes and tails for showing; muck out stalls and replenish bedding; clean and organize tack; and manage the stores of supplies and feed.

People considering this career field should be flexible, reliable, and have lots of physical energy; they should have a good attitude to cope with the wide variety of tasks that grooms are asked to perform. The level of horse experience required depends upon the position. While show, hunt, and race-track grooms are expected to have strong horse experience and skills, other horse facilities may hire entry-level grooms.

Education and Training

Many grooms learn on-the-job, although trade schools and some colleges offer classes for professional grooms. Also, a four-year degree in equine studies is valuable for someone considering this field, especially if you are hoping to move into higher-level professional groom positions.

Salary

According to a 2003 survey by the Equistaff online equine employment agency, the average salary for grooms/stablehands is $16,216. Twenty-nine percent of respondents reported that their employers provided housing and utilities; 43 percent received medical and dental insurance; and 52 percent received additional perks, such as riding lessons, board for their horses, breeding rights, and use of a vehicle.

Resources

Contact stables and farms in your area, equine employment agencies, and horse publications.

Horse Packer and Guide

About the Job

Packers and guides are employed by outfitting companies that take hunters, fly-fishers, hikers, photographers, and campers on days-, weeks- or months-long trips into the backcountry. In addition to wilderness skills, horse experience, and hunting or fishing skills, packers and guides must be dependable and have excellent people skills. Packers are generally responsible for loading and caring for the pack mules and horses that transport gear, supplies, and game during these trips; guides lead excursions, help hunters locate game, advise on good fishing spots, and find wildlife for viewing for photographers and campers. Depending on the outfitting company, the guide may also be the cook. Overall, all staff on outfitting trips are expected to pitch in wherever and whenever assistance is needed.

EDUCATION AND TRAINING

A high school diploma and backcountry experience, on-the-job training, or attendance at an outfitter and guide training school (see Web site listed below) are important. College classes in wildlife management or similar areas are helpful.

SALARY

Monthly salaries for first-year guides are generally in the $800 to $1,200 range, according to Royal Tine Guide and Packer School (see Web site below for contact information). Room and board are often included in addition to the base salary.

RESOURCES

Royal Tine
PO Box 809
Philipsburg, MT 59858
www.royaltine.com

ELM Outfitter and Guide Training, Inc.
P.O. Box 627
Corvallis, MT 59828
www.elmoutfitter-guidetraining.com

Performers and Stunt Doubles

ABOUT THE JOB

Expert riders are used in movies and television as doubles and stunt riders for actors who are scheduled to perform stunts. Many times, doubles and stunt riders are former or current professional riders in a variety of horse sports; stunt riders may also perform stunts that do not involve horses. Besides excellent horsemanship ability, it is necessary for these individuals to be comfortable in front of the camera. Networking skills are important in finding work in this competitive field. Other performance and riding jobs include circus acts and medieval festivals that include jousting on horseback.

EDUCATION AND TRAINING
A high school diploma is necessary; also, one should become familiar with the movie and television industry.

SALARY
No information available.

RESOURCES
Stuntmen's Association of Motion Pictures
10660 Riverside Drive 2nd Floor, Suite E
Toluca Lake, CA 91602
www.stuntmen.com

United Stuntmen's Association
2723 Saratoga Lane
Everett, WA 98203
www.stuntschool.com

Polo Jobs

ABOUT THE JOB
Many jobs in polo are voluntary or appointed, though larger polo clubs may have paying positions, such as club managers. Amateur players or clubs wishing to play in high goal tournaments hire professional polo players. Professionals in turn may hire grooms and stable hands to help care for their ponies. Some players are hired in dual roles, such as player/groom or player/trainer, player/instructor, or player/sales person. Players may or may not be required to bring their own string of ponies when accepting a position with a club. Other positions in the sport that may be paid include referee, umpire, scorekeeper, timekeeper, and judge.

EDUCATION AND TRAINING

A high school diploma is required. Depending on the groom position, little to strong polo knowledge and experience may be required in addition to an ability to exercise polo ponies. Aspiring professional players must be experts in the game and know its rules.

SALARY

Grooms—Average of $1,500 monthly.

Players—Varies, from approximately $3,500 per game into the six figures for top professional players, according to www.sportpolo.com

RESOURCES

United States Polo Association
Suite 505
771 Corporate Drive
Lexington, KY 40503
www.us-polo.org

Public Riding Stable Operator

ABOUT THE JOB

Riding stables rent horses to the general public by the hour, half day, or full day. They may also offer riding lessons, horse training, and boarding. Owning a public riding stable requires a major financial investment in horses and property, access to trails, insurance coverage in case of accidents—which can be challenging to obtain—and city licensing and permits. Riding stable operators must have strong horse experience to choose horses for their operations that are good on the trail and can be handled by beginning through advanced riders. They must be able to recognize which horses are appropriate for which riders, have good communication skills, and the assertiveness (and patience) to deal with individuals who may exaggerate their riding abilities (potentially putting themselves and others at risk).

Aspiring riding stable owners should have managerial skills to supervise grooms, stable hands, trail guides, riding instructors, and others in their employ. A background in stable management, marketing, and business is also important, as is an understanding of insurance regulations related to horse rentals.

EDUCATION AND TRAINING

A high school diploma or higher is required. A degree in equine studies or administration, focusing on stable management, or a business or marketing degree is helpful.

SALARY

Income will be based upon the rates you charge, minus your expenses. Many stables charge from $20 per hour and up for one-hour rentals, depending on location.

RESOURCES

Stable Management Magazine
45 Main Street North
P.O. Box 644
Woodbury, CT 06798
www.stable-management.com

Riding Camp Counselor

ABOUT THE JOB

Working as a camp counselor is seasonal and usually occurs during the summer months when children are out of school for the summer. Horse camps may focus specifically on riding, or they may integrate other activities into the camp experience, with a percentage of time dedicated to horses. Counselors are needed to care for children, lead camp activities, help with horses, and perform a variety of other duties.

Camp counselors must be flexible, as they are frequently called upon to pitch in whenever and wherever necessary. Camp counselors should genuinely like children, be patient and enthusiastic, and have some horse experience.

EDUCATION AND TRAINING

A high school diploma or higher is necessary, depending on the position. First-aid and CPR training are also typically required.

SALARY

Salary may be paid weekly, monthly, or by season (which is from the beginning of June through mid-August). Room and board is usually included. Sometimes end-of-summer bonuses or a share of tips are offered. A sample salary for a season as a camp counselor at a Colorado camp is $1,500; for a junior counselor it's $1,300, plus room and board. Salaries will vary based on location, activities, and length of the season.

RESOURCES
American Camping Association
5000 State Road 67 North
Martinsville, IN 46151-7902
www.acacamps.org

Riding Camp Director

ABOUT THE JOB
Camp directors oversee all facets of summer riding camps. This includes hiring and supervising camp staff, overseeing horse care, organizing the program of activities, and ensuring that campers have a safe and enjoyable experience. Strong organizational and people skills, a genuine interest in children, and horse experience are essential. Prior teaching and management experience is a plus.

EDUCATION AND TRAINING
A bachelor's degree in equine studies, administration, or business is essential; CPR and first-aid training; riding instructor certification.

SALARY
Salaries will vary based on location, activities, and length of the season. A sample salary is $2,800 for the season; room and board is often included.

RESOURCES
American Camping Association
5000 State Road 67 North
Martinsville, IN 46151-7902
www.acacamps.org

Career Spotlight

Roger N. Felch, PhD, C Bar T Trail Ranch Camp Director

Roger N. Felch runs the western horseback riding camp that his father started in 1958 in Idledale, Colorado. C Bar T campers, ages 11 to 17, are responsible for their own horses as they participate in a continuous horseback pack trip through the high mountain backcountry of the Colorado National Forest. Roger was "raised" with the camp since he was six years old, spending his summers there first as a camper, then as a wrangler, trail guide, counselor, and since 1979 as director and outfitter/guide. Growing up on a working horse ranch gave Roger experience in all aspects of ranch management, including feeding, veterinary work, shoeing, riding, tack repair, and fabrication. With an academic expertise in geophysics, having earned a PhD from Pennsylvania State University, Roger teaches high school chemistry and Earth and environmental science during the school year. He currently owns 29 Morgan or Morgan-cross horses, ages one to 30 years old, along with four mules and two Belgian draft horses.

Q. In what part of Colorado is your camp located and where does the pack trip go?

A. The Base Ranch is in Idledale, just west of Denver in the foothills, but the camp is an extended pack trip through the central Colorado Rockies. Our most recent trip started at Camp Hale (midway between Minturn and Leadville) and ended at Erickson Springs, near Paonia.

Q. What made you decide to go into this field?

A. My dad started the camp. I loved the horses and grew up with the experience. It's difficult for me to imagine a summer without C Bar T, horses, and the high mountain backcountry.

Q. What does your job involve?

A. As director, I am responsible for planning the camp program and trail route, breeding, raising, training, and shoeing horses for the camp's use and for acquiring the permits from the Forest Service, Social Services, and other regulatory agencies.

As outfitter/guide, I instruct campers in riding our horses, tacking them up for mountain travel, and respecting the wilderness as we travel through it. I lead the group on the trail and offer assistance in cultivating individual interests (such as fly-fishing, photography, and geology) as opportunities present themselves along the way.

Q. What is your typical workday like?

A. The day begins early for me. I arise; get a fire going (or stove, if a fire ban is in effect) to boil buckets of wash water. When ready, I awaken the group with, "Good Morning, C Bar T! Rise and shine! Sunlight's a-burnin'!" While the campers are rolling their sleeping bags and taking down tarps, and the counselor readies breakfast, I begin sorting what needs to be stowed on the pack animals. After breakfast and dishes are done, we take horses off the picket lines and pack up for the day's ride which can last anywhere from three to eight hours. Lunch sometimes happens en route, sometimes after we arrive in camp. Once we reach our evening's campsite, I set up a portable electric fence, and campers take turns watching horses as they graze. During that time, pack gear is unloaded, saddles are hung in trees, tarps are set up, and personal gear is stowed underneath. After three to five hours of grazing, horses are gathered and tied to the picket lines. Afterwards, there's usually time to fish a bit before dinner, and then wonderful stories of the day's adventures are recounted around the fire. It doesn't take long before everyone feels exhaustion from the day and retires for the evening. The sameness of each day's schedule is remarkable, given the uniqueness of each day's experience!

Q. How long is a trip, and how many campers are involved? What parts of the country/world do the campers come from?

A. In the early days of the camp, sessions lasted over nine weeks with upward of 40 campers. In recent years, our trail trips have been two to four weeks in length, with a maximum of nine campers in each session (USFS regulations limit the numbers). Campers come from all over the world, though in recent years, more have come from Colorado.

Q. How many wranglers, cooks, and other workers are there on a trail trip?

A. I wrangle; there's usually one head counselor, who also cooks; and one or two staff assistants, all of whom have been exemplary campers in previous years. All together, there can be no more than 11 human heartbeats!

Q. What do you enjoy most about the work?

A. Being outdoors in the mountains with my horses, and sharing the experience with interested teenagers.

Q. What do you like least about the work?

A. Dealing with regulations, insurance, and paperwork.

Q. How would you describe the most interesting trail camp trip you've been on?

A. Doing a camp session for adults was far more interesting and challenging than I had imagined possible after working exclusively with teenagers.

Q. What is the most rewarding part of your job?

A. Witnessing the growth and emerging confidence in inexperienced campers.

Q. What is the most challenging part of your job?

A. Keeping everybody safe.

Q. Do you have any other horse industry work experience?

A. I packed an adult group for the very first Certified Horsemanship Association Pack and Trail clinic, which certified prospective instructors.

Q. What is the biggest achievement of your career?

A. I have never lost a horse on the trail, and my campers have never suffered any serious injuries.

Q. What advice would you give to someone interested in working for a trail camp?

A. Be prepared for mounting obstacles in the form of monumental regulations and vanishing insurance. It appears to be a doomed enterprise by today's standards.

Q. What education and/or experience do you recommend for someone interested in working in this field?

A. Years of experience with horses and wilderness travel. Also, one must enjoy sharing that experience with people. There is really no education substitute for experience.

Riding Instructor

ABOUT THE JOB

Riding instructors work with students at all levels to help them develop or improve their riding skills. Instructors work as employees at established riding schools, stables, dude and guest ranches, and children's summer camps, or they are self-employed, traveling from barn to barn or holding classes at facilities of their own. Instructors who are employed by others usually have additional tasks around the barn, such as stable management, horse training and exercising, and other things as determined by the employer, but they have the advantage of regular paychecks and more regular hours.

Instructors often find it difficult to make a full-time living on instruction alone, supplementing their incomes by trading horses, training, farm sitting, stable management, doing clinics, or working in jobs outside the horse industry. Strong communication and teaching skills, strict attention to safety, and a great deal of patience are required. Self-employed riding instructors should know how to market themselves and have basic business skills.

The instructor's experience and qualifications determine the highest level of students she'll teach as well as her certification level if she is certified.

EDUCATION AND TRAINING

On-the-job training as an apprentice or working student, or being self-taught through years spent working with horses is requisite; a college degree in equine studies with an emphasis on riding and riding instruction is also helpful. Classes in education, business, and marketing are also helpful.

Though certification is not required to teach riding in the United States, and there are many good instructors who are not certified, certification is recommended as a way for instructors to enhance their skills; it can also be a valuable marketing tool. Potential clients who are not familiar with an instructor may look to certification as a requirement, as it demonstrates to them that the instructor is qualified to teach. Additionally, certification through an organization can reduce the cost of the riding instructor's insurance, which is necessary for protection in case of an accident.

SALARY

The American Riding Instructors Association compiled the following rates from the results of a recent nationwide survey: $5 to $40 for a half hour private lesson ($20 median), $10 to $75 for a one-hour private lesson ($30 median). The average number of lessons taught per week was 15.

While the top rate in the survey was $75 for a one-hour private lesson, this is not an average rate. Many factors come into play when setting rates, including the demand in the area for instruction, area of the country, and reputation of the school and/or instructor.

A 2003 survey by Equistaff, an online horse industry employment service, states that instructors receive an average annual salary of $17,549. Twelve percent of respondents reported the extra benefit of housing; 47 percent received benefits such as board for their horses, breeding rights, or use of a vehicle; 35 percent reported receiving the traditional benefits of medical and dental insurance.

RESOURCES

American Riding Instructors Association
28801 Trenton Court
Bonita Springs, FL 34134-3337
www.riding-instructor.com

CHA, The Association for Horsemanship Safety
5318 Old Bullard Road
Tyler, TX 75703
www.cha-ahse.org

American Association for Horsemanship Safety (AAHS)
P.O. Box 39
Fentress, TX 78622
www.horsemanshipsafety.com

United States Dressage Federation
220 Lexington Green Circle, Suite 510
Lexington, KY 40503
www.usdf.org

Career Spotlight

DESAIX TANKERSLEY HILL, RIDING INSTRUCTOR

Riding instructor deSaix Tankersley Hill has been training hunters and teaching hunt-seat equitation for 15 years. Born in upstate New York, but raised mostly in Baton Rouge, Louisiana, deSaix started riding her aunt's horse when she was only two years old and has continued riding ever since. By the time she was 12, she was teaching other riders and training horses, already realizing her life's vocation. In addition to teaching, deSaix also competes in hunt-seat, hunt-seat equitation, and jumpers. She has two Thoroughbreds—24-year-old Ambrose and 13-year-old Murphy—as well as an 8-year-old Welsh Pony named Twinkles. A new mother, deSaix is surrounded by an active horse-involved family, including her husband, an equine veterinarian (see profile of Josh Hill in Chapter 9); her brother, a farrier; and her mother (see profile of Lanier Cordell in Chapter 15), who serves on numerous horse-related boards.

Q. What does your job involve?

A. Planning lessons and teaching beginners through advanced riders in hunt seat and hunt seat equitation. I teach both children and adults.

Q. What is your typical workday like?

A. I plan and teach lessons, select lesson horses, oversee tacking-up, and handle billing.

Q. How many hours per week do you typically work?

A. I average 25 to 30 hours per week.

Q. What do you enjoy most about your work?

A. Working with the horses and the students.

Q. What do you like least about your work?

A. Dealing with the unrealistic expectations of riders and parents.

Q. What is your educational background?

A. I have a Bachelor of Arts in equine studies from Virginia Intermont College and am certified by the American Riding Instructors Association in hunt-seat for beginners through advanced.

Q. What sparked your interest in horses?

A. I have always loved animals and horses in particular. Fortunately, my aunt had a horse in her backyard so I was able to ride as often as I wanted from a very early age.

Q. When did you know you wanted to teach riding?

A. I have been teaching riders since I was 12 years old. I have always enjoyed it and never wanted to do anything other than teach, train horses, and ride.

Q. What is your most memorable moment as a horsewoman?

A. Getting my very first horse.

Q. What is the most rewarding aspect of working in the horse industry?

A. You can take your dog to work and ride horses.

Q. What is the most challenging part of your job?

A. Juggling a new baby and scheduling lessons that are convenient to students and my baby-sitter.

Q. What is the biggest achievement of your career?

A. Turning around a riding program at an all girls' school and making it successful.

Q. What is the most challenging obstacle in your career?

A. Dealing with "civilians" who pay the bills, but who don't really understand the horses or the horse industry.

Q. What has driven you to excel in your career?

A. My passion for the horses and the desire to create a really comfortable, healthy environment for the horses and the students. I also would have done anything to be able to take part in a school-based riding program when I was in school, instead of being the only person in my school who liked horses.

Q. What education and experience do you recommend for someone interested in becoming a certified riding instructor?

A. You don't have to have a college education, but I have to say that what I learned earning my bachelor's in equine studies at Virginia Intermont College really filled in a lot of gaps that I don't think experience alone can fill. I learned so much more about nutrition, how to keep a horse healthy, and liability issues that even the most experienced and knowledgeable trainers don't tend to know. I also believe that certification that requires extensive testing is invaluable, and that you should make an effort to continue your education by attending professional-level workshops and clinics.

Q. What personal strengths or skills should someone have who is considering this field?

A. Lots of patience and good communication and organizational skills.

Q. If you could do it over, is there anything you would have done differently to reach your career goal?

A. I can't think of a thing because everything, including mistakes, taught me something valuable that made me better prepared for the next hurdle.

Q. What do you think the job outlook is for your career area in the horse industry?

A. As long as people love horses and want to ride, I think there will be opportunities for good riding instructors and trainers. Unfortunately, liability issues add a lot of pressure that didn't exist in the past. And I think that the more educated and discriminating students and parents become, the higher the bar is raised for instructors and all the other horse industry professionals. I think the growth in the number of college degree programs in equine studies has also raised the bar by improving the knowledge instructors have about teaching skills, safety, horse care, and instruction.

Career Spotlight

DODI L. STACEY, RIDING INSTRUCTOR CERTIFIER AND HORSE PACKER

Dodi L. Stacey has been a riding instructor and horse packer for over 25 years. Notably involved in the Certified Horsemanship Association (CHA), she now devotes her time to certifying riding instructors in English, western, trail riding, and disability specialties. Dodi grew up in the Ozarks near Forsyth, Missouri, and now lives in Colorado Springs, Colorado. Although she has owned and ridden horses since childhood, Dodi's initial career plans did not revolve around horses: she majored in English, drama, and physical education, with the goal of being a high school educator. While focusing on raising her family, she worked temporarily as a substitute teacher. Acting as an art and drama consultant at a Girl Scout camp led her to her ultimate career with horses. Fulfilling the Girl Scout camp's needs for someone to run its riding program, and later, to be a counselor at a specialty packing camp, Dodi was thrilled to be experiencing her dream career—combining her passion for horses, children, teaching, and outdoor living. In addition to working directly with riders, Dodi also has served on various riding association committees. Dodi's dedication to developing and improving certification standards and programs has contributed to the safety of riders around the world. She has one horse now—the same one for 27 years—Lad's Vandy Bar.

Q. What does your job involve?

A. At this point in my life, I am partially retired. Now the main thrust of my career is certifying riding instructors. I travel throughout the United States and Canada certifying these instructors through the Certified Horsemanship Association (CHA) during five-to-six day clinics. I certify instructors in the four disciplines at four levels: according to individual ability; for horsemanship safety; effectiveness as an instructor; and ability to be creative and fun in their teaching. I still do a little teaching and some correction training of horses with mild problems.

Q. What made you decide to pursue these areas?

A. I must be honest here. I do not believe that I made these decisions as much as God put me in a situation and gave me the incentive and ability to expand on them. My parents gave me my first horse when I was eight years old and I have ridden throughout my life. When I was put in a position where I had to teach, I found out that I could combine my love of horses and my love of children into a career. My very supportive husband told me to "go for it!"

Q. How did you get your first job as an instructor? How did you get your first job as a packer?

A. I was working as a drama and art consultant for two weeks at an established Girl Scout camp to pay the camp fee for one of my two daughters when the facility lost most of its riding staff and had no staff left that was old enough to legally head the program. They asked me to take the instructor job, as they knew I rode horses. I took the position and loved it.

As a packer, again, the Girl Scout Council was looking for someone to be the counselor at a specialty packing camp of 12 advanced girls in the horsemanship program. I could combine camping with horses and girls! I was taught to pack on-the-job by Roger Felch of C Bar T Trail Camp (see profile of Roger in this chapter), who provided the horses for the Girl Scouts on this seven-day packing trip into the Colorado high country.

Q. What is your typical workday like?

A. Currently, I have one horse in training. I spend two to three hours a day working with him at the stable where I board. When I had my own facility I spent the day feeding at 7:30 A.M., cleaning stalls, riding training horses, teaching lessons, hauling hay and feed, feeding in the evening about 7:00 P.M., and I'd end my day at 9:30 or 10:00 P.M. by checking the horses in the barn to be sure all was well with them.

During a certification clinic, I spend five to six days in a row watching instructors teach practice lessons and evaluating progress from 8:00 A.M. to 5:30 P.M. Then, in the evenings, I lecture on various riding and teaching related subjects for another two hours.

Q. How many hours/days per week do you typically work?

A. I will spend about two hours a day per horse. With severe degenerative arthritis, I am very limited in what I can do. I used to spend about 10 hours a day, sometimes more and sometimes less, when I had my own facility. When I am conducting certification clinics, the day is 10 to 12 hours long. Pack trips required me to be on duty 24 hours a day, every day spent on the trail.

Q. What do you enjoy most about your work?

A. Incorporating my love for horses, children, outdoor living/camping, and teaching into a satisfying and fulfilling life.

Q. What do you like least about your work?

A. Telling riding instructors that I cannot certify them at as high a level as they would like—or think that they are qualified to be—at certification clinics. I would much prefer to make people happy.

Q. Do you have any other horse industry experience?

A. I attended a Certified Horsemanship Association (CHA) clinic in 1980, where I received my certification as a Clinic Instructor in the Standard certification program (arena instruction). I have been very involved with that organization ever since. I assisted in the development of the majority of CHA's manuals.

I served as Chairwoman for the CHA committees that developed the CHA Trail Program and the Program for Certification of Instructor for Riders with Disabilities, developing certification standards and clinic formats in these two disciplines. I participated in developing and improving the standards for certification in CHA's certification of riding instructors. I served on the ADA compliance committee for the North American Horseman's Association (NAHA) and chaired the Certified Horsemanship Association (CHA) ADA Committee. I served for a year on the North American Riding for the Handicapped (NARHA) task force, and reviewed and reorganized their certification program. I served CHA as a Regional Director for four years, as Board Member for 15 years, and as President (two years as President Elect, two years as President, and two years as Past President).

Q. What is your overall background with horses?

A. I have owned and ridden horses for 53 years. I worked at Gary Foreman (son of well-known trainer Monte Foreman) Stables, cleaning up to 46 stalls a day in exchange for western riding lessons. I rode for Susan Noble and learned to ride and jump hunt-seat.

I have attended many clinics to improve my riding knowledge in western, hunt-seat, and dressage. I have had lessons in riding and training Paso Fino horses.

Q. What is your most memorable moment as a horsewoman?

A. There have been so many in so many areas that it is hard to pick one. On a horse, it has to be the first time I experienced a suspended trot on a fourth-level dressage horse. In packing, it was when I realized that I could look at the way a pack sat on a horse before we left camp and know that it was well-balanced enough to stay on while riding trails in the Rocky Mountains at 13,000 feet.

In my career, it was receiving the North American Horsemen's Association "1999 Horsewoman of Distinction" award for: "dedication to the betterment of the horse industry, by teaching, analyzing, and promoting the safest horsemanship practices, the service given to unite the horse industry, the sensitivity shown for people, horses, and key issues; and for her integrity and warmth uniting to provide an exceptional role model within the horse industry."

Other memorable moments included receiving the Certified Horsemanship Association award for "2002 Volunteer of the Year" in a beautiful ceremony via the phone during the 2002 CHA Annual Conference; and the "Elizabeth Hayden Award," the Mile-Hi Girl Scout Council's highest award for volunteers in the early '90s.

Q. What is the most rewarding part of your job?

A. Seeing the light come on in a student's eyes when she finally owns the difficult riding skill that I have been attempting to share with her! Also, feeling the horse move freely under me when I am able to clearly communicate to him what I am expecting him to do!

Q. What is the most challenging part of your job?

A. Telling students where and how they need to improve teaching or riding skills, while making them feel good about themselves and their abilities.

Q. What is the biggest achievement of your career?

A. Improving the safety and overall riding experience of thousands of riders around the world through certification and education of riding instructors.

Q. What is the most challenging obstacle in your career?

A. Achieving a balance between continuing my riding education and career while being a good mother and wife.

Q. What education and/or experience do you recommend for someone interested in teaching riders or horse packing?

A. First of all, get a good college education in any field that holds your interest and that can support you. If you major in equestrian science, minor in a field that will help you find a job outside of the horse industry, if necessary. You can also major outside the horse industry and get a minor in a horse program. Then, there is always simply including as many horsemanship-related courses, teaching courses, and psychology courses as possible. If you plan on owning your own facility, a business and marketing degree would really help! Intern under as highly respected and a safe certified trainer and instructor as possible. This will provide you with a real perspective of what is actually expected of you without being the person "in charge," and it has the valuable benefit of continuing your horsemanship education. Watch every possible riding lesson given by anyone! You can learn something from everyone!

Few universities offer an education in horse packing. There used to be a couple of universities that offered classes, so contact the school you plan on attending and ask. Really, the best way to learn packing is to go west and get a job with an outfitter and learn on the job.

Q. What personal traits should someone have who is considering this field?

A. You must love horses and working with people. You must be a self-starter. You must have a lot of patience. You must accept accountability when things go wrong as well as when they are going right! (It is not always the horse's or student's fault when they don't learn.) And finally, you must be willing to work hard for long hours.

Q. If you could do it over, is there anything you would have done differently to reach your career goal?

A. Only that I wish I had become a professional in the horse industry when I was much younger!

Q. Is there anything else you would like to say about your career?

A. I said previously that I wish I had been younger when I began my career in the horse industry. I do, however, realize that I had many benefits from getting a late start. I was not faced with the choice of family or horses, but was able to have a totally fulfilling career and a family because of the maturity and experience I had when I entered the industry.

Working in the horse industry is not for the faint-hearted! It is a very demanding career! I know horse people who have traded family life for a career in the industry. I know others who were unsuccessful in juggling horses and family. Horses will not take care of you when you are old and gray. Yes, you can derive comfort from them, but they cannot go the doctor with you or give you comfort and help in times of extreme stress.

I am so thankful for my four children, and now in my retirement years, my children's spouses and my grandchildren. I am thankful also for the wonderful husband who has supported me as I struggled with the career and family and handed out the dollars when they were needed to continue my education and/or pay my horse bills. I am thankful that I am able to look back on my life with no regrets.

When you are considering your career choice, take the time to look down life's road and see where you want to be in the later years. Be prepared to support yourself and your horses when the money gets tight by having a good education that will bring in funds when needed. Be sure that your spouse/prospective spouse is supportive of you, your horses, and your career. I would recommend taking time out from your career to have a family if you want, but make the decision before entering the field. Then, go for it!

Stable Hand

ABOUT THE JOB

Stable hands are the "girl Friday" positions of the horse world. This entry-level job may encompass a combination of duties, such as feeding and watering horses, mucking stalls and sweeping aisles, light facility maintenance, grooming, foal sitting, operating farm equipment, unloading and stacking bedding and feed, and generally doing anything that needs to be done around the barn, farm, or other horse facility. These positions are fairly common, and though the pay is low, the opportunities to learn and advance can be quite good. Many stable hands are provided room and board as part of their compensation. Flexibility, willingness to take direction, and a positive attitude are important for this type of job.

The most entry-level of these positions may not require horse care experience. However, having horse experience will increase your chances of getting into a large or well-respected facility, where you can assume and take on more advanced responsibilities.

EDUCATION AND TRAINING

A high school diploma is helpful.

SALARY

According to a 2003 survey by the Equistaff online equine employment agency, the average salary for grooms/stable hands is $16,216. Twenty-nine percent of respondents reported that their employers provided housing and utilities; 43 percent received medical and dental insurance; and 52 percent received additional perks such as riding lessons, board for their horses, breeding rights, and use of a vehicle.

RESOURCES

Look into equine employment agencies and horse publications; also, search for jobs on the Internet under "stable hand" or for stables in your area.

Stable (or Barn) Manager

ABOUT THE JOB

Stable managers keep the daily operations humming smoothly at breeding, boarding and training barns, riding schools, racetracks, and other horse facilities. Depending on the size of the operation and the number of employees, stable managers may do some or all of the following: oversee horse care; schedule the farrier and veterinarian; groom, exercise and turn out horses; order feed, bedding, and other supplies; attend to minor injuries and administer medication; handle record-keeping and paperwork; teach riding lessons; handle public relations and marketing; handle sales; train horses; coordinate clinics and horse shows; and supervise other barn employees. The hours can be long and being on call is common. Stable managers may live on-site, with room and board included in their compensation. Strong organizational and management skills, a flexible personality, and being good with people are essential, as is extensive horse experience.

EDUCATION AND TRAINING
Strong experience with horses is essential, plus management and other applicable skills or a four-year degree in equine studies or equine administration or similar with stable management classes, plus a horse background.

SALARY
Positions start at $400 per week and up.

RESOURCES
Contact equine employment agencies for jobs in this category, stables in your area, or search on the Internet for stable or barn manager jobs.

Career Spotlight

KIMBERLY P. STANFORD, RIDING SCHOOL BARN MANAGER AND
RIDING INSTRUCTOR

Kimberly P. Stanford manages the barn at the Huntington Beach Riding School in California. Located at the Huntington Beach Equestrian Center, the school teaches hunt-seat and hunt-seat equitation to beginning through advanced riders and has 11 lesson horses. In addition to her work managing the riding school and its horses, this Southern California native also teaches riding lessons to students. She started working in this position full-time in September 2002. Though Kimberly is formally educated as a dental assistant—she worked as an oral and maxillofacial surgical and anesthesia assistant prior to joining the staff at the riding school—she has years of horse experience beginning when she was just a child. In addi-

tion to her current job in the horse industry, she helped with the family business of riding prospective purchases when she was younger. Kimberly is married and has a teenage daughter.

Q. What is your background with horses?

A. Ever since I can remember, I had a fascination with horses. I rode them at fairs, petting zoos, and rental trail rides any chance I got. In second grade, I started riding lessons at the local equestrian center; by fifth grade, I had my own horse. From that time on, I moved to show barns. We purchased four more horses and that's when my real intense training started. I rode any horse and had some of the best training from excellent instructors. As my show accomplishments increased, so did my horsemanship skills.

By the time I started high school, I dreamed of being an instructor of hunt-seat equitation. During those years, some of my barn buddies would ask me to give them flat lessons on their hack days. I really enjoyed constructing exercises to help them with weak points, then seeing them strengthen their riding by accomplishing the goals we were both working toward. I became quite sure of my career path. During this period, my father had started an equine business that would eventually become the family horse brokerage/investment/training business.

Then I had an accident at a local horse show. My horse, Reserve Bid, and I crashed at an oxer. Though I had fallen so many times to that point that I lost count, this fall was the most harmful. I fractured my back—two badly compressed lumbar—and spent 14 months in a back brace. We kept some of the horses and I kept hanging around to watch and learn from the lessons, but I didn't realize that the psychological damage was done. When I could do it physically, I returned to riding and had a real hard time with my confidence over fences. I showed a little bit, but was embarrassed that I couldn't do what I was doing before, so I drifted away from riding. A few years later, a local trainer who I had known since I began riding asked me to work part-time as a schooling rider at her barn. I did it for a few days, jumped the horses, and then psychologically froze again. At that point, I left the field for more than 15 years. Occasionally, my father would ask me to come along to watch some Grand Prix in which my old barn pal Richard Spooner was competing. I didn't go because I felt ashamed of myself and scared to death. I never told my dad why I wouldn't go.

Q. How did you get back into riding?

A. My daughter wanted to start riding when she was 13. I finally gave in to the desire to be back around horses. After two weeks of watching my daughter ride, I had to get on too. My old friend and barn mom, who was there for me years ago, Ginny Spooner of J. Alden enterprises and Huntington Beach Riding School, was there for me again. We started lessons. After two years of being back in the saddle and working substitute lessons for other instructors, Ginny offered me the barn manager/riding instructor position.

Q. What does your job involve?

A. As barn manager for the riding school horses, I keep an eye on their well-being. I manage their workload, watch for any health issues that may arise, and treat or call the vet as necessary. I had to get to know the horses as individuals: their temperaments, moods, physical conditions, eating habits, vices, and any special needs. I need to know the norm so if there is a problem, it can be identified and treated as quickly as possible. School horses work very hard and deserve to be cared for as well as any show horse.

As riding school manager, I take care of public relations, phone communications, appointments, and scheduling appropriate lesson horses according to the ability and skill level of the riders. The safety of the horse and rider is one of the school's number one concerns. I supervise to make sure that the basics are being taught and the student progresses at a rate appropriate for her skill level.

Q. What is a typical workday like?

A. I arrive at 8 or 9 A.M., check for phone messages, and return the most urgent calls. Then, I go around and check the horses to make sure they're feeling well. If I suspect a problem, the horse is taken out of the stall right away for a closer look. If all is well, I return to the office to look at the lesson schedule for the day. I assign horses to students. Every time I enter the office throughout the day, I check the phone and return more calls. I then proceed to work as my own groom. I like to give the horses as much attention as the horses in show training barns. They will have turn-outs, baths, clippings, schooling, and tune-up training by me or an elevated student doing volunteer work for the school. I take care of any treatments needed. With 11 horses, there's often at least one that needs special attention due to injury or a health issue. If the vet comes to examine a horse, I will work as her assistant, which is interesting and educational. When the school groom is here, I supervise his care of the horses. I monitor the feed and supplement schedule to ensure it's adhered to by the staff. On weekdays, the school opens in the early afternoon for lessons. I start my own students and also monitor that my fellow riding instructors are teaching the basics and progressing the students safely. Once the school is open, public relations also start. (Most of the time, instructing students is easier than communicating with the nonriding parents and spouses on the outside of the arena.) At the end of the day, I check payments and finish up with phone calls and give final instructions to the groom. I usually leave about 7 P.M. if all is well. If we have a sick horse, I may be there a lot later and come back many times in the middle of the night.

Q. How many hours/days per week do you work?

A. My days are quite long, eight to 12 hours plus additional time if there is a problem. I'm scheduled to work five days a week, but if I'm at the stable when my daughter is riding, I always check in with the school and take care of anything that needs prompt attention.

Q. What do you enjoy most?

A. I love the work I do for the horses. Each one of them is so different. Getting to know their personalities—we bond like close friends. They know we work together and when they work well, they are rewarded. I've worked hard to gain their respect and want for them to work well for me on-ground or in the saddle.

Q. What do you like least?

A. I really get frustrated when parents or nonriding supporters get pushy about a student's progress. Some people just don't understand that safety should be number one and that pushing a student too fast before she has the skill can be dangerous for horse and rider.

Q. What is your most memorable moment as a horsewoman?

A. As of now, the hundreds of show ribbons that are mementos of my past show experiences. Most recently is coming back to the business and helping at the side of the show ring. I coached a student last summer in her first "A" circuit show; she did very well, pinning high in the classes, and I was so proud of her.

Q. What is the most rewarding part of your job?

A. Working with students at shows using my previous years of experience and coaching the students while they prepare to enter the arena. We work as a team. They come to me seeking advice on how to ride a course or how to deal with a difficult situation; we discuss it, and come up with a plan. When the round goes well we are all happy.

The training of the horses is also very rewarding. Some come out of pasture, need to be retrained, and have a proper nutritional program established. They need to be worked into the routine of the school. The ones who meld into the school's routine and learn to tolerate the beginners are special horses.

Q. What is the most challenging part of your job?

A. The most challenging part of the job so far is teaching the "not so natural" riding student. As long as they really have the drive to learn, though, I will have the passion to teach them.

Q. What is the most challenging obstacle in your career?

A. The psychological issues of my accident years ago.

Q. What advice would you give to someone interested in working as a barn manager and/or instructor?

A. Pursue your own riding as far as you can. Train under the best trainers you can. Take clinics offered by respected trainers. Work as an assistant under a trainer who will sponsor you while you strive for your goals. Watch lessons given by others. There are many schools that specialize in equine sciences along with business classes. And don't stop because of a problem that you have with your own training. Seek help early so you can continue to grow toward your goals.

Q. What personal strengths or traits should someone have who is considering this field?

A. This field isn't just a job, it's a lifestyle. The loved ones around you need to understand how time-consuming this work will be for you. You need to like physical activity. This will make you strong. You need to be brave. You should have good people skills. Remember, it's the students and owners who make this business possible for instructors and trainers. Learning to network with others—trainers, vets, tack shop owners, etc.—is important. You never know when you may need advice from someone.

Q. If you could do it over, is there anything you would have done differently to reach your career goal?

A. I would have seen a sports psychologist earlier and continued to work in the field.

Q. Is there anything else you would like to say about your career or your life with horses?

A. Even though I did take a long time off before coming back to the business, I always dreamed of coming back. It never left my life mentally. While the fire of passion for the horse business burned in my soul during the years I was gone, I knew one day that I would come back. I never knew when it was going to happen, but now that I'm here, I'm more mature and devoted than ever.

Trail Guide

ABOUT THE JOB

Trail guides work at public riding stables, dude ranches, and guest ranches. They take riders of all levels on guided trail rides. Trail guides should be knowledgeable about the countryside in which they are riding, so they can answer questions from riders. Some rides include overnight stays or longer; these packing trips involve additional duties, such as setting up camp and cooking. Prior to rides, trail guides determine the experience levels of riders and assign them to appropriate mounts. They also groom and tack up horses. Trail guides should be patient, have good communication skills, be safety conscious, and have excellent horsemanship skills. CPR and first-aid certification and wilderness survival skills are also helpful and may be required, depending on the job. Most trail guide jobs are seasonal.

EDUCATION AND TRAINING

A high school diploma plus experience; certification is available through CHA First-aid and CPR certification are desirable.

SALARY

Trail guides may be paid $1,500 and up for a camp season.

RESOURCES

CHA, The Association for Horsemanship Safety
5318 Old Bullard Road
Tyler, TX 75703
www.cha-ahse.org

The Dude Ranchers' Association
P.O. Box 2307
Cody, Wyoming 82414
www.duderanch.org

Travel Agent

ABOUT THE JOB

Equine travel agents work for agencies specializing in horseback riding vacations throughout the world. They advise travelers on available vacations and make travel arrangements for individuals and groups interested in riding adventures that range from horseback safaris to dude ranch vacations to dressage camps. While travel agents do visit vacation destinations to evaluate them, the majority of their time is spent at the agency meeting with clients and doing the necessary duties (paperwork, computer, and phone work) to promote and book trips.

Travel professionals should have good writing, verbal, sales, and computer skills, as well as a general knowledge of geography. Experience as a traveler is an asset. Riding skills and an interest in horses are important.

EDUCATION AND TRAINING

A high school diploma and on-the-job training and/or travel agent courses through a trade school, adult-education program, or college are helpful. A few schools offer bachelor's and master's degrees in travel and tourism. Courses in business management, marketing, and accounting are also helpful, especially for individuals interested in starting their own agencies.

The American Society of Travel Agents offers online home-study courses in specialty areas, including one that discusses dude ranches. The Travel Institute (formerly The Institute of Certified Travel Agents) offers experienced agents advanced study courses leading to the designation of Certified Travel Counselor (CTC); it also offers destination specialist programs. Both organizations list schools and training programs on their Web sites. Their contact information is listed below.

Licensing laws vary from state to state. There are currently 14 states with regulations over travel sellers: California, Delaware, Florida, Hawaii, Illinois, Iowa, Massachusetts, New York, Ohio, Oregon, Pennsylvania, Rhode Island, Virginia, and Washington. Contact the Department of Commerce or other appropriate agency in your state for more information.

SALARY

The median annual salary is $25,150.

RESOURCES

American Society of Travel Agents
1101 King St., Suite 200
Alexandria, VA 22314
www.astanet.com

The Travel Institute
148 Linden St.
P.O. Box 812059
Wellesley, MA 02181-0012
www.icta.com

Wrangler

ABOUT THE JOB

Wranglers commonly work on guest or dude ranches, for outfitters, and at summer horse camps. (This term is also used in the cattle industry to describe someone responsible for a herd of livestock.) Wranglers take care of the day-to-day needs of the horses on the ranch, ensure that tack is clean and safe, assist guests, and plan ranch activities and trail rides. Wranglers often act as trail guides as well.

Sometimes experience in singing, playing guitar, or western dancing can be helpful in finding employment, as dude and guest ranches often provide this type of entertainment to guests. Strong riding skills and horse care and handling knowledge are essential. People interested in working for dude and guest ranches, summer camps, and outfitters must have an enthusiastic atti-tude, excellent people skills, and a willingness to pitch in wherever and whenever help is needed. A neat and clean appearance is expected and some ranches and summer camps have very specific guidelines as to dress, makeup, facial hair, and hairstyle. This job is usually seasonal. (Also, see descriptions for trail guide, horse packer and outfitter, and horse camp counselor.)

EDUCATION AND TRAINING

A high school diploma, plus experience is important. First aid and CPR cer-tification is desirable.

SALARY

A sample salary for a wrangler is $2,000 for a summer camp season.

CHAPTER 19

Transportation and Facilities Careers

— — —

Horses are bought and sold, moved to farms for breeding and foaling, and taken to competitions throughout the country, making reliable transportation a necessity in the industry. Because of this need, there are several careers for those who know horses and know how to get them safely from place to place. On the opposite end of the spectrum, when horses aren't traveling, their owners must have a place to keep them. Thus, there are numerous job opportunities open to those who are experts in building, designing, and landscaping horse properties. Whether on the go or at home, horses have facility needs that qualified people must address.

Architect

ABOUT THE JOB

Architects in the horse industry specialize in designing equestrian facilities such as barns, arenas, hay and equipment buildings, paddocks, and farmhouses. Horse experience is necessary to fully understand the day-to-day facility needs of the horse owner, the horse disciplines that must be accommodated, and safety issues.

Some architects are self-employed while others work for architectural design firms; those who work for themselves must have the skills to market and manage their own businesses. All architects must have good design, engineering, supervisory, computer, and communication skills.

Architecture is a competitive field. It is helpful to have experience in an architectural firm during school, as well as freehand drawing, computer-aided design, and drafting technology skills.

EDUCATION AND TRAINING

A five-year Bachelor of Architecture or a six-year Master of Architecture is required. Some students preparing for architecture careers pursue four-year liberal arts degrees followed by a three- or four-year master's program in architecture. An internship (usually three years long) is required by most states before a student can sit for the Architect Registration Examination and earn state licensing. In most states, you must earn the professional architecture degree from a school with a program accredited from the National Architectural Accrediting Board.

SALARY

The median annual salary for architects is $52,510.

RESOURCES

The American Institute of Architects
1735 New York Ave. NW
Washington, D.C. 20006
www.aia.org

National Council of Architectural Registration Boards
Intern Development Program

1801 K Street NW, Suite 1100K
Washington, D.C. 20006
www.ncarb.org

The Internet Community for Architecture and Construction
P.O. Box 18350
Irvine, CA 92623
www.akropolis.net

Commercial Horse Transporter

ABOUT THE JOB

Horse transportation companies carry horses throughout the country to shows, rodeos, races, new homes, and other events. Positions available with horse transportation companies include drivers, equine attendants, and office workers.

Owning a horse transportation company takes a large investment in money and excellent business and marketing skills. Registration with the Department of Transportation is a requirement, as is insurance to protect your business. Horse transporters must be aware of the types of health certificates and veterinary paperwork required from owners to ship horses on commercial carriers, as well as any additional paperwork required by some states when owners transport their own hay or grain with their horses. Carriers charge rates based on the number of miles to be traveled, the type of stall used, and the number of horses being shipped. Horse transporters should have a strong background with horses to better understand the concerns of their clients and be able to handle the horses if the carrier owner is also a driver.

EDUCATION AND TRAINING

A four-year degree in commercial transportation or related field or business is ideal, as well as previous experience in animal transportation.

SALARY

No information available.

Career Spotlight

ANDRE DELAHOUSSAYE, HORSE TRANSPORTER, BOARDING STABLE OWNER, AND HORSEMAN

Andre Delahoussaye has spent his life surrounded by horses. He owns and manages Christiana Farm, a boarding facility located on 48 rolling acres in Broussard, Louisiana. In addition to running the farm, Andre spends much of his time on the road transporting horses for breeders, trainers, and others while his wife oversees operations at home with the help of several part-time stable workers. This busy horseman also works with horse owners to resolve problems such as trailer loading. Andre first learned horsemanship from his father, who breeds horses as a hobby, and from several local horse people whom he admired. Andre rode racehorses and got his professional jockey's license as a teenager, though he quit riding in 1996, when he got married and had children. Andre is the father of two young boys.

Q. What is your background with horses?

A. I've been around horses all my life and I've learned to work and connect with them. I've learned from experience and experienced people. And I'm not ashamed to call someone if I need help.

Q. What does your job involve?

A. I spend most of my time doing horse transportation. Eighty to 85 percent of my time is spent on the road. Some people hire others, but I do all the horse hauling myself. For me to trust someone else driving my clients' horses is slim to none. A typical road trip involves driving for hours, while stopping to water and care for the horses along the way. I recently had a client move from Louisiana to Wisconsin. I drove straight through for 17 hours, stopping only to care for the horses. I have a few part-time workers who help with the boarding facility and my wife is in charge when I am on the road. We are now boarding 24 horses and I also take horses in to correct problems.

Q. Do you consider yourself a trainer?

A. Should I? Yes. Do I? No. I was taught as a jockey and a horseman, not a trainer. There are so many trainers I've seen who are irresponsible. Anyone can be a horseman or a trainer but it takes a natural gift to really be one. These days, true horsemen are the last of a dying breed, especially around here.

When I was in New York, Kentucky, and Virginia, and working with the horsemen there, I saw that they take time with their horses—they don't run their horses into the ground until they can't run anymore. I worked for a trainer in the North once as an exerciser. He had a sour horse. I suggested he take the blinkers off and change the bit. He did that and the horse became easy to handle, worked well; all he needed was different equipment. He asked me to jockey the horse and I did later, after I had gained more experience galloping. When that horse tired of running, they retired him to a nice place. They have fun with their horses—it isn't just about money

Q. What training methods do you use?

A. You must build a relationship with a horse—let him know he can trust you—to get him to do what you need him to do, such as loading in a trailer or crossing a pond. You can't physically control a 1,000-pound or 1,500-pound horse, so you have to learn to communicate with him. I don't believe in hitting a horse on the head and neck—it makes him head shy. Get his attention in other ways. If you make a horse want to do something he will do it, but don't scare him into doing it. Show him he can do it and he will trust you. I love John Lyons's methods. I don't train like him, but I take parts of his methods and use them. I respect him highly. There is another gentleman whose method of communicating with the horse I like, though I don't care for all his training methods, such as tying up. I take parts of different methods and use them.

Q. How do you transport the horses?

A. I have one truck and a six-horse trailer. I'm also in the process of purchasing another truck and trailer.

Q. What do you like most about your work?

A. To enjoy my work and make money at the same time is a privilege. I love my job and I love horses. I wouldn't give it up for anything.

Q. What do you find most challenging about your work?

A. Dealing with the people, not the horses. It's easy to get a horse to communicate with you, but hard to get someone who thinks he knows it all to listen to you.

Q. What do you find most rewarding?

A. To connect and communicate with a horse in a sense only the horse and I can understand. This gives me a great sense of accomplishment. The best is to accomplish something with the horse and know that the horse is safe and happy.

Q. What would you say to someone interested in horse transport?

A. Ask yourself these questions: Can you accept spending 90 percent of your time away from your family? Do you have the patience to deal with horses and people? This business goes through up and down cycles; can you live with that and can you put up with the expense of upkeep and equipment? You have to take care of your equipment or you won't have a business.

Most importantly, you must have respect for the horses. There are some drivers who wouldn't know if a horse flipped over in the trailer. You must be sensitive enough to feel the horse move his foot in the trailer. When you get to that point, then you know you can do it. You must care about the horse first. If something happens to a horse while he is being hauled or boarded, I take care of the horse first and then notify the owner.

I take care of horses like they are my own. If one goes down, I blame myself. We had a horse at the farm being boarded that died of an aneurysm and even after I found out what caused the death, I still blamed myself. A death of a horse is hard to accept.

Finally, you have to consider your family and make time for them. I was raised the old-fashioned way and this is very important.

Q. What personality characteristics should a person have who is considering this field?

A. You've got to have a positive attitude and be there to do it right. When I transport a horse, I want the horse to be happy and I want the owner to be happy, so I'm going to do it the right way. I'll work with the horse to get him to load in the trailer by building a relationship with the horse and letting him know he can trust me.

Q. What is your most memorable moment in the horse industry?

A. My mom passed away in 1994. Prior to her becoming sick, I quit high school and got my GED. She had given me a list of things she wanted me to accomplish. One of them was that she wanted me to breed her favorite mare to a stallion, Explosive Wagon, who was standing in Texas. Dad thought the horse was small and ugly and wouldn't pay the stud fee. So I paid it. That year we had five babies at our farm, including the Explosive Wagon baby. When I first looked at that foal, named Explosive Run, I liked him. When he was a yearling mom fell sick. She told me to race him. When it came time to break him as a 2–year old, mom had passed on. I won the race on him at Evangeline Downs. To finish that race and know I did it, to beat the horses I beat, which were top-of-the-line horses, was fantastic. I got him going and never whipped him again. I let him be a horse. I really made a connection with that little horse.

Construction Manager/Contractor

ABOUT THE JOB

Construction contractors and crews build equestrian facilities, including arenas, barns, farmhouses, and equipment buildings. Construction managers/contractors may own their own business, be employed by a construction or contracting firm, or be an independent contractor hired by the owner of a firm. They are responsible for planning and overseeing projects, including hiring and managing people, materials, and equipment with an eye toward safety, as well as managing budgets, schedules, and contracts. Workers on construction projects include masons, carpenters, painters, electricians, and plumbers.

Construction managers/contractors work from field offices set up at the construction site and spend much of their time outdoors. They are often on call to deal with issues that may arise during construction. Horse experience is desirable for construction managers/contractors who must understand the needs of horse owners.

EDUCATION AND TRAINING

Many construction managers begin their careers as tradespeople and work their way up. More and more, however, employers are looking for candidates with a combination of construction work experience and education. Most often a bachelor's degree in construction science, construction management, or civil engineering is desired.

SALARY

The median annual salary for construction managers is $58,250. According to a 2001 salary survey by the National Association of Colleges and Employers, candidates with a bachelor's degree in construction science/management received job offers averaging $40,740 per year.

RESOURCES

American Council for Construction Education
1300 Hudson Lane, Suite 3
Monroe, LA 71201
www.acce-hq.org

Construction Management Association of America
7918 Jones Branch Dr., Suite 540
McLean, VA 22102
www.cmaanet.org

Farm Fencing Contractor

ABOUT THE JOB

Fencing contractors supply fencing for horse properties. They must be familiar enough with horses and horse behavior to help clients select fencing that is safe to their horses and appropriate for their properties. In addition to the business owner, fencing companies may employ installers, salespeople, yard foremen, and others, depending on the company's size.

An individual starting his own fencing business must have marketing and business skills to be successful, as well as an in-depth knowledge of the fencing industry and the different types of fencing available for horse properties and other agricultural uses. Working your way up at a fencing company is a good way to learn all aspects of the business. To find fencing companies, look in horse directories and magazines as well as farming, ranching, and agricultural publications. Also, the American Fence Association lists fencing contractors on its Web site.

EDUCATION AND TRAINING

On-the-job training is important. Though a degree is not required for business owners, a bachelor's degree in agriculture or business, with an agricultural focus, is helpful.

SALARY

Fencing company owners' salaries will vary, depending on the size of their operation, their marketing ability, and the area of the country. The median annual salary for fence installers is $21,900.

RESOURCES

American Fence Association
800 Roosevelt Rd., Bldg. C-20
Glen Ellyn, IL 60137
www.americanfenceassociation.com

Landscape Architect

About the job

Landscape architects design the grounds, including vegetation and walkways, for farms, ranches, and other equestrian facilities. They must be familiar with the flowers, shrubs, and trees that are dangerous to horses and other animals. Landscape architects also work with architects, surveyors, and engineers to determine the best placement for roads and buildings at new building sites.

While this may sound like a career where much of the time is spent outdoors, it isn't. Landscape architects spend the majority of their time in offices creating plans and designs, preparing cost estimates, researching, and attending meetings with clients and others involved in the project. They do spend time visiting the project sites to ensure that their designs are properly incorporated into the landscape and to oversee the actual landscaping work. About one-quarter of landscape architects are self-employed, while the rest work for landscaping firms.

Aspiring landscape architects should appreciate nature, be creative and have good communication skills because presentations to clients are required.

Education and training

A minimum of a bachelor's degree in landscape architecture (a list of schools offering architecture degrees is available from the American Society of Landscape Architects Web site) is requisite; a master's degree is desirable. Licensing or registration is required in 46 states.

Salary

The median annual salary is $43,540.

Resources

American Society of Landscape Architects
636 Eye St., NW
Washington, D.C. 20001
www.asla.org

Council of Landscape Architectural Registration Boards
144 Church St., NW, Ste. 201
Vienna, VA 22180
www.clarb.org

Transportation Driver

About the Job

Transportation drivers, employed by animal transportation companies, travel throughout the country carrying horses from one location to another. They may drive tractor-trailer rigs, horse vans, or small trucks with trailers. Drivers spend many consecutive days on the road, covering long distances to reach their destinations. They must be able to safely load and unload horses, supply feed and water, and be equipped to handle possible emergencies; sometimes, they must administer medication or treat injuries. Excellent driving skills, good health and vision, and a blemish-free driving record are important for this career, as is horse experience.

Education and Training

A high school diploma is ideal, plus on-the-job experience and/or vocational school. Classes in automotive mechanics are also helpful. A commercial driver's license is usually required.

Salary

The median hourly wage is $15.25.

Resources

National Horse Carriers Association
18 Mechanic Street
Amenia, New York, 12501
www.nationalhorsecarriers.com

Animal Transportation Association
111 East Loop North
Houston, TX 77029
www.aata-animaltransport.org

Who's Who in Live Animal Trade and Transport
Handbook of Live Animal Transport
P.O. Box 441110
Ft. Washington, MD 20749
www.lattmag.com/

APPENDIX A
HORSE REGISTRIES AND ASSOCIATIONS

Akhal-Teke Association of America
405 Page Creek Road
Cave Junction, OR 97523
www.akhal-teke.org

American Andalusian Horse Association
6020 Emerald Lane
Sykesville, MD 21784-8501

American Association of Owners & Breeders of Peruvian Paso Horses
P.O. Box 189
Ramona, CA 92065-0189
916-687-6232
www.aaobpph.org

American Azteca Horse International Association
2218 Jackson Blvd., Suite 3
Rapid City, SD 57702-3452
605-342-2322
www.americanazteca.com

American Bashkir Curly Registry
P.O. Box 246
371 Clark St.
Ely, NV 89301-0246
775-289-4999
www.abcregistry.org

American Buckskin Registry Association, Inc.
1141 Hartnell Ave.
Redding, CA 96002-2113
530-223-1420
www.americanbuckskin.com

American Connemara Pony Society
2360 Hunting Ridge Road
Winchester, VA 22603
540-662-5953
www.acps.org

American Council of Spotted Asses
P.O. Box 121
New Melle, MO 63365
319-735-5533
www.spottedass.com

American Cream Draft Horse Association
193 Crossover Road
Bennington, VT 05201
802-447-7612
www.americancreamdraft.org

American Dartmoor Pony Association
203 Kendall Oaks Dr.
Boerne, TX 78006
704-894-5672
www.imh.org/imh/bw/dart.html

The American Donkey and Mule Society, Inc.
P.O. Box 1210
Lewisville, TX 75067
972-219-0781
www.lovelongears.com

American Equine Registration Service
375 Burton Road
Reidsville, NC 27320-7771
336-939-2022
www.registerhorse.com

American Gaited Mules Association
P.O. Box 764
Shelbyville, TN 37160

American Hackney Horse Society
4059 Iron Works Pkwy., Suite 3
Lexington, KY 40511-8462
859.255.8694
www.hackneysociety.com

The American Haflinger Registry
2746 State Route 44
Rootstown, OH 44272
330-325-8116
www.haflingerhorse.com

The American Hanoverian Society, Inc.
4067 Iron Works Pkwy., Suite 1
Lexington, KY 40511-8483
859-255-4141
www.hanoverian.org

American Holsteiner Horse Association
222 E. Main St., Suite1
Georgetown, KY 40324-0722
502-863-4239
www.holsteiner.com

American Horizon Horse Registry
P.O. Box 564
Belen, NM 87002-0564
505-864-4778

American Indian Horse Registry, Inc.
9028 State Park Road
Lockhart, TX 78644-4310
512-398-6642
www.indianhorse.com

American Mammoth Jackstock Registry
P.O. Box 1190
Enumclaw, WA 98022
360-825-1550
www.amjr.us

American Miniature Horse Association, Inc.
5601 S. I-35 W
Alvarado, TX 76009
817-783-6403
www.amha.com

American Miniature Horse Registry
81-B Queenwood Road
Morton, IL 61550
309-263-4044
www.shetlandminiature.com/amhr.shtml

American Morgan Horse Association, Inc.
P.O. Box 960
Shelburne, VT 05482-0960
802 985 8897
www.morganhorse.com

American Mustang and Burro Association
P.O. Box 788
Lincoln, CA 95648
530-633-9271
www.bardalisa.com

American Paint Horse Association
P.O. Box 961023
Fort Worth, TX 76161-0023
817-834-2742
www.apha.com

American Part-Blooded Horse Registry
13100 SE River Road
Portland, OR 97222-8031
503-698-8615
www.apbhorseregistry.com

The American Pinto Arabian Registry
3524 E. Highway 34
Ennis, TX 75119-1440
972-975-4670
www.apar.topcities.com/Main.html

American Quarter Horse Association
P.O. Box 200
Amarillo, TX 79168-0001
806-376-4811
www.aqha.com

American Registry of Arab Bred Sporthorses
15 St. Michael Ct.
San Ramon, CA 94583

**American Remount Association Part
  Thoroughbred Stud Book, Inc.**
P.O. Box 1901
Middleburg, VA 22117-1901
301-791-1238

American Saddlebred Horse Association
4093 Iron Works Pkwy.
Lexington, KY 40511-8434
859-259-2742
www.saddlebred.com

American Shetland Pony Club
81-B E. Queenwood
Morton, IL 61550
309-263-4044
www.shetlandminiature.com

American Shire Horse Association
P.O. Box 2134
North Platte, NE 69103
970-876-5980
www.shirehorse.org

American Show Pony Registry
81-B E. Queenwood
Morton, IL 61550
309-263-4044
www.shetlandminiature.com/aspr.shtml

American Sportpony Registry
P.O. Box 211735
Royal Palm Beach, FL 33421-1735
561-667-0561
www.americansportpony.com

American Suffolk Horse Association
4240 Goehring Road
Ledbetter, TX 78946-5004
979-249-5795
www.suffolkpunch.com

American Tarpan Studbook Association
150 Joan St.
Medford, WI 54451
715-748-9952

American Trakehner Association, Inc.
1514 W. Church St.
Newark, OH 43055
740-344-1111
www.americantrakehner.com

American Walking Pony Registry
P.O. Box 5282
Macon, GA 31208-5282
912-7443-2321

American Warmblood Registry, Inc.
P.O. Box 211735
Royal Palm Beach, FL 33421-1735
209-245-3565
www.americanwarmblood.com

American Warmblood Society
2 Buffalo Run Road
Center Ridge, AR 72027-8347
501-893-2777
www.americanwarmblood.org

American Welara Registry
P.O. Box 401
Yucca Valley, CA 92286-0401
760-364-2048
www.welararegistry.com

American White & American Creme Horse Registry
Rt. 1, P.O. Box 20
Naper, NE 68755-2020
402-832-5560

Appaloosa Horse Club, Inc.
2720 W. Pullman Road
Moscow, ID 83843-0903
208-882-5578
www.appaloosa.com

Appaloosa Sport Horse Association
3380 Saxonburg Blvd.
Glenshaw, PA 15116
412-767-4616
www.netrax.net/~aliasme

AraAppaloosa and Foundation Breeders International
RR 8, P.O. Box 317
Fairmont, WV 26554
304-366-8766

Arabian Breeders Association
P.O. Box 43
Millville, CA 96062
www.arabian-breeders.com

Arabian Horse Association
10805 E. Bethany Dr.
Aurora, CO 80014-2605
303-696-4599
www.arabianhorses.org

Arabian International Registry
P.O. Box F
Rumford, ME 04276-3018
207-369-2798

Arabian Jockey Club
12000 Zuni St.
Westminster, CO 80234
303-743-6246
www.arabianracing.org

Arabian Sport Horse Association Inc.
6145 Whaleyville Blvd.
Suffolk, VA 23438
757-986-4486
www.ashai.org

Azteca Horse Owners Association Inc.
P.O. Box 998
Ridgefield, WA 98642-0998
612-462-1949
www.azteca-horse.com

Belgian Draft Horse Corporation of America
P.O. Box 335
Wabash, IN 46992-0335
206-563-3205
www.belgiancorp.com

Belgian Warmblood Breeding Association/North American District
136 Red Fox Trail

Chapin, SC 29036
803-345-5588
www.belgianwarmblood.com

Caspian Horse Society of the Americas
18156 FM 359
Hempstead TX 77445
936-931-2424
www.caspianhorse.com

Chilean Corralero Registry International
4121 Washington Road
Wisconsin Rapids, WI 54494
715-424-4060

Chincoteague Pony Association
P.O. Box 407
Chincoteague, VA 23336-0407
757-336-6161
www.chincoteaguechamber.com/map-assn.html

Cleveland Bay Horse Society of North America
P.O. Box 483
Goshen, NH 03752
603-863-5193
www.clevelandbay.org

Clydesdale Breeders of the U.S.A.
17346 Kelley Road
Pecatonica, IL 61063
815-247-8780
www.clydesusa.com

Colorado Ranger Horse Association, Inc.
RR 1, P.O. Box 1290
Wampum, PA 16157-9610
724-535-4841
www.coloradoranger.com

Dales Pony Association of North America
P.O. Box 733
Walkerton, ON N0G 2V0, Canada
705-541-9106
www.dalesponyassoc.com

The Dutch Warmblood Studbook in North America
609 E. Central
Sutherlin, OR 97479
541-459-3232
www.nawpn.org

Falabella Miniature Horse Association
33222 N. Fairfield Road
Round Lake, IL 60073
847-546-6688
www.falabellafmha.com

Federation of North American Sport Horse Registries
4067 Iron Works Pkwy., Suite 1
Lexington, KY 40511
www.sporthorsefederation.org

The Florida Cracker Horse Association, Inc.
P.O. Box 186
Newberry, FL 32669-0186
352-472-2228
www.fcha.flahorse.com/spotlight.htm

The Foundation Quarter Horse Registry
P.O. Box 230
Sterling, CO 80751
970-521-7822
www.fqhrregistry.com

The Friesian Horse Association of North America
P.O. Box 11217
Lexington KY 40574-1217
www.fhana.com

Friesian Horse Society
8502 E. Chapman Ave., Suite 140
Orange, CA 92869
250-295-3102
www.friesianhorsesociety.com

Gaited Horse International Association
507 N. Sullivan Road
Veradale, WA 99037
509-928-5690
www.gaitedhorse.com

Galiceno Horse Breeders Association
P.O. Box 219
Godley, TX 76044-0219
817-389-3547

Gotland-Russ Association of North America, Inc.
RR 1, P.O. Box 174
Triadelphia, WV 26059-9720
304-547-9028
www.gotlands.org

Half Saddlebred Registry of America
4093 Iron Works Pkwy.
Lexington, KY 40511
859-259-2742
www.asha.net

Harnessbred Breeders Affiliation
18481 Elm Creek Road
Moody, TX 76557
254-853-2806
www.fortstoreyranch.com

Hungarian Horse Association of America
HC 71, P.O. Box 108
Anselmo, NE 68813
308-749-2411
www.horseplaza.com/cfusion/template/hhaa/index.cfm

Iberian Warmblood Registry
P.O. Box 204
Glenoma, WA 98336
www.iberianwarmblood.com

International Andalusian and Lusitano Horse Association
101 Carnoustie N., Suite 200
Birmingham, AL 35242
205-995-8900
www.ialha.com

International Buckskin Horse Association
P.O. Box 268
Shelby, IN 46377-0268
219-552-1013
www.ibha.net

International Champagne Horse Registry
P.O. Box 4430
Paso Robles, CA 93447-4430
www.ichregistry.com

The International Colored Appaloosa Association, Inc.
P.O. Box 99
Shipshewana, IN 46565
219-825-3331
www.icaainc.com

International Generic Horse Association
P.O. Box 6778
Dept. AHC
San Pedro, CA 90734-6778

310-719-9094
www.igha.org

International Miniature Trotting & Pacing Association, Inc.
18481 Elm Creek Road
Moody, TX 76557
254-853-3744
www.fortstoreyranch.com/impta.html

International Morab Breeders Association and Registry
S. 101 W. 34628 Hwy.
Eagle, WI 53119-1857
262-594-3667
www.morab.com

International Quarter Pony Association
P.O. Box 125
Sheridan, CA 95681
www.netpets.org/~iqpa

International Sport Horses of Color
P.O. Box 294
Newcastle, CA 95658
916-645-6909
www.shoc.org

International Sporthorse Registry and Oldenburg Registry North America
939 Merchandise Mart
Chicago, IL 60654
312-527-6544
www.isroldenburg.org

Irish Draught Horse Society, N.A.
5480 Major Lane
Platteville, WI 53818
608-348-2519
www.irishdraught.com

The Jockey Club
821 Corporate Dr.
Lexington, KY 40503-2794
212-371-5970
www.jockeyclub.com

The Jockey Club-Executive Offices
40 E. 52nd St.
New York, NY 10022-6123
212-371-5970
www.jockeyclub.com

Lipizzan Association of North America
P.O. Box 1133
Anderson, IN 46015-1133
765-644-3904
www.lipizzan.org

Mangalarga Marchador Horse Association of America
P.O. Box 770955
Ocala, FL 34477
352-368-5815
www.mmhaa.net

Mangalarga Paulista Horse Association of America
P.O. Box 80762
Atlanta, GA 30366-0762
770-893-4304

Missouri Fox Trotting Horse Breed Association, Inc.
P.O. Box 1027
Ava, MO 65608-1027
417-683-2468
www.mfthba.com

Mountain Pleasure Horse Association
P.O. Box 79
Wellington, KY 40387
859-768-9224
www.mtn-pleasure-horse.org

The National Chincoteague Pony Association
2595 Jensen Road
Bellingham, WA 98226
360-671-8338
www.pony-chincoteague.com

The National Foundation Quarter Horse Association
P.O. Box P
Joseph, OR 97846
541-426-4403
www.nfqha.com

National Pinto Arabian Registry
9706 County Road 2440
Royse City, TX 75189-3084
972-636-9006
www.pintoarabianregistry.com

National Pinto Horse Registry
P.O. Box 486
Oxford, NY 13830-0486
607-334-4964

National Show Horse Registry
10368 Bluegrass Pkwy.
Louisville, KY 40299
502-266-5100
www.nshregistry.org

National Spotted Saddle Horse Association
P.O. Box 898
Murfreesboro, TN 37133-0898
615-890-2864
www.nssha.com

National Standardbred Pleasure Horse Organization
41 West Summit St., Suite 17
South Hadley, MA 01075
413-534-4354
www.spho.org

New Forest Pony Association, Inc.
P.O. Box 206
Pascoag, RI 02859-1210
401-568-8238
www.newforestpony.net

Nokota Horse Conservancy
5330 Homeville Road
Oxford, PA 19363-1033
701-782-4323
www.nokotahorse.org

North American Mustang Association and Registry
P.O. Box 850906
Mesquite, TX 75185-0906
972-289-9344

North American Selle Francais Association, Inc.
P.O. Box 604
Round Hill, VA 20142-0604
540-338-0166
www.sellefrancais.org

North American Single-Footing Horse Association
2995 Clark Valley Road
Los Osos, CA 93402
805-528-7308
www.singlefootinghorse.com

Norwegian Fjord Horse Registry
1203 Appian Dr.
Webster, NY 14580-9129
716-872-4114
www.nfhr.com

Palomino Horse Association
HC 63, P.O. Box 24
Dornsife, PA 17823
570-758-3067
www.palominohorseassoc.com

Palomino Horse Breeders of America, Inc.
15253 E. Skelly Dr.
Tulsa, OK 74116-2637
918-438-1234
www.palominohba.com

Paso Fino Horse Association, Inc.
101 North Collins St.
Plant City, FL 33563-3311
813-719-7777
www.pfha.org

Percheron Horse Association of America
P.O. Box 141
Fredericktown, OH 43019-0141
740-694-3602
www.percheronhorse.org

Performance Horse Registry
4047 Iron Works Pkwy.
Lexington, KY 40511-8483
859-258-2472
www.usef.org

Peruvian Paso Horse Registry of North America
3077 Wiljan Ct., Suite A
Santa Rosa, CA 95407-5702
707-579-4394
www.pphrna.org

Peruvian Paso Part-Blood Registry of North America
3077 Wiljan Ct., Suite A
Santa Rosa, CA 95407-5702
707-579-4394
www.pphrna.org

Pintabian Horse Registry, Inc
P.O. Box 360
Karlstad, MN 56732-0360

Pinto Horse Association of America, Inc.
1900 Samuels Ave.
Fort Worth, TX 76102-1141
817-336-7842
www.pinto.org

Pony of the Americas Club, Inc.
5240 Elmwood Ave.
Indianapolis, IN 46203-5990317-788-0107
www.poac.org

Purebred Morab Horse Association/Purebred Morab Horse Registry
P.O. Box 10
Sherwood, WI 54169
920-853-3086
www.puremorab.com
www.morabnet.com

Racking Horse Breeders' Association of America
67 Horse Center Road
Decatur, AL 35603
256-353-7225
www.rackinghorse.com

Rocky Mountain Horse Association
P.O. Box 129
Mt. Olivet, KY 41064
606-724-2354
www.rmhorse.com

Shire Sport-Horse Registry
P.O. Box 2134
North Platte, NE 69103
970-384-1511
www.shirehorse.org

Spanish-Barb Breeders Association International, Inc.
HCR 31, P.O. Box 95A
Caballo, NM 87931-9702
601-372-8801

Spanish Gaited Ponies Registry
P.O. Box 270
Creston, CA 93432-0270

The Spanish Mustang Registry, Inc.
11790 Halstad Ave.
Lonsdale, MN 55046-4246
www.spanishmustang.org

The Spanish-Norman Horse Registry
P.O. Box 985
Woodbury, CT 06798-3216
203-266-2028
www.spanish-norman.com

Spotted Saddle Horse Breeders & Exhibitors
Association
P.O. Box 1046
Shelbyville, TN 37162
931-684-7496
www.sshbea.org

Swedish Warmblood Association of North
America
P.O. Box 788
Socorro, NM 87801
505-835-1318
www.wbstallions.com/wb/swana

Tennessee Walking Horse Breeders' and
Exhibitors' Association
P.O. Box 286
Lewisburg, TN 37091-0286
931-359-1574
www.twhbea.com

United States Icelandic Horse Congress
38 Park St.
Montclair, NJ 07042
973-783-3429
www.icelandics.org

United States Lipizzan Registry
707 Thirteenth St., Suite 275
Salem, OR 97301-4005
503-589-3172
www.lipizzan-uslr.com

United States Trotting Association
750 Michigan Ave.
Columbus, OH 43215-1191
614-224-2291
www.ustrotting.com

Walkaloosa Horse Association
2995 Clark Valley Road
Los Osos, CA 93402
805-528-3128
www.walkaloosaregistry.com

Walking Horse Owners' Association
304-A W. Thompson Lane

Murfreesboro, TN 37129
615-494-8822
www.walkinghorseowners.com

Welsh Pony and Cob Society of America
P.O. Box 2977
Winchester, VA 22604-2977
540-667-6195
www.welshpony.org

Westfalen Horse Association
716 N. McQueen Road
Chandler, AZ 85222
480-963-1310
www.wwwarmbloods.com/westfalen/

Wild Horses of America Registry
6212 E. Sweetwater Ave.
Scottsdale, AZ 85254-4461
602 991 0273

APPENDIX B
EDUCATIONAL ORGANIZATIONS

Affiliated National Riding Commission
1900 Association Dr.
Reston, VA 20191
www.anrc.org

American Association for Horsemanship
Safety, Inc.
P.O. Box 39
Fentress, TX 78622-0039
512-488-2220
www.horsemanshipsafety.com

American Association of Riding Schools, Inc.
8375 Coldwater Road
Davison, MI 48423-8966
810-653-1440
www.ucanride.com

American Farrier's Association
4059 Iron Works Pkwy., Suite 1
Lexington, KY 40511-8434
859-233-7411
www.americanfarriers.org

American Horse Council
1616 H St., 7th Floor
Washington, D.C. 20006-3805
202-296-4031
www.horsecouncil.org

American Riding Instructor Certification Program (ARICP)
28801 Trenton Ct.
Bonita Springs, FL 34134-3337
239-948-3232
www.riding-instructor.com

American Riding Instructors Association (ARIA)
28801 Trenton Ct.
Bonita Springs, FL 34134-3337
239-948-3232
www.riding-instructor.com

American Youth Horse Council, Inc.
577 N. Boyero Ave.
Pueblo West, CO 81007
719-547-7677
www.ayhc.com

The Brotherhood of Working Farriers Association
14013 East Hwy. 136
LaFayette, GA 30728
706-397-8047
www.bwfa.net

CHA (Certified Horsemanship Association)
5318 Old Bullard Road
Tyler, TX 75703-3612
800-399-0138
www.cha-ahse.org

Communicating for Agriculture Exchange Program
112 E. Lincoln Ave.
P.O. Box 677
Fergus Falls, MN 56537-0677
218-739-3241
http://ca.cainc.org/

Farriers' National Research Center and School, Inc.
14013 East Hwy., Suite136
LaFayette, GA 30728
706-397-8047
www.bwfa.net/fnrc

Harness Horse Youth Foundation
16575 Carey Road
Westfield, IN 46074
317-867-5877
www.hhyf.org

Horsemanship Safety Association, Inc.
P.O. Box 2710
Lake Placid, FL 33862-2710
941-465-0289

National 4-H Council
7100 Connecticut Ave.
Chevy Chase, MD 20815-4999
301-961-2973
www.fourhcouncil.edu

National FFA Organization
P.O. Box 68960
Indianapolis, IN 46268-0960
317-802-6060
www.ffa.org

New Horizons Equine Education Center
425 Red Mountain Road
Livermore, CO 80536-9998
970-484-9207
www.newhorizonsequine.com

North American Riding For the Handicapped Association
P.O. Box 33150
Denver, CO 80233
303-452-1212
www.narha.org

United States Pony Clubs, Inc
4041 Iron Works Pkwy.
Lexington, KY 40511-8462
859-254-7669
www.ponyclub.org

APPENDIX C
HEALTH AND RESEARCH ORGANIZATIONS

American Association of Equine Practitioners
4075 Iron Works Pkwy.
Lexington, KY 40511-8434
859-233-0147
www.aaep.org

American Farriers' Association
4059 Iron Works Pkwy., Suite 1
Lexington, KY 40511-8434
859-233-7862
www.americanfarriers.org

American Medical Equestrian Association
5318 Old Bullard Road
Tyler, TX 75703
1-866-441-2632
www.law.utexas.edu/dawson/amea/amea.htm

American Quarter Horse Foundation
P.O. Box 200
Amarillo, TX 79168
806-376-4811
www.aqha.org

American Veterinary Medical Association
Communications Division
1931 N. Meacham Road, Suite100
Schaumburg, IL 60173-4360
806-376-4811
www.avma.org

Association for Equine Sports Medicine
3579 E. Foothill, Suite 288
Pasadena, CA 91107

Cornell Equine Research Park
Cornell University
One Bluegrass Lane
Ithaca, NY 14850
607-255-7753
www.vet.cornell.edu/public/cuerp

Farriers' National Research Center and School, Inc.
14013 East Hwy. 136
La Fayette, GA 30728
706-397-8047
www.bwfa.net/fnrc

Grayson-Jockey Club Research Foundation, Inc.
821 Corporate Dr.
Lexington, KY 40503-2794
859-224-2850
http://home.jockeyclub.com/grayson.html

Kentucky Association of Equine Practitioners
1901 Ferguson Road
Lexington, KY 40511

**Maxwell H. Gluck Equine Research Center
University of Kentucky College of Agriculture
Dept. of Veterinary Science**
108 Gluck Equine Research Center
Lexington, KY 40546-0099
859-257-4757
www.ca.uky.edu

Morris Animal Foundation
45 Inverness Dr., E.
Englewood, CO 80112-5480
800-243-2345
www.morrisanimalfoundation.org

United States Animal Health Association
P.O. Box K227
8100 Three Chopt Road, Suite 203
Richmond, VA 23288
804-285-3210
www.usaha.org

University of Arizona - Race Track Industry Program
Education Bldg. 69, Rm. 104
Tuscon, AZ 85721-0069
520-621-5660
www.ag.arizona.edu/rtip

University of California - Center for Equine Health
One Shields Ave.
Davis, CA 95616-8589
530-752-6433
www.vetmed.ucdavis.edu/ceh

University of Kentucky Equine Research Foundation
805 S. Limestone St.
Lexington, KY 40536-0339
859-257-1308
www.ca.uky.edu/agcollege/vetscience/home.htm

APPENDIX D
Horse Publications
Annual and Directories
United States

AAEP Membership Directory
American Association of Equine Practitioners
4075 Iron Works Pkwy.
Lexington, KY 40511-8434
859-233-0147
www.aaep.org

AAEP Proceedings Book
4075 Iron Works Pkwy.
Lexington, KY 40511-8434
859-233-0147
www.aaep.org

All About Horses: A Complete Directory for the NJ Equine Industry
1400 Washington St.
Hoboken, NJ 07030-1601

American Steeplechasing
National Steeplechase Association
400 Fair Hill Dr.
Elkton, MD 21921-2569
410-392-0700
www.nationalsteeplechase.com

American Veterinary Medical Association Membership Directory and Resource Manual
Membership & Field Services
American Veterinary Medical Association
1931 N. Meacham Road, Suite100
Schaumburg, IL 60173
847-925-8070
www.avma.org

American Warmblood Society Annual Sport Horse Guide
American Warmblood Society
2 Buffalo Run Road
Center Ridge, AR 72027
501-893-2777
www.americanwarmblood.org

Annual Breeders Guide
International Sporthorse Registry and Oldenburg Verband N.A.
939 Merchandise Mart
200 World Trade Center
Chicago, IL 60654
321-527-6544
www.isroldenburg.org

The Barn Book
P.O. Box 221
Loxahatchee, FL 33470
561-793-9654
www.thebarnbook.com

The Blood-Horse Auctions
Thoroughbred Owners and Breeders Association
P.O. Box 4038
1736 Alexandria Dr.
Lexington, KY 40544-4038
859-276-6729
www.bloodhorse.com

The Blood-Horse: Nicks, An Annual Guide to Sire and Broodmare Sire Crosses
Thoroughbred Owners and Breeders Association
P.O. Box 4038
1736 Alexandria Dr.
Lexington, KY 40544-4038
859-276-6729
www.bloodhorse.com

The Blood-Horse Sires
Thoroughbred Owners and Breeders Association
P.O. Box 4038
1736 Alexandria Dr.
Lexington, KY 40544-4038
859-276-6729
www.bloodhorse.com

The Blood-Horse Stakes
Thoroughbred Owners and Breeders Association
P.O. Box 4038
1736 Alexandria Dr.
Lexington, KY 40544-4038
859-276-6729
www.bloodhorse.com

The Blood-Horse Stallion Register
Thoroughbred Owners and Breeders Association
P.O. Box 4038
1736 Alexandria Dr.
Lexington, KY 40544-4038
859-276-6729
www.bloodhorse.com

The Blood-Horse: The Source for North American Racing and Breeding
Thoroughbred Owners and Breeders Association
P.O. Box 4038
1736 Alexandria Dr.
Lexington, KY 40544-4038
859-276-6729
www.bloodhorse.com

California Horseman's Directory
9131 Chesapeake Dr.
San Diego, CA 92123
858-268-0397
www.cahorse.com

Directory of ARICP Certified Riding Instructors
American Riding Instructor Certification Program
28801 Trenton, Ct.
Bonita Springs, FL 34134-3337

239-948-3232
www.riding-instructor.com

The Dude Rancher Directory
Dude Rancher's Association
P.O. Box G471
LaPorte, CO 80535-0471
307-587-2339
www.duderanch.org

Equine School and College Directory
Harness Horse Youth Foundation
14950 Greyhound Dr., Suite 210
Carmel, IN 46032-1091
317-867-5877
www.hhyf.org

Farrier Supplies and Services Directory
American Farriers Association and American
    Farriers Journal
P.O. Box 624
Brookfield, WI 53008-0624
262-782-4480
www.lesspub.com

The Guide to the Alaska Horse Community
710 N. Harriette
Wasilla, AK 99654-7627

**Harness Tracks of America World Racing
    Directory**
Harness Tracks of America
4640 E. Sunrise, Suite 200
Tucson, AZ 85718-4576

Horse Industry Directory
American Horse Council
1700 K St., N.W., Suite 300
Washington DC 20006-3805
202-296-4031
www.horsecouncil.org

**The Horse: The Source, An Annual Source and
    Buyer's Guide For Equine Products,
    Equipment and Services**
P.O. Box 4038
1736 Alexandria Dr.
Lexington, KY 40544-4038
800-866-2361
www.thehorse.com

Jim Balzotti's Custom Ranch Vacations
5 Barker St.
Pembroke, MA 02359
800-829-0715
www.jimbalzotti.com

**Just Horses: A Directory of Equine Businesses
    for Connecticut, Massachusetts, Rhode
    Island and Eastern New York**
P.O. Box 10
Huntington, MA 01050-0010
www.justhorses.com

Kentucky Thoroughbred Farm Managers' Club
600 Elsmere Park
Lexington, KY 40508-1406
859-296-4279
www.ktfmc.org

Maine Stable Guide
P.O. Box 2248
South Portland, ME 04116-2248
207 799 7041
www.wordplaypublishing.com

Meadowlands Harness Source
100 Rt. 10 West
East Hanover, NJ 07936

**Missouri Equine Council Horse Industry
    Directory**
Missouri Equine Council, Inc.
P.O. Box 608
Fulton, MO 65251
800-313-3327
www.mo-equine.org

**Nationwide Overnight Stabling Directory and
    Equestrian Vacation Guide**
Equine Travelers of America, Inc.
P.O. Box 322
Arkansas City, KS 67005-0322
620-442-8131
www.overnightstabling.com

New Jersey Standardbred Stallion Register
Standardbred Breeders and Owners Association
    of New Jersey
P.O. Box 839
Freehold, NJ 07728-0839

The Northern Virginia Horseman's Reference
P.O. Box 218
Aldie, VA 20105

Paddock Magazine
Oak Tree Racing Association
P.O. Box 60014
Arcadia, CA 91066-6014
625-574-7223
www.oaktreeracing.com

The Reach - The Driving World Directory
P.O. Box 932
Kendallville, IN 46755-0932

Show Circuit
P.O. Box 1457
Lake Ozark, MO 65049

The SMR Annual
Spanish Mustang Registry, Inc.
11790 Halstad Ave.
Lonsdale, MN 55046
www.spanishmustang.org

Tack 'n Togs Merchandising Buyers Guide
P.O. Box 2400
Minnetonka, MN 55343-2400
952-930-4390
www.tackntogs.com

Tennessee Horse Source
Tennessee Horse Council
P.O. Box 69
College Grove, TN 37046-0069
615-297-3200
www.tnhorsecouncil.com

Texas Horseman's Directory
P.O. Box 625
Cypress, TX 77410-0625
www.texashorsemansdirectory.com

TRA Directory and Record Book
Thoroughbred Racing Associations of North
    America, Inc.
420 Fair Hill Dr., Suite 1
Elkton, MD 21921-2573
www.tra-online.com

Trotting and Pacing Guide
United States Trotting Association
750 Michigan Ave.

Columbus, OH 43215-1191
614-224-2291
www.ustrotting.com

U.S. Stabling Guide
5 Barker St.
Pembroke, MA 02359
800-829-0715
www.jimbalzotti.com

USDF Directory
United States Dressage Federation
P.O. Box 6669
Lincoln, NE 68506-0669
859-971-2277
www.USDF.org
Foreign Horse Publications

ANNUAL AND DIRECTORIES INTERNATIONAL

British Equestrian Directory
Stockfeld Park
Wetherby, West Yorkshire, LS22 4AW
England
01937-587-062
www.beta-uk.org

British Horse
The British Horse Society
Stoneleigh Deer Park
Kenilworth, Warwickshire CV8 2XZ
England
08701-202244
www.bhs.org.uk

Canadian Arabian News
Canadian Arabian Horse Registry
37 Athabascan Ave., Suite 113
Sherwood Park, AB T8A 4H3
Canada
780-416-4990
www.cahr.ca

The Canadian Horse Annual
Horse Publications Group
225 Industrial Pkwy. S.
P.O. Box 670
Aurora, ON L4G 4J9
Canada
800-505-7428
www.horse-canada.com

Canadian Rodeo News
Canadian Professional Rodeo Association
2116 Twenty-seventh Ave., Suite 223
Calgary, AB T2E 7A6
Canada
403-250-7440
www.rodeocanada.com

Canadian Thoroughbred
225 Industrial Pkwy.
P.O. Box 670
Aurora, ON L4G 4J9
Canada
800-505-7428
www.horse-canada.com

Carriage Driving
7 Barnak Business Centre, Blakey Road
Salisbury, Wiltshire SP1 2LP
England
44-0-1722-422107
www.carriage-driving.com

Corinthian Horse Sport
225 Industrial Pkwy.
P.O. Box 670
Aurora, ON L4G 4J9
Canada
800-505-7428
www.horse-canada.com

Endurance World
P.O. Box 5882
Abu Dhabi, United Arab Emirates
925-229-9960
www.endurance-world.com

The Exmoor Gathering
North American Exmoors
P.O. Box 155
Ripley, ON N0G 2R0
Canada

FEI Bulletin
Federation Equestre Internationale
24 Ave. Mon Repos
P.O. Box 157
CH-1000 Lausanne 5
Switzerland
41-21-310-47-47
www.horsesport.org

Gait Post
105-26730 Fifty-Sixth Ave.
Langley, BC V4W 3X5
Canada
800-663-4802
www.gaitpost.com

Highland Pony Gazette
Denmill, Alford
Aberdeenshire AB33 8EP
United Kingdom
01738-451861
www.highland-pony.demon.co.uk

Horse & Country
422 Kitley Line 3
Toledo, ON K0E 1Y0
Canada
613-275-1684
www.horseandcountry.net

**Horsepower Magazine for Young Horse
Lovers**
P.O. Box 670
Aurora, ON L4G 4J9
Canada
800-505-7428
www.horse-canada.com

Horses All
278 Nineteenth St., NE
Calgary, AB T3E 8P7
Canada
403-248-9993
www.horsesall.com

Horsewyse Magazine
P.O. Box 4170
Knox City Shopping Center
Wantirna, South Victoria 3152
Australia
03-9801-6800
www.horsewyse.com.au

Northern Horse Review
Bay 114, 3907-3A St. NE
Calgary, AB T2E 6S7
Canada
403-250-1128
www.northernhorsereview.com

Polo Quarterly
PQ International
PQ House 22 Rowena Crescent
Battersea, London SW11 2 PT
United Kingdom
44-020-7924-2550
www.poloworld.co.uk

The Scottish Equestrian Magazine
The Native Pony Magazine
Hillaine Publishing
26 Blairs Road, Letham
Forfar, Angus DD8 2PE
Scotland
0845-130-7669
www.scotequest.com

Show Trail
Saskatchewan Horse Federation
2205 Victoria Ave.
Regina, SK S4P 0S4
Canada
306-780-9244
www.saskhorsefed.com

NEWSLETTERS

A Dream Walking
American Walking Pony Registry
P.O. Box 5282
Macon, GA 31208-5282

AAEP Report
American Association of Equine Practitioners
4075 Iron Works Pkwy.
Lexington, KY 40511
859-233-0147
www.aaep.org

Actiongram
910 Currie St.
Fort Worth, TX 76107
817-336-1130
www.livestockpublications.com

AHPA News
American Horse Protection Association, Inc.
1000 Twenty-Ninth St., NW T-100
Washington, DC 20007-3820

AIF Newsletter
Animal Industry Foundation

1501 Wilson Blvd., Suite 1100
Arlington, VA 22209-0522

The ALBC News
American Livestock Breeds Conservancy
P.O. Box 477
Pittsboro, NC 27312-0477
919-542-5704
www.albc-usa.org

American Indian Horse News
American Indian Horse Registry, Inc.
9028 State Park Road
Lockhart, TX 78644-4310
512-398-6642
www.indianhorse.com

American Medical Equestrian Association News
American Medical Equestrian Association
5318 Old Bullard Road
Tyler, TX 75703
1-866-441-2632
www.utexas.edu

The AMHA Network
American Morgan Horse Association, Inc.
P.O. Box 960
Shelburne, VT 05482-0960
802-985-4944
www.morganhorse.com

Animalnews
Morris Animal Foundation
45 Inverness Dr. E.
Englewood, CO 80112-5480
800-243-2345
www.morrisanimalfoundation.org

Appaloosa Network
9915 White Rock Road
Conroe, TX 77306-7683

Arabian Jockey Club News
Arabian Jockey Club
10805 E. Bethany Dr.
Aurora, CO 80014
303-696-4568
www.arabianracing.org

Backyard Race Horse Newsletter
3708 Crystal Beach Road
Winter Haven, FL 33880

863-299-8448
www.backyardracehorse.com

Bellwether
University of Pennsylvania School of Veterinary
    Medicine
3800 Spruce St.
Philadelphia, PA 19104-6010
215-898-4680
www.vet.upenn.edu

Bugle
Bay State Trail Riders Association
24 Glenn St.
Douglas, MA 01516-2410
http://users.rcn.com/bstra/

Caution: Horses
American Association for Horsemanship Safety,
    Inc.
P.O. Box 39
Fentress, TX 78622
512-488-2220
www.law.utexas.edu/dawson/

CHA - The Instructor
CHA - The Association for Horsemanship Safety
    and Education
5318 Old Bullard Road
Tyler, TX 75703
800-399-0138
www.cha-ahse.org

**Christian Harness Horsemen's Association
    Newsletter**
Christian Harness Horsemen's Association
1846 Ross Road
Sunbury, OH 43074
740-965-1356
www.ohha.com/chha/chha.html

The Clydesdale News
Clydesdale Breeders of the U.S.A.
17346 Kelley Road
Pecatonica, IL 61063
815-247-8780
www.clydesusa.com

Collegiate Arena
National Intercollegiate Rodeo Association
2316 East Gate North, Suite 160
Walla Walla, WA 99362-2246

509-529-4402
www.collegerodeo.com

Colorado State Trails News
Colorado State Trails Programs
1313 Sherman St., Rm. 618
Denver, CO 80203
303-866-3311
www.dnr.state.co.us

Colorado West Paint Horse Club News
3273 J Road
Hotchkiss, CO 81419
970-242-9019
www.paintedpastime.com/CWPHC.html

Counciletter
Wisconsin State Horse Council
132A S. Ludington St.
Columbus, WI 53925
920-623-0393
www.wisconsinstatehorsecouncil.org

Covertside
Masters of Foxhounds Association of America
P.O. Box 363
Millwood, VA 22646
540-955-5680
www.mfha.com

The Crabbet Influence in Arabians Today
P.O. Box 188
Battle Ground, WA 98604
360-687-1600
www.crabbet.com

Curly Cues
American Bashkir Curly Registry
P.O. Box 246
Ely, NV 89301-0453
775-289-4999
www.abcregistry.org

Delaware Thoroughbred Horsemen's Journal
Delaware Thoroughbred Horsemen's
    Association
777 Delaware Park Blvd.
Wilmington, DE 19804
302-994-2521
www.dtha.com

East Coast Pro Rodeo News
13613-13 Hwy. 74
Indian Trail, NC 28079
704-882-6994
www.arealcowboystore.com

Equine Industry Program News
Department of Equine Administration - University
of Louisville
Louisville, KY 40292-0001
502-852-6440
www.cbpa.louisville.edu/eip

Equine Insider
Equine Resources Internationals, LLC
621 Wollaston Road
Kennett Square, PA 1948-1679
610-444-7554
www.equineresources.com

Equine Law & Business Letter
P.O. Box 4285
Charlottesville, VA 22905
804-295-4991

Equine Research & Service Report
University of Kentucky
805 South Limestone St.
Lexington, KY 40536-0339
589-257-1308
www.ca.uky.edu/agcollege/vetscience/home.htm

ESQHA News
Empire State Quarter Horse Association
4530 New Road
Williamson, NY 14589
716-773-4813
www.esqha.org

Georgia Horse Council News
Georgia Horse Council
1970- C Centennial Olympic Pkwy.
Conyers, GA 30013
770-922-3350
www.georgiahorsecouncil.com

The Gotland Glimpses
Gotland Russ Association of North America, Inc.
53 Weathersfield Lane
Amissville, VA 20106
505-672-1318
www.gotlands.org

HHAA Newsletter
Hungarian Horse Association of America
P.O. Box 108
Anselmo, NE 68813

Horse Law News
P.O. Box 579
Redwood City, CA 94064-0579
909-817-9616

The Horse Report
University of California - Equine Research Laboratory
Center for Equine Health
School of Veterinary Medicine, UCD
One Shields Ave.
Davis, CA 95616-8589
530-752-6433
www.vetmed.ucdavis.edu/ceh

The Horsemen's Newsletter
Maryland Thoroughbred Horsemen's Association
6314 Windsor Mill Road
Baltimore, MD 21207
410-265-6842
www.mdhorsemen.com

HSA News
Horsemanship Safety Association, Inc.
P.O. Box 2710
Lake Placid, FL 33862-2710
941-465-0289

Icelandic Horse Trekkers Newsletter
Icelandic Horse Trekkers
P.O. Box 986
Kearney, MO 64060-0986

Idaho Horse Council Newsletter
Idaho Horse Council
500 Chinden Blvd., Suite F
Boise, ID 83714
208-323-8184
http://members.dallypost.com/ihc/aboutus.php

IHIC Iowa Horse Industry Council
57154 Two Hundred and Forty Fifth St.
Ames, IA 50010

IHSA News
Intercollegiate Horse Show Association
Smoke Run Farm
Hollow Road

P.O. Box 741
Stony Brook, NY 11790-0741
www.isha.com

Impulsion
American Holsteiner Horse Association
222 E. Main St., Suite1
Georgetown, KY 40324-1712
502-863-4239
www.holsteiner.com

International Equine Science
1687 Symonds Mill Road
Wolcott, VT 05680

Kansas Horse Council Connection
Kansas Horse Council
P.O. Box 1612
Manhattan, KS 66505-1612
785-776-0662
www.kansashorsecouncil.com

Kentucky Horse Park News
Kentucky Horse Park
4089 Iron Works Pkwy.
Lexington, KY 40511-8400
800-678-8813
www.kyhorsepark.com

KTA Wire
Kentucky Thoroughbred Association and
Kentucky Thoroughbred Owners and
  Breeders, Inc.
4089 Iron Works Pkwy.
Lexington, KY 40511-8400
859-381-1414
www.kta-ktob.com

Lloyd's Equine Disease Quarterly
108 Gluck Equine Research Center
Lexington, KY 40546-0099
859-257-4757
www.uky.edu

The Meadow Muffin Reports
National Association of Competitive Mounted
  Orienteering
503 One Hundred and Seventy-First Ave., SE
Tenino, WA 98589-9711
800-354-7264
www.nacmo.org

The MEC Masthead
Missouri Equine Council, Inc.
9870 SE Twenty-Eighth Road
St. Joseph, MO 64507
800-313-3327
www.mo-equine.org

Minnesota Horse Council "For Horses Sake"
Minnesota Horse Council
2230 Van Dyke St.
Maplewood, MN 55109-2704
www.mnhorsecouncil.org

Mississippi Horse Council Newsletter
Mississippi Horse Council
1924 McCullough Blvd.
Tupelo, MS 38801
763-428-7532
www2.netdoor.com/~mhc/

The Morab Perspective
International Morab Breeders Association and
  International Morab Registry
RR 3 P.O. Box 235
Ava, MO 656080-9553
417-683-4426
www.morab.com

MTA Newsletter
Minnesota Thoroughbred Association
P.O. Box 508
1100 Canterbury Road
Shakopee, MN 55379-0508
952-496-3770
www.mtassoc.com/index.jsp

NAIWPN Newsletter
Dutch Warmblood Studbook in North America
P.O. Box O
Sutherlin, OR 97479
541-459-3232
www.nawpn.org

NAMAR Newsletter
North American Mustang Association and Registry
P.O. Box 850906
Mesquite, TX 75185-0906
972-298-9344

NARHA News
North American Riding for the Handicapped
  Association
P.O. Box 33150

Denver, CO 80233
800-369-7433
www.narha.org

NASFA Newsletter
North American Selle Francais Association, Inc.
P.O. Box 604
Round Hill, VA 20142
540-338-0166
www.sellefrancais.org

The National Mounted Courier
National Mounted Services Organization
P.O. Box 358
643 Main St.
Sparkill, NY 10976-0358

National Sporting Library Newsletter
102 The Plains Road
Middleburg, VA 20118-1335
540-687-6542
www.nsl.org

NCHC Newsletter
North Carolina Horse Council
P.O. Box 12999
Raleigh, NC 27605-2999
919-854-1990
www.nchorsecouncil.com

The New Forester
New Forest Pony Association, Inc.
P.O. Box 206
Pascoag, RI 02859
www.newforestpony.net/info/

New Mexico Horse Council News
New Mexico Horse Council
1501 Los Arboles, NW
Albuquerque, NM 87107-1017
505-344-8548
www.nmhorsecouncil.org

NSHA Newsletter
Nassau-Suffolk Horseman's Association
2 Carll Ct.
Northport, NY 11768-1649
516-868-9600
www.nshaonline.org

NYSHC Newsletter
New York State Horse Council, Inc.

853 Cooley Road
Parksville, NY 12768
845-942-0420
www.nyshc.org

O.D. News (Old Dominion News)
Old Dominion 100-Mile Endurance Ride, Inc.
149 Spring St.
Herndon, VA 20170
703-435-1953
www.olddominionrides.org

OHA Newsletter
Oregon Horsemen's Association
32302 S. Rachael Larkin Road
Molalla, OR 97038
www.oregonhorsemen.com

OHC Newsletter
Ohio Horseman's Council
P.O. Box 81
London, OH 43140
740-385-5306
www.ohiohorsemanscouncil.com

Over the Fence
Michigan Horse Council
P.O. Box 22008
Lansing, MI 48909-2008
231-821-2487
www.michiganhorsecouncil.com

Owner Breeder
P.O. Box 1927
Fremont, CA 94538
800-354-9206
www.brisnet.com/cgi-bin/static.cgi?page=obi

Pacesetter
Standardbred Breeders and Owners Association
of New Jersey
P.O. Box 839
Freehold, NJ 07728-0839

The Palomino Parade
Palomino Horse Association
P.O. Box 24
Dornsife, PA 17823
570-758-3067
www.palominohorseassoc.com

PCQHRA Newsletter
Pacific Coast Quarter Horse Racing Association
P.O. Box 919
Los Alamitos, CA 90720-0919
714-236-1755
www.pcqhra.org

Pedlines
P.O.Box 672
Antioch, CA 94509
www.reines-de-course.com/pedlines.htm

Percheron News
Percheron Horse Association of America
P.O. Box 141
Fredericktown, OH 43019-0141
740-694-2602
www.percheronhorse.org

Pintabian Ink Spot
Pintabian Horse Registry
P.O. Box 360
Karlstad, MN 56732-0360

Pony Expression/Horses People Love
The Horse Protection League
P.O. Box 741089
Arvada, CO 80006
303-216-0141
www.hpl-colo.org

POPS Newsletter
Promoters of Palomino Saddlebreds, Inc.
P.O. Box 177
Oxford Junction, IA 52323
310-486-2072

Rangerbreds In the News
Colorado Ranger Horse Association
P.O. Box 1290
Wampum, PA 16157-9610
724-535-4841
www.coloradoranger.com

RCI Bulletin
Association of Racing Commissioners
    International, Inc.
2 Paragon Center, Suite 200
2343 Alexandria Dr.
Lexington, KY 40504-3276
859-224-7070
www.arci.com

Renews
Thoroughbred Retirement Foundation
PMB 351, 450 Shrewsbury Plaza
Shrewsbury, NJ 07702-4332
www.trfinc.org/releases.htm

Research Today
Grayson-Jockey Club Research Foundation, Inc.
821 Corporate Dr.
Lexington, KY 40503-2794
859-224-2700
www.jockeyclub.com

RTCA Winner's Circle
Race Track Chaplaincy of America, Inc.
P.O. Box 91640
Los Angeles, CA 90009
310-419-1640
www.racetrackchaplaincy.org

Saddle Bags
P.O. Box 518
Parker, CO 80138

Savvy Up
P.O. Box 3729
Pagosa Springs, CO 81147
800-642-3335
www.parelli.com/literature/newsletter/savvy_up.
    htm

SCHC Newsletter
South Carolina Horsemen's Council
P.O. Box 160
Lexington, SC 29071
803-356-4535
www.schorsecouncil.net

SDHC Newsletter
South Dakota Horse Council
P.O. Box 25
Hayti, SD 57241
605-783-3832

Side-Saddle News
International Side-Saddle Organization
90 Cumberland Ave.
Estell Manor, NJ 08319
609-476-2976
www.sidesaddle.com

Single-Footing Express
North American Single-Footing Horse Association
2995 Clark Valley Road
Los Osos, CA 93402
805-528-7308
www.walkaloosaregistry.com

The South Carolina Market Bulletin
South Carolina Department of Agriculture
P.O. Box 11280
Columbia, SC 29211-1280
803-734-2186
www.scda.state.sc.us/marketbulletin/marketbulletin.htm

Spotted Saddle Horse News
Spotted Saddle Horse Breeders & Exhibitors
    Association
P.O. Box 1046
Shelbyville, TN 37162
931-684-7496
www.sshbea.org

The SSHC Newsletter
Sunshine State Horse Council, Inc.
P.O. Box 4158
N. Fort Meyers, FL 33918-4158
239-731-2999
www.sshc.org

SWANA News
Swedish Warmblood Association of North
    America
P.O. Box 788
Socorro, NM 87801
505-835-1318
www.wbstallions.com/wb/swana

TBH Marketwatch
P.O. Box 4038
Lexington, KY 40544-4038
859-276-6729
http://marketwatch.bloodhorse.com/

Tennequine Report
P.O. Box 69
College Grove, TN 37046-0069
615-297-3200
www.tnhorsecouncil.com

The TIA Newsletter
Thoroughbred Information Agency

2600 S. Town Center Dr., Suite 1034
Las Vegas, NV 89135
707-585-2569
www.thoroughbredinfo.com

TQHA Newsletter
Texas Quarter Horse Association
P.O. Box 16229
Austin, TX 78761
512-458-5202
www.tqha.com

Track Topics
Harness Tracks of America, Inc.
4640 East Sunrise, Suite 200
Tuscon, AZ 85718-4576
520-529-2525
www.harnesstracks.com

Trotnews
Trail Riders of Today
7928 Bennett Branch Road
Mt. Airy, MD 21771
301-588-8768
www.trot-md.org

United States Animal Health Association
    Newsletter
United States Animal Health Association
P.O. Box K227
8100 Three Chopt Road, Suite 203
Richmond, VA 23288
804-285-3210
www.usaha.org/links.html

USET News
United States Equestrian Team
P.O. Box 355
Pottersville Road
Gladstone, NJ 07934
908-234-1251
www.uset.org

Veterinary Medicine
Tufts University School of Veterinary Medicine
200 Westboro Road
North Grafton, MA 01536-1895
508-839-5302
http://vet.tufts.edu/index.php

Virginia Horse Center Foundation Post
Virginia Horse Center

P.O. Box 1051
Lexington, VA 24450-1051
540-464-2951
www.horsecenter.org

Virginia Horse Council News
Virginia Horse Council
7025 Owl Lane
Marshall, VA 20115-2233
540-351-0278
www.virginiahorse.com

VTA News Bulletin
Virginia Thoroughbred Association
P.O. Box 858
Warrenton, VA 20188
540-351-0278
www.vabred.org

Walkaloosa Horse Association Newsletter
Walkaloosa Horse Association
2995 Clark Valley Road
Los Osos, CA 93402
805-528-7308
www.walkaloosaregistry.com

Warhorse
Arkansas Horse Council
P.O. Box 737
Jasper, AR 72641-0737
870-446-6226
www.twb.net/ahc

Warmblood Whisper
American Warmblood Society
2 Buffalo Run Road
Center Ridge, AR 72027
501-893-2777
www.americanwarmblood.org/whisper

Western-English Industry Report
Western-English Retailers Association
P.O. Box 2348
Weatherford, TX 76086

WSHC Newsletter
Washington State Horse Council
2363 Mountain View Road, E
Port Orchard, WA 98366-8320
360-769-8083
www.horsemansyellowpages.com/wasthrscncl/

PERIODICALS

Alaska Horse Journal
310 N. Harriette
Wasilla, AK 99654-7627
907-376-4470
www.alaskahorsejournal.com

AMBA Journal
American Mustang and Burro Association, Inc.
P.O. Box 788
Lincoln, CA 95648
530-633-9271
www.bardalisa.com

America's Barrel Racer
201 W. Moore, Suite 200
Terrell, TX 75160

America's Horse
American Quarter Horse Association
1600 Quarter Horse Dr.
Amarillo, TX 79104
806-376-4811
www.aqha.com

The American Connemara
American Connemara Pony Society
2360 Hunting Ridge Road
Winchester, VA 22603-2453
540-662-5953
www.acps.org/

American Cowboy
P.O. Box 6630
Sheridan, WY 82801
307-672-7766
www.americancowboy.com

American Farriers Journal
American Farriers Association
P.O. Box 624
Brookfield, WI 53008-0624
800-645-8455
www.americanfarriers.com

The American Hanoverian
The American Hanoverian Society
4067 Iron Works Pkwy., Suite 1
Lexington, KY 40511
859-255-4141
www.hanoverian.org

The American Quarter Horse Journal
American Quarter Horse Association
P.O. Box 32470
Amarillo, TX 79120-2470
806-376-4811
www.aqha.org

The American Quarter Horse Racing Journal
American Quarter Horse Association
P.O. Box 32470
Amarillo, TX 79120
806-376-4811
www.aqha.com/racing

The American Saddlebred
American Saddlebred Horse Association
4093 Iron Works Pkwy.
Lexington, KY 40511-8434
859-259-2742
www.saddlebred.com

The American Trakehner
American Trakehner Association
1514 W. Church St.
Newark, OH 43055
740-344-1111
www.americantrakehner.com

American Turf Monthly
299 East Shore Road
Great Neck, NY 11023
516-773-4075
www.americanturf.com/

Appaloosa Journal
Appaloosa Horse Club, Inc.
2720 W. Pullman Road
Moscow, ID 83843-0903
208-882-5578
www.appaloosajournal.com

Arabian Horse Express
512 Green Bay Road, Suite 302
Kenilworth, IL 60043

Arabian Horse Newspaper
P.O. Box 380
Dublin, TX 76446-0380
254-785-2251
www.arabianhorsenewspaper.com

Arabian Horse Times
1050 Eighth St., NE
Waseca, MN 56093
800-248-4637
www.ahtimes.com

Arabian Horse World
1316 Tamson Dr., Suite101
Cambria, CA 93428
805-771-2300
www.ahwmagazine.com

Arabian Horse Magazine
Arabian Horse Association
10805 E. Bethany Dr.
Aurora, CO 80014-2605
303-696-4500
www.iaha.com

Arabian Horse World Quarterly
1316 Tamson Dr., Suite101
Cambria, CA 93428
805-771-2300
www.ahwmagazine.com

Arizona Horse Connection
1130 Red Cinder Road
Chino Valley, AZ 86323
800-284-1792
www.angelfire.com/az/PaintHorse/

The Arizona Horseman
Arizona State Horsemen's Association
P.O. Box 31758
Phoenix, AZ 85046-1758
602-390-6806
www.azsthorseassoc.com/

The Arizona Thoroughbred
Arizona Thoroughbred Association, Inc.
P.O. Box 41774
Phoenix, AZ 85050-1774
602-942-1310
www.atba.net

Aside World
The World Sidesaddle Federation, Inc.
P.O. Box 1104
Bucyrus, OH 44820
419-284-3176
www.sidesaddle.org

Barrel Horse News
Cowboy Publishing
P.O. Box 9768
Fort Worth, TX 76147-2768
817-569-7116
http://barrelhorsenews.com/

Bitterroooo Reader: Horses and Stories
P.O. Box 622
Moorpark, CA 93020

The Blood-Horse
Thoroughbred Owners and Breeders Association
P.O. Box 4038
Lexington, KY 40544-4038
859-276-6729
www.bloodhorse.com

Blue Ribbon Magazine
P.O. Box 389
Lexington, KY 40588
859-258-9420
www.bluegrasshorseman.com

Brayer
American Donkey and Mule Society
P.O. Box 1210
Lewisville, TX 75067
972-219-0781
www.geocities.com/lovelongears

California Horsetrader
P.O. Box 462950
Escondido, CA 92046-2950
760-546-1184
www.horsetrader.com

The California Thoroughbred
California Thoroughbred Breeders Association
P.O. Box 60018
Arcadia, CA 91066-6018
800-573-2822
www.ctba.com

The Calvary Journal
The United States Calvary Association
P.O. Box 2325
Fort Riley, KS 66442-0325
785-784-5797
www.uscalvary.org

Carriage Driving World
P.O. Box 36
Springtown, TX 76082
817-523-4111
www.carriagedrivingworld.com

The Carriage Journal
The Carriage Association of America, Inc.
177 Pointers-Auburn Road
Salem, NJ 08079-4312
856-935-1616
www.caaonline.com

Cascade Horseman
P.O. Box 1390
541-885-4410
Klamath Falls, OR 97601-1390
www.heraldandnews.com

The Central States Horseman
9509 Gravois Road
St. Louis, MO 63123
314-683-0682
http://ettfmo.tripod.com/ettu/id27.html

Christian Ranchman
P.O. Box 7557
Fort Worth, TX 76111-7557
817-236-0023
www.cowboysforchrist.net

The Chronicle of the Horse
P.O. Box 46
Middleburg, VA 20118
540-687-6341
www.chronofhorse.com

The Classical Horse
P.O. Box 1129
Lakeside, CA 92040
619-443-5030
www.theandalusian.com

Conquistador - The World of Spanish Horses
P.O. Box 666
3029 W Hwy. 154
Los Olivos CA 93441-0666
805-686-4616
www.conquistador.com

Cutting Horse Chatter
National Cutting Horse Association
260 Bailey Ave.
Fort Worth, TX 76107-1862
817-244-6188
www.nchacutting.com

Daily Racing Form
100 Broadway, 7th Floor
New York, NY 10005
800-306-3676
www.drf.com

Discover Horses at Kentucky Horse Farm
Kentucky Horse Park
656 Quince Orchard Road, Suite 600
Gaithersburg, MD 20878
301-977-3900
www.imh.org/khp

Draft Horse Journal
P.O. Box 670
2700 Fifth Ave., NW
Waverly, IA 50677
319-352-4046
www.drafthorsejournal.com

Dressage Today
656 Quince Orchard Road, Suite, 600
Gaithersburg, MD 20878-1472
301-977-3900
www.primedia.com/

Driving Digest
P.O. Box 110
New London, OH 44851-0110
419-929-6781
www.drivingdigest.com

DVM The Newsmagazine of Veterinary Medicine
7500 Old Oak Blvd.
Cleveland, OH 44130
440-891-2675
www.dvmnewsmagazine.com/dvm/

The Eastern Equerry
P.O. Box 367
Epping, NH 03042
800-403-6777
www.easternequerry.com

Endurance News
American Endurance Ride Conference
11960 Heritage Oak Place, Suite 9
Auburn, CA 95603
866-271-AERC
www.aerc.org

Equestrian Connection
8331 Allene Creek Ct.
Citrus Heights, CA 95610-0759

Equestrian Trails
Equestrian Trails, Inc.
13741 Foothill Blvd., #100
Sylmar, CA 91342-3015
818-362-6819
www.eti.av.org

Equiculture
1505 Knoxlyn Road
Gettysburg, PA 17325
717-642-6836
www.equiculture.com

The Equiery
P.O. Box 610
Lisbon, MD 21765
800-244-9580
www.equiery.com

Equine and Bovine Magazine
P.O. Box 661
Pendleton, SC 29670
877-258-8363
www.equinebovine.com

The Equine Images
1736 Alexandria Dr.
Lexington, KY 40504
800-866-2361
www.eclipsepress.com

Equine Journal
103 Roxbury St.
Keene, NH 03431
800-742-9171
www.equinejournal.com

The Equine Journal
P.O. Box 5299
Laguna Beach, CA 92652
949-494-2033
www.theequinejournal.com

The Equine Marketer
P.O. Box 3107
West Chester, PA 19381
610-431-6800
www.equinemarketer.com

Equine Review
3910 Delaney Ferry Road
Versailles, KY 40383
859-873-1988
www.wehn.com

Equine Times
331 East Bell
P.O. Box 130
Camden, MI 49232-0008
517-368-0365
www.equinetimes.com

The Equine Trader
P.O. Box 125
Cedar Grove, NC 27231
919 732 1830
www.horsebreed.com/equinetrader

The Equinews
3910 Delaney Ferry Road
Versailles, KY 40383
859-873-1988
www.ker.com

Equus
656 Quince Orchard Road, Suite 600
Gaithersburg, MD 20878-1472
301-977-3900
www.equisearch.com/magazines/Equus/con-
tacts/

Horse & Rider
P.O. Box 4101
Golden, CO 80401
720-836-1256
www.cowles.com

Horse Bits
9417 Preston Hill Rd
Camden, NY 13316
315-245-5086

Horse Circuit News
8098 E. 400
New Castle, IN 47362
800-537-3958
www.horsecircuitnews.com

Horse Directory, Long Island's Equine
  Magazine
P.O. Box 60
Eastport, NY 11941
631-878-3013
www.lihorsedirectory.com

The Horse Gazette
6395 Mondean St.
San Antonio, TX 78240-2565
210-641-9928
www.horsegazette.com

The Horse Gazette
P.O. Box 8446
Monterey, CA 93943-8446
877-624-6241
www.horsegazette.com/

Horse Illustrated
P.O. Box 6050
Mission Viejo, CA 92690-6050
949-855-8822
www.horseillustratedmagazine.com

Horse Journal
6538 Van Buren Road
Warners, NY 13164-9747
315-468-0627

Horse Journal Quarterly
416 NE Wilshire Blvd.
Burleson, TX 76028
www.horsejournal.com

Horse News
8 Minneakoning Road
Flemington, NJ 08822
908-782-4747
www.horsenewsonline.com

Horse Power All Breed Newspaper
P.O. Box 510365
Salt Lake City, UT 84151-0365

Horse Professional
3300 N. Central Ave., Suite 2500
Phoenix, AZ 85012
www.horseprofessional.com

Horse Talk
P.O. Box 1037
Locust Grove, VA 22508

540-548-4613
www.horsetalkmagazine.com

Horse Talk Magazine
Greater Houston Horse Council
P.O. Box 924305
Houston, TX 77292
281-681-6171
www.ghhc.com

Horse World
730 Madison St.
Shelbyville, TN 37162-1007

The Horse: Your Guide to Equine Health Care
Blood-Horse, Inc.
1736 Alexandria Dr.
Lexington, KY 40544-4680
800-866-2361
www.thehorse.com

Horse'n Around
P.O. Box 304
125 North Main, MN 56018
507-526-7390
www.horsenaround.com

The Horse's Maine
P.O. Box 506
New Gloucester, ME 04260
207-926-3036
www.horsesmaine.com

The Horseman and Fair World
P.O. Box 8480
Lexington, KY 40533
859-276-4026
www.harnessracing.com

Horsemen's Corral
P.O. Box 110
211 W. Main St.
New London, OH 44851-0110
419-929-3800
www.horsemenscorral.com

The Horsemen's Journal
P.O. Box 202290
Austin, TX 78720-2290
512-258-7271
www.hbpa.org/HorsemensJournalDisplay.asp

Horsemen's Newsletter of the Southeast
5512 Galway Dr.
Charlotte, NC 28215
704-564-4493

Horsemen's Roundup
201 E. Markham, Suite 200
Little Rock, AR 72201

The Horsemen's Voice
3060 Los Lentes, SE
Los Lunas, NM 87031
505-565-3222
www.horsemensvoice.com

The Horsemen's Yankee Pedlar
83 Leicester St.
North Oxford, MA 01537
508-987-5886
www.pedlar.com

Horsepeople
One Gannett Dr.
White Plains, NY 10604
914-696-8262

HORSEpower Magazine
P.O. Box 391
Clarion, IA 50525-0319
515-532-2105
www.horsepowermagazine.net

Horses USA
P.O. Box 6050
Mission Viejo, CA 92690
949-855-8822
www.fancypubs.com

Horsesouth Magazine
277 Damascus Road
Blue Ridge, GA 30513
706-492-5911
www.horsesouth.com

The Horsetrader
P.O. Box 462950
Escondido, CA 92046
760-546-1184
http://horsetrader.com/

Hunter & Sport Horse
12204 Covington Road

Fort Wayne, IN 46814
800-554-7470
www.hunterandsporthorsemag.com

Icelandic Horse and Travel Magazine
P.O. Box 142059
Spokane, WA 99214-2059
509-927-0404
www.icelandichorseandtravel.com/

Illinois Racing News
111 Shore Dr.
Burr Ridge, IL 60521
630-887-7722
www.illinoisracingnews.com

Illinois Standardbred and Mid-America
Harness News
Illinois Harness Horseman's Association
P.O. Box 399
Downers Grove, IL 60515-4267
888-601-7223
www.midamericaharness.trot.net

In & Around Horse Country
60 Alexandria Pike
Warrenton, VA 22186
540-347-3141

Iowa Quarter Horse Magazine
Iowa Quarter Horse Association
21955 H Ave.
Grundy, IA 50638
641-869-3733
www.barhonline.com

The Jockey News
Jockeys' Guild
P.O. Box 250
Lexington, KY 40588-02520

John Lyons Perfect Horse
P.O. Box 420235
Palm Coast, FL 32142-0235
800-424-7887
www.perfecthorse.com/

PERIODICALS

The Journal of American Shetland
Pony/American Miniature Horse
P.O. Box 887

Warrenville, IL 60555
815-748-5013
www.shetlandminiature.com/journal.shtml

Journal of Equine Veterinary Science
P.O. Box 1209
Wildomar, CA 92595-1209
www.j-evs.com

Just About Horses
Breyer Animal Creations
14 Industrial Road
Pequannock, NJ 07440
973-694-5006
www.breyerhorses.com

Just Horses
P.O. Box 6662
Boise, ID 83701-0662
208-336-6707

Keeneland
Keeneland Association
P.O. Box 1690
Lexington, KY 40505
859-254-3412
www.keenland.com

The Lariat Horsemens Newspaper
P.O. Box 229
Beaverton, OR 97075-0229
503-644-2233

Literally Horses
208 Cherry Hill St.
Kalamazoo, MI 49006

Lone Star Horse Report
P.O. Box 470215
Fort Worth, TX 76147

Louisiana Horse
Louisiana Thoroughbred Breeders Association
P.O. Box 2098
Hammond, LA 70404-2098
800-772-1195

The Maryland Horse
Maryland Horse Breeder's Association, Inc.
P.O. Box 427
Lutherville-Timonium, MD 21094-0427
410-252-2100
www.mdhorsebreeders.com

Maverick Press
220 Livestock Exchange Bldg.
4701 Marion St.
Denver, CO 80216
212-840-0660
www.karabanequestriannetwork.com/Members/
    maverick.html

Michigan Harness Horseman
4650 Moore St.
P.O. Box 349
Okemos, MI 48864
517-349-2920
www.ambersystems.com/mhha

Michigan Quarter Horse Journal
Michigan Quarter Horse Association
P.O. Box 278
Greenville, MI 48838
616-225-8211
www.miquarterhorse.com

Michigan Thoroughbred
Throroughbred Owners & Breeders Association of
    Michigan
4800 Harvey St.
Muskegon, MI 49444
231-798-7721

Mid-Atlantic Thoroughbred
Maryland Horse Breeders Association
P.O. Box 427
Lutherville-Timonium, MD 21094-0427
410-252-2100
www.mdhorsebreeders.com

The Mid-South Horse Review
P.O. Box 519
Somerville, TN 38068
901-465-4042
www.midsouthhorsereview.com

Midwest Horseman
P.O. Box 3223
Springfield, MO 65808-3223
www.mwha.net/

Midwest Sporthorse Journal
4826 South Hill Dr.
Madison, WI 53705
608-232-2922
www.sporthorse1.com/journal

Miniature Donkey Talk
1338 Hughes Shop Road
Westminster, MD 21158
410-857-9145
www.miniaturedonkey.net

The Miniature Horse Voice
P.O. Box 857
Loris, SC 29569
843-756-6464
www.smallhorse.com/minivoice

The Miniature Horse World
5601 S. Interstate 35 W
Alvarado, TX 76009
817-783-5600
www.amha.com

Missouri Fox Trotting Horse Breed Association
P.O. Box 1027
Ava, MO 65608-1027
417-83-2468
www.MFTHBA.com

Montana Horseman's Journal
P.O. Box 507
Stanford, MT 59479-0507
406-566-2200
www.mthorseman.com/articles/savvy.htm

The Morgan Horse
American Morgan Horse Association
P.O. Box 960
Shelburne, VT 05482-0960
802-985-4944
www.morganhorse.com

Mountain Horse Connection
2805 Lancaster Road
Danville, KY 40422
859-238-7754
www.naturalgait.com

Mules and More, Inc.
P.O. Box 460
Bland, MO 65014-0460
573-646-3934
www.mulesandmore.com

NARHA Strides
North American Riding for the Handicapped
    Association
P.O. Box 33150

Denver, CO 80233
800-369-7433
www.narha.org

The National Horseman
16101 N. 82nd St., Suite 10
Scottsdale, AZ 85260-1830
480-922-5202
www.tnh1865.com

National Spotted Saddle Horse Journal
P.O. Box 898
Murfreesboro, TN 37133-0898
615-890-2864

Natural Horse Magazine
P.O. Box 10
Holtwood, PA 17532
800-660-8923
www.naturalhorse.com

Nevada Valley Horse News
7350 Rome Blvd.
Las Vegas, NV 89131

New York Horse
1753 Dugan Road
Clayville, NY 13322
315-822-3071
www.newyorkhorse.com

NHRSA Times
National High School Rodeo Association, Inc.
12001 Tejon St., Suite 128
Denver, CO 80234
303-452-0820
www.nhsra.org

NLBRA News
National Little Britches Rodeo Association
1045 W. Rio Grande
Colorado Springs, CO 80906-1212
719-389-0333
www.nlbra.com

The Northwest Horse Source
P.O. Box 717
Blaine, WA 98231
360-332-5579
www.nwhorsesource.com

Northwest Horse Trader Magazine
P.O. Box 12628
Salem, OR 97309-0628

Northwest Rider Magazine
P.O. Box 1446
Queen Creek, AZ 85242
877-904-1890
www.nwrider.com

NRHA Reiner
National Reining Horse Association
3000 NW 10th St.
Oklahoma City, OK 73107-5302
405-946-7400
www.207.30.41.224/nrhahome.asp

The NSBA - Way to Go
National Snaffle Bit Association
4815 S. Sheridan, Suite 109
Tulsa, OK 74145
918-270-1469
www.nsba.com

Nuestro Caballo
Peruvian Paso Registry of North America
3077 Wiljan Ct. Suite A
Santa Rosa, CA 95407-5702
707-579-4394
www.pplrna.org

Ohio Quarter Horse Association News
Ohio Quarter Horse Association
101 Tawa Road, P.O. Box 209
Richwood, OH 43344-0209
740-943-2346
www.oqha.com

Ohio Thoroughbred
Ohio Thoroughbred Breeders Association
6024 Harrison Ave., Suite 13
Cincinnati, OH 45248
513-574-0440
www.otbo.com

Oregon Horse Magazine
Oregon Thoroughbred Breeders Association
P.O. Box 17248
Portland, OR 97217
503-285-0658
www.thoroughbredinfo.com/showcase/otba.htm

Paint Horse Journal
American Paint Horse Association
P.O. Box 961023
Fort Worth, TX 76161-0023
817-834-2742
www.painthorsejournal.com

Palomino Horses Magazine
Palomino Horse Breeders of America, Inc.
117 E. Hill St.
Oklahoma City, OK 73105
405-528-3100
www.palominohba.com

Paso Fino Horse World
Paso Fino Horse Association
101 N. Collins St.
Plant City, FL 33566-3311
813-719-7777
www.pfha.org

The Pegasus Equine Express!
P.O. Box 355
Moody, AL 35004
www.thepegasus.netfirms.com

The Pennsylvania Equestrian
P.O. Box 8412
Lancaster, PA 17604-8412
717-898-5874
www.pennsylvaniaequestrian.com

Performance Horse
P.O. Box 7426
Eugene, OR 97401
800-352-0636
www.performancehorse.com

Peruvian Digest
3095 Burleson-Retta Road
Burleson, TX 76028
817-447-2703
www.peruviandigest.com

POA Magazine
Pony of the Americas Club, Inc.
5240 Elmwood Ave.
Indianapolis, IN 46203-5990
317-788-0107
www.poac.org

Polo Players' Edition
3500 Fairlane Farms Road, Suite 9
Wellington, FL 33414

561-793-9524
www.poloplayersedition.com

Practical Horseman
P.O. Box 589
Unionville, PA 19375
610-380-8304
www.primedia.com/divisions/cmmg/practical-horseman

Prorodeo Sports News
Professional Rodeo Cowboys Association
101 ProRodeo Dr.
Colorado Springs, CO 80919
719-593-8840
www.prorodeo.com

The Pyramid Report & The Stallion Guide
The Pyramid Society
4067 Iron Works Pkwy., Suite 2
Lexington, KY 40511
859-231-0771
www.pyramidsociety.org

Quarter Horse News
2112 Montgomery
Fort Worth, TX 76147-2707
817-569-7116
http://quarterhorsenews.com

The Racking Review
P.O. Box 2507
Murfreesboro, TN 37133
www.therackingreview.com

The Record Stockman
P.O. Box 1209
Wheat Ridge, CO 80034
303-425-5777
www.recordstockman.com

Ride!
728 Cherry St.
Chico, CA 95928
800-267-8373
www.ridemagazine.com

Ride With Bob Avila
Winsor Publishing
720 Front St.
Louisville, CO 80027-1805
877-467-7300
www.horse.com

Riding Instructor
American Riding Instructor Certification Program
28801 Trenton Ct.
Bonita Springs, FL 34134-3337
239-948-5053
www.riding-instructor.com

Rocky Mountain Horse Connection
380 Perry St., Suite 210
Castle Rock, CO 80104
303-663-1300
www.horseconnection.com

Rocky Mountain Quarter Horse
318 Livestock Exchange Bldg.
Denver, CO 80216-2140
303-296-1143
www.quarterh.com/rmqha.htm

Rocky Mountain Rider Magazine
P.O. Box 1011
Hamilton, MT 59840-1011
800-509-1537
www.rockymountainrider.com

Ropers Sports News
24080 N. Ray Road
Lodi, CA 95242
209-333-2924
www.roperssportsnews.com

Rural Heritage
281-D Dean Ridge Lane
Gainesboro, TN 38562-5039
931-268-0655
www.ruralheritage.com

Saddle & Bridle
375 Jackson Ave.
St. Louis, MO 63130-4243
314-725-9115
www.saddleandbridle.com

Saddle Horse Report
P.O. Box 1007
730 Madison St.
Shelbyville, TN 37160-1007
931-684-8123
www.saddlehorsereport.com/default.aspx

Savvy
P.O. Box 3729

Pagosa Springs, CO 81147
800-642-3335
www.parelli.com

The Sentinel, Voice of the Horse Industry
Libertyville Saddle Shop
P.O. Box M
Libertyville, IL 60048-4913
800-872-3353
www.saddleshop.com

The Shop Talk!
Saddle, Harness and Allied Trades Association
1101 Broad St.
Oriental, NC 28751
252-249-3409
www.proleptic.net/contact_us.asp

Show Ring Horse News Magazine
P.O. Box 1541
Columbus, IN 47202-1541
800-487-1920
http://showringhorsenews.com/site/index.html

Small Farm Today
3903 W. Ridge Trail Road
Clark, MO 65243-9525
800-633-2535
www.smallfarmtoday.com

Southeast Equine Monthly
P.O. Box 1333
Columbia, SC 29202
803-771-8415
www.thestate.com

The Southeast Horse Report
P.O. Box 10329
Brooksville, FL 34603-0329
www.southeasthorse.com

Southern California Riding Magazine
9131 Chesapeake Dr.
San Diego, CA 92123
888.272.0472
www.ridingmagazine.com

The Southern Horse Connection
P.O. Box 1000
102 N. Goodman St.
Sparks, GA 31647-1000
1-888-784-3713
www.southernhorseconnect.com

The Southern Horseman
P.O. Box 71
3839 Old Hwy. 45 North
Meridian, MS 39302-0071
601-693-6607
www.southernhorseman.com

Southwest Horse Trader
P.O. Box 1865
Spendora, TX 77372-1865
1-866-357-7948
www.swhorsetrader.com

Spanish-Barb Journal
Spanish-Barb Breeders Association
    International, Inc.
13862 Gulf Haven Road
Gulfport, MS 39503-1110
352-622-5878

Speedhorse - Racing Report
P.O. Box 1000
Norman, OK 73070-1000
405-573-1050

Spin to Win
720 Front St.
Louisville, CO 80027-1805
800-317-3682

Spotted Saddle Horse News
P.O. Box 1046
Shelbyville, TN 37162
931-684-7496
www.sshbea.org

Stable Management
45 Main St. N.
Woodbury, CT 06798
203-263-0888
www.stable-management.com

Stable Mates
5665 Hwy. 9, #103-360
Alpharetta, GA 30004
800-782-6283
www.stablemates.com

The Star Ledger
One Star-Ledger Plaza
Newark, NJ 07102
1-888-782-7533
www.starledger.com

Steed Read Horseman's Classified, LLC.
P.O. Box 2057
Salem, CT 06420
860-859-0770
www.steedread.com

Steeplechase Times
364 Fair Hill Drive, Suite F
Elkton, MD 21921
410-392-5867
www.steeplechasetimes.com

Stock Horse News
National Reined Cow Horse Association
13181 US Highway 177
Byares OK 74831
580-759-3868
www.nrcha.com

Tack 'n Togs Merchandising
P.O. Box 2400
Minnetonka, MN 55343-2400
952-930-4390
www.tackntogs.com

Take The Lead
Indiana Horse Council, Inc.
225 S. East St., Suite 738
Indianapolis, IN 46202-4059
317-692-7115
www.indianahorsecouncil.org

The Team Penner
P.O. Box 473
Greenville, IN 47124

The Texas Thoroughbred
Texas Thoroughbred Association
P.O. Box 14967
Austin, TX 78761
512-458-6133
www.texasthoroughbred.com

Thoroughbred Daily News
27 Monmouth St., 2nd floor
Red Bank, NJ 07701
732-747-8060
www.thoroughbreddailynews.com

The Thoroughbred Journal
American Thoroughbred Horse Registry
P.O. Box 851
Syracuse, NY 13209

315-488-0973
www.athj.com

Thoroughbred Times
P.O. Box 8237
Lexington, KY 40533-8237
859-260-9800
www.thoroughbredtimes.com

Times: In Harness
8125 Old Jonestown Road
Harrisburg, PA 17112-9713
171-469-2000
www.timesite.com

Trail Blazer
4241 N. Covina Circle
Prescott, AZ 86314
212-840-0660
www.karabanequestriannetwork.com/Members/
    trail_blazer.html

The Trail Rider
P.O. Box 5089
Alexandria, LA 71307
800-448-1154
www.trailridermagazine.com

Tri-State Livestock News
P.O. Box 129
Sturgis, SD 57785
800-253-3656
www.tsln.com

U.S. Horse Market
P.O. Box 608
Union, OR 97883
541-562-9360
www.ushorsemarket.com/

U.S. Equestrian Magazine
U.S. Equestrian, Inc.
4047 Iron Works Pkwy.
Lexington, KY 40511-8483
859-258-2472
www.equestrian.org

USDF Connection
United States Dressage Federation
220 Lexington Green Circle, Suite 510
Lexington, KY 40503
859-971-2277
www.usdf.org

USPC News
United States Pony Clubs
4041 Iron Works Pkwy.
Lexington, KY 40511-8483
859-254-7669
www.ponyclub.org

Vaulting World
American Vaulting Association
One Liberty Road
Petaluma, CA 94952
707-795-8019
www.americanvaulting.org

Virginia Horse Journal
Virginia Horse Council
P.O. Box 858
Warrenton, VA 20188
540-351-0278
www.virginiahorse.com

Voice of the Tennessee Walking Horse
Tennessee Walking Horse Breeders' and
    Exhibitors' Association
P.O. Box 286
250 N. Ellington Pkwy.
Lewisburg, TN 37091-0286
800-467-0232
www.twhbea.com

Walking Horse Report
P.O. Box 1007
Shelbyville, TN 37160-1007
931-684-8123
www.walkinghorsereport.com

Warmblood Magazine
384 Bullsboro Dr., Suite 301
Newnan, GA 30263
www.warmboodmagazine.com

Warmblood News
P.O. Box 211735
Royal Palm Beach, FL 33421
561-333-5848
www.americanwarmblood.com

Washington Thoroughbred
Washington Thoroughbred Breeders Association
P.O. Box 1499
Auburn, WA 98071-1499
253-288-7878
www.washingtonthoroughbred.com

Welara Journal
American Welara Pony Society
P.O. Box 401
Yucca Valley, CA 92286-0401
www.welararegistry.com

Western & English Today
8214 Westchester Dr., Suite 800
Dallas, TX 75225
214-750-1844
www.wetoday.com

Western Horseman
3850 North Nevada Ave.
Colorado Springs, CO 80907
719-633-5524
www.westernhorseman.com

The Whip
American Driving Society
2324 Clark Road
Lapeer, MI 48446
810-664-8666
www.americandrivingsociety.com

Wire to Wire
Florida Thoroughbred Breeders' and Owners'
    Association
801 SW 60th Ave.
Ocala, FL 34474-1827
352-629-2160
www.wiretowire.net

Wisconsin Horsemen's News
P.O. Box 152
Waupaca, WI 54981

Women's Pro Rodeo News
Women's Professional Rodeo Association and
    Professional Women's Rodeo Association
1235 Lake Plaza Dr., Suite 134
Colorado Springs, CO 80906
719-576-0900
www.wpra.com

The Wrangler Horse and Rodeo News
P.O. Box 6070
Riverton, WY 82501
800-927-7578
www.thewrangler.com

Young Rider
BowTie Inc.
P.O. Box 8237
Lexington, KY 40533
859-260-9800
www.fancypubs.com

APPENDIX E
LIBRARIES AND MUSEUMS

**American Quarter Horse Heritage Center &
    Museum**
2601 I-40 East
Amarillo, TX 79104
806-376-5181
www.imh.org/imh/qhm/qhhome.html

American Saddle Horse Museum
4093 Iron Works Pkwy.
Lexington, KY 40511-4909
800-829-4438
www.americansaddlebred.com

American Work Horse Museum
P.O. Box 88
Peaonian Springs, VA 22129-0088
www.horsecenter.com

Appaloosa Museum and Heritage Center
2720 W. Pullman Road
Moscow, ID 83843-0903
208-882-8150
www.appaloosa.com

Arabian Horse Trust
12000 Zuni St.
Westminster, CO 80234
303-450-4710
www.arabianhorsetrust.com

Austin Carriage Museum
Florida Carriage Driving Center
Continental Acres Equine Resort
3000 Marion County Road
P.O. Box 68
Weirsdale, FL 32195
352-750-1763

Autry Museum of Western Heritage
4700 Western Heritage Way
Los Angeles, CA 90027

323-667-2000
www.autry-museum.org

Carleton F. Burke Memorial Library
201 Colorado Place
Arcadia, CA 91007-2604
818-445-7800
www.ctba.com

The Carolina Cup Racing Museum
P.O. Box 280
Camden, SC 29020
803-432-6513
www.carolina-cup.org/nsm/

Carriage Museum of America - Library
P.O. Box 417
Bird-in-Hand, PA 17505
717-656-7019
www.carriagemuseumlibrary.org

Cowboy Artists of America Museum
1550 Bandera Hwy.
Kerrville, TX 78028
830-896-2553
www.caamuseum.com/test/default.htm

Eiteljorg Museum of American and Western Art
500 W. Washington St.
Indianapolis, IN 46204
317-636-9378
www.eiteljorg.org

Favell Museum of Western Art
125 W. Main St.
Klamath Falls, OR 9601
541-882-9996
http://kfalls.unclewebster.com/lc/bus/461/

The Harness Racing Museum and Hall of Fame
240 Main St.
Goshen, NY 10924-0590
845-294-6330
www.harnessmuseum.com

International Museum of the Horse
Kentucky Horse Park
4089 Iron Works Pkwy.
Lexington, KY 40511-8434
800-678-8813
www.kyhorsepark.com

The John A. Morris Memorial Library
Gluck Equine Research Center
University of Kentucky
Lexington, KY 40546-0099
859-257-1192
www.uky.edu/Ag/VetScience/morris.htm

The Justin Morgan Memorial Museum
P.O. Box 519
Shelburne, VT 05482-0519

Keeneland Association Library
P.O. Box 1690
Lexington, KY 40588-1690
800-456-3412
www.keeneland.com

Kentucky Derby Museum Corporation
P.O. Box 3513
Louisville, KY 40201-3513
502-637-7097
www.derbymuseum.org

The Leanin' Tree Museum of Western Art
P.O. Box 9500-W
Boulder, CO 80301
303-530-5124
www.leanintree.com/museum

Museum of the Horse
P.O. Box 40
Ruidoso Downs, NM 88346
505-378-4142

The Museum of Hounds and Hunting
Morven Park
P.O. Box 6228
Leesburg, VA 20178-7433
703-777-3282
www.morvenpark.org

National Cowboy & Western Heritage Museum
1700 NE 63rd St.
Oklahoma City, OK 73111
405-478-2250
www.cowboyhalloffame.org/index2.html

National Museum of Racing, Inc.
191 Union Ave.
Saratoga Springs, NY 12866-3566
518-584-0400
www.racingmuseum.org

National Museum of the Morgan Horse
122 Botswick Road
Shelburne, VT 05482-0519802-985-8665
www.morganmuseum.org

The National Sporting Library
102 The Plains Road
Middleburg, VA 20118-1335
540-687-6542
www.nsl.org

Phippen Museum of Western Art
4701 Hwy 89 North
Prescott, AZ 86301
928-778-1385
www.phippenartmuseum.org

Phoenix Art Museum
1625 N. Central Ave.
Phoenix, AZ 86301
602-257-1222
www.phxart.org

Pony Express National Memorial
P.O. Box 244
St. Joseph, MO 64502
816-279-5059

APPENDIX F

RACING

Poplar Hill
Carriage and National Historical Landmark
7606 Woodyard Road
Clinton, MD 20735-1955
301-856-0358
www.poplarhillonhlk.com

Pro Rodeo Hall of Fame and Museum of the American Cowboy
101 Pro Rodeo Dr.
Colorado Springs, CO 80919
719-593-8840
www.prorodeo.com

The Show Jumping Hall of Fame and Museum, Inc.
38 Mechanic St., Suite 101
Foxboro, MA 02035-2042
www.showjumpinghalloffame.net

William P. Kyne Memorial Thoroughbred Racing Library
Bay Meadows Race Course
P.O. Box 5050
San Mateo, CA 94402-0050
415-574-7223

The World Sidesaddle Federation Library
P.O. Box 1104
Bucyrus, OH 44820419-284-3176
www.sidesaddle.com

RACETRACKS

Anthony Downs
Thoroughbred, Quarter Horse, Arabian
521 E. Sherman
Anthony, KS 67003-0444
316-842-5989
www.ohmygosh.com/anthonydowns/

Aqueduct
Thoroughbred
11000 Rockaway Blvd.
Jamaica, NY 11417
718-641-4700
www.nyra.com/aqueduct/

Arapahoe Park
Thoroughbred, Quarter Horse, Paint, Appaloosa, Arabian
26000 E. Quincy Ave.
Aurora, CO 80016
303-690-2400
www.wembleyusa.com

Arlington Park
Thoroughbred
2200 W. Euclid
Arlington Heights, IL 60004
847-255-4300

Atlantic City Racecourse
Thoroughbred
4501 Black Horse Pike
Mays Landing, NJ 08330
609-641-2190

Balmoral Park
Harness
26435 S. Dixie Hwy.
Crete, IL 60417
708-672-7544
www.balmoralpark.com

Bangor Raceway
Harness
52 Main St.
Bangor, Maine 04401-6890
207-947-6744
www.bangorraceway.com

Bay Meadows
Thoroughbred
2600 S. Delaware St.
San Mateo, CA 94403
650-574-7223
www.baymeadows.com

Belmont Park
Thoroughbred
2150 Hempstead Pike
Flmont, NY 11003
516-488-6000
www.nyra.com/belmont/

Beulah Park
Thoroughbred, Quarter Horse
3664 Grant Ave.
Grove City, OH 43123
614-871-9600
www.beulahpark.com

Blue Ribbon Downs
Thoroughbred, Quarter Horse, Paint, Appaloosa
3700 W. Cherokee
Salislaw, OK 74955
918-775-7771
www.blueribbondowns.net

Bluegrass Downs
Harness
P.O. Box 7907
Paducah, KY 42002-7907
502-444-7117

Buffalo Raceway
Harness
5600 McKinley Pkwy.
Hamburg, NY 14075
716-649-1280
www.buffaloraceway.com/

Calder Race Course/Tropical Park
Thoroughbred
21001 NW. 27th Ave.
Miami, FL 33055-0808
305-625-1311
www.calderracecourse.com

Canterbury Park
Thoroughbred, Quarter Horse
1100 Canterbury Road
Shakopee, MN 55379
952-445-7223
www.canterburypark.com

Charles Town Races
Thoroughbred
U.S. Rt. 340
Charles Town, WV 25414
800-795-7001
www.ctownraces.com

Chippewa Downs
Thoroughbred, Quarter Horse
701-228-2642

Churchill Downs
Thoroughbred
7000 Central Ave.
Louisville, KY 40208-1200
502-636-4400

Colonial Downs
Thoroughbred, Harness
10515 Colonial Downs Pkwy.
New Kent, VA 23124
804-966-7223
www.colonialdowns.com

Del Mar
Thoroughbred
2260 Jimmy Durante Blvd.
Del Mar, CA 92014-0700
858-755-1141
www.delmarracing.com

Delaware Park
Thorougbred
777 Delaware Park Blvd.
Stanton, DE 19804
(302) 994-2521
www.delpark.com

Delta Downs
Thoroughbred, Quarter Horse, Paint
2717 Hwy. 3063
Vinton, LA 70668
337-589-7441
www.deltadowns.com

Dover Downs
Harness
1131 North DuPont Hwy.
Dover, DE 19901
800-711-5882
www.doverdowns.com

Downs at Albuquerque
Thoroughbred, Quarter Horse
201 California St. NE
Albuquerque, NM 87198
505-266-5555
www.abqdowns.com

Ellis Park
Thoroughbred
3300 U.S. Hwy 41
Henderson, KY 42419-0033
812-425-1456
www.ellisparkracing.com

Emerald Downs
Thoroughbred
2300 Emerald Downs Dr.
Auburn, WA 98071-0617
253-288-7000
www.emdowns.com

Eureka Downs
Thoroughbred, Quarter Horse, Paint, Appaloosa
210 N. Jefferson St.
Eureka, KS 67405
620-583-5528
www.eurekadowns.com

Evangeline Downs
Thoroughbred, Quarter Horse
P.O. Box 90270
Lafayette, LA 70509-0270
337-896-7223
www.evangelinedowns.com

Fairmount Park
Thoroughbred
9301 Collinsville Road
Collinsville, IL 62234
618-345-4300
www.fairmountpark.com

Finger Lakes
Thoroughbred
5857 Route 96

Farmington, NY 14425
716-924-3232
www.fingerlakesracetrack.com

Fonner Park
Thoroughbred
700 E. Stolley Park Road
Grand Island, NE 68802
308-382-4515
www.fonnerpark.com

Fort Pierre
Thoroughbred, Quarter Horse
P.O. Box 426
Fort Pierre, SD 57532
605-223-2178

Freehold Raceway
Harness
130 Park Ave.
Freehold, NJ 07728
732-462-3800
www.freeholdraceway.com

Golden Gate Fields
Thoroughbred
1100 Eastshore Hwy.
Albany, CA 94710
510-559-7345
www.ggfields.com

Great Lakes Downs
Thoroughbred
4800 S. Harvey St.
Muskegon, MI 49444
231-799-2400
www.greatlakesdowns.com

Gulfstream Park
Thoroughbred
901 S. Federal Hwy.
Hallendale, FL 33009-7124
954-454-7000
www.gulfstreampark.com

Harrington Raceway
Harness
15 W. Rider Road
Harrington, DE 19952
302-398-7223
www.harringtonraceway.com

Hawthorne
Thoroughbred, Harness
3501 S. Laramie Ave.
Cicero, IL 60804
708-780-3700
www.hawthorneracecourse.com

Hazel Park
Harness
1650 E. Ten Mile Road
Hazel Park, MI 48030
248-398-1000
www.hazelparkraceway.com

Hialeah Park
Thoroughbred
105 E. 21st St.
Hialeah, FL 33011
305-885-8000
www.hialeahpark.com

Hollywood Park
Thoroughbred
1050 S. Prairie Ave.
Inglewood, CA 90306-0369
310- 419-1500
www.hollywoodpark.com

Hoosier Park
Thoroughbred, Harness, Quarter Horse
4500 Dan Patch Circle
Anderson, IN 46013
800-380-0467
www.hoosierpark.com

Horsemen's Atokad Downs
Thoroughbred
P.O.Box 518
S. Sioux City, NE 68776
402-471-2571

Horsemen's Park
Thoroughbred
6303 Q. St.
Omaha, NE 68117
402-731-2900

Jackson Raceway
Harness
P.O. Box 881
Jackson, MI 49204
517-788-4500

Keeneland
Thoroughbred
4201 Versailles Road
Lexington, KY 40592-1690
859-254-3412

Kentucky Downs
Thoroughbred
5629 Nashville Road
Franklin, KY 42135
207-586-7778
www.kentuckydowns.com

Laurel Race Course
Thoroughbred
P.O. Box 130
Laurel, MD 20725
301-725-0400
www.marylandracing.com

Lebanon Raceway
Harness
P.O. Box 58
Lebanon, OH 45036
513-932-4936
www.thelebanonraceway.com/

Les Boise Park
Thoroughbred, Quarter Horse, Appaloosa, Paint
5610 Glenwood Road
Boise, ID 83714
208-376-7223
www.lesboispark.org

Lone Star Park
Thoroughbred, Quarter Horse, Arabian, Paint
1000 Lone Star Pkwy.
Grand Prairie, TX 75050
972-263-7223
www.lonestarpark.com

Los Alamitos
Quarter Horse, Arabian, Thoroughbred, Paint and
    Appaloosa
4961 Katella Ave.
Los Alamitos, CA 90720
714-236-4317
www.losalamitos.com

Louisiana Downs
Thoroughbred, Quarter Horse
8000 E. Texas St.

Bossier City, LA 71171-5519
318-742-5555
www.ladowns.com

Manor Downs
Thoroughbred, Quarter Horse
9211 Hill Lane
Manor, TX 78653
512-272-5581
www.manordowns.com

Maywood Park
Harness
8600 W. North Ave.
Melrose Park, IL 60160
708-343-4800
www.maywoodpark.com

Meadowlands
Thoroughbred, Harness
50 Rte. 120
East Rutherford, NJ 07073
201-935-8500
www.thebigm.com

The Meadows
Harness
P.O. Box 499
Meadow Lands, PA 15347
724-225-9300

Monmouth Park
Thoroughbred
P.O. Box MP
Oceanport, NJ 07757-1298
732-222-5100
www.monmouthpark.com

Monticello Raceway
Harness
P.O. Box 5013
Monticello, NY 12701
914-794-4100
www.monticelloraceway.com/Home/home.htm

Mount Pleasant Meadows
Thoroughbred, Quarter Horse, Arabian,
   Appaloosa
500 N. Mission Road
Mount Pleasant, MI 48804-0220
517-773-0012

Mountaineer Race Track
Thoroughbred
Rt. 2
Chester, WV 26034
304-387-2400
www.mtgaming.com

North Dakota Horse Park
Thoroughbred
901 Twenty-Eight St. SW
Fargo, ND 58103
701-277-3872
www.northdakotahorsepark.org/index.php

Northfield Park
Harness
P.O. Box 374
Northfield, OH 44067
330-467-4101
www.northfieldpark.com/nfld.htm

Northville Downs
Harness
301 S. Center St.
Northville, MI 48167
248-349-1000
www.northvilledowns.com

Oaklawn Park
Thoroughbred
2705 Central Ave.
Hot Springs, AR 71902
501-623-4411
www.oaklawn.com

Ocean Downs
Harness
10218 Racetrack Road
Berlin, MD 21811-3233
410-641-0600
www.oceandowns.com

Penn National
Thoroughbred
Rt. 743
Grantville, PA 17028
717-469-2211
www.pnrc.com

Philadelphia Park
Thoroughbred
3001 St. Road

Bensalem, PA 19020-2096
215-639-9000
www.philadelphiapark.com

Pimlico Race Course
Thoroughbred
5200 Park Heights Ave.
Baltimore, MD 21215
410-542-9400
www.marylandracing.com

Platte County Ag Park
Thoroughbred
822 Fifteenth St.
Columbus, NE 68601
402-564-0133
www.agpark.com/main.htm

Pocatello Downs
Quarter Horse, Paint, Appaloosa
10588 Fairgrounds Road
Pocatello, ID 83204
208-238-1721

Pocono Downs
Harness
1280 Hwy. 315
Wilkes-Barre, PA 18702
570-825-6681
www.poconodowns.com

Pompano Park
Harness
1800 SW 3rd St.
Pompano Beach, FL 33069
954-972-2000
www.pompanopark.com

Portland Meadows
Thoroughbred, Quarter Horse
1001 N. Schmeer Road
Portland, OR 97217
503-285-9144
www.portlandmeadows.com

Prairie Meadows
Thoroughbred, Quarter Horse, Harness
One Prairie Meadows Dr.
Altoona, IA 50009-0901
515-967-1000
www.prairiemeadows.com

Raceway Park
Harness
5700 Telegraph Road
Toledo, OH 43612
419-476-7751
www.racewayparktoledo.com/

The Red Mile
Harness
1200 Red Mile Road
Lexington, KY 40504
859-255-0752
www.tattersallsredmile.com/

Remington Park
Thoroughbred, Quarter Horse, Paint, Appaloosa
One Remington Pl.
Oklahoma City, OK 73111
405-424-1000
www.remingtonpark.com

Retama Park
Thoroughbred, Quarter Horse
One Retama Pkwy.
Selma, TX 78154
210-651-7000
www.retamapark.com

River Downs
Thoroughbred
6301 Kellogg Ave.
Cincinnati, OH 45230-0286
513-232-8000
www.riverdowns.com

Rockingham Park, Salem New Hampshire
Thoroughbred
P.O. Box 47
Salem, NH 03079
603-898-2311
www.rockinghampark.com

Rosecroft Raceway
Harness
6336 Rosecroft Drive
Fort Washington, MD 20744
301-567-4000
www.rosecroft.com/default.htm

Ruidoso Downs
Quarter Horse
P.O. Box 449

Ruidoso, NM 88346
505-378-4431
www.ruidownsracing.com

Saginaw Raceway
Harness
2701 E. Genesee St.
Saginaw, MI 48601
989-755-3451
www.saginawraceway.com

Sam Houston Race Park
Thoroughbred, Quarter Horse, Arabian
7575 Sam Houston Pkwy.
Houston, TX 77064
281-807-8700
www.samhoustonracepark.com

Sandy Downs Racing
Quarter Horse, Paint, Appaloosa
6855 S. 15 East
Idaho Falls, ID 83404-7694
208-524- 3737

Santa Anita Thoroughbred
285 W. Huntington St.
Arcadia, CA 91007-3439
626-574-7223
www.santaanita.com

Saratoga Race Course
Thoroughbred, Harness
P.O. Box 564
Saratoga Springs, NY 12866
518-584-6200
www.nyra.com/saratoga/

Scarborough Downs
Harness
U.S. Rte. 1
Scarborough, ME 04074
207-883-4331
www.scarboroughdowns.com

Scioto Downs
Harness
6000 S. High St.
Columbus, OH 43207
614-491-2515
www.sciotodowns.com/

Sports Creek Raceway
Harness

4290 Morrish Road
Swartz Creek, MI 48473-1391
810-635-3333

Suffolk Downs
Thoroughbred
111 Waldemar Ave.
East Boston, MA 02128
617-567-3900
www.suffolkdowns.com

Sun Ray Park
Thoroughbred, Quarter Horse
39 Road 5568
Farmington, NM 87401-1466
505-566-1200
www.sunraygaming.com

Sunland Park
Thoroughbred, Quarter Horse
P.O. Box 1
Sunland Park, NM 88063
505-874-5200
www.sunland-park.com

Tampa Bay Downs
Thoroughbred, Arabian
11225 Race Track ROAD
Oldsmar, FL 34677
813-855-4401
www.tampadowns.com

Thistledown, North Randall
Thoroughbred
21501 Emery Road
North Randall, OH 44128
216-662-8600
www.thistledown.com

Thunder Ridge
Harness
164 Thunder Road
Prestonburg, KY 41653
859-886-7223

Turf Paradise
Thoroughbred, Quarter Horse, Arabian
1501 W. Bell Road
Phoenix, AZ 85023-3411
602-942-1101
www.turfparadise.com

Turfway Park
Thoroughbred
7500 Turfway Road
Florence, KY 41042
859-371-0200

Vernon Downs
Harness
P.O. Box 860
Vernon, NY 13476
315-829-2201
www.vernondowns.com

Will Rogers Downs
Thoroughbred
20900 S. 4200 Road
Claremore, OK 74018
918-343-5900
www.willrogersdowns.com

The Woodlands
Thoroughbred, Quarter Horse
9700 Leavenworth Road
Kansas City, KS 66112
913-299-9797
www.woodlandskc.com

Wyoming Downs
Thoroughbred, Quarter Horse
10180 Hwy. 89 N.
Evanston, WY 82931
307-789-0511
www.wyomingdowns.com

Yonkers Raceway
Harness
810 Central Ave.
Yonkers, NY 10704
914-968-4200
www.yonkersraceway.com

Fairs/Fairgrounds with Racing

Albuquerque State Fair
Thoroughbred, Quarter Horse
201 California St. NE
Albuquerque, NM 87198
505-266-5555
www.abqdowns.com

Apache County Fair
Thoroughbred, Quarter Horse, Paint, Mule

825 W. 4th St. North
St. Johns, AZ 85936-0357
928-337-4364

Brown County Fairgrounds
Thoroughbred, Quarter Horse
25 Market St.
Aberdeen, SD 57401
800-272-3247
www.brown.sd.us/fair

Cal Expo
Thoroughbred, Quarter Horse, Appaloosa
1600 Exposition Blvd.
Sacramento, CA 95815
916-263-4677
www.calfairs.com

Capital Racing—Cal Expo
Harness
1600 Exposition Blvd.
Sacramento, CA 95815
916-263-4677
www.calfairs.com

Cassia County Fair
Thoroughbred, Quarter Horse, Arabian,
    Appaloosa, Paint
1101 Elba Ave.
Burley, ID 83318
208-678-8610
www.cassiacounty.org/fair/default.htm

Cochise County Fair
Thoroughbred, Quarter Horse
3677 N. Leslie Canyon Road
Douglas, AZ 85607-6304
520-364-3819

Coconino Fair
Thoroughbred, Quarter Horse, Paint, Mule
HC 30 P.O. Box 3A
Flagstaff, AZ 86001
928-774-5139

Columbia County Fairgrounds
Thoroughbred, Quarter Horse, Arabian
P.O. Box 74
St. Helens, OR 97051
503-397-4231
www.co.columbia.or.us/Fairgrounds/Fairgrounds.asp

Crooked River Roundup
Thoroughbred, Quarter Horse, Appaloosa
P.O. Box 536
Prineville, OR 9774
800-4BULLRIDES
www.crookedriverroundup.com

Cumberland Fairgrounds
Harness
39 Samuel Road
Portland, ME
207-797-0899
www.cumberlandfair.com

Eastern Idaho Fair
Thoroughbred, Quarter Horse, Arabian,
    Appaloosa, Paint
P.O. Box 250
Blackfoot, ID 83221
208-785-2480
www.idaho-state-fair.com/index2.html

Elko County Fair
Thoroughbred, Quarter Horse
Fair Grounds
Elko, NV 89801
775-738-3616

Fair Meadows
Thoroughbred, Quarter Horse, Paint, Appaloosa
4145 E. 21st St.
Tulsa, OK 74114
918-744-6999
www.fairmeadows.com

Fairplex Fairgrounds
Thoroughbred, Quarter Horse, Arabian,
    Appaloosa
1101 W. McKinley Ave.
Pomona, CA 91769
909-865-4545
www.fairplex.com

Farmington Fairgrounds
Harness
229 S. Strong Road
Farmington, ME 04938-5103
207-778-9595

Fresno Fair, Fresno
Thoroughbred, Appaloosa, Quarter Horse,
    Arabian, Mule
1121 Chance Ave.

Fresno, CA
559-650-3331
www.fresnofair.com

Fryeburg Fairgrounds
Harness
P.O. Box 78
Fryeburg, ME 04037
207-935-3268
www.fryeburgfair.com

Gem County Fairgrounds
Thoroughbred, Quarter Horse, Arabian,
    Appaloosa, Paint
3103 W. Idaho Blvd.
Emmett, ID 83617
208-265-5560

Gila County Fair
Thoroughbred, Quarter Horse, Paint, Mule
P.O. Box 2193
Globe, AZ 85502-2193
928-425-2772

Gillespie County Fair
Thoroughbred, Quarter Horse, Paint, Appaloosa
P.O. Box 526
Fredericksburg, TX 78624
830-997-2359
www.gillespiefair.com

Graham County Fair
Thoroughbred, Quarter Horse, Paint, Mule
527 E. Armory
Safford, AZ 85546-2231
928-428-6240

Greenlee Fairgrounds
Thoroughbred, Quarter Horse, Paint, Mule
P.O. Box 123
Duncan, AZ 85534-0123
928-359-2032

Harney County Fair
Thoroughbred, Quarter Horse, Mule
Fairgrounds Road
Burns, OR 97720
541-573-6166

Humboldt County Fair
Mule
480 E. Haskell St.

Winnemucca, NV 89445
775-623-2220

Humboldt Fair
Thoroughbred, Quarter Horse, Arabian,
   Appaloosa
1250 Fifth St.
Ferndale, CA 95536
707-786-9525
www.calfairs.com

Jerome County Fair
Thoroughbred, Quarter Horse, Appaloosa, Paint
200 N. Fir St.
Jerome, ID 83338-1700
208-324-7057

Josephine County Fair
Thoroughbred, Quarter Horse, Appaloosa
1451 Fairgrounds Road
Grants Pass, OR 97527
541-476-3215

La Paz Fair
Thoroughbred, Quarter Horse
1501 W. Bell Road
Phoenix, AZ 85023
602-942-1101
www.turfparadise.com

Marias Fair
Thoroughbred, Quarter Horse, Paint, Appaloosa,
   Mule
28082 U.S. Hwy. 2
Shelby, MT 59474
406-337-2692

Maricopa Fair
Thoroughbred, Quarter Horse
1501 W. Bell Road
Phoenix, AZ 85023
602-942-1101
www.turfparadise.com

Mohave County Fair
Thoroughbred, Quarter Horse, Paint, Mule
2600 Fairgrounds Blvd.
Kingman, AZ 86401-4169
928-753-2636

Montana State Fair
Thoroughbred, Quarter Horse
P.O. Box 1888

Great Falls, MT 59403
406-452-8955
www.mtexpopark.com/2003/index.html

Navajo County Fair
Thorougbred, Quarter Horse
1501 W. Bell Road
Phoenix, AZ 85023
602-942-1101
www.turfparadise.com

Nebraska State Fair Thoroughbred
Twenty-Seventh St.
Lincoln, NE 68501-1223
402-474-5371
www.statefair.org

New Orleans Fairground
Thoroughbred, Quarter Horse
1757 Gentilly Blvd.
New Orleans, LA 70119
504-904-5515
www.fgno.com

Northern Maine Fair
Harness
68 Ward St.
Presque Isle, ME 04769
207-764-1830

Oneida County Fair
Quarter Horse, Paint, Appaloosa
459 S. Main St.
Malad City, ID 83252-1398
208-766-4706

Pinal Fair
Thoroughbred, Quarter Horse
1501 W. Bell Road
Phoenix, AZ 85023
602-942-1101
www.turfparadise.com

Pleasanton
Thoroughbred, Quarter Horse, Arabian,
   Appaloosa
4501 Pleasanton Ave.
Pleasanton, CA 94566
925-426-7519
www.calfairs.com

Queen City Racing
Thoroughbred, Quarter Horse, Paint, Appaloosa,
   Mule

P.O. Box 9706
Helena, MT 59604
406-457-9492

Rillito Park (Pima Fair)
Thoroughbred, Quarter Horse
4502 N. 1st Ave.
Tucson, AZ 85718
520-293-5211

Rupert Fairgrounds
Quarter Horse, Paint, Appaloosa
P.O. Box 263
Rupert, ID 83350
208-524-3737

San Joaquin County Fair
Thoroughbred, Quarter Horse, Arabian,
    Appaloosa
1658 S. Airport Way
Stockton, CA 95206
209-466-5041
www.calfairs.com

San Mateo County Expo Center
Thoroughbred, Quarter Horse, Appaloosa
2495 S. Delaware St.
San Mateo, CA 94403
650-574-3247
www.sanmateoexpo.org/

Santa Cruz County Fair
Thoroughbred, Quarter Horse
P.O. Box 85
Sonoita, AZ 85637-0085
520-455-5553

Skowhegan Fair
Harness
P.O. Box 39
Skowhegan, ME 04976
207-474-2947
www.skowheganstatefair.com

Solano County Fair
Thoroughbred, Quarter Horse, Arabian,
    Appaloosa
900 Fairgrounds Dr.
Vallejo, CA 94589707-644-4455
www.scfair.com

Sonoma County Fair
Thoroughbred, Quarter Horse, Arabian,
    Appaloosa
1350 Bennett Valley Road
Santa Rosa, CA 95403
707-545-6206
www.sonomacountyfair.com

Sun Downs
Thoroughbred, Quarter Horse, Arabian
P.O. Box 6662
Kennewick, WA 99336-0639
509-582-5434

Syracuse Mile-New York State Fairgrounds
Harness
581 State Fair Blvd.
Syracuse, NY 13209
800-475-3247
www.nysfair.org/state_fair/2004

Tillamook County Fair
Thoroughbred, Quarter Horse, Appaloosa
P.O. Box 455
Tillamook OR, 97141
503-842-2272
www.wcn.net/tillamookfair/main.htm

Timonium Fairgrounds
Thoroughbred
220 York Road
Timonium, MD 21094-0188
410-252-0200
www.marylandstatefair.com

Topsham Fair Harness
614 Meadow Road
Topsham, ME 04086
207-725-2735

Union Fairgrounds
Harness
P.O. Box 421
Union, ME 04862
207-236-8009
www.unionfair.org/directions.cfm

Waitsburg Race Track
Thoroughbred, Quarter Horse, Arabian
P.O. Box 391
Waitsburg, WA 99361-0391
509-337-6623

Walla Walla Race Track
Thoroughbred, Quarter Horse, Arabian
P.O. Drawer G
Walla Walla, WA 99362
509-527-3247

Western Montana Fair
Thoroughbred, Quarter Horse, Arabian, Paint,
    Appaloosa, Mule
1101 S. Ave.W.
Missoula, MT 9801-7907
406-421-3247
www.westernmontanafair.com

Windsor Fairground
Harness
Rt. 32
Windsor, ME 04363
207-549-3137

Yavapai Downs (Yavapai Fair)
Thorougbred, Quarter Horse
P.O. Box 26557
Prescott Valley, AZ 86312
928-775-8000
www.yavapaidownsatpv.com

Yellowstone Downs
Thoroughbred, Quarter Horse, Paint, Appaloosa
P.O. Box 1138
Billings, MT 59103
406-656-1619

Yuma County Fair
Thoroughbred, Quarter Horse
P.O. Box 26557
Prescott Valley, AZ 86312
928-775-8000
www.yavapaidownsatpv.com

APPENDIX G
RACING ORGANIZATIONS

American Mule Racing Association
P.O. Box 660651
Sacramento, CA 95866-0651
916-263-1529
www.muleracing.org

American Paint Horse Association
P.O. Box 961023
Fort Worth, TX 76161-0023

817-834-2742
www.apha.com

American Quarter Horse Association
P.O. Box 200
Amarillo, TX 79168-0001
800-376-4811
www.aqha.com

American Quarter Horse Race Track
    Association
P.O. Box 200
Amarillo, TX 79168-0001
800-376-4811
www.aqha.com

American Quarter Horse Racing Council
P.O. Box 200
Amarillo, TX 79168-0001
800-376-4811
www.aqha.com

Appaloosa Horse Club, Inc.
P.O. Box 8403
2720 W. Pulman Road
Moscow, D 83843-0903
208-882-5578
www.appaloosa.com

Arabian Jockey Club
10805 E Bethany Dr.
Aurora, CO 80014
303-696-4568
www.arabianracing.org

Arabian Racing Association of California
4961 Katella Ave.
Los Alamitos, CA 90720-2721
714-820-2817
www.arac.org

Association of Racing Commissioners
    International
2343 Alexandria Dr.
Lexington, KY 40504-3276
859-224-7070
www.arci.com

Breeders Crown
1200 Tices Lane, Suite 204
East Brunswick, NJ 08816-1335
732-249-8500
www.hambletonian.org

Breeders' Cup Limited/ NTRA
2525 Harrodsburg Road
Lexington, KY 40504
859-223-5444
www.ntra.com

The Hambletonian Society
1200 Tices Lane, Suite 204
East Brunswick, NJ 08816-1335
732-249-8500
www.hambletonian.org

Harness Horsemen International
14 Main St.
Robbinsville, NJ 08691-1410
609-259-3717

Harness Racing Communications
41 Rt. 34
Colts Neck, NJ 07722-1736
732-780-3700
www.ustrotting.com

Harness Tracks of America, Inc.
4640 East Sunrise, Suite 200
Tuscon, AZ 85718-4576
520-529-2525
www.harnesstracks.com

The Jockey Club
40 E. 52nd St.
New York, NY 10022-5911
212-371-5970
www.jockeyclub.com

Jockey's Guild, Inc.
250 W. Main St., Suite 1820
Lexington, KY 40588-0250
859-259-3211

Maryland Million Ltd.
30 E. Padonia Road, Suite303
Timonium, MD 21094-0365
410-252-2100
www.mdhorsebreeders.com

The National H.B.P.A., Inc.
4063 Ironworks Pkwy.
Bldg. B., Suite 2
Lexington, KY 40511859-259-0451
www.hbpa.org

The National Racing Compact
P.O. Box 184
New Kent, VA 23124
www.racinglicense.com

National Steeplechase Association
400 Fair Hill Dr.
Elkton, MD 21921-2569
410-392-0700
www.nationalsteeplechase.com

National Thoroughbred Racing Association
2525 Harrodsburg Road, Suite 500
Lexington, KY 40504
859-223-5444
www.ntra.com

North American Pari-Mutuel Regulators
 Association
P.O. Box 446
Cheyenne, WY 82003
888-NAPRA50
www.napraonline.com/PublicPages/2001web/
 home.asp

Pacific Coast Quarter Horse Racing Association
P.O. Box 919
Los Alamitos, CA 90720-0919
714-236-1755
www.pcqhra.org

Race Track Chaplaincy
P.O. Box 91640
Los Angeles, CA 90009
714-778-2229
www.racetrackchaplaincy.org

Racing Fans Club of America
P.O. Box 6158
Philadelphia, PA 19115-6158

Thoroughbred Club of America, Inc.
P.O. Box 8098
Lexington, KY 40533-8098
859-254-4282

Thoroughbred Horsemen's Associations, Inc.
10500 Little Patuxent Pkwy., Suite 650
Columbia, MD 21044-3502
410-740-4900

Thoroughbred Owners and Breeders
 Association

P.O. Box 4367
Lexington, KY 40544-4367
859-276-2291
www.toba.org

Thoroughbred Racing Associations
420 Fair Hill Dr., Suite 1
Elkton, MD 21921-2573
410-392-9200
www.tra-online.com

Thoroughbred Racing Protective Bureau, Inc.
420 Fair Hill Dr., Suite1
Elkton, MD 21921-2573
410-398-2261
www.trpb.com

Triple Crown Productions, LLC
700 Central Ave.
Louisville, KY 40208-1200
502-636-4405
www.kyderby.com

United States Harness Writers Association, Inc.
P.O. Box 1314
Mechanicsburg, PA 17055
717-766-3219
www.ustrotting.com/ushwa/ushwa.htm

United States Trotting Association
750 Michigan Ave.
Columbus, OH 43215-1191
614-224-2291
www.ustrotting.com

APPENDIX H
RODEO ORGANIZATIONS

International Professional Rodeo Association
P.O. Box 83377
Oklahoma City, OK 73148
405-235-6540
www.iprarodeo.com

Midstates Rodeo Association (MSRA)
4408 Prices Creek Road
Lewisburg, OH 45338
937-962-2530
www.midstatesrodeo.com

National High School Rodeo Association

12001 Tejon St., Suite 128
Denver, CO 80234
303-452-0820
www.nhsra.org

National Intercollegiate Rodeo Association
2316 East Gate N., Suite 60
Walla Walla, WA 99362
509-529-4402
www.collegerodeo.com

National Little Britches Rodeo
1045 W. Rio Grande
Colorado Springs, CO 80906-1212
719-389-0333
www.nlbra.org

National Pro Rodeo Association (NPRA)
P.O. Box 212
Mandan, ND 58554
701-663-4973
www.npra.com

Northwest Professional Rodeo Association
21905 Buckhorn Lane
Fossil, OR 97830
541-384-2855
www.nwprorodeo.com

Professional Rodeo Cowboys Association, Inc.
101 Pro Rodeo Dr.
Colorado Springs, CO 80919-9989
719-593-8840
www.prorodeo.com

**Professional Western Rodeo Association
(Pro-West)**
P.O. Box 427
Moses Lake, WA 98837
509-766-2855
www.pro-west.net

**Women's Professional Rodeo Association
(WPRA/PWRA)**
1235 Lake Plaza Dr., Suite 134
Colorado Springs, CO 80906
719-576-0900
www.wpra.com

Working Ranch Cowboys Association (WRCA)
2750 Duniven Circle, Suite B
Amarillo, TX 79109
806-374-9722
www.wrca.org

APPENDIX I
SALES COMPANIES

Arizona Thoroughbred Breeders Association
P.O. Box 41774
Phoenix, AZ 85080-1774
602-942-1310
www.atba.net

C.T.B.A. Sales
201 Colorado Place
Arcadia, CA 91007-2604
800-573-2822
www.ctba.com

Fasig-Tipton Company Inc.
2400 Newtown Pike
Lexington, KY 40511
859-255-1555
www.fasigtipton.com

Illinois Thoroughbred Breeders and Owners Foundation
P.O. Box 336
Caseyville, IL 62232-0336
618-344-3427
www.illinoisracingnews.com

Keeneland Association, Inc.
P.O. Box 1690
Lexington, KY 40588-1690
859-254-3412
www.keeneland.com

Kentucky Standardbred Sales Company LLC
1251 Red Mile Road
Lexington, KY 40508
606-255-8537
www.kentuckystandardbred.com

National Cutting Horse Association
260 Bailey Ave.
Fort Worth, TX 76107-1862
817-244-6188
www.nchacutting.com

National Equine Sales, Inc.
2040 W. Blee Road
Springfield, Oh 45502-8715
800-451-5264
www.nationalequine.com

Ocala Breeders' Sales Company, Inc.
P.O. Box 99
Ocala, FL 34478-0099
352-237-2754
www.obssales.com

Pacific Coast Quarter Horse Racing Association—Sales Division
P.O. Box 919
Los Alamitos, CA 90720-0919
714-236-1755
www.pcqhra.org

Tattersalls Horse Sales
P.O. Box 420
Lexington, KY 40585-0420
914-773-7777
www.tattersallsredmile.com

Texas Thoroughbred Association
P.O. Box 14967
Austin, TX 78761-4967
512-458-6133
www.texasthoroughbred.com

Triangle Sales Company
43207 Benson Park Road
Shawnee, OK 74801-9317
405-275-2196
www.trihorse.com

Washington Thoroughbred Breeders Association
P.O. Box 1499
Auburn, WA 98071-1499
253-288-7878
www.washingtonthoroughbred.com

APPENDIX J
SCHOOLS
Colleges and universities with two- and four-year and advanced degree programs in equine areas, animal science or agriculture

Abraham Baldwin Agriculture College
2802 Moore Hwy.
Tifton, GA 31794
229-386-3236
http://stallion.abac.peachnet.edu

Alfred University
One Saxon Dr.
Alfred, NY 14802
607-871-2111
www.alfred.edu

Auburn University
Auburn, AL 36849
334-844-4000
www.auburn.edu

Averett University
420 W. Main St.
Danville, VA 24541
800-AVERETT
www.averett.edu

Berry College
2277 Martha Berry Hwy., NW
Mount Berry, GA 30149
706-232-5374
www2.berry.edu

Black Hawk College
1501 Illinois Hwy. 78
Kewanee, IL 61443
309-796-5000
www.BHC.edu

Bridgewater College
402 E. College St.
Bridgewater, VA 22812
540-828-8000
www.bridgewater.edu

Brigham Young
Provo, UT 84602
801-378-4636
www.byu.edu

Cal Poly Pomona
3801 W. Temple Ave.
Pomona, CA 91768
909-869-7659
www.csupomona.edu

Cal Poly San Luis Obispo
Agricultural Dept., Bldg. 10
San Luis Obispo, CA 93407
805-756-2803
www.cagr.calpoly.edu

California State University, Fresno
California Agricultural Technology Institute
5241 N. Maple Ave.
Fresno, CA 93740
559-278-4240
www.CSUFresno.edu

Cazenovia College
22 Sullivan St.
Cazenovia, New York 13035
315-655-7000
www.cazcollege.edu

Centenary College
400 Jefferson St.
Hackettstown, NJ 07840
908-852-1400
www.centenarycollege.edu

Central Texas College
P.O. Box 1800
Killeen, TX 76540
254-526-7161
www.ctcd.cc.tx.us

Central Wyoming College
2660 Peck Ave.
Riverton, WY 82501
800-735-8418
www.cwc.whecn.edu

Clemson University
College of Agriculture, Forestry and Life Sciences
P.O. Box 345125
Clemson, SC 29634
864-656-3311
www.clemson.edu

College of Southern Idaho
P.O. Box 1238
Twin Falls, ID 83303
208-732-6221
www.csi.edu

Colorado State University
College of Agricultural Sciences
Fort Collins, CO 80523
970-491-1101
www.colostate.edu

Cornell University
College of Agriculture and Life Sciences
274 Roberts Hall

Ithaca, NY 14853
607-254-5137
www.cals.cornell.edu

Delaware Valley College
700 E. Butler Ave.
Doylestown, PA 18901
215-345-1500
www.devalcol.edu

Dodge City Community College
2501 N. 14th Ave.
Dodge City, KS 67801
620-225-1321
www.dccc.cc.ks.us

Ellsworth Community College
1100 College Ave.
Iowa Falls, IA 50126
800-322-9235
www.iavalley.cc.ia.us/ecc/

Feather River College
570 Golden Eagle Ave.
Quincy, CA 95971
1-800-442-9799
www.frcc.cc.ca.us

**Iowa State University of Science and
    Technology**
College of Agriculture
Ames, IA 50011
515-294-4111
www.ag.iastate.edu

Johnson & Wales University
8 Abbott Park Pl.
Providence, RI
1-800-DIAL-JWU
www.jwu.edu

Judson College
1151 N. State St.
Elgin, IL 60123
847-695-2500
www.judson-il.edu

Kemptville College—University of Guelph
P.O. Box 2003
Kemptville, ON K0G 1J0, Canada
613-258-8336
www.kemptvillec.uoguelph.ca

Kansas State University
College of Agriculture
117 Waters Hall
Manhattan, KS 66506
785-532-6151
www.ag.ksu.edu

Kirkwood Community College
6301 Kirkwood Blvd.
P.O. Box 2068
Cedar Rapids, IA 52406
319-398-5517
www.kirkwood.edu

Lake Erie College
391 W. Washington St.
Painesville, OH 44077-3309
440-296-1856
www.lec.edu

Laramie County Community College
1400 E. College Dr.
Cheyenne, WY 82007
800-522-2993
www.lccc.cc.wy.us

Louisiana State University
College of Agriculture
104 Agricultural Administration Bldg.
Baton Rouge, LA 70803
225-578-2065
www.coa.lsu.edu/indexframe1024.html

Louisiana Tech University
P.O. Box 3178
Ruston, LA 71272
1-800-LATECH-1
www.latech.edu

Michigan State University
College of Agriculture and Natural Resources
102 Agriculture Hall
East Lansing, MI 48824-1039
517-355-0232
www.canr.msu.edu/about.htm

Middle Tennessee State University
1301 E. Main St.
Murfreesboro, TN 37132
615-898-2300
www.mtsu.edu

Midway College
512 E. Stephens St.
Midway, KY 40347-1120
1-800-755-0031
www.midway.edu

Mississippi State University
College of Agriculture and Life Sciences
Mississipi State, MS 39762
662-325-2323
www.msstate.edu

Montana State University
P.O. Box 172860
Bozeman, MT 59717-2860
406-994-3681
www.montana.edu

Morehead State University
150 University Blvd.
Morehead, KY 40351
800-585-6781
www.morehead-st.edu

Mount Holyoke College
50 College St.
South Hadley, MA 01075-1488
413-583-2000
www.mtholyoke.edu

Mount Ida College
777 Dedham St.
Newton Center, MA 02459
617-928-4500
www.mountida.edu

Murray State University
P.O. Box 9
Murray, KY 42071
800-272-4MSU
www.murraystate.edu

New Mexico State University
College of Agriculture and Home Economics
Las Cruces, NM 88003-8001
505-646-0111
www.cahe.nmsu.edu

North Carolina State University
College of Agriculture and Life Sciences
115 Patterson Hall
Raleigh, NC 27695
919-515-2614
www.cals.ncsu.edu

North Central Texas College
1525 W. California St.
Gainesville, TX 76240
940-668-7731
www.nctc.edu

North Dakota State University
College of Agriculture, Food Systems and Natural
    Resources
1301 Twelfth Ave.
Fargo, ND 58105
800-488-NDSU
www.ndsu.nodak.edu

Northeast Louisiana University
700 University Ave.
Monroe, LA 71209
318 342 1766
www.nlu.edu

Northwest College
231 W. 6th St.
Powell, WY 82435
307-754-6000
www.northwestcollege.org

Northwest Missouri State University
800 University Dr.
Maryville, MO 64468-6001
800-633-1175
www.nwmissouri.edu

Ohio State University
100 Agricultural Administration Bldg.
2120 Fyffe Road
Columbus, OH 43210
614-292-6891
www.cfaes.osu.edu

Ohio University Southern Campus
Athens, OH 45701
740-593-1000
www.ohio.edu

Olds College
4500-50 Street
Olds, AB T4H 1R6
Canada
800-661-6537
www.oldscollege.ab.ca

Oklahoma State University
324 Student Union

Stillwater, OK 74078
405-744-6858
www.okstate.edu

Oregon State University
Withycombe Hall
Corvallis, OR 97331
541-737-1000
http://oregonstate.edu

Otterbein College
Dept. of Equine Science
Westerville, OH 43081-2006
614-823-1517
www.otterbein.edu

Parkland College
2400 W. Bradley Ave.
Champaign, IL 61821-1899
217-351-2200
www.parkland.edu

Pennsylvania State University
College of Agricultural Sciences
University Park, PA 16802
814-865-7521
www.cas.psu.edu

Purdue University
615 W. State St.
West Lafayette, IN 47907
765-494-4600
www.purdue.edu

Rocky Mountain College
1511 Poly Drive
Billings, MT 59101
800-877-6259
www.rocky.edu

Saint Andrews Presbyterian College
1700 Dogwood Mile
Lauringburg, NC 28352
910-277-5555
www.sapc.edu

Saint Mary-of-the-Woods College
Saint Mary-of-the-Woods, IN 47876
812-535-5151
www.smwc.edu

Salem International University
223 W. Main St.
Salem, WV 26426-0500
800-283-4562
www.salemiu.edu

South Dakota State University
P.O. Box 2207
Brookings, SD 57007
800-952-3541
www3.sdstate.edu

Southern Illinois University
College of Agricultural Sciences
Carbondale, IL 62901-6899
618-536-4405
www.siu.edu

Southwest Missouri State University
901 S. National Ave.
Springfield, MO 65804
417-836-5000
www.smsu.edu

State University of New York
College of Agriculture and Technology
Cobleskill, NY 12043
518-255-5323
www.cobleskill.edu

Stephen F. Austin State University
SFA Station
Nacogdoches, TX 75962
936-468-3401
www.sfasu.edu

Stephens College
1200 E. Broadway
Columbia, MO 65215
800-876-7207
www.stephens.edu

Sul Ross State University
P.O. Box C-114
Alpine, TX 79832
432-837-8011
www.sulross.edu/pages/991.asp

Sweet Briar College
P.O. Box 6
Sweet Briar, VA 24595-0006
800-381-6742
www.sbc.edu

Teikyo Post University
800 Country Club Road
Waterbury, CT 06723
203-596-4500
www.teikyopost.edu

Texas A&M University
2112 TAMU
College Station, TX 77843
979-845-2211
www.agprogra.tamu.edu

Texas Tech University
2500 Broadway
Lubbock, TX 79409
806-742-2011
www.ttu.edu

Truman State University
158 Barnett Hall
Kirksville, MO 63501-0828
800-452-6678
www.truman.edu/agriculture

Tuskegee University
College of Agricultural, Environmental and
    Natural Sciences
Tuskegee, Al 36088
334-727-8157
www.tusk.edu

University of Arizona
Education Bldg. 69, Rm. 104
Tucson, AZ 85721-0069
520-621-7621
www.ag.arizona.edu

University of California, Davis
One Shields Ave.
Davis, CA 95616
530-752-0107
www.caes.ucdavis.edu

University of Connecticut
College of Agriculture and Natural Resources
Stoors, CT 06269
860-486-2919
www.canr.uconn.edu

University of Delaware
College of Agriculture and Natural Resources
113 Townsend Hall
Newark, DE 19717

302-831-2501
http://ag.udel.edu

University of Findlay
Equestrian & Pre-Veterinary Studies
1000 Main St.
Findlay, OH 45840
800-472-9502
www.findlay.edu

University of Florida
Gainesville, FL 32611
352-392-3261
www.ufl.edu

University of Georgia
College of Agricultural and Environmental
    Sciences
Tifton, GA 30602
706-542-3000
http://uqacescn.ces.uga.edu/caeshome

University of Idaho
College of Agricultural & Life Sciences
P.O. Box 442335
Moscow, ID 83843
208-885-6681
www.ag.uidaho.edu

University of Illinois
College of Agricultural, Consumer &
    Environmental Studies
1207 W. Gregory Dr.
Urbana-Champaign, IL 61820
217-333-1000
www.aces.uiuc.edu

University of Kentucky
College of Agriculture
Lexington, KY 40506
859-257-3469
www.ca.uky.edu

University of Louisville
Department of Equine Business
Louisville, KY 40292-0001
502-852-8440
http://cbpa.louisville.edu/eip

University of Maine
College of Natural Sciences, Forestry and
    Agriculture
5782 Winslow Hall

Orono, ME 04469
207-581-3206
www.nsfa.umaine.edu

University of Maryland
Institute of Applied Agriculture - Equine Business
  Management
2115 Jull Hall
College Park, MD 20742
301-405-1000
www.iaa.umd.edu

University of Massachusetts
Amherst, MA 01003
413-545-0111
www.umass.edu

University of Minnesota—Crookston
Equine Industries Management
2900 University Ave.
Crookston, MI 56717-5001
800-UMC-MINN
www.crk.umn.edu

University of Missouri
Columbia, MO 65211
573-882-2121
www.missouri.edu

University of Nebraska
College of Agricultural Sciences and Natural
  Resources
103 Ag Hall
Lincoln, NE 68583
800-742-8800
http://casnr.unl.edu/index.htm

University of Nevada
1664 N. Virginia St.
Reno, NV 89557
775-784-1110
www.unr.edu/content

University of New Hampshire
College of Life Sciences and Agriculture
Durham, NH 03824
603-862-1360
www.colsa.unh.edu

University of Rhode Island
Kingston, RI 02881
401-874-1000
www.uri.edu

University of Tennessee
Institute of Agriculture
Knoxville, TN 37996
865-974-1000
www.utk.edu

University of Vermont
College of Agriculture and Life Sciences
Burlington, VT 05405
802-656-3131
www.uvm.edu/cals

University of Wisconsin
College of Agricultural and Life Sciences
140 Agricultural Hall
Madison, WI 53706
608-262-4930
www.cals.wisc.edu

University of Wyoming
College of Agriculture
Laramie, WY 82070
307-766-1121
www.uwyo.edu

Utah State University
4800 Old Main Hill
Logan, UT 84322
435-797-2215
www.usu.edu

Virginia Intermont College
1013 Moore St.
Bristol, VA 24201
800-451-1VIC
www.vic.edu

**Virginia Polytechnic Institute and State
  University**
College of Agriculture and Life Sciences
Blacksburg, VA 24061
540-231-6503
www.cals.vt.edu

Washington State University
College of Agriculture and Home Economics
P.O. Box 646242
Pullman, WA 99164-1067
509-335-4561
www.cahe.wsu.edu

Wesleyan College
4760 Forsyth Road

Macon, GA 31210
800-447-6610
www.wesleyan-college.edu

West Texas A&M University
2501 Fourth Ave.
Canyon, TX 79016-0001
806-651-2000
www.wtamu.edu

Western Kentucky University
One Big Red Way
Bowling Green, KY 42101-3579
270-745-0111
www.wky.edu

William Woods University
Division of Equestrian Studies
One University Ave.
Fulton, MO 65251-1098
800-995-3159
www.williamwoods.edu

Wilmington College
320 N. DuPont Hwy.
New Castle, DE 19720
302-328-9401
www.wilmcoll.edu

Wilson College
1015 Philadelphia Ave.
Chambersburg, PA 17201
717-264-4141
www.wilson.edu

Colleges and universities with pre-veterinary programs

Auburn University
Auburn, AL 36849
333-844-4000
www.auuburn.edu

Berry College
2277 Martha Berry Hwy., NW
Mount Berry, GA 30149
706-232-5374
www.berry.edu

Brigham Young
Provo, UT 84602
801-378-4636
www.byu.edu

Cal Poly Pomona
3801 W. Temple Ave.
Pomona, CA 91768
909-869-7659
www.csupomona.edu

California State University, Fresno
California Agricultural Technology Institute
5241 N. Maple Ave.
Fresno, CA 93740
559-278-4240
www.CSUFresno.edu

Clemson University
College of Agriculture, Forestry and Life Sciences
P.O. Box 345125
Clemson, SC 29634
864-656-3311
www.clemson.edu

Colorado State University
Fort Collins, CO 80523
970-491-1101
www.colostate.edu

Cornell University
College of Agriculture and Life Sciences
274 Roberts Hall
Ithaca, NY 14853
607-254-5137
www.cals.cornell.edu

Delaware Valley College
700 E. Butler Ave.
Doylestown, PA 18901
215-345-1500
www.devalcol.edu

Fairmont State College
1201 Locust Ave.
Fairmont, WV 26554
304-367-4000
www.fscwv.edu

Iowa State University of Science and Technology
College of Agriculture
Ames, IA 50011
515-294-4111
www.ag.iastate.edu

Kansas State University
College of Agriculture

117 Waters Hall
Manhattan, KS 66506
785-532-6151
www.ag.ksu.edu

Lake Erie College
391 W. Washington St.
Painesville, OH 44077-3309
440-296-1856
www.lec.edu

Louisiana State University
College of Agriculture
104 Agricultural Administration Bldg.
Baton Rouge, LA 70803
225-578-2065
www.coa.lsu.edu/indexframe1024.html

Louisiana Tech University
P.O. Box 3178
Ruston, LA 71272
800-LATECH-1
www.latech.edu

Mercy College
555 Broadway
Dobbs Ferry, NY 10522
800-MERCY-NY
www.mercynet.edu

Michigan State University
College of Agriculture and Natural Resources
102 Agriculture Hall
East Lansing, MI 48824-1039
517-355-0232
www.canr.msu.edu/about.htm

Middle Tennessee State University
1301 E. Main St.
Murfreesboro, TN 37132
615-898-2300
www.mtsu.edu

Mississippi State University
Mississippi State, MS 39762
662-325-2323
www.msstate.edu

Montana State University
P.O. Box 172860
Bozeman, MT 59717-2860
406-994-3681
www.montana.edu

Morehead State University
150 University Blvd.
Morehead, KY 40351
800-585-6781
www.morehead-st.edu

Mount Ida College
777 Dedham St.
Newton Center, MA 02459
617-928-4500
www.mountida.edu

Murray State University
P.O. Box 9
Murray, KY 42071
800-272-4MSU
www.murraystate.edu

New Mexico State University
College of Agriculture and Home Economics
Las Cruces, NM 88003-8001
505-646-0111
www.cahe.nmsu.edu

North Carolina State University
College of Agriculture and Life Sciences
115 Patterson Hall
Raleigh, NC 27695
919-515-2614
www.cals.ncsu.edu

North Dakota State University
College of Agriculture, Food Systems and Natural
    Resources
1301 Twelfth Ave.
Fargo, ND 58105
800-488-NDSU
www.ndsu.nodak.edu

Northeast Louisiana University
700 University Ave.
Monroe, LA 71209
318-342-1766
www.nlu.edu

Northwestern State University of Louisiana
Natchitoches, LA 71497
318-357-6011
www.nsula.edu

Ohio State University
100 Agricultural Administration Bldg.
2120 Fyffe Road

Columbus, OH 43210
614-292-6891
www.cfaes.osu.edu

Oklahoma State University
324 Student Union
Stillwater, OK 74078
405-744-6858
www.okstate.edu

Oregon State University
Withycombe Hall
Corvallis, OR 97331
541-737-1000
http://oregonstate.edu

Otterbein College
Dept. of Equine Science
Westerville, OH 43081-2006
614-823-1517
www.otterbein.edu

Pennsylvania State University
College of Agricultural Sciences
University Park, PA 16802
814-865-7521
www.cas.psu.edu

Purdue University
615 W. State St.
West Lafayette, IN 47907
765-494-4600
www.purdue.edu

Quinnipiac College
275 Mount Carmel Ave.
Hamden, CT 06518
203-582-8200
www.quinnipiac.edu

Saint Andrews Presbyterian College
1700 Dogwood Mile
Lauringburg, NC 28352
910-277-5555
www.sapc.edu

South Dakota State University
P.O. Box 2207
Brookings, SD 57007
800-952-3541
www3.sdstate.edu

Southern Illinois University
College of Agricultural Sciences

Carbondale, IL 62901-6899
618-536-4405
www.siu.edu

Southwest Missouri State University
901 S. National Ave.
Springfield, MO 65804
417-836-5000
www.smsu.edu

State University of New York
College of Agriculture and Technology
Cobleskill, NY 12043
518-255-5323
www.cobleskill.edu

Stephens College
1200 E. Broadway
Columbia, MO 65215
800-876-7207
www.stephens.edu

Sul Ross State University
P.O. Box C-114
Alpine, TX 79832
432-837-8011
www.sulross.edu/pages/991.asp

Teikyo Post University
800 Country Club Road
P.O. Box 2540
Waterbury, CT 06723
203-596-4500
www.teikyopost.edu

Texas A&M University
2112 TAMU
College Station, TX 77843
979-845-2211
www.agprogra.tamu.edu

Texas Tech University
2500 Broadway
Lubbock, TX 79409806-742-2011
www.ttu.edu

Tufts University
Medford, MA 02155
617-628-5000
www.tufts.edu

Tuskegee University
College of Agricultural, Environmental and
  Natural Sciences

Tuskegee, AL 36088
334-727-8157
www.tusk.edu

University of Arizona
Education Bldg. 69, Rm. 104
Tucson, AZ 85721-0069
520-621-7621
www.ag.arizona.edu

University of California, Davis
One Shields Ave.
Davis, CA 95616
530-752-0107
www.caes.ucdavis.edu

University of Connecticut
College of Agriculture and Natural Resources
Stoors, CT 06269
860-486-2919
www.canr.uconn.edu

University of Delaware
College of Agriculture and Natural Resources
113 Townsend Hall
Newark, DE 19717
302-831-2501
http://ag.udel.edu

University of Findlay
Equestrian & Pre-Veterinary Studies
1000 Main St.
Findlay, OH 45840
800-472-9502
www.findlay.edu

University of Florida
Gainesville, FL 32611
352-392-3261
www.ufl.edu

University of Georgia
College of Agricultural and Environmental
    Sciences
Tifton, GA 30602
706-542-3000
http://ugacescn.ces.uga.edu/caeshome

University of Illinois
College of Agricultural, Consumer &
    Environmental Studies
Urbana-Champaign, IL 61820

217-333-1000
www.aces.uiuc.edu

University of Kentucky
College of Agriculture
Lexington, KY 40506
859-257-3469
www.ca.uky.edu

University of Louisville
Department of Equine Business
Louisville, KY 40292-0001
502-852-8440
http://cbpa.louisville.edu/eip

University of Maine
College of Natural Sciences, Forestry and
    Agriculture
5782 Winslow Hall
Orono, ME 04469
207-581-3206
www.nsfa.umaine.edu

University of Maryland
Institute of Applied Agriculture—Equine Business
    Management
2115 Jull Hall
College Park, MD 20742
301-405-1000
www.iaa.umd.edu

University of Massachusetts
Amherst, MA 01003
413-545-0111
www.umass.edu

University of Missouri
Columbia, MO 65211
573-882-2121
www.missouri.edu

University of Nevada
1664 N. Virginia St.
Reno, NV 89557
775-784-1110
www.unr.edu/content

University of Rhode Island
Kingston, RI 02881
401-874-1000
www.uri.edu

University of Tennessee
Institute of Agriculture
Knoxville, TN 37996
865-974-1000
www.utk.edu

University of Vermont
College of Agriculture and Life Sciences
Burlington, VT 05405
802-656-3131
www.uvm.edu/cals

University of Wisconsin
College of Agricultural & Life Sciences
140 Agricultural Hall
Madison, WI 53706
608-262-4930
www.cals.wisc.edu

Utah State University
4800 Old Main Hill
Logan, UT 84322
435-797-2215
www.usu.edu

Washington State University
College of Agriculture and Home Economics
P.O. Box 646242
Pullman, WA 99164-1067
509-335-4561
www.cahe.wsa.edu

West Texas A&M University
2501 Fourteenth Ave.
Canyon, TX 79016-0001
806-651-2000
www.wtamu.edu

Wilson College
1015 Philadelphia Ave.
Chambersburg, PA 17201
717-264-4141
www.wilson.edu

Veterinary technology or technician schools with American Veterinary Medical Association accreditation

Alfred State College
Agriculture Science Bldg.
Alfred, NY 14801

607-587-4544
www.alfredstate.edu

Argosy University
1515 Central Pkwy.
Eagan, MN 55121
888-844-2004
www.argosyu.edu

Athens Technical College
800 US Hwy. 29 N.
Athens, GA 30601
706-355-5000
www.athens.tec.ga.us

Baker College of Flint
1050 W. Bristol Road
Flint, MI 48507
810-766-4000
www.baker.edu/visit/flint.html

Baker College of Muskegon
1903 Marquette Ave.
Muskegon, MI 49442
800-937-0337
www.baker.edu/visit/main.html

Becker College
3 Paxton St.
Leicester, MA 01524
877-5BECKER
www.beckercollege.com

Bel-Rea Institute of Animal Technology
1681 S. Dayton St.
Denver, CO 80247
303-751-8700
www.bel-rea.com

Blue Ridge Community College
P.O. Box 80
Weyers Cave, VA 24486
888-750-2722
www.br.cc.va.us

Brevard Community College
1519 Clearlake Road
Cocoa, FL 32922
321-632-1111
www.brevaRoadcc.fl.us

Brigham Young University
Provo, UT 84602

801-378-4636
www.byu.edu

California State Polytechnic University
College of Agriculture
3801 W. Temple Ave.
Pomona, CA 91768
909-869-7659
www.csupomona.edu

Camden County College
P.O. Box 200
Blackwood, NJ 08012
856-227-7200
www.camdencc.edu

Cedar Valley College
3030 N. Dallas Ave.
Lancaster, TX 75134
877-353-3482
http://ollie.dcccd.edu/vettech/default1.htm

Central Carolina Community College
1105 Kelly Dr.
Sanford, NC 27330
800-682-8353
www.ccarolina.cc.nc.us

Colby Community College
1255 S. Range
Colby, KS 67701
785-462-3984
http://Colbycc.org/www/vet/vettech.html

College of Southern Idaho
315 Falls Ave.
Twin Falls, ID 83303-1238
208-733-9554
www.csi.cc.id.us

Colorado Mountain College
Spring Valley Campus
3000 County Road 114
Glenwood Springs, CO 81601
800-621-8559
www.coloradomtn.edu

Columbia State Community College
P.O. Box 1315
Columbia, TN 38401
931-540-2722
www.coscc.cc.tn.us

Columbus State Community College
550 E. Spring St.
Columbus, OH 43216
800-621-6407
www.cscc.edu

Community College of Denver
1070 Alton Way, Bldg. 849
Denver, CO 80230
303-556-2600
www.ccd.rightchoice.org

Cosumnes River College
8401 Center Pkwy.
Sacramento, CA 95823
916-691-7344
www.crc.losrios.edu/

Cuyahooga Community College
700 Carnegie Ave.
Cleveland, OH 44115
800-954-8754
www.tri-c.cc.oh.us

Delaware Technical and Community College
P.O. Box 610, Rt. 18
Georgetown, DE 19947
302-856-5400
www.dtcc.edu

Eastern Wyoming College
3200 W. C St.
Torrington, WY 82240
307-532-8330
http://Ewcweb.ewc.whecn.edu

Essex Campus of the Community College of Baltimore County
7201 Rossville Blvd.
Baltimore, MD 21237
410-780-6313
www.ccbcmd.edu

Fairmont State College
1201 Locust Ave.
Fairmont, WV 26554
304-367-4000
www.fscwv.edu

Foothill College
12345 El Monte Road
Los Altos Hills, CA 94022
650-949-7777
www.foothill.fhda.edu

Fort Valley State University
1005 State University Dr.
Fort Valley, GA 31030
478-825-6344
www.fvsu.edu

Front Range Community College
4616 S. Shields
Ft. Collins, CO 80526
970-226-2500
www.frcc.cc.co.us

Gaston College
201 Hwy. 321 S.
Dallas, NC 28034-1499
704-922-6200
www.gaston.cc.nc.us

Globe College
7166 Tenth St.
Oakdale, MN 55128
1-800-231-0660
www.globecollege.com

Gwinnet Technical College
5150 Sugarloaf Pkwy.
Lawrenceville, GA 30043
770-962-7580
www.gwinnetttechnicalcollege.com

Harcum College
750 Montgomery Ave.
Bryn Mawr, PA 19010-3476
610-525-4100
www.harcum.edu

Hartnell College
156 Homestead Ave.
Salinas, CA 93901
831-755-6700
www.hartnell.cc.ca.us

Hinds Community College
P.O. Box 10461
Raymond, MS 39154
800-HINDSCC
www.hinds.cc.ms.us

Holyoke Community College
303 Homestead Ave.
Holyoke, MA 01040-1099
413-538-7000
www.hcc.mass.edu

Jefferson College
1000 Viking Dr.
Hillsboro, MO 63050
636-797-3000
www.jeffco.edu

Joliet Junior College
1215 Houbolt Road
Joliet, IL 60431
815-729-9020
www.jjc.cc.il.us

Johnson College
3427 N. Main Ave.
Scranton, PA 18508
570-342-6404
www.johnsoncollege.com

Kirkwood Community College
6301 Kirkwood Blvd.
Cedar Rapids, IA 52406
319-398-5517
www.kirkwood.cc.ia.us

La Guardia Community College
The City University of New York
31-10 Thomson Ave.
Long Island City, NY 11101
718-482-7206
www.lagcc.cuny.edu

Lehigh Carbon & Northhampton Community Colleges
4525 Education Park Dr.
Schnecksville, PA 18078
610-799-2121
www.lccc.edu

Lincoln Memorial University
6965 Cumberland Gap Pkwy.
Harrogate, TN 37752
800-325-0900
http://www.lmunet.edu

Los Angeles Pierce College
6201 Winnetka Ave.
Woodland Hills, CA 91371
818-710-4253
www.macrohead.com/rvt

Macomb Community College
14500 E. Twelve Mile Road

Warren, MI 48088
866-622-6624
www.macomb.cc.mi.us

Madison Area Technical College
3550 Anderson
Madison, WI 53704
800-322-6282
www.madison.tec.wi.us/matc

Manor College
700 Fox Chase Road
Jenkintown, PA 19046
215-885-2360
www.manor.edu

Maple Woods Community College
2601 NE Barry Road
Kansas City, MO 64156
816-437-3000
www.kcmetro.edu

Medaille College
18 Agassiz Circle
Buffalo, NY 14214
800-292-1582
www.medaille.edu

Median School of Allied Health Careers
125 Seventh Street
Pittsburgh, PA 15222
800-570-0693
www.medianschool.com

Mercy College
555 Broadway
Dobbs Ferry, NY 10522
800-MERCY-NY
www.mercynet.edu

Miami-Dade Community College
Medical Center Campus
950 NW 20th St.
Miami, Fl 33127
306-237-4141
www.mdcc.edu/medical/aht/vettech

Michigan State University
College of Veterinary Medicine
G100 Vet Med Center
East Lansing, MI 48824
517-355-6509
www.cvn.msu.edu/vettech

Midland College
3600 N. Garfield
Midland, TX 79705
432-685-4500
www.midland.edu

Mt. San Antonio College
1100 N. Grand Ave.
Walnut, CA 91789
909-594-5611
www.mtsac.edu

Morehead State University
Department of Agriculture & Human Sciences
325 Reed Hall
Morehead, KY 40351
606-783-2662
www.morehead-st.edu

Mount Ida College
777 Dedham St.
Newton, MA 02459
617-928-4500
www.mountida.edu

Murray State College
1 Murray Campus
Tishomingo, OK 73460
580-371-2371
www.msc.cc.ok.us

National American University
Allied Health Division
321 Kansas City St.
Rapid City, SD 57701
605-394-4800
www.national.edu/veterinary_tech.html

Nebraska College of Technical Agriculture
RR 3 P.O. Box 23A
Curtis, NE 69025
800-3CURTIS
www.ncta.unl.edu

New Hampshire Community Technical College
277 Portsmouth Ave.
Stratham, NJ 03885-2297
800-522-1194
www.stratham.tec.nh.us

Newberry College
2100 College St.
Newberry, SC 29108

800-845-4955
www.newberry.edu

North Dakota State University
Van Es Laboratories
1301 Twelfth Ave.
Fargo, ND 58105
701-231-7511
www.ndsu.nodak.edu

Northeast Community College
801 E. Benjamin Ave.
Norfolk, NE 68702-0469
402-371-2020
www.northeastcollege.com

Northern New Jersey Consortium for Veterinary Technician Education
400 Paramus Road
Paramus, NJ 07652
201-447-7100
www.bergen.cc.nj.us

Northern Virginia Community College
Loudoun Campus
1000 Harry Flood Byrd Hwy.
Sterling, VA 20164-8699
703-450-2500
www.nv.cc.va.us

Northwest Mississippi Community College
4975 Hwy. 51 N.
Senatobia, MS 38668
662-562-3200
www.northwestms.edu

Northwestern State University of Louisiana
Department of Life Sciences
Natchitoches, LA 71497
800-327-1903
www.nsula.edu

NW Connecticut Community Technical College
Park Place E.
Winsted, CT 06098
860-738-6438
www.nwctc.commnet.edu/vettech

Oklahoma State University
900 N. Portland Ave.
Oklahoma City, OK 73107
405-947-4421
www.osuokc.edu

Palo Alto College
1400 W. Villaret Blvd.
San Antonio, TX 78224-2499
210-208-8000
www.accd.edu

Parkland College
2400 W. Bradley Ave.
Champaign, IL 61821
800-346-8089
www.parkland.cc.il.us

Pierce College at Ft. Steilacoom
9401 Farwest Dr. SW
Lakewood, WA 98498
253-964-6500
www.pierce.ctc.edu

Pima Community College
8181 E. Irvington Road
Tucson, AZ 85709-4000
520-206-4530
www.pima.edu

Portland Community College
P.O. Box 19000
Portland, OR 97219
866-922-1010
www.pcc.edu

Purdue University
School of Veterinary Medicine
615 W. State St.
West Lafayette, IN 47907
765-494-4600
www.vet.purdue.edu/vettech/index.html

Quinnipiac University
275 Mt. Carmel Ave.
Hamden, CT 06518
203-582-8200
www.quinnipiac.edu

Raymond Walters College
9555 Plainfield Road
Blue Ash, OH 45236-1096
513-745-5600
www.rwc.uc.edu

Ridgewater College
2101 Fifteenth Ave. NW
Willmar, MN 56201
320-231-5114
www.ridgewater.mnscu.edu

Snead State Community College
P.O. Box 734
Boaz, AL 35957
256-593-5120
www.snead.cc.al.us

St. Petersburg College
P.O. Box 13489
St. Petersburg, FL 33733
727-341-3653
www.spjc.edu/hec/vettech/vt1.html

State University of New York
College of Technology
Delhi, NY 13753
800-96-DEHLI
www.delhi.edu

Stautzenberger College
5355 Southwyck Blvd.
Toledo, OH 43614
800-552-5099
www.stautzen.com

Suffolk County Community College
Western Campus
Crooked Hill Road516-451-4110
Brentwood, NY 11717
www.sunysuffolk.edu/About/

Sul Ross State University
School of Agriculture & Natural Resource Science
P.O. Box C-114
Alpine, TX 79832
432-837-8011
www.sulross.edu/pages/991.asp

Tomball College
30555 Tomball Pkwy
Tomball, TX 77375-4036
281-351-3300
wwwtc.nhmccd.edu

Tri-County Technical College
P.O. Box 587
Pendleton, SC 29670
864-646-8361
www.tctc.edu

Trident Technical College
1001 South Live Oak Dr.
Moncks Corner, SC 29461

843-574-6111
www.tridenttech.edu

Tulsa Community College
7505 W. 41st St.
Tulsa, OK 74107
918-585-7000
www.tulsa.cc.ok.us

University of Maine at Augusta
85 Texas Ave., 217 Belfast Hall
Bangor, ME 04401-4367
207-262-7800
www.uma.maine.edu/bangor

University of Puerto Rico
Medical Sciences Campus
P.O. Box 365067
San Juan, PR 00936-5067
787-765-2363
http://medweb.rcm.upr.edu

Vatterott College
225 N. 80th St.
Omaha, NE 68114402-392-1300
www.vatterott-college.com

Vermont Technical College
Veterinary Technology Program
Randolph Center, VT 05061
802-728-1000
www.vtc.vsc.edu

Wayne County Community College
c/o Wayne State University
Div. of Laboratory Animal Resources
5901 Conner
Detroit, MI 48213
313-922-3311
www.wccc.edu

Wilson College
1015 Philadelphia Ave.
Chambersburg, PA 17201
800-421-8402
www.wilson.edu

Yakima Valley Community College
P.O. Box 22520
Yakima, WA 98907-2520
509-574-4600
www.yvcc.cc.wa.us

Yuba College
2088 N. Beale Road
Marysville, CA 95901
530-741-6700
www.yuba.cc.ca.us

United States veterinary schools

Auburn University
College of Veterinary Medicine
Auburn University, AL 36849
334-844-4546
www.vetmed.auburn.edu

Colorado State University
College of Veterinary Medicine & Biomedical
   Sciences
1601 Campus Delivery
Fort Collins, CO 80523-1601
970-491-7051
www.cvmbs.colostate.edu

Cornell University
College of Veterinary Medicine
Ithaca, NY 14853
607-253-3000
www.vet.cornell.edu

Iowa State University
College of Veterinary Medicine
Chirstensen Dr.
Ames, IA 50011
515-294-1242
www.vetmed.iastate.edu

Kansas State University
College of Veterinary Medicine
101 Trotter Hall
Manhattan, KS 66506
785-532-4335
www.vet.ksu.edu

Louisiana State University
School of Veterinary Medicine
Skip Bertman Dr.
Baton Rouge, LA 70803
225-578-9900
www.vetmed.lsu.edu

Michigan State University
College of Veterinary Medicine

Office of the Dean
G100 Vet Med Center
East Lansing, MI 48824
517-355-6509
www.cvm.msu.edu

Mississippi State University
College of Veterinary Medicine
Office of the Dean
P.O. Box 9825
Mississippi State, MS 39762-9825
662-325-1131
www.cvm.msstate.edu

North Carolina State University
4700 Hillsborough St.
Raleigh, NC 27606
919-513-6212
www.cvm.ncsu.edu

Ohio State University
College of Veterinary Medicine
1900 Coffey Road
Columbus, OH 43210
614-292-1171
www.vet.ohio-state.edu

Oklahoma State University
Veterinary Medicine
110 McElroy Hall
Stillwater, OK 74078
405-744-6653
www.cvm.okstate.edu

Oregon State University
College of Veterinary Medicine
Oregon State University
200 Magruder Hall
Corvallis, OR 97331-4801
541-737-2098
www.vet.orst.edu

Purdue University
School of Veterinary Medicine
1240 Lynn Hall, Rm.1176
West Lafayette, IN 47907
800-213-2859
www.vet.purdue.edu

Texas A&M University
College of Veterinary Medicine
Suite 101—VMA
College Station, TX 77843

979-845-5051
www.cvm.tamu.edu

Tufts University
School of Veterinary Medicine
North Grafton, MA 01536
508-839-5302
www.tufts.edu/vet

Tuskegee University
College of Veterinary Medicine, Nursing & Allied
　　Health
Tuskegee, AL 36088
334-727-8174
www.tusk.edu/Global/category.asp

University of California, Davis
School of Veterinary Medicine
Office of the Dean
One Shields Ave.
Davis, CA 95616
530-752-1360
www.vetmed.ucdavis.edu

University of Florida
The College of Veterinary Medicine
Campus Box 10012
Gainesville, FL 32610
352-392-4700
www.vetmed.ufl.edu

University of Georgia
The College of Veterinary Medicine
Athens, GA 30602
706-542-5728
www.vet.uga.edu

University of Illinois at Urbana-Champaign
College of Veterinary Medicine
3503 Veterinary Medicine Basic Sciences Bldg.
2001 S. Lincoln Ave.
Urbana, IL 61801
217-333-2760
www.cvm.uiuc.edu

University of Minnesota
College of Veterinary Medicine
1365 Gortner Ave.
St. Paul, MN 55108
612-624-4747
www.ahc.umn.edu/ahc_content/colleges/vetmed

University of Missouri-Columbia
W-203 Veterinary Medicine Bldg.
Columbia, MO 65211
573-884-5044
www.cvm.missouri.edu

University of Pennsylvania
School of Veterinary Medicine
3800 Spruce St.
Philadelphia, PA 19104
215-898-5434
www.vet.upenn.edu

University of Tennessee
College of Veterinary Medicine
2407 River Dr.
Knoxville, TN 37996
865-974-VETS
www.vet.utk.edu

University of Wisconsin
School of Veterinary Medicine
2015 Linden Dr.
Madison, WI 53706
608-263-2525
www.vetmed.wisc.edu

Virginia Tech and University of Maryland
Virginia-Maryland Regional College of Veterinary
　　Medicine
Duck Pond Drive (0442)
Blacksburg, VA 24061
540-231-7666
www.vetmed.vt.edu

Washington State University
College of Veterinary Medicine
Pullman, WA 99164
509-335-9515
www.vetmed.wsu.edu

Western University of Health Sciences
College of Veterinary Medicine
Admissions Office, 309 E. 2nd St.
Pomona, CA 91766
909-623-6116
www.westernu.edu/cvm.html

Non-U.S. veterinary schools with American Veterinary Medical Association accreditation

Massey University
Institute of Veterinary, Animal and Biomedical
    Sciences
College of Sciences
Private Bag 11-222
Palmerston North
New Zealand
64-6-350-4219
http://lvabs.massey.ac.nz

Murdoch University
Division of Veterinary and Biomedical Sciences
South St.
Murdoch 6150
West Australia
61-08-9360-6000
wwwvet.murdoch.edu.au

Ontario Veterinary College
University of Guelph
Guelph, ON N1G 2W1
Canada
519-824-4120
www.ovcnet.uoguelph.ca

State University of Utrecht
Faculty of Veterinary Medicine
P.O. Box 80163
3508 TD Utrecht
The Netherlands
31-30-253-4851
www.vet.uu.nl

University of Edinburgh
Faculty of Veterinary Medicine
The Royal (Dick) School of Veterinary Studies
Summerhall, Edinburg EH9 1QH
Scotland
44-0-131-650-6130
www.vet.ed.ac.uk

University of Glasgow
Veterinary School
Bearsden Road, Glasgow G61 1QH
Scotland
44-0-141-330-5777
www.gla.ac.uk

University of London
The Royal Veterinary College
London, England NW1 0UT
44-0-170-166-6333
www.rvc.ac.uk

University of Montreal
Faculty of Veterinary Medicine
3200 Sicotte St.
Saint-Hyacinthe, QC J2S 7C6
Canada
450-773-8521
www.umontreal.ca/ang

University of Prince Edward Island
Atlantic Veterinary College
550 University Ave.
Charlottetown, Prince Edward Island C1A 4P3
Canada
902-566-0882
www.upei.ca/~avc

University of Saskatchewan
Western College of Veterinary Medicine
52 Campus Dr.
Saskatoon, Saskatchewan, Canada S7N 5B4
306-966-7447
www.usask.ca/wcvm

Land grant colleges and universities

Alabama A&M University
Alcorn State University
Auburn University
Clemson University
College of Agriculture
College of Tropical Agriculture and Human
    Resources
Colorado State University
Delaware State University
Diné College, Arizona (formerly Navajo
    Community College)
Florida A&M University
Fort Valley State University
Haskell Indian Nations University
Iowa State University
Kansas State University
Kentucky State University
Langston University
Lincoln University
Louisiana State University
Louisiana State University Agricultural Center
Michigan State University
Mississippi State University
Montana State University—Bozeman
Montana Tribal Colleges
Nebraska Indian Community College
New Mexico State University

New Mexico Tribal Colleges
North Carolina A&T University
North Carolina State University
North Dakota State University
North Dakota Tribal Colleges
Northwest Indian College
Oklahoma State University
Oregon State University
Penn State University
Prairie View A&M University
Purdue University
Rutgers State University
South Carolina State University
South Dakota State University
South Dakota Tribal Colleges
Tennessee State University
Texas A&M University
Tuskegee University
Southern University and A&M College
University of Alaska—Fairbanks
University of Arizona
University of Arkansas
University of Arkansas Pine Bluff
University of California—Berkeley
University of California—Davis
University of California—Riverside
University of Connecticut
University of Delaware
University of the District of Columbia.
University of Florida
University of Georgia
University of Hawaii
University of Idaho
University of Illinois
University of Kentucky
University of Maine
University of Maryland
University of Maryland Eastern Shore
University of Massachusetts
University of Minnesota
University of Missouri
University of Nebraska—Lincoln
University of Nevada—Reno
University of New Hampshire
University of Rhode Island
University of Tennessee
University of Vermont
University of Wisconsin—Madison
University of Wyoming
Utah State University
Virginia Polytechnic Institute and State University
Virginia State University

Washington State University
West Virginia State College
West Virginia University
Wisconsin Tribal Colleges
Yale University, Connecticut

Colleges in the U.S. Territories

American Samoa Community College
College of Micronesia—Kolonia
Northern Marianas College
University of Guam
University of the Virgin Islands

Schools teaching specialties and trades

Dentistry

Academy of Equine Dentistry
P.O. Box 999
Glenns Ferry, ID 83623
208-366-2550
www.horsedentistry.com

The American School of Equine Dentistry
P.O. Box 126
Brunswick, MD 21716
540-668-6505
www.amscheqdentistry.com

Farriery

American Master Farrier School
415 Hazzard St.
Milton, DE 19968
302-684-1747

American School of Equine Services
6710 Sage Ct.
Adamstown, MD 21710

Auburn Horseshoeing School
770 Lee Road, Suite191
Auburn, AL 36830
334-502-4007

Butler Graduate Farrier Training
P.O. Box 1390
Laporte, CO 80535
970-221-2834

C.S. Mott Community College
1401 E. Court St., Suite 1117
Flint, MI 48503
810-762-0200
www.mcc.edu/indexmain.shtml

Cal Poly San Luis Obispo
Extended Education—Horseshoeing Unit
San Luis Obispo, CA 93407
805-756-2419
www.animalscience.calpoly.edu/areas_of_study/eq
    uine/eq_overview.html

Casey & Son Horseshoeing School
14013 E. Hwy. 136
La Fayette, GA 30728
706-397-8909
www.caseyhorseshoeing.com

Colorado School of Trades
1575 Hoyt St.
Lakewood, CO 80215-2996
800-234-4594
www.horse-horseshoeing.com

Colorado State University
Equine Sciences Dept.
Fort Collins, CO 80523
970-491-8373
http://equinescience.colostate.edu

Cornell University
Cornell University Farrier Short Course
Ithaca, New York 14853
607-253-3127
www.vet.cornell.edu/hospital/farrier.htm

Cowtown Horseshoeing School
P.O. Box 481
S. Sunday Creek
Miles City, MT 59301
406-232-3362

Danny Ward's Horseshoeing School
51 Ward Road
Martinsville, VA 24114
276-638-1908

Dawson Community College
P.O. Box 421
300 College Dr.
Glendive, MT 59330
800-821-8320
www.dawson.cc.mt.us

East Texas Horseshoeing Clinics
Rt. 4, P.O. Box 731
Atlanta, TX 75551
903-796-9308
www.angelfire.com/in2/eth/index.html

Eastern School of Farrier Science
P.O. Box 1368
50 Ward Road
Martinsville, VA 24112
276-638-1908

Ellsworth Community College
1100 College Ave.
Iowa Falls, IA 50126
800-322-9235
www.iavalley.cc.ia.us/ecc

Equine Educational Services
P.O. Box 413, Dept. HS
O'Fallon, IL 62269

Equine Research Center
50 McGilvray St.
Guelph, ON N1G 2W1, Canada
519-824-4120
www.erc.on.ca/new_home

Fairview College
Equine Studies
P.O. Box 3000
Fairview, AB T0H 1L0, Canada
780-835-6600
www.fairviewc.ab.ca/programs/equine

Far Hills Forge
7 Timberline Road
Asbury, 08802
908-537-9041
www.horseshoes.com/supplies/alphabet/farhills-
    forge/pages

Feather River College
570 Golden Eagle Ave.
Quincy, CA 95971
800-442-9799
www.frcc.cc.ca.us

Heartland Horseshoeing School
327 SW 1st Lane
Lamar, MO 64759
417-682-6896
www.mofoxtrot.com/heartland

Hill Country Horseshoeing School
257 Camino Real
Kerrville, TX 78028
888-806-3330
www.hillcountryhorseshoeingschool.com

Indian River Community College
Dixon Hendry Campus
2229 NW 9th Ave.
Okeechobee, FL 34972
863-763-8017
www.ircc.cc.fl.us/atircc/welcome/dixonhendry.html

Kentucky Horseshoeing School
P.O. Box 120, Hwy. 53
Mount Eden, KY 40046
502-738-5257
www.kyhorseshoeing.com

Kwantlen College, Langley Campus
P.O. Box 9030
Surrey, BC V3W 2M8, Canada
604-599-2100
www.kwantlen.bc.ca/calendar/farrprg.html

Lamar Community College
2401 S. Main St.
Lamor, CO 81052
719-336-2248
www.lcc.cccoes.edu/contact/Home.htm

Laramie County Community College
1400 E. College Dr.
Cheyenne, WY 82007
800-522-2993
www.lccc.cc.wy.us

Linn-Benton Community College Farrier School
6500 SW Pacific Blvd.
Albany, OR 97321
541-917-4811
www.linnbenton.edu/programs

Lookout Mountain School of Horseshoeing
400 Lewis Road
Gadsen, AL 35904
256-546-2036
www.horseshoeingschool.com

Maritime Horseshoeing School, Ltd.
RR1, Westville
Pictou County, NS B0K 2A0, Canada

Maryland Horseshoeing School
11200 Wolfsville Road
Smithsburg, MD 21783
301-416-0800
www.lrn2shoe.com

Merced College
School of Farriery
3600 M St.
Merced, CA 95348-2898209-384-6000
www.merced.cc.ca.us/academics/index.html

Meredith Manor International Equestrian Center
Rte. 1, P.O. Box 66
Waverly, WV 26184
800-679-2603
www.meredithmanor.com

Mesa Technical College
911 S. 10th St.
Tucumcari, NM 88401
505-461-4413
www.mesatc.cc.nm.us

Midwest Horseshoeing School
2312 South Maple Ave.
Macomb, IL 61455
309-833-4063
www.centaur.org/mhs

Minnesota School of Horseshoeing
6250 Riverdale Dr. NW
Ramsey, MN 55303
763-427-5850
www.horseshoes.com/schools/minnesota/home-page.htm

Mission Farrier School
4404 Two Hundred-Sixtieth Ave. NE
Redmond, WA 98053
425-898-7757

Montana State University Horseshoeing School
Dept. of Animal & Range Sciences
P.O. Box 172900
Bozeman, MT 59717-2900
406-994-3721
http://animalrange.montana.edu/horseshoe.htm

New England School of Horseshoeing
4 Dresser Hill Road
Charlton, MA 01507
508-248-6145

North Carolina School of Horseshoeing & Lameness
1165 Oberby Road
Walnut Cove NC 27052
307-754-6601

Northwest College
231 W.6th St.
Powell, WY 82435
307-754-6000

Northwest Community College
P.O. Box 1277
Houston, BC V0J 1Z0, Canada
877-277-2288
www.nwcc.bc.ca

Northwest School of Horseshoeing
Rte. 2, P.O. Box 232A
Walla Walla, WA 99362

Oklahoma Farriers College, Inc.
Rte. 2, P.O. Box 88
Sperry, OK 74073
918-288-7221

Oklahoma Horseshoeing School
26446 Horseshoe Circle
Purcell, OK 73080
800 538 1383
www.horseshoes.com/schools/okschool/contents/contents.htm

Oklahoma State Horseshoeing School
Rte. 1, P.O. Box 28-B
Ardmore, OK 73401800-634-2811

Olds College
4500-50 St.
Olds, AB T4H 1R6
Canada
800-661-6537
www.oldscollege.ca/careers/programs/AdvancedFarrier.asp

Pacific Coast Horseshoeing School
9625 Florin Road
Sacramento, CA 95829-1009
916-366-6064
www.farrierschool.com

Pikes Peak Community College
P.O. Box 17

Colorado Springs, CO 80906-5498
800-456-6847
www.ppcc.cccoes.edu

ShurShod Horseshoeing School
P.O. Box 119
Cimarron, KS 67835
417-462-7848
www.horseshoes.com/schools/shurshod/home-page.htm

Sierra Horseshoelng School
Rte. 2, P.O. Box 22-B
Bishop, CA 93514
760-872-1279
www.sierrahorseshoeing.com

Sul Ross State University
Range Animal Science Center
P.O. Box C-11
Alpine, TX 79832
432-837-8011
www.sulross.edu/pages/991.asp

Tennessee State Blacksmith & Farrier School
3780 Shepardsville Hwy.
Bloomington Springs, TN 38545
931-653-4341
http://tsbfs.com/founder.html

Tucson School of Horseshoeing
2230 N. Kimberlee Road
Tucson, AZ 85749
800-657-2779
www.tucsonhorseshoeing.com

Turley Forge Blacksmithing School
919A Chicoma Vista
Santa Fe, New Mexico 87507
505-471-8608

Victory Mountain Forge Farrier School
9163 E. Merrick Road
Lava Hot Springs, ID 83246
208-776-9825

Village Farrier Hoof Care School
51566 Range Road, Suite 223
Sherwood Park, AV T8C 1H4, Canada

Walla Walla Community College
500 Tausick Way

Walla Walla, WA 98362
509-522-2500
www.wallawalla.cc

Western's School of Horseshoeing
2801 W. Maryland Ave.
Phoenix, AZ 85017-1204
602-242-2560

Wolverine Farrier School
3104 E. Stevenson Lake Road
Clare, MI 48617
www.wfschool.com

Massage Therapy

Aspen Equine Studies Inc.
5821 County Road 331
Silt, CO. 81652
970-876-5839
www.equinemassageschool.com

D'Arcy School of Equine Massage
627 Maitland St.
London, Ontario N5Y 2V7
Canada
519-673-4420
www.serix.com/~darcyinc/home.htm

Don Doran's Equine Sports Massage Programs
9791 NW 160th St.
Reddick, FL 32686
352-591-4735
www.equinesportsmassage.com

Equissage
P.O. Box 447
Round Hill, VA 20142
800-843-0224
www.equissage.com

EquiTouch Systems
P.O. Box 7701
Loveland, CO 80537
800-483-0577
www.equitouch.net

Full Circle School of Alternative Therapies
P.O. Box 989
Corvallis, MT 59828
877-926-6210
www.fullcircleschool.com

Geary Whiting's Equine Massage School
P.O. Box 435
Douglas City, CA 96024
530-623-6485
www.gearywhiting.com

Racing

Hawkeye Hill Racing School
Rt. 1, P.O. Box 382
Commiskey, IN 47227

Paradise Ranch Racing School
Equestrian Center "C"
382200 Paradise Ranch Road
Castaic, CA 91384

Therapuetic Riding

Cheff Therapuetic Riding Center
8450 N. 43rd St.
Augusta, MI 49012
269-731-4471
www.cheffcenter.com

Equine homestudy schools

Aspen Equine Studies, Inc.
Equine Massage
5821 County Road 331
Silt, CO 81652
www.equinemassageschool.com

Equine Education Institute
Farriery
P.O. Box 68
Ringwood, IL 60072
815-653-2382
www.horseshoes.com/supplies/alphabet/
    equineeducationinstitute

Global Equine Academy
P.O. Box 205
Beulah, WY 82712
307-283-2587
www.globalequineacademy.com

New Horizons Equine Education Center
425 Red Mountain Road
Livermore, CO 80536-9998
970-484-9207
www.newhorizonsequine.com

Penzance Equine Solutions
200 South St.
Douglas, MA 01516
508-476-1317
www.kersur.net/~santa

Professional Career Development Institute
430 Technology Pkwy.
Norcross, GA 30092-3406
800-223-4542
http://www.pcdi-homestudy.com

Intercollegiate Horse Show Association Colleges & Universities

Zone 1
Region 1
Brown University
Connecticut College
Johnson & Wales University
Roger Williams University
Teikyo Post
Trinity College
University of Connecticut
University of Rhode Island
Wesleyan University
Region 2
Bates College
Bowdoin College
Colby College
Dartmouth College
Middlebury College
Mount Ida College
University of Maine at Orono
University of New Hampshire
University of Vermont
Region 3
Amherst College
Becker College
Clark University
College of the Holy Cross
Elms College
Landmark College
Massachusetts College of Liberal Arts
Mount Holyoke College
Smith College
Springfield College
University of Massachusetts/Amherst
Westfield State College
Williams College

Region 4
Boston University
Endicott College
Framingham State College
Harvard University
Massachusetts Institute of Technology
Stonehill College
Tufts University
University of Massachusetts Dartmouth
Wellesley College
Wheaton College

Zone 2
Region 1
Centenary College
College of Saint Elizabeth
Columbia University
Drew University
Manhattanville College
Marist College
New York University
Pace University
Sarah Lawrence College
State University of New York, New Paltz
The Cooper Union
United States Military Academy
Vassar College
William Paterson University
Region 2
Alfred University
Cazenovia College
Nazareth College of Rochester
Rochester Institute of Technology
St. Lawrence University
State University of New York at Geneseo
State University of New York at Oswego
Syracuse University
University of Ottawa
University of Rochester
Region 3
Binghamton University
Colgate University
Cornell University
Hartwick College
Ithaca College
Rensselaer Polytechnic Institute
Siena College
Skidmore College
State University of New York, Morrisville
State University of New York, Cobleskill
State University of New York, Morrisville

Zone 3

Region 1

Dowling College
Fairfield University
Hofstra University
Long Island University
Molloy College
Nassau Community College
Sacred Heart University
St. Johns University
St. Josephs College
Stony Brook University
Yale University

Region 2

Arcadia University
Bryn Mawr College
Bucks County Community College
Delaware Valley College
Franklin and Marshall College
Gettysburg College
Haverford College
Rider University
Temple University
University of Delaware
University of Pennsylvania
Washington College

Region 3

Allegheny College
California University of Pennsylvania
Dickinson College
Duquesne College
Edinboro University of Pennsylvania
Indiana University of Pennsylvania
Juniata College
Pennsylvania State University
Pennsylvania State University—Fayette Campus
Seton Hill University
Slippery Rock University
The University of Pittsburgh
Washington and Jefferson College
West Virginia University
Westminster College
Wilson College

Region 4

Bloomsburg University
Bucknell University
Cedar Crest College
DeSales University
East Stroudsburg University
Kutztown University
Lehigh University
Princeton University

Rutgers University
University of Scranton

Zone 4

Region 1

Christopher Newport University
College of William and Mary
Goucher College
Hood College
Johns Hopkins University
Mary Washington College
Mount Saint Mary's College
St. Mary's College of Maryland
Sweet Brian College
University of Maryland
University of Richmond

Region 2

Bridgewater College
Hollins University
James Madison University
Longwood University
Lynchburg College
Radford University
Randolph-Macon Woman's College
University of Virginia
Washington and Lee University

Region 3

Appalachian State University
Duke University
Elon University
North Carolina State University
St. Andrews Presbyterian College
University of North Carolina at Chapel Hill
University of North Carolina at Greensboro
Virginia Intermont College
Virginia Tech
Wake Forest University
Western Carolina University

Zone 5

Region 1

Maryville College
Middle Tennessee State University
Mississippi State University
Murray State University
Rhodes College
Tennessee Tech University
University of Tennessee, Knoxville
University of Tennessee, Martin
University of the South
Vanderbilt University
Western Kentucky University

Region 2

Anderson College
Auburn University
Augusta State University
Berry College
Clemson University
Converse College
Erskine College
Judson College
Lander College
Presbyterian College
University of Georgia
University of South Carolina
Wallace State College

Region 3

College of Charleston
Emory University
Florida State University
Georgia Institute of Technology
Georgia Southern University
Georgia State University
Rollins College
Savannah College of Art and Design
University of Miami
University of Florida
Wesleyan College

Zone 6

Region 1

Denison University
Hiram College
Kent State University
Kenyon College
Lake Erie College
Oberlin College
Ohio University
Salem International University
The Ohio State University
University of Akron

Region 2

Miami University
Midway College
Morehead State University
Ohio University Southern
University of Cincinnati
University of Kentucky
University of Louisville
Wilmington College

Region 3

Grand Valley State University
Hillsdale College
Michigan State University
Ohio Wesleyan University

Otterbein College
Saginaw Valley State University
University of Findlay
University of Michigan
Western Michigan University
Virginia Intermont College
Virginia Tech
Wake Forest University
Western Carolina University

Zone 7

Region 1

Colby Community College
Colorado College
Colorado State University
Laramie County Community College
Nebraska College of Technical Agriculture
New Mexico State University
United States Air Force Academy
University of Colorado at Boulder
University of Denver
University of Wyoming

Region 2

Louisiana State University
North Central Texas College
Oklahoma State University
Southeastern Oklahoma State University
Stephen F. Austin State University
Sul Ross State University
Tarleton State University
Texas A& M University
Texas A & M University-Corpus Christi
Texas Tech University
University of Texas at Austin
West Texas A&M University

Zone 8

Region 1

Bakersfield College
California State University, San Luis Obispo
College of the Sequoias
Fresno State
Stanford University
University of California, Davis
University of California, Santa Cruz
University of Nevada, Reno

Region 2

California State University Pomona
Mt. San Antonio College
Pepperdine University
The University of San Diego
University of California, San Diego
University of Southern California

Region 3
College of Southern Idaho
Montana State University, Bozeman
University of Montana
University of Montana Western
Utah State University
Region 4
Linn Benton Community College
Oregon State University
Seattle University
University of Oregon
University of Washington
Washington State University

Zone 9

Region 1
Ball State University
Butler University
Earlham College
Indiana University
Indiana University-Purdue University Indianapolis
Northwestern University
Parkland
Purdue University
Saint Mary-of-the-Woods College
Taylor University
University of Illinois
University of Notre Dame
Region 2
Black Hawk College
Illinois Wesleyan University
Iowa State University
Kansas State University
Northern Illinois University
Southern Illinois University at Carbondale
Southwest Missouri State University
Truman State University
Region 3
Carleton College
Ellsworth Community College
Gustavus Adolphus College
Saint Cloud State University
South Dakota State University
Southeast Community College
University of Minnesota, Crookston
University of Nebraska
University of Wisconsin, Madison
University of Wisconsin, River Falls

United States Polo Association member schools

California
California Poly Polo Club, San Luis Obispo

Santa Barbara Community College, Santa Barbara
Stanford University Polo Club, Stanford
University of California, Davis
University of California, Santa Barbara
University of Southern California, Los Angeles
Colorado
Colorado State University Polo Club, Ft. Collins
Connecticut
University of Connecticut Polo Club, Storrs
Yale Polo & Equestrian Center, New Haven
Georgia
University of Georgia, Monroe
Indiana
Culver Academies Polo Club, Culver
Purdue Intercollegiate Polo Club, West Lafayette
Maryland
Garrison Forest School Polo Club, Garrison
Michigan
Michigan State University Polo Club, East Lansing
New Mexico
New Mexico State University, Las Cruces
New York
Cornell Polo Club, Ithaca
Skidmore College Polo Club, Saratoga Springs
Ohio
Ohio State University Polo Club, Columbus
Oklahoma
University of Oklahoma Polo Club, Norman
Oregon
Oregon State University Polo Club, Corvallis
Pennsylvania
Valley Forge Military Academy Polo Club, Wayne
Texas
Texas A&M University Polo Club, College Station
Texas Tech Polo Club, Lubbock
University of Texas Polo, Austin
Virginia
University of Virginia Polo Club, Charlottesville
Washington
Washington State University Polo Club, Pullman
Washington, D.C.
Georgetown University Polo Club, Washington

National Intercollegiate Rodeo Association schools

Big Sky Region
Dawson Community College
Miles Community College
Montana State University
Montana State University, Northern
Northwest College
University of Montana

University of Montana, Western

Central Plains Region

Bacone College

Colby Community College

Connors State College

Dodge City Community College

Eastern Oklahoma State College

Fort Hays State University

Fort Scott Community College

Garden City Community College

Kansas State University

Murray State College

Northwest Missouri State University

Northwestern Oklahoma State University

Oklahoma State University

Panhandle State University

Pratt Community College

Rogers State College

Southeastern Oklahoma State University

Southwestern Oklahoma State University

Western Oklahoma State College

Central Rocky Mountains Region

Casper College

Central Wyoming College

Chadron State College

Colorado State University

Eastern Wyoming College

Lamar Community College

Laramie County Community College

Mesa State College

Northeastern Junior College

Sheridan College

University of Colorado

University of Southern Colorado

University of Wyoming

Great Plains Region

Black Hills State University

Dakota Wesleyan University

Dickinson State University

Iowa State University

Lake Area Technical Institute

Mitchell Technical Institute

National American University

Nebraska College of Technical Agriculture

North Dakota State University

Northeast Community College

South Dakota State University

University of Minnesota, Crookston

University of Nebraska, Lincoln

University of Wisconsin, River Falls

Western Dakota Technical Institute

Grand Canyon Region

Central Arizona College

Cochise Community College

Dine Community College

New Mexico State University

Northland Pioneer College

Pima Community College

Scottsdale Community College

University of Arizona

University of New Mexico

Northwest Region

Blue Mountain Community College

Central Washington University

Columbia Basin College

Eastern Oregon University

Lewis-Clark State College

Southern Oregon University

Spokane Community College

Treasure Valley Community College

University of Idaho

Walla Walla Community College

Washington State University

Ozark Region

Abraham Baldwin Agricultural College

Arkansas State University

East Central Community College

Faulkner State Community College

Michigan State University

Missouri Valley College

Murray State University

Northwest MS Community College

Southern Arkansas University

Southwest Missouri State University

Troy State University

University of Tennessee, Martin

University of West Alabama

Rocky Mountain Region

Boise State University

College of Eastern Utah

College of Southern Idaho

Dixie College

Great Basin College

Idaho State University

Rick's College

Salt Lake Community College

Snow College

Southern Utah University

Southern Utah State University

Utah State University

Utah State University, Uintah Basin

Utah Valley State College

Weber State University

Southern Region

Alvin Community College

Angelina College

Hill College
McNeese State University
North Central Texas College
Northeast Texas Community College
Northwestern State University
Prairie View A&M University
Sam Houston State University
Southwest Texas Junior College
Southwest Texas State University
Stephen F. Austin State University
Texas A&M University, College Station
Texas A&M University, Kingsville
Tyler Junior College
Wharton County Junior College
Southwest Region
Angelo State University
Cisco Junior College
Eastern New Mexico University
Frank Phillips Junior College
Hardin-Simmons University
Howard County Junior College
Mesalands Community College
New Mexico Junior College
Odessa College
South Plains College
Sul Ross State University
Tarleton State University
Texas Technical University, Lubbock
Vernon Regional Junior College
Weatherford College
West Texas A&M University
Western Texas College
West Coast Region
Cal Poly State University, Pomona
Cal Poly State University, San Luis Obispo
California State Fresno
Lassen College
Pierce College
University of Nevada, Las Vegas
West Hills College

APPENDIX L
SHOW AND SPORT
ORGANIZATIONS

American Driving Society
2324 Clark Road
Lapeer, MI 48446
810-664-8666
www.americandrivingsociety.org

American Endurance Ride Conference
11960 Heritage Oak Pl., Suite 9
Auburn, CA 95603
866-271-AERC
www.aerc.org

American Hunter and Jumper Foundation
335 Lancaster St.
P.O. Box 369
West Boylston, MA 01583-0369
508-835-8813
www.ryegate.com/AHJF/ahjf.htm

American Morgan Horse Association, Inc.
P.O. Box 960
Shelburne, VT 05482-0960
802-985-49440
www.morganhorse.com

American Paint Horse Association
P.O. Box 961023
Fort Worth, TX 76161-0023
817-834-2742
www.apha.com

American Quarter Horse Association
P.O. Box 200
Amarillo, TX 79168-0001
806-376-4811
www.aqha.org

American Royal Association
1701 American Royal Ct.
Kansas City, MO 64102-1097
816-221-9800

American Saddlebred Grand National
4093 Iron Works Pkwy.
Lexington, KY 40511-8434
859-259-2742
www.saddlebred.com/Prizes/asgn.html

American Vaulting Association
One Liberty Road
Petaluma, CA 94952
707-953-8821
www.americanvaulting.org

American Warmblood Society
2 Buffalo Run Road
Center Ridge, AR 72027-8347
209-245-3565
www.americanwarmblood.org

Appaloosa Horse Club, Inc.
2720 W. Pullman Road
Moscow, ID 83843-0903
208-882-5578
www.appaloosa.com

The Augusta Futurity
Atlantic Coast Cutting Horse Association
P.O. Box 936
Augusta, GA 30903-0936
706-823-3417
www.augustafuturity.com

Barrel Futurities of America, Inc.
4701 Parsons Road
Springdale, AR 72764-0227
479-756-9524
www.barrelfuturitiesofamerica.com

Cal-Western Appaloosa Show Horse Association, Inc.
P.O. Box 10908
San Bernardino, CA 92423-0908
909-794-0022
www.cal-westernappaloosa.com

The Carriage Association of America, Inc.
177 Pointers-Auburn Road
Salem, NJ 08079-4312
856-935-1616
www.caaonline.com

Del Mar National Horse Show
2260 Jimmy Durante Blvd.
Del Mar, CA 92014-2216
858-755-1161
www.sdfair.com

Gladstone Equestrian Association
P.O. Box 119
Gladstone, NJ 07934-0119
908-234-0151
www.gladstonedriving.com

Houston Livestock Show & Rodeo
P.O. Box 20070
Houston, TX 77225-0070
832-667-1000
www.rodeohouston.com

Intercollegiate Horse Show Association
Smoke Run Farm

P.O. Box 741
Stony Brook, NY 11790-0741
www.ihsa.com

International Arabian Horse Association
10805 E. Bethany Dr.
Aurora, CO 80014-2605
303-696-4500
www.iaha.com

International Buckskin Horse Association
P.O. Box 268 Shelby, IN 46377-0268
219-552-1013
www.ibha.net

International Equestrian Drill Team Alliance
483 SW Leona Dr.
Port St. Lucie, FL 34953-6052
877-838-8509
www.iedta.org

International Hunter Futurity
P.O. Box 13244
Lexington, KY 40583-3244
800-852-1162
www.inthf.org

International Livestock Exposition & Wild West Show
209 Bruns Lane
Springfield, IL 62702-4612
217-787-4653
www.theexpo.org

The International Side-Saddle Organization
90 Cumberland Ave.
Estell Manor, NJ 08319
609-476-2976
www.sidesaddle.com

Masters of Foxhounds Association of America
P.O. Box 363
Millwood, VA 22646
540-955-5680
www.mfha.com

National Barrel Horse Association
P.O. Box 1988
Augusta, GA 30903-1988
706-722-7223
www.NBHA.com

National Cutting Horse Association
260 Bailey Ave.
Fort Worth, TX 76107
817-244-6188
www.nchacutting.com

National Horse Show Commission
P.O. Box 167
Shelbyville, TN 37162

The National Hunter and Jumper Association
P.O. Box 1015
Riverside, CT 06878-1015
203-869-1225
www.nhja.com

National Reined Cow Horse Association
13181 U.S. Hwy 177
Byars, OK 74831
580-759-4949
www.nrcha.com

National Reining Horse Association
3000 NW 10th St.
Oklahoma City, OK 73107-5302
405-946-7400
www.nrha.com

National Snaffle Bit Association
4815 S. Sheridan, Suite 109
Tulsa, OK 74145
918-270-1469
www.nsba.com

National Western Stock Show
4655 Humboldt St.
Denver, CO 80216-2818
303-297-1166
www.nationalwestern.com

North American Riding For the Handicapped Association
P.O. Box 33150
Denver, CO 80233
800-369-7433
www.narha.org

Palomino Horse Association
HC 63, P.O. Box 24
Dornsife, PA 17823
570-758-3067
www.palominohorseassoc.com

Palomino Horse Breeders of America
15253 E. Skelly Dr.
Tulsa, OK 74116-2637
918-438-1234
www.palominohba.com

Performance Horse Registry
4047 Iron Works Pkwy.
Lexington, KY 40511-8483
859-258-2472
www.usef.org

Professional Horsemen's Association of America, Inc.
23 Juniper Meadow Road
Washington Depot, CT 06794
860-868-9904
www.nationalpha.com/purpose.html

Promoters of Palomino Saddlebreds, Inc.
P.O. Box 177
Oxford Junction, IA 52323-0177

The Pyramid Society
P.O. Box 11941
Lexington, KY 40579-1941
859-231-0771
www.pyramidsociety.org

Southwestern Exposition and Livestock Show
P.O. Box 150
Fort Worth, TX 76101-0150

Tennessee Walking Horse National Celebration
P.O. Box 1010
Shelbyville, TN 37162
931-684-5915
www.twhnc.com/eventcalendar.htm

United Professional Horsemen's Association, Inc.
4059 Iron Works Pkwy., Suite 2
Lexington, KY 40511-8434
859-231-5070
www.upha.com

United States Dressage Federation
220 Lexington Green Circle, Suite 510
Lexington KY 40503
859-971-2277
www.usdf.org

United States Equestrian Team
Pottersville Road
Gladstone, NJ 07934
908-234-1251
www.uset.org

United States Eventing Association, Inc.
525 Old Waterford Road, NW
Leesburg, VA 20176-2050
703-779-0440
www.eventingusa.com

United States Polo Association
771 Corporate Dr., Suite 505
Lexington, KY 40503
859-219-1000
www.uspolo.org

U.S. Equestrian, Inc.
4047 Iron Works Pkwy.
Lexington, KY 40511-8483
859-258-2472
www.usef.org

Virginia Horse Shows Association
32 Ashby St.
Warrenton, VA 20186
540-349-0910
www.vhsa.com

Walking Horse Trainer's Association, Inc.
P.O. Box 61
Shelbyville, TN 37162-0061
931-684-5866
www.walkinghorsetrainers.com

Washington International Horse Show
16063 Comprint Circle
Gaithersburg, MD 20877
301-987-9400
www.wihs.org

The World Sidesaddle Federation, Inc.
P.O. Box 1104
Bucyrus, OH 44820
419-284-3176
www.sidesaddle.org

APPENDIX M
STATE ORGANIZATIONS

State Extension Specialists

Alabama
Auburn University
Dept. of Animal and Dairy Sciences
Auburn, AL 36849-5415
334-844-4000
www.auburn.edu

Arkansas
University of Arkansas
Cooperative Extension Service
P.O. Box 391
Little Rock, AR 72203-0391
501-671-2000
www.uaex.edu

California
University of California Davis
Dept. of Animal Science
One Shields Ave.
Davis, CA 95616-8521
530-752-1011
www.ucdavis.edu

Colorado
Colorado State University
Dept. of Animal Sciences
Fort Collins, CO 80523-1171
970-491-1101
www.colostate.edu

Connecticut
University of Connecticut
Dept. of Animal Science
U-4040, 3636 Horsebarn Road Extension
Storrs, CT 06269-4040
860-486-2000
www.uconn.edu

Florida
University of Florida
P.O. Box 110910
Gainesville, FL 32611-0691
352-392-3261
www.ufl.edu

Georgia
University of Georgia
Dept. of Animal Science
425 River Road

Athens, GA 30602-2771
706-542-3000
www.uga.edu

Idaho
University of Idaho
P.O. Box 442335
Moscow, ID 83843
208-885-6111
www.ag.uidaho.edu

Illinois
University of Illinois
388 Animal Science Lab
1207 W. Gregory Dr.
Urbana, IL 61801-3838
217-333-1000
www.uiuc.edu

Iowa
Iowa State University
Animal Science Dept.
119 Kildee Hall
Ames, IA 5001-3150
515-294-4111
www.iastate.edu

Kentucky
University of Kentucky
Dept. of Animal Science
912 W. P. Garrigus Bldg.
Lexington, KY 40546-0215
859-257-3469
www.ca.uky.edu

Maine
University of Maine
Kennebec County Extension
125 State St., 3rd Fl.
Augusta, ME 04330-5692
207-622-7546
www.umext.maine.edu/counties/kennebec.htm

Maryland
University of Maryland
11975 Homewood Road
Ellicott City, MD 21042-1545
301-405-1000
www.umd.edu

Massachusetts
University of Massachusetts
P.O. Box 37605

Amherst, MA 01003-7605
www.umass.edu

Michigan
Michigan State University
Dept. of Animal Science
1287 Anthony Hall
East Lansing, MI 48824-1225
517-355-2308
www.msu.edu

Mississippi
Mississippi State University
Animal & Dairy Sciences
P.O. Box 9815
Mississippi State, MS 39762-9815
662-325-2323
www.msstate.edu/dept/ads

Missouri
University of Missouri
Animal Sciences Dept.
S. 103 Animal Science Center
Columbia, MO 65211-5300
573-882-2121
www.missouri.edu/index.cfm

Montana
Montana State University
P.O. Box 172860
Bozeman, MT 59717
406-994-3681
www.montana.edu

Nebraska
University of Nebraska
Animal Science Complex, C204
Lincoln, NE 68583-0908
402-472-7211
www.unl.edu

New Hampshire
University of New Hampshire
Dept. of Animal and Nutritional Sciences
Kendall Hall
129 Main St.
Durham, NH 03824-3590
603-862-3757
www.unh.edu

New Jersey
Rutgers University

Animal Science Dept., Cook College
84 Lipman Dr.
New Brunswick, NJ 08901-8525
732-932-9100
www.rutgers.edu

New Mexico
New Mexico State University
P.O. Box 30003
Department 3-I
Las Cruces, NM 88003-0003
505-646-0111
www.nmsu.edu

New York
Cornell University
149 Morrison Hall
Ithaca, NY 14853-4801
607-255-2862
www.ansci.cornell.edu

North Carolina
North Carolina State University
P.O. Box 7523
Raleigh, NC 27695-7523
919-515-2011
www.ncsu.edu

Ohio
Ohio State University
2029 Fyffe Road
Columbus, OH 43210-1095
614-292-OHIO
www.osu.edu

Oklahoma
Oklahoma State University
Animal Science Dept.
101 Animal Science Bldg.
Stillwater, OK 74078-0425
405-744-6062
www.ansi.okstate.edu

Oregon
Oregon State University
Horse Center, Dept. of Animal Sciences
Withycombe Hall 112
Corvallis, OR 97331-6702
541-737-4411
www.orst.edu

Pennsylvania
Pennsylvania State University
Dept. of Dairy & Animal Sciences

324 Henning Bldg.
University Park, PA 16802-3503
814-863-3665
www.psu.edu

South Carolina
4-H Horse Specialist
P.O. Box 246
Greenwood, SC 29648-0246
864-656-3311
www.clemson.edu

South Dakota
South Dakota State University
Animal and Range Sciences Dept.
P.O. Box 2170
Brookings, SD 57007-0392
605-688-5165
www.sdstate.edu

Tennessee
University of Tennessee
Institute of Agriculture
5201 Marchant Dr.
Nashville, TN 37211-5112
865-974-7321
www.utk.edu

Texas
Texas A&M University
Dept. of Animal Science
Kleberg Ctr., Rm. 249
College Station, TX 77843-2471
979-845-1541
www.tamu.edu

Utah
Utah State University
4815 Old Main Hill
Logan, UT 84322-4815
435-797-1000
www.usu.edu

Vermont
University of Vermont
655 Spear St.
Burlington, VT 05405-0107
802-656-3131
www.uvm.edu

Virginia
Virginia Tech
Animal & Poultry Science Dept.

3460 Litton Reaves Hall, Rm. 380
Blacksburg, VA 24061-0306
540-231-6311
www.vt.edu

Wisconsin
University of Wisconsin
Dept. of Animal Sciences
1675 Observatory Dr.
Madison, WI 53706-1284
608-263-4300
www.uwex.edu

Wyoming
University of Wyoming
College of Agriculture Coop. Ext. Service
P.O. Box 3354
Laramie, WY 82071-3354
307-766-4133
www.uwyo.edu

State Horse Councils

Alabama Horse Council
4994 County Road, Suite 1082
Cullman, AL 35179
256-747-4937
www.alabamahorsecouncil.org

Arizona State Horsemen's Association
P.O. Box 31758
Phoenix, AZ 85046-1758
602-390-6806
www.azsthorseassoc.com

Arkansas Horse Council
P.O. Box 737
Jasper, AR 72641-0737
870-446-6226
www.twb.net/ahc

California State Horsemen's Association
264 Clovis Ave., Suite 109
Clovis, CA 93612
559-325-1055
www.californiastatehorsemen.com

Colorado Horse Council, Inc.
420 E. 58th Ave.
Denver, CO 80216
303-292-4981
www.cohoco.com

Connecticut Horse Council, Inc.
P.O. Box 57
Durham, CT 06422-0057
860-282-0468
www.cthorsecouncil.org

Delaware Equine Council
P.O. Box 158
Harrington, DE 19952
302-284-4457
www.delawareequinecouncil.org

Florida—Sunshine State Horse Council, Inc.
Palm Beach County Horse Industry Council, Inc.
P.O. Box 4158
N. Fort Myers, FL 33918-4158
239-731-2999
www.sshc.org

Georgia Horse Council, Inc.
1970-C Olympic Centennial Pkwy.
Conyers, GA 30013
770-922-3350
www.georgiahorsecouncil.com

Idaho Horse Council
5000 Chinden Blvd., Suite F
Boise, ID 83714
208-323-8148
www.dallypost.com/ihc/aboutus.php

Illinois—Horsemen's Council of Illinois
P.O. Box 1605
Springfield, IL 62705-1605
217-585-1600
www.horsemenscouncil.org

Indiana Horse Council, Inc.
225 S. East St., Suite 738
Indianapolis, IN 46202-4059
317-692-7115
www.indianahorsecouncil.org

Iowa Horse Industry Council
1817 E. 30th St.
Des Moines, IA 50317-8613

Kansas Horse Council
P.O. Box 1612
Manhattan, KS 66505-1612
785-776-0662
www.kansashorsecouncil.com

Kentucky Horse Council
P.O. Box 11706
Lexington, KY 40577-1706
800-459-4677
www.kentuckyhorse.org

Maine Farm Bureau Horse Council
4 Gabriel Dr.
Augusta, ME 04330-9332
207-622-4111
www.mainehorsecouncil.org

Maryland Horse Council, Inc.
P.O. Box 233
Lisbon, MD 21765
410-489-7826
www.mdhorsecouncil.org

**Massachusetts Bay State Trail Riders
Association**
24 Glenn St.
Douglas, MA 01516-2410
508-476-3960
http://users.rcn.com/bstra/home.html

Michigan Horse Council
P.O. Box 22008
Lansing, MI 48909-2008
231-821-2487
www.michiganhorsecouncil.com

Minnesota Horse Council "For Horses Sake"
Minnesota Horse Council
2230 Van Dyke St.
Maplewood, MN 55109-2704
763-755-7729
www.horses-mn.org

Mississippi Horse Council
1924 McCullough Blvd.
Tupelo, MS 38801
662-842-9346
www2.netdoor.com/~mhc

Missouri Equine Council, Inc.
P.O. Box 681
Republic, MO 65738-0681
800-313-3327
www.mo-equine.org

Nebraska Horse Council
P.O. Box 81481
Lincoln, NE 68501
402-826-5610
www.nebraskahorsecouncil.org

Nevada—Horse Council of Nevada, Inc.
P.O. Box 33171
Las Vegas, NV 89133
702-656-5177

New England Horsemen's Council
P.O. Box 70
Sandown, NH 03841-2038
603-887-NEHC
www.nehc.info

New Hampshire Horse Council
465 White Plains Road
Webster, NH 03303
603-239-4628
www.nhhorsecouncil.com

New Jersey Horse Council, Inc.
24 Beth Dr.
Moorestown, NJ 08057-3021
856-231-0771
www.njhorsecouncil.com

New Mexico Horse Council, Inc.
P.O. Box 10206
Albuquerque, NM 87184
505-345-8959
www.nmhorsecouncil.org

New York State Horse Council, Inc.
760 Webster Road
Webster, NY 14580
845-942-0420
www.nyshc.org

North Carolina Horse Council
P.O. Box 12999
Raleigh, NC 27605-2999
919-854-1990
www.nchorsecouncil.com

Ohio Horseman's Council
9830 Roley Road
Logan, OH 43138
740-385-5306
www.ohiohorsemanscouncil.com

Oklahoma Horse Industry Council, Inc.
9801 Ritter Road
Oklahoma City, OK 73162
580-233-2538
www.oklahomahorseindustrycouncil.com

Oregon Horsemen's Association, Inc.
32302 S. Rachael Larkin Road
Mollala, OR 97038
www.oregonhorsemen.com

Pennsylvania Equine Council
P.O. Box 21
Dallas, PA 18612
888-304-0281
www.pennsylvaniaequinecouncil.com

South Carolina Horsemen's Council
P.O. Box 160
Lexington, SC 29071
803-356-4535
www.schorsecouncil.org

South Dakota Horse Council
P.O. Box 25
Hayti, SD 57241
605-783-3832
www.sdhorsecouncil.org

Tennessee Horse Council
P.O. Box 69
College Grove, TN 37046-0069
615-395-7650
www.tnhorsecouncil.com

Texas—Greater Houston Horse Council
P.O. Box 924305
Houston, TX 77292-4305
281-681-6171
www.ghhc.com

Utah Horse Council
3268 S. 1000 W.
Syracuse, UT 84075
www.utahhorsecouncil.org

Virginia Horse Council
P.O. Box 665
Mineral, VA 23117
540-894-0735
www.virginiahorse.com

Washington State Horse Council
2363 Mt. View Road, E.
Port Orchard, WA 98366-8320
360-769-8083
www.horsemansyellowpages.com/wasthrscncl

Wisconsin State Horse Council
132A S. Ludington St.
Columbus, WI 53925-1516
920-623-0393
www.wisconsinstatehorsecouncil.org

Horse Facilities

Arkansas State Fairgrounds
P.O. Box 166660
Little Rock, AR 72216-6660
501-372-8341
www.arkfairgrounds.com

Florida Agriculture Center & Horse Park
5800 Veterans Memorial Dr.
Tallahassee, FL 32309-9507
850-893-0579

Garrison Livestock Arena
Clemson University
P.O. Box 340322
Clemson, SC 29634-0322
864-646-2717
www.clemson.edu/garrison

Georgia National Fairgrounds & Agricenter
P.O. Box 1367
Perry, GA 31069
478-987-3247
www.gnfa.com

Governor James B. Hunt Horse Complex
North Carolina State Fair
1025 Blue Ridge Blvd.
Raleigh, NC 27607-3999
919-733-4845
www.ncstatefair.org/hunthors.htm

Hoosier Horse Park
4500 Dan Patch Circle
Anderson, Indiana 46013
800-526-RACE
www.hoosierpark.com

Horse Park of New Jersey at Stone Tavern, Inc.
P.O. Box 548
Allentown, NJ 08501
609-259-0170
www.horseparkofnewjersey.com

Kentucky Horse Park
4089 Iron Works Pkwy.
Lexington, KY 40511-8434
800-678-8813
www.kyhorsepark.com

Oregon State Fairgrounds
2330 17th St., NE
Salem, OR 97303-3201
503-947-3247
www.fair.state.or.us

Senator Bob Martin Eastern Agricultural
    Center
P.O. Box 310
Williamston, NC 27892
919-792-5802
www.martincountync.com/mc/mc-agcenter

Virginia Horse Center
P.O. Box 1051
Lexington, VA 24450
540-464-2950
www.horsecenter.org

Western North Carolina Agri-Center
1301 Fanning Bridge Road
Fletcher, NC 28732-9215

State Horse Fairs and Exhibitions

Alabama
Alabama Horse Fair
Garret Coliseum
P.O. Box 70026
Montgomery, AL 36107
205-678-2882
www.aces.edu

Arkansas
Arkansas Equine Expo
White County Fairgrounds
Searcy, AR 72143
870-446-6226
www.horseandpetexpo.com

Arkansas State Horse Show
Barton Coliseum
2600 Howard St.
Little Rock, AR 72206
501-372-8341
www.arkfairgrounds.com

California
Equine Affaire
Fairplex
1101 W. McKinley Ave.
Pomona, CA 91768
740-845-0085
www.equineaffaire.com

Western States Horse Expo
P.O. Box 517
Coloma, CA 95613
530-295-1424
www.horsexpo.com

Colorado
Rocky Mountain Horse Expo
National Western Complex
420 E. 58th Ave.
Denver, CO 80216
303-292-4981
www.rockymountainhorseexpo.com

Delaware
Delaware State Fair
P.O. Box 28
Harrington, DE 19952-0028
302-398-3269
www.delawarestatefair.com

Georgia
Georgia Horse Fair
Georgia National Fairgrounds and Agricenter
P.O. Box 1367
Perry, GA 31069-1367
800-922-0145
www.gnfa.com

Southern National Expo
Georgia National Fairgrounds and Agricenter
Perry, GA
P.O. Box 1367
Perry, GA 31069-1367
410-451-9674
www.sne.com

Idaho
Idaho Horse Expo
Canyon County Fairgrounds
Caldwell, ID 83606
208-323-8148
www.idahohorseexpo.com

Western Idaho Horse Fair and Trade Show
Western Idaho Fairgrounds Expo Bldg.
8699 S. Gantz
Boise, ID 83704
888-684-5172
www.horseaffairs.com

Illinois
Illinois Horse Fair
Illinois State Fairgrounds
801 Sangamon Ave.
Springfield, IL 62706
217-498-8000
www.illinoishorse.com/fair

Indiana
Hoosier Horse Fair & Expo
Indiana State Fairgrounds
1202 E. 28th St.
Indianapolis, IN 46205
317-692-7115
www.in.gov/statefair/events/horsefair/ Iowa

Iowa
Iowa Horse Fair
Iowa State Fairgrounds
P.O. Box 57130
Des Moines, IA 50317-0003
515-233-4541
www.iowahorsecouncil.com

Kansas
EquiFest of Kansas
Kansas Coliseum
1229 E. 85th St.
Valley Center, KS 67147
Wichita, KS
785-776-0662
www.kansashorsecouncil.com/equifest/equifestofk
    s.html

Kentucky
Kentucky State Fair
Kentucky International Convention Center
221 Fourth St.
Louisville, KY 40202
502-367-5000
www.kyfairexpo.org

Maryland
Horse World Expo
Maryland State Fairgrounds

P.O. Box 188
Timonium, MD 21094-0188
301-916-0852
www.horseworldexpo.com

Massachusetts
Equine Affaire
Eastern States Exposition
1305 Memorial Ave.
West Springfield, MA 01089
740-845-0085
www.equineaffaire.com

Michigan
Horse Spectacular
Novi Expo Center
43700 Expo Center Dr.
Novi, MI 48375
800-878-5131
www.horsespectacular.com

MHC Horse Expo
MSU Pavilion
1290 Anthony Hall
E. Lansing, MI 48824
248-437-1525
www.equi-sense.com/HorseExpo.html

Minnesota
Minnesota Horse Expo
Minnesota State Fairgrounds
1265 Snelling Ave.
St. Paul, MN
952-922-8666
www.mnhorseexpo.org

Mississippi
Dixie National Livestock Show and Rodeo
P.O. Box 892
Jacksonville, MS 39205
601-961-4000
www.mdac.state.ms.us/Library/BBC/FairComm/Fa
    irComm.html

Missouri
Equine Education Days
Boone County Fairgrounds
5212 N. Oakland Gravel Road
Columbia, MO 65202
800-313-3327
http://boonecountyfairgrounds.com/ Nebraska

Nebraska
Horse Expo
Lancaster Event Center
P.O. Box 29167
Lincoln, NE 68529
402-238-2698
www.nebraskahorsecouncil.org

Nebraska State Fair
State Fair Park
1600 Court St.
Lincoln, NE 68508-1098
402-473-4104
www.statefair.org

Nevada
Nevada State Fair
Reno Livestock Events Center
1350 N. Wells Ave.
Reno, NV 89512
775-688-5767
www.nevadastatefair.org

New Jersey
Horse World Expo
Convention Center at Raritan Center
50 Atrium Dr.
Somerset, NJ 08873-4163
www.horseworldexpo.com

New Mexico
New Mexico State Fair
P.O. Box 8546
Albuquerque, NM 87198
505-265-1791
www.nmstatefair.com

New York
New York State Fair, Open Horse Show
Empire Expo Center
581 State Fair Blvd.
Syracuse, NY 13209
800-475-FAIR
http://nysfair.org

North Carolina
Carolina Classic Horse Expo
LJVM Coliseum Complex
2825 University Pkwy.
Winston-Salem, NC 27105
336-352-5000
www.cchexpo.com

North Dakota
North Dakota State Fair
North Dakota State Fair Center
P.O. Box 1796
Minot, ND 58702
701-857-7620
www.ndstatefair.com

Ohio
Equine Affair
Ohio Expo Center
2720 State Rte. 56 SW
London, Ohio 43140
740-845-0085
www.equineaffaire.com

Oregon
Greater Northwest Equine Expo
Linn County Fairgrounds & Expo Center
3700 Knox Butte Road
Albany, OR 97321
765-655-2107
www.showmasters.com

Oregon State Fair
Oregon State Fair & Expo Center
2330 Seventeenth St. NE
Salem OR 97303
503-947-3247

Pennsylvania
Pennsylvania Horse Expo
Fort Washington Expo Center
1100 Virginia Dr.
Fort Washington, PA 19034
800-360-3976
www.horseandpetexpo.com

South Dakota
Sioux Empire Fair
W.H. Lyons Fairgrounds
4000 W. 12th St.
Sioux Falls, SD 57106
605-367-7178
www.tahssd.itgo.com

South Dakota State Fair
South Dakota State Fairgrounds
P.O. Box 1275
Huron, SD 57350
800-529-0900
www.sdstatefair.com

Tennessee
Volunteer Horse Fair
Middle Tennessee Livestock Center
MTSU Campus
Murfreesboro, TN 37130
615-297-3200
www.tnhorsecouncil.com/VolunteerHorseFair/Volu
 nteerHorseFair.html

Texas
Houston Livestock Show and Rodeo
Reliant Stadium
P.O. Box 20070
Houston, TX 77225-0070
832-667-1000
www.hsr.com

San Antonio Livestock Show
SBC Center at Freeman Coliseum Grounds
3201 Houston St.
San Antonio, TX 78219
210-225-0575
www.sarodeo.com

Southwestern Exposition Livestock Show and
 Rodeo
Will Rogers Center
P.O. Box 150
Forth Worth, TX 7601-0150
817-877-2400
www.fwstockshowrodeo.com

Virginia
State Fair Horse Show
Richmond Raceway Complex
8407 Erle Road
Mechanicsville, VA 23116
804-569-3220
www.statefair.com/index.asp

Washington
The Puyallup Fair
Western Washington Fairgrounds
P.O. Box 430
Puyallup, WA 98371
253-841-5045
www.thefair.com

West Virginia
West Virginia State Fair
State Fair Events Center
P.O. Drawer 986

Lewisburg, WV 24901
304-645-1090
www.wvstatefair.com

Wisconsin
Midwest Horse Fair
Alliant Energy Center
1919 Alliant Energy Center Way
Madison, WI 53713
920-623-5515
www.midwesthorsefair.com

Wyoming
Wyoming State Fair & Rodeo
Wyoming State Fair Park
P.O. Drawer 10
Douglas, WY 82633
307-358-2398
www.wystatefair.com

Horse Specialists

Delaware
Dr. C. Melvin Rietmour
University of Delaware
Rm. 34 Townsend Hall
Newark, DE 19717-1303
302-831-2791
www.udel.edu

Florida
Florida Dept. of Agriculture and Consumer
 Services
Paul Davis
Rm. 431 Mayo Bldg.
Tallahassee, FL 32399-0800
850-487-2779
www.doacs.state.fl.us

Maryland
University of Maryland
Malcolm Commer, Ph.D.
11975 Homewood Road
Ellicott City, MD 21042
301-405-1000
www.umd.edu

New Jersey
New Jersey Dept. of Agriculture
Division of Markets
P.O. Box 330
Trenton, NJ 08625-0330

609-984-5367
www.state.nj.us/agriculture/markets/index.html

North Carolina
North Carolina Dept. of Agriculture
P.O. Box 27647
Raleigh, NC 27611
919-733-7125
www.ncdamarkets.org

South Carolina
South Carolina Dept. of Agriculture
P.O. Box 11280
Columbia, SC 29211-1280
803-734-2182
www.scda.state.sc.us

Tennessee
Tennessee Dept. of Agriculture, Marketing Div.
P.O. Box 40627
Nashville, TN 37204-0627
1-800-342-8206
http://picktnproducts.org

Vermont
University of Vermont
Animal Service Dept.
200A Terill Hall, 570 Main St.
Burlington, VT 05401-0148
802-656-3131
www.asci.uvm.edu/equine

Virginia
Virginia Dept. of Agriculture and Consumer
   Services
Equine Marketing
1100 Bank St., Suite1004
Richmond, VA 23219-1164
804-786-2373
www.state.va.us/~vdacs

State Veterinarians

Alabama
Animal Industry Division
P.O. Box 3336
Montgomery, AL 36109-3336
334-240-7255
www.agi.state.al.us/Animal.htm

Alaska
ADEC Division of Environmental Health
500 S. Alaska St., Suite A

Palmer, AK 99645
907-745-3236
www.state.ak.us/dec/deh/animal/home.htm

Arizona
Department of Agriculture
1688 W. Adams
Phoenix, AZ 85007-2617
602-542-4293
http://agriculture.state.az.us/ASD/state_vet.htm

Arkansas
Arkansas Livestock and Poultry Commission
P.O. Box 8505
Little Rock, AR 72205-8505
501-224-2836
www.arlpc.org/vets/index.asp

California
California Dept. of Food and Agriculture
1420 Howe Avenue, Suite 6
Sacramento, CA 95825
916-263-2610
www.vmb.ca.gov

Colorado
Colorado Dept. of Agriculture
700 Kipling St., Suite 4000
Lakewood, CO 80215
303-239-4100
www.ag.state.co.us

Connecticut
Connecticut Dept. of Agriculture
765 Asylum Ave.
Hartford, CT 06105-2822
860-713-2514
www.state.ct.us/doag

Delaware
Delaware Dept. of Agriculture
2320 S. Du Pont Hwy.
Dover, DE 19901-5515
302-698-4500
www.dda.state.de.us

Florida
Division of Animal Industry
407 S. Calhoun St.
Tallahassee, FL 32399-0800
850-410-0900
www.doacs.state.fl.us

Georgia
Dept. of Agriculture
19 Martin Luther King Jr. Dr.
Atlanta, GA 30334-4201
404-656-3685
www.agr.state.ga.us

Hawaii
Division of Animal Industry
99-941 Halawa Valley St.
Aiea, HI 96701-5602
808-483-7100
www.hawaiiag.org

Idaho
Idaho Division of Animal Industries
P.O. Box 790
Boise, ID 83701
208-332-8540
www.agri.state.id.us/animal/animalindustriesTOC.htm

Illinois
Bureau of Animal Health
P.O. Box 19281
Springfield, IL 62794-9281
217-782-4944
www.agr.state.il.us/AnimalHW

Indiana
Board of Animal Health
805 Beachway Dr., Suite 50
Indianapolis, IN 46224-7785
317-227-0300
www.boah.state.in.us

Iowa
Dept. of Agriculture
Wallace State Office Bldg.
502 E. 9th and Grand
Des Moines, IA 50319-0001
515-281-5305
www.idals.state.ia.us

Kansas
Kansas Animal Health Dept.
708 S. Jackson
Topeka, KS 66603-3714
785-296-2326
www.accesskansas.org

Kentucky
Kentucky Dept. of Agriculture
Animal Health Division

100 Fairoaks Lane, Suite 252
Frankfort, KY 40601
502-564-3956
www.kyagr.com

Louisiana
Animal Health Division
P.O. Box 4048
Baton Rouge, LA 70821-1951
225-925-3962
www.ldaf.state.la.us

Maine
Maine Dept. of Agriculture
Division of Animal Health and Industry
28 State House Station
Augusta, ME 04333-0028
207-287-3701
www.state.me.us

Maryland
Maryland Dept. of Agriculture
50 Harry S. Truman Pkwy.
Annapolis, MD 21401-7080
410-841-5810
www.mda.state.md.us

Massachusetts
Bureau of Animal Health
Dept. of Food and Agriculture
251 Causeway St., Suite500
Boston, MA 02114-2151
617-626-1700
www.state.ma.us

Minnesota
Minnesota Board of Animal Health
90 W. Plato Blvd.
St. Paul, MN 55107-2094
651-296-2942
www.bah.state.mn.us

Mississippi
Board of Animal Health
P.O. Box 3889
Jackson, MS 39207-3889
601-359-1160
www.mdac.state.ms.us

Montana
Dept. of Livestock, Animal Health Division
P.O. Box 202001
Helena, MT 59620-2001

406-444-7323
www.discoveringmontana.com/liv/aboutdol/con-
tact.asp

Nebraska
Bureau of Animal Industry
P.O. Box 94787
Lincoln, NE 68509-4787
402-471-2351
www.agr.state.ne.us

Nevada
Division of Animal Industry
350 Capitol Hill Ave.
Reno, NV 89502-2992
775-688-1180
http://agri.state.nv.us/indexa.htm

New Hampshire
Division of Animal Industry
P.O. Box 2042
Concord, NH 03301-2042
603-271-2404
www.state.nh.us

New Jersey
Dept. of Agriculture
Division of Animal Health
P.O. Box 330
Trenton, NJ 08625-0330
609-292-3965
www.ag.state.nj.us

New Mexico
Dept. of Agriculture
MSC APR P.O. Box 30005
Las Cruces, NM 88003-8005
505-646-2642
www.state.nm.us

New York
Division of Animal Industry
One Winners Circle
Albany, NY 12235-0001
518-457-3502
www.agmkt.state.ny.us/AI/AIHome.html

North Carolina
North Carolina Department of Agriculture and
    Consumer Services
P.O. Box 26026
Raleigh, NC 27611-6026
919-733-7601
www.agr.state.nc.us/vet

North Dakota
North Dakota Dept. of Agriculture
600 E. Blvd. Ave., Dept. 602
Bismarck, ND 58505-0020
800-242-7535
www.agdepartment.com

Ohio
Ohio Dept. of Agriculture
Division of Animal Industry
8995 E. Main St.
Reynoldsburg, OH 43068-3399
614-728-6220
www.state.oh.us/agr/AnimalIndustryDiv.html

Oklahoma
Animal Industry Division
2800 N. Lincoln Blvd.
Oklahoma City, OK 73105
405-521-3864
www.oda.state.ok.us/aind.htm

Oregon
Animal Health and Identification Division
Oregon Dept. of Agriculture
635 Capitol St., NE
Salem, OR 97301-2532
503-986-4680
www.od.state.or.us

Pennsylvania
Pennsylvania Dept. of Agriculture
Bureau of Animal Health & Diagnostic Service
2301 N. Cameron St.
Harrisburg, PA 17110-9408
717-783-6677
www.state.pa.us

Rhode Island
Division of Agriculture, Animal Health Section
235 Promenade St.
Providence, RI 02908-6047
401-222-6047
www.info.state.ri.us/default.htm

South Carolina
Clemson Livestock, Poultry Health Programs
P.O. Box 102406
Columbia, SC 29224-2406
803-788-2260
www.clemson.edu

South Dakota
Dept. of Animal Health

411 S. Fort St.
Pierre, SD 57501-4503
605-773-3321
www.state.sd.us

Tennessee
Dept. of Agriculture
P.O. Box 40627
Nashville, TN 37204-0627
615-837-5103
www.state.tn.us

Texas
Texas Animal Health Commission
333 Guadalupe Street Tower III, Suite 810
Austin, TX 78701
800-821-3205
www.tbvme.state.tx.us

Utah
Utah Dept. of Agriculture and Food
Division of Animal Industry
P.O. Box 146500
Salt Lake City, UT 84114-6500
801-538-7160
http://ag.utah.gov/animind/animal_ind.html

Vermont
Dept. of Agriculture—Food and Markets
116 State St., Drawer 20
Montpelier, VT 05620-2901
802-828-2416
www.vermontagriculture.com

Virginia
Division of Animal Industry Services
Dept. of Agriculture and Consumer Services
P.O. Box 1163
Richmond, VA 23218-1163
804-786-2481
www.vdacs.state.va.us

Washington
Food Security and Animal Health
Dept. of Agriculture
P.O. Box 42560
Olympia, WA 98504-2560
360-902-1878
http://agr.wa.gov/default.htm

West Virginia
West Virginia Dept. of Agriculture
1900 Kanawha Blvd.

E. Charleston, WV 25305-0172
304-558-2214
www.wvagriculture.org/divisions/
  animal_health.html

Wisconsin
Animal Health Division
P.O. Box 8911
2811 Agriculture Dr.
Madison, WI 53708-8911
608-224-4879
www.datcp.state.wi.us/core/agriculture

Wyoming
Wyoming Livestock Board
2020 Carey Ave., 4th Floor
Cheyenne, WY 82002-0051
307-777-7515
http://wlsb.state.wy.us

State Racing Commissions

Alabama, Birmingham Racing Commission
2101 Sixth Ave., Suite 725
Birmingham, AL 35203
205-328-7223
www.mindspring.com/~brc

Arizona Department of Racing
1110 W. Washington, Suite 260
Phoenix, AZ 85007
602-364-1700
www.racing.state.az.us

Arkansas State Racing Commission
P.O. Box 3076
Little Rock, AR 72203-3076
501-324-9058
www.state.ar.us/dfa/racing

California Horse Racing Board
1010 Hurley Way, Suite300
Sacramento, CA 95825-3215
916-263-6000
www.chrb.ca.gov

Colorado Racing Commission
1881 Pierce St., Suite108
Lakewood, CO 80214-1494
303-205-2990
www.revenue.state.co.us/racing_dir/coracing.html

Connecticut Division of Special Revenue
P.O. Box 310424
Newington, CT 06131-0424
860-594-0500
www.dosr.state.ct.us/CONTACTU.htm

Delaware Harness Racing Commission
2320 S. DuPont Hwy.
Dover, DE 19901-5515
302-698-4500
www.state.de.us

Delaware Thoroughbred Racing Commission
2320 S. DuPont Hwy.
Dover, DE 19901-5515
302-698-4500
www.state.de.us

Florida Division of Pari-mutuel Wagering
1940 N. Monroe St.
Tallahassee, FL 32399-1027
850-487-1395
www.state.fl.us/dbpr/pmw/index.shtml

Idaho Horse Racing Commission
P.O. Box 700
Meridian, ID 83680-0700
208-884-7080
www.isp.state.id.us

Illinois Racing Board
100 Randolph St., Suite 11-100
Chicago, IL 60601
312-814-2600
www.state.il.us/agency/irb

Indiana Horse Racing Commission
ISTA Center150 W. Market, Suite530
Indianapolis, IN 46204
317-233-3119
www.in.gov/ihrc

Iowa Racing and Gaming Commission
717 E. Court Ave., Suite B
Des Moines, IA 50309
515-281-7352
www.state.ia.us/irgc

Kansas Racing and Gaming Commission
3400 SW Van Buren St.
Topeka, KS 66611-2228
785-296-5800
www.accesskansas.org/krc

Kentucky Racing Commission
4063 Iron Works Pkwy., Bldg. B
Lexington, KY 40511-8434
859-246-2040
http://krc.ppr.ky.gov

Louisiana State Racing Commission
320 N. Carrollton Ave., Suite 2-B
New Orleans, LA 70119-5106
859-246-2040
www.state.la.us

Maine State Harness Racing Commission
28 State House Station
Augusta, ME 04333-0028
207-287-3221
www.state.me.us/agriculture

Maryland Racing Commission
500 N. Calvert St.
Baltimore, MD 21202-3561
410-230-6330
www.dllr.state.md.us/racing/index.html

Massachusetts State Racing Commission
One Ashburton Pl., Rm. 1313
Boston, MA 02108-1501
617-727-2581
www.state.ma.us/src

Michigan Office of Racing Commissioner
37650 Professional Center Dr., Suite 105A
Livonia, MI 48154-1100
734-462-2400
www.michigan.gov/mda

Minnesota Racing Commission
P.O. Box 630
Shakopee, MN 55379-0630
952-496-7950
www.mnrace.commission.state.mn.us

Montana Board of Horse Racing
Dept. of Livestock
1424 Ninth Ave.
Helena, MT 59620-0512
406-444-4287
www.state.mt.us

Nebraska State Racing Commission
P.O. Box 95014
Lincoln, NE 68509-5014
402-471-4155
www.horseracing.state.ne.us

Nevada Gaming Commission
557 W. Silver St., Suite 207
Elko, NV 89801
775-738-7191
http://gaming.state.nv.us

New Hampshire Pari-Mutuel Commission
244 N. Main St.
Concord, NH 03301-5041
603-271-2158
www.state.nh.us/nhpmc

New Jersey Racing Commission
P.O. Box 088
Trenton, NJ 08625-0088
609-292-0613
www.state.nj.us

New Mexico Racing Commission
P.O. Box 8576
Albuquerque, NM 87198-8576
888-627-7250
www.nmrc.state.nm.us

New York State Racing and Wagering Board
One Watervliet Ave. Ext., Suite 2
Albany, NY 12206-1668
518-453-8460
www.racing.state.ny.us

North Dakota Racing Commission
500 N. 9th St.
Bismarck, ND 58501-4509
701-328-4633
www.ndracingcommission.com

Ohio State Racing Commission
State Office Tower
77 S. High St., 18th Fl.
Columbus, OH 43215
614-466-2757
www.state.oh.us/rac/commission.stm

Oklahoma Horse Racing Commission
Shepherd Mall
2614 Villa Prom
Oklahoma City, OK 73107-2421
405-943-6472
www.ohrc.org/INTRO.HTML

Oregon Racing Commission
800 NE Oregon St., Suite 310
Portland, OR 97232-2162

503-731-4052
www.oregonvos.net/~orc

Pennsylvania State Harness Racing Commission
2301 N. Cameron St.
Harrisburg, PA 17110-9408
717-787-5196
www.agriculture.state.pa.us

Pennsylvania State Horse Racing Commission
2301 N. Cameron St.
Harrisburg, PA 17110-9408
717-787-1942
www.agriculture.state.pa.usRhode Island
    Department of Business Regulation, Division of

Racing and Athletics
233 Richmond St.
Providence, RI 02903-4230
401-222-2246
www.dbr.state.ri.us

South Dakota Commission on Gaming
118 W. Capitol
Pierre, SD 57501-5070
605-773-6050
www.state.sd.us/drr2/reg/gaming/gam-hom.htm

Texas Racing Commission
P.O. Box 12080
Austin, TX 78711-2080
512-833-6699
www.txrc.state.tx.us

Vermont Racing Commission
128 Merchants Row
Rutland, VT 05701-5912
802-786-5050
http://vermont.gov

Virginia Racing Commission
10700 Horsemen's Road
New Kent, VA 23124
804-966-7400
www.vrc.state.va.us

Washington Horse Racing Commission
6326 Martin Way E., Suite 209
Lacey, WA 98516
360-459-6462
http://access.wa.gov

West Virginia Racing Commission
106 Dee Dr.
Charleston, WV 25311
304-558-2150
www.wvf.state.wv.us/racing/main.htm

Wisconsin Division of Gaming, Dept. of Administration
2005 W. Beltline Hwy., Suite 201
Madison, WI 53708-8979
608-270-2555
www.doa.state.wi.us/gaming/index.asp

Wyoming State Pari-Mutuel Commission
2515 Warren Ave., Suite 301
Cheyenne, WY 82002-0060
307-777-5887
http://parimutuel.state.wy.us

APPENDIX N
TRAIL ORGANIZATIONS

American Recreation Coalition
1225 New York Ave. NW, Suite 450
Washington D.C. 20005
202-682-9530
www.funoutdoors.com

Back Country Horsemen of America
P.O. Box 1367
Graham, WA 98338-1367
888-893-5161
www.backcountryhorse.com

BlueRibbon Coalition
P.O. Box 5449
Pocatello, ID 83202-0003
208-237-1008
www.sharetrails.org

Coalition for Recreational Trails
22377 Belmont Ridge Road
Ashburn, VA 20148-4501
703-858-4501
www.nrpa.org

Equestrian Land Conservation Resource
P.O. Box 423
Elizabeth, IL 61028
815-858-3501
www.elcr.org

Heritage Trails Fund
1350 Castle Rock Road
Walnut Creek, CA 94598
925-937-7661

Icelandic Horse Trekkers Association
P.O. Box 986
Kearney, MO 64060-0986

Illinois Trail Riders
3855 Somerset Road
Harrisburg, IL 62946-5446
618-252-7338
www.illinoistrailriders.com

National Association of Competitive Mounted Orienteering
503 One Hundred and Seventy First Ave., SE
Tenino, WA 98589-9711
800-354-7264
www.nacmo.org

National Association of State Trail Administrators
701 Ivanhoe St.
Denver, CO 80220-5339
303-321-8082
www.americantrails.org

North American Single-Footing Horse Trail, Field and Pleasure Division
6120 Cutler Lake Road
Blue Rock, OH 43720-9740
740-674-4555
www.oqha.com/bid.htm

North American Trail Ride Conference
P.O. Box 224
Sedalia, CO 80135
303-688-1677
www.natrc.org

Roundup Riders of the Rockies, Heritage, and Trails Foundation, Inc.
1733 S. Unita Way
Denver, CO 80231

Trail Riders of Today
7928 Bennet Branch Road
Mount Airy, MD 21771
www.trot-md.org/links/trotlnk1.html

APPENDIX O
TRANSPORTATION COMPANIES

Air Equine Services
P.O. Box 2096
Del Mar, CA 92014-1396
858-350-2050
www.airequine.com/introduction.htm

Alex Nichols Agency, Inc.
50 Carnation Ave.
Floral Park, NY 11001
516-488-8080
www.alexnicholsagency.com

All-State Horse Express Transportation
P.O. Box 18400
Colorado Springs, CO 80935
800-451-7696
www.horse-express.com

American Equine Services, Inc.
Horse Transport
93 Thornton Road
Thornton, PA 19373
610-459-1555
www.horsemovers.com

B&B Horse Transportation
509 Fountain Ave.
Georgetown, KY 40324
606-229-2337
www.polocenter.com

Bill Roberts Horse Transportation, Inc.
1831 Bashor Road
Goshen, IN 46526
574-533-4390
www.premierequine.com

B.J. Sunshine Ranch
P.O. Box 1525
Sanford, FL 40702
606-526-9408
www.polocenter.com

Bob Hubbard Horse Transportation, Inc.
3730 S. Riverside Ave.
Colton, CA 92324-3344
800-472-7786
www.bobhubbardhorsetrans.com

Bobby Ostrov Horse Transportation
941 SW 80th St.
Ocala, Fl 34480
352-854-0224
www.polocenter.com

Brook Ledge, Inc.
P.O. Box 56
Oley, PA 19547-0056
800-523-8143
www.brookledge.com

Carabajal Horse Hauling
10108 Meacham Road
Bakersfield, CA 93312
661-978-7343
http://ushorsehauler.com/horsehauling.htm

Coleman Horse Transportation Inc.
P.O. Box 15602
Ft. Wayne, IN 46885
219-493-4051
www.polocenter.com

Cowboy Express
HC 73, P.O. Box 520
Hysham, MT 59038
406-342-5489
www.cowboy-express.com/pages/1/index.htm

D&D Horse Transport
P.O. Box 1921
Oakdale, CA 95361
209-881-0212
www.polocenter.com

DC Wimpfheimer Horse Transportation
1305 Garfield St.
Hollywood, FL 33019
305-417-2092
www.polocenter.com

Drexler Horse Transportation
12 N288 Waughon Road
Hampshire, IL 60140
847-683-4464
www.drexlerhorsetransportation.com

Elite Horse Transport
5810 Gilliam Road
Orlando, FL 32818
407-810-7830
www.polocenter.com

Equine Express, N.A., Inc.
P.O. Box 501
Pilot Point, TX 76258
800-545-9098
www.cyberhorse.com/equine/eqex.htm

Flying Dutchman Equine Van Line
P.O. Box 4250
Midway, KY 40347
606-254-2591
www.polocenter.com

4M Horse Transportation LLC.
P.O. Box 3500, Suite 191
Sisters, OR 97759
877-4M-HORSE
www.horse-Transport.com

Goodpaster Horse Transport
Lexington, KY
859-421-3166
www.polocenter.com

Glenbrook Farm
15922 Seventy-Sixth St.
Live Oak, FL 32060
904-362-6903
www.glenbrookfarm.com

Global Horse Transport
P.O. Box 358
Lindenhurst, NY 11757-0358
631-957-6710
www.globalhorsetransport.com

Greenbriar Stablemate Farm, Inc
Trucking Service
3390 Eager Road
Jamesville, NY 13078
www.equineonly.com

Hacienda Siesta Alegre
P.O. Box 1876
Rio Grande, PR 00745
787-876-7740
www.haciendasiestaalegre.com

Hal Sullens Horse Transportation
P.O. Box 12875
Lexington, KY 40583
800-567-3978
www.polocenter.com

Happy Horse Equine Services, Inc.
7370 NW 36th St.
Miami, FL 33166
305-597-7115
www.polocenter.com

H.H. Hudson Horse Transport
5879 NW County Road, Suite 326
Ocala, Fl 34478
352-732-3902
www.polocenter.com

Hill Horse Transport
486 Maupin Road
Lancaster, KY 40444
606-792-6509
www.polocenter.com

Horse America, Inc.
51 Atlantic Ave., Suite 203
Floral Park, NY 11001

Horse Heaven
5243 Adams Road
New Plymouth, ID 83655
800-390-9451
www.horseheaven.net

International Racehorse Transport
200 S. 4th St.
Geneva, IL 60314
630-262-1221
www.polocenter.com

Interstate Equine Travel
P.O. Box 177
Hardinsburgh, IN 47125
812-472-3117
www.polocenter.com

Jamison Express Equine Transportation
P.O. Box 275
Huxley, IA 50124
515-597-3655
www.polocenter.com

Jet Pets, Inc.
20 Garden Dr.
Tullamarine, Victoria 304
Australia
613-9330-1541
https://secure.jetpets.com.au

Judge Manning Horse Transportation, Inc.
18 Mechanic St.
Amenia, NY 12501
845-373-8700
www.judgemanning.com

KLM Cargo
Worldwide Horse Transportation
3500 Inner Loop Road
Atlanta, GA 30326
404-762-3028
www.polocenter.com

Kum Horse Transport
P.O. Box 14133
Louisville, KY 40214
502-448-9612
www.polocenter.com

Lazy J Ranch Horse Transportation
5580 W. 500 St.
North Judson, IN 46366
877-786-1777
www.ljranch.com

Lockwood Horse Vans Inc.
911 S. Lily Lake Road
McHenry, IL 60050
815-385-2731
www.polocenter.com

Lorraine Horse Transport
9226 NW Hwy. 27
Ocala, FL 34482
352-622-2214
www.polocenter.com

Lucky Me Acres
13151 SE 125 Lane
Dunnellon, FL 34431
352-465-3762
www.minidonks.com

Lufthansa Cargo
3400 Peachtree Ave., Suite 1225
Atlanta, GA 30326
404-814-5313
www.polocenter.com

Mersant International Ltd.
158-12 Rockaway Blvd.
Jamaica, NY 11434-4840
718-978-8200
www.mersant.com

Moments Notice Equine Transport
103 Redden Lane
Middletown, DE 19709
302-376-5766
www.polocenter.com

Nation-Wide Horse Transportation, Inc.
P.O. Box 5368
Colorado Springs, CO 80911-5368
719-392-1888
www.nationwidehorse.com

Okoboji Equine Transportation
5229 NW 114th St.
Grimes, IA 50111
515-202-2596
www.polocenter.com

Perry Transport Limited
P.O. Box 880
Nobleton, ON L0G 1N0, Canada
905-859-0333
www.perryt.com

Peter J. Rabusin Horse Transportation
12285 NW 35th St.
Ocala, FL 34482
352-629-5958
www.polocenter.com

PonyXpress Horse Transportation
www.ponyx.com

Rapid Roany Horse Express
4378 Mount House Road
Tracy, CA 95376
877-I-HAUL-2-U
www.polocenter.com

Reese's All State Horse Transport
P.O. Box 18400
Colorado Springs, CO 80935
800-451-7696
www.polocenter.com

Rob Nuttall Bloodstock Travel
143 North Upper St.
Lexington, KY 40597
606-252-2245
www.polocenter.com

Rocking H Horse Packers
HC 02, P.O. Box 7636
Palmer, AK 99645

907-745-4911
www.ushorses.com/RockingH

Rocking Horse Transportation Inc.
1016 Adley Wyatt Dr.
Breaux Bridge, LA 70517
318-228-7169
www.polocenter.com

Sandy's Horse Hauling
18111 Middleton Road
Middleton, ID 83687
208-585-6369
http://horses-etc.com/Horse_Transportation.shtml

SPS Horse Transportation
1810 S. Washington Fields Road
Washington, UT 84780
435-313-1118
www.ut-biz.com/sps

Tally-Ho Horse Transport
P.O. Box 567
Hamilton, GA 31811
706-628-5505
www.polocenter.com

Texas Equine Transportation
3151 FM 316
Mabank, TX 75147
903-887-5207
www.texasequinetransport.com

Three Way Horse Transportation
7655 Calhan Road
Calhan, CO 80808
719-548-9333
www.polocenter.com

Triple Barrel Farm Inc.
1211 B Grande Anse Hwy.
Breaux Bridge, LA 70517
318-667-6803
www.polocenter.com

Triton International Inc.
1060 W. Florence Ave.
Inglewood, CA 90301
310-337-0022
www.polocenter.com

William J. Barnes Agency, Inc.
220 Golf Edge

Westfield, NJ 07090-1806
908-232-7650
www.WJBAgency.com

WJ Barry Horse Transportation Inc.
21 Jansen St.
Danbury, CT 06810
203-792-2288
www.polocenter.com

Worley's Hauling
P.O. Box 1525
Corbin, KY 40702
606-526-9408
www.polocenter.com

Your Horse Haulers
3564 Hwy. 87 S
Roundup, MT 59072
800-426-0658
www.horsehaulers.net

INDEX